Select World Constitutions

Select World Constitutions

Volume I

Introduction by

U.N. Gupta

ATLANTIC

PUBLISHERS & DISTRIBUTORS (P) LTD

Published by

ATLANTIC

PUBLISHERS & DISTRIBUTORS (P) LTD

7/22, Ansari Road, Darya Ganj,
New Delhi-110002
Phones : +91-11-40775252, 23273880, 23275880, 23280451
Fax : +91-11-23285873
Web : www.atlanticbooks.com
E-mail : orders@atlanticbooks.com

Branch Office
5, Nallathambi Street, Wallajah Road,
Chennai-600002
Phones : +91-44-64611085, 32413319
E-mail : chennai@atlanticbooks.com

Printed in India at Glorious Printers, A-13, D.S.I.D.C.,
Jhilmil Industrial Area, Delhi-110095

Preface

A Constitution can be defined as the system of laws and basic principles that a country or an organization is governed by. There are 192 states in the world, and each state has its Constitution having certain identifiable characteristics depending upon the theories that have been preferred by its framers. There are democracies, monarchies, federal states, republics, autocracies, federation of communities and religious states. Within each of these categories there are different shades on the basis of which each state can be identified and studied.

The general features of the Constitution include, *inter alia*, the relative importance of legislative, executive and judicial branches of government along with the purposes or ideals sought to be achieved by the state such as freedom of the individual, equality, maintenance of public order and promotion of civil liberties. However, in many new states formed after the breaking up of large empires, the political theories have been put on the back-burner, and new set-ups that facilitate rapid economic growth are now being preferred. Many new as well as old states are now giving precedence to a combination of different constitutional theories to suit their socio-political, religious and economic heritage. Most of the former colonies and dominions of British empire such as Australia, Canada, India, Sri Lanka and Republic of South Africa opted to be socialist states though their polities are modeled on the British parliamentary system.

The Constitution of any state is a political document which is sacrosanct for the state and can only be changed either by a political upheaval or amended by a procedure provided to do so. The rudimentary idea around a Constitution is that it should have a long continuity if not permanency. The Constitutions which are changed frequently lose their sanctity. This happens when a state has long or several transitional periods as in the case of Pakistan and Afghanistan.

Select World Constitutions, in two Volumes, encompasses the main provisions and articles of 13 landmark Constitutions of the world. Volume I covers the Constitutions of United Kingdom, United States of America, Australia, Federal Republic of Germany, Canada, South Africa, and Japan. Volume II includes the Constitutions of France, Swiss Confederation (Switzerland), People's Republic of China, Sri Lanka, Kingdom of Bhutan, and Singapore. The Constitutions of Pakistan and Nepal—two important countries of the Indian subcontinent—have not been included because they continue to be in a fluid state with persistent political uncertainties. The Constitution of India has been deliberately kept outside the purview of this book as such a detailed and well-written Constitution is being given in an exclusive Volume.

The book is a wonderful admixture of different Constitutions representing democracy—both with parliamentary as well as presidential form of government, monarchy, commonwealth of dominions as in Australia, and Stalinist Marxism as in China. Various constitutional theories of executive, legislative and judicial powers, separation of powers between the units and the federation, legal rights, civil liberties and duties, and many other aspects of functioning of a political system can be studied in this book.

It will prove immensely useful to the students and teachers of political science and researchers in this field. It is an ideal reference source for legislators, lawyers and those concerned with the working of a political system. Common readers will also find it inculcating and informative.

U.N. Gupta

Contents

Introduction

U.N. Gupta

Every State, there are 192 states in the world community now, has a political Constitution. A state has a defined territory, fixed population, a government which protects its people and has international status and recognition. In return, the government rules over its people. In democracies, the government is 'by the people for the people'. It may or may not be 'of the people'. In autocracies the rulers are heads of the State, are absolute state power wielders and are either monarchs or dictators. The monarchs may or may not be acceptable to people while dictators always impose themselves on people. Now since the 1960s monarchs are generally nominal heads of their state and are normally backed by a Constitution. Even the dictators prefer to have a Constitution for the State in order to justify their status and give legal validity or sanction to their actions; Stalin of Soviet Russia, Hitler of Nazi Germany, Mussolini of Fascist Italy, Fidel Castro of Cuba or Musharraf of Pakistan all wielded or wield power under a formal Constitution for their state, generally of their own making.

What are the basic features of a Constitution for a State, for this there are precepts of constitutional theory which have evolved during last four or five centuries. All states have their constitutions based on one, other or mixed variants of these precepts. These principles are identifiable and help in comparative understanding or evaluation of different Constitutions. The Constitutions of some selected states are parts of this book.

Constitutional Theory

Each Constitution of the nation-member of the contemporary world polity has identifiable characteristics depending on the constitutional theories that have been preferred by its framers. There are monarchies, federal states, republican states, autocracies, federation of communities, democracies, religious states and so on. There are different shades within each category and so the Constitutions of some of these states of the present 192 states of the world can be or are to be identified, studied and noticed since these are of interest to us. The general features of Constitutions including the relative importance of legislative, executive and judicial branches of government along with the purposes or ideals sought to be achieved by the state such as freedom of individual, equality, maintenance of public order or promotion of civil liberties among others are expressed as constitutional theory. Every country has its own peculiarities and political problems. Breaking of empires has given rise to new undeveloped States and these have had to choose between monarchial, democratic, socialist, communist form of polity and constitutional organization and models are now available in practice. Contemporary race for rapid economic development of states is also reflected in constitutional setup and prospects of modern states. Political theories have taken a backbench nowadays. The Constitutional Theory brings out salient features of constitutionalism and it is seen that new and old states take help of the peculiarities of the systems to suit their socio-political, religious and economic heritage or environment. Full time Marxist States are now becoming multiparty democratic welfare States and capitalist States are liberalizing *laissez-faire* to state financed welfare for their ordinary citizens.

State and Constitutional State: Basically, a system of written political Constitution for every State was initiated in the 1770s when the thirteen British colonies in North America had decided to separate from British Empire in 1776, had declared independence and had adopted a republican Constitution without a king to rule over them. Till then monarchies were absolute power centers without a written code of conduct and had independent place in international relations based on a lineage for heritage. Break up of monarchies was associated with the rise of the sense of statehood. The term 'state' since French Revolution of 1789 also connotes the impact of the people on the government machinery. The 1783 Constitution of the USA is the first written Constitution which defined the government authorities, their powers and their relative standing along with the Bill of Rights of people. With the USA becoming independent, a constitutional state system had come into existence. This evolution was fortified by the French Revolution of 1789, which saw the end of monarchy there and establishment of another republic. Basically, a republic is a constitutional State; it has pre-established permanent political institutions under a 'Constitution' that defines their functions. Since the nineteenth century modern constitutional theory based on rationalist thinking has evolved the state on the basis of nationalism, natural rights of people and representative democracy, much as professed by Plato in his *Republic* in fifth century BC.

With the rise of nationalism as basis for a nation State around 1850, a new generation of states has come into existence. The new rationale was that people of a territory or of similar language, traditions and cultural background have a common nationality and are entitled to have self-government through the right of self-determination and to form a separate state identity.[1] Alien rule meaning subjugation became a detested political situation in Europe. Under this movement of nationalism the European monarchs were forced to accept and incorporate a parliamentary system of government as in England. The freedom movements since then led to the claim for the formation of new states; otherwise people were living in subjugation. Under the Covenant of League of Nations at the end of First World War, the trend for breaking empires of defeated states, viz. Germany, Italy and Ottoman, in favour of

1. However, in international relations, particularly in commercial treaties term state or the name of territory, viz. Germany, England, Portugal, Spain, Denmark, etc. was used instead of the name of the Kings or signatories. Internally in England the generalized terms 'Crown', 'Rex' or 'Regina' were used instead of name of King or Queen.

independent nation status for European territories and colonies was set on the basis of nationality of people.. This trend was further improved under the Charter of United Nations Organization (UNO) and under its impact all European empires were broken down and ultimately around 145 more new states have come into existence. Remarkably, 'states' and not other entities can be members of United Nations Organization. For them the United Nations has provided much of the background constitutional theory concepts with emphasis on democracy and elaborated human, civil or economic rights for the people. When there is upheaval in a state, the UNO acts under its powers and a new constitutional setup is provided for the state as happened in Congo, in former Yugoslavia or in Afghanistan.[2] However, whether the new state is monarchial or republican is immaterial for UNO but all the Constitutions of world are set in practice within the framework of this improvised statehood with variations here and there that have some impact of concepts and contents of state sovereignty also.

---

2. It can in brief be mentioned here that Afghanistan had monarchy till 1980 with parliamentary form of government and guarantee of civil liberties. Under the Fourth Afghan Constitution of 1973 the former Prime Minister Dawood overthrew the monarchy and declared Afghanistan a republic. In 1976 a presidential government was then formed under the domination of the official Revolutionary National Party. In 1978, however, when President Dawood began an effort to loosen ties with the Soviet Union, leftist military officers toppled him in a coup. The coup brought the communist P.D.P.A. to power; the new communist leaders established a single-party government, "the new-style state of the Democratic Republic of Afghanistan", in which the executive entirely dominated the legislature and the judiciary. This was resented by West. In 1980 a temporary Constitution "Fundamental Principles of the Democratic Republic of Afghanistan" was adopted. The expressed aim was to guide the Afghans in the creation of a society of human beings free from exploitation of one another. The Fourth Afghan Constitution was based on the political structure that was already in existence. The Fifth Afghan Constitution was made in 1987, after Najibullah had replaced Kaarmal as president. After a Civil War, under the Bonn Agreement sponsored by the UNO, the present Constitution of Afghanistan (2004) has come into action with Karzai as President.

Nature of Constitutions: Constitution of any State is a political document which is sacrosanct for the state and can be changed either by a political upheaval or by the procedure provided by it. A Constitution is framed and adopted by referendum, popularly appointed Assembly or even by forced acquiescence to a dictator. In all circumstances it is the source or reservoir of 'basic validity' for all political and administrative authorities that rule the state. A Constitution defines and links different constitutional institutions and their powers and duties. It is an organic[3] "instrument by which the fundamental powers of the government are established, limited and defined; and by which these powers are distributed among several departments for more safe and useful exercise for the benefit of the body politic". Constitution is regarded to be supreme law; there is no other higher law in the state. Its validity cannot be challenged by any institution of the state while the validity of a law can be challenged in courts of law. The validity of a Constitution is inherent within itself. It is regarded to be the 'Basic Law' of a State. Any other institution has to have its authority: an order is binding or a law is valid only insofar as it is in conformity with the Constitution. It being a document must be written or documented and ought to be handy or discernible to all who are interested in it. But there have been and there are states that function without a written Constitution. Many times those States which have a set Constitution have revolution type of intermissions when the old Constitution is out of form and new Constitution has not been framed or promulgated: Dictatorship replacing democracy or monarchy replacing republican Constitution. However, as observed earlier, a Constitution for the country may also be forced on people as all dictators have done.

3. Justice Miller quoted in Bernard Schwartiz, *The Powers of Governments*, Vol. 1, p. 1.

The states have existed or continue to exist with an unwritten Constitution. The states of Afghanistan, France,[4] Pakistan, Russia, China, Bangladesh or Nepal among several other contemporary countries have had periods of no written Constitution, suspended or a Constitution not in force. Relevant to this book (Part II), following states have operative Constitutions:

1. Islamic Republic of Afghanistan: Sixth (Current) Constitution 2003-2004.[5]
2. Commonwealth of Australia: Constitution Act, 1900.
3. People's Republic of Bangladesh: Basic Constitution[6] 1972.
4. The Kingdom of Bhutan: Dynastic Absolute Monarchy to become Constitutional Monarchy by a Constitution (18 August 2005) to be operative in 2008 after referendum.
5. The Dominion of Canada: The British North America Act, 1867.
6. The People's Republic of China: (Current) Constitution 1982 with further revisions in 1988, 1993, 1999 and 2004.
7. The Republic of France[7] : Fifth Constitution 1958.

---

4. During Second World War, while the country was in occupation from 1940 to 1945 the French Constitutional Law of 1940 had been constituted. Government of Petain that had collaborated with Nazi Germany and this regarded to be a period of no formal Constitution for mainland France and its occupied Colonies. Afterwards from 2 November, 1945 to 27 October, 1946 the post-WWII provisional government of President Charles de Gaulle had functioned.
5. Third Constitution 1964; Fourth Constitution 1973; Fifth Constitution 1987.
6. Currently suspended under Emergency of January 2007.
7. Earlier: Constitution of the French Fourth Republic, 27 October, 1946; French Third Republic, 24 and 25 February, and 16 July, 1875; and Constitution the Second French Republic, 4 November, 1848.

8. Federal Republic of Germany:[8] Basic Law 1949.
9. Japan: Monarchy (under) Constitution of 1946.
10. Kingdom of Nepal: Constitutional Monarchy: Constitution of Nepal (19 November 1990); New Constitution [Secular republic] (2007) to come into force after election in April 2008.
11. Islamic Republic of Pakistan: The [Democratic][9] Constitution of 1973.
12. Federation of Russia: Commonwealth of Independent States (CIS): (Present)[10] Constitution adopted by national referendum on 12 December 1993.
13. Republic of Singapore[11]: Independence Act of 1965.
14. Union of South Africa: Current[12] Constitution of May 1996.
15. Sri Lanka: Constitution of 7 September 1978.
16. Confederation of Switzerland: Federal Constitution of 1874.
17. United Kingdom: Eleven Constitutional Documents of UK are cited in Part III of the Book.[13]
18. United States of America.[14]

---

8. Germany was known as Prussian Empire till 1919, it became Weimar Republic (1919) which Hitler overthrew. Present Constitution (1946) is called Basic Law. The Basic Law of 1949 has remained the Constitution of united Germany with necessary minor changes.
9. It replaced the 1962 Constitution establishing military dictatorship, which in turn had replaced original (First Democratic) Constitution of 1956.
10. It replaces Constitution of 'The Union of Soviet Socialist Republics' (USSR) 1936. Not included in Part II of the book.
11. Earlier, ruled under Rendel Constitution 1955 and State of Singapore Act 1958 enacted by British Parliament.
12. It replaces the Constitution of 7 September 1978.
13. These alongwith uncodified 'Conventions of the Constitution' constitute the framework of British Constitution.
14. Constitution adopted on 17 September 1787, effective from 4 March 1789.

It is noted that up till the beginning of twentieth century most of the monarchies and dictatorships did not have written Constitutions. Contemporarily England, Bhutan and Nepal are kingdoms which do not have formal written or documented Constitutions, though the monarchies are constitutional and the States have international identity. The last two of these three are in process of adopting a formal Constitution.

The rudimentary idea around a Constitution remains that it should have a long continuity if not permanency. The Constitutions which are changed frequently lose sanctity, a feeling that is naturally considered to be attached to them. This happens when a State has long or several transitional periods. For example, Afghanistan or Pakistan have remained constitutionally unstable. The answer to this problem is desired to be achieved by many State Constitutions, for example, constitutional changes requiring referendum or acceptances by constituent units of a federated State are ideas to this end. Some Constitutions take certain aspects to be beyond change, for example, the Fifth Constitution of France makes republican nature of the Constitution and makes detachment of existing territories of France beyond the power and scope of revision or amendment. The Constitution of India[15] has been interpreted to mean that the term 'amendment' does not imply 'abrogation' of the Constitution and therefore, after amendment the amended Constitution should basically remain the same, that is, the 'basic structure of the Constitution cannot be amended'.[16] Similarly the Constitution of Switzerland does not give plenary powers of amendment to the Federal authorities or to the people and maintains the Confederation nature of union permanent.

Economic Organization of State and Constitutions: The end of monarchial autocratic States has led to republicanism. However, the new States in the name of social and economic development of people have given economics or economic functionalism to be the base for whole of constitutionalism: Capitalism for USA and West;

15. Not included in the book.
16. The federal character, right to equality, secularism, democratic form of government and judicial power of review have been held to be part of basic structure of Indian Constitution.

Marxism for communist states, viz. now communist China, Cuba or North Korea; and socialism for Eire, India, Sri Lanka, Union of South Africa and other states. Capitalism based on principle of *laissez-faire* has meant non-interference by the State in the economic activities leaving full scope for competitive 'Benthamite Individualism' and later to 'Collectivism'. The latter has led to use of the 'coercive machinery of State in the economic interests of the community'; and Marxist or Communist states provided extreme form of economic organization for the state of which People's Republic of China continues to be a contemporary adherent. Socialism and earlier Syndicalism combine economic development with democracy that is, the economic activity of the State should be controlled by people through their active participation in government. The British parliamentary system became a model for constitutionalism of this kind of economic organization. Most of the former colonies and dominions of British Empire such as Australia, Canada, India, Sri Lanka or Republic of South Africa profess to be socialist states. These states have mixed economies, that is, there is a public sector and a private sector for economic activities within the state and harmony between the two is maintained by the Parliament or National Assembly representing the people.

Patterns of Constitutions: First, primarily all the modern Constitutions are either monarchial or republican. Monarchial Constitutions are leftovers or are in continuity of ancient and medieval era political organizations of people in kingdoms, and now their presence is only in Europe and in Asia. For example, England, Saudi Arabia, Nepal, Thailand or Japan have established monarchies which have adapted themselves in one way or the other to modern constitutionalism, that is, State exists for welfare of people and to rule by representative government. The USA was first republican state formed in 1787 followed by France in 1789. French revolution gave out the political philosophy that absolute monarchs were anti-people and the people should 'recover' their liberty by overthrowing the dynasties. In reaction alongwith the European monarchs had formed the Holy Alliance in 1815 at the Congress of Vienna by Prussia, Austria, Russia and Great Britain that regarded French republicanism to be a symbol of despotism opposed to Christian morality and decided to resist and end it with armies. This Holy Alliance was opposed by the USA with its 'Monroe Doctrine' that declared that effort by European monarchs to maintain their empires in North, Central and South America would be resisted by it. The history of Europe of a century after Napoleon's defeat in 1815 is of tussle between monarchies and republicans. Later, as the result of First World War (1914-1918), which was won with the assistance of USA, most of the monarchial states of Europe including Germany had turned republican. After the Russian Revolution of 1917, Russia had become a republican state. The end of Second World War further extended republican constitutionalism or monarchies pledged to democracy of parliamentary type. Most of the 140 new states formed under the impact of the Charter of United Nations Organization have republican Constitution and profess to be democratic.

Second, 'democratic' constitutions have either parliamentary form of government, presidential form of government or admixture of the two, and are analyzed subsequently. The professed theory or purpose of democracy is to enable people to choose their government or rulers and to maximize interdependence between the two. Democracy as an ideal is a unity or via media in social, economic and above all political diversity. It is not a static system but has a succession of virtues desired by a people or society with change of times. It is founded in the informed and vigilant civil society with freedom of speech and expression; democracy is also an associate of 'rule of law' system. Democracy is a pluralist rule by people for themselves. Generally it is unity in diversity when all distinct interests are politically allowed free play and have equal chances of forming the government. There is no political cleavage among rich and poor, among people of different religious, social or cultural faith. There are no political minorities. In practicality it implies that all citizens have equal opportunity to become and can become President or Prime Minister of the country depending only on the mandate of political electorate. There is no political regimentation in a democracy. True democracy means several organized political parties with different manifesto and each one hopes to come into power on next election. The voting rights are not selective but qualifying age and some other basic factors, like criminal conviction or insanity, are only hurdles.

It is to be noted that 'freedom for people' and 'democracy' are not same or synonymous concepts. While the end of state is recognized to be the welfare and freedom of people the 'democracy' involves a 'process for government through elected representatives of people'. A democracy may be religion, race, tribe or Marxism oriented and the minorities, contrary to principles of equality, may be inhumanly treated by the elected government. Basically, all states are free to give voting rights to adults or to limit the right of franchise to select. Many democracies have denied franchise to women. It is known Nazi Government of Hitler was elected government that systematically eliminated Jews giving rise to 'crimes against humanity'. The Marxist communist states, like erstwhile USSR, or contemporary China,[17] are one-party elected totalitarian governments that do not allow political dissention or opposition and place natural freedoms of their people under state fiat since by theory there is no distinction between people and their government. Elected governments are supposed to express and further fundamental freedoms of whole people of the state but these states function like autocrats and ignore, deny or abrogate the freedoms in the name of 'democratic will of the people'. It is a situation outside of constitutional theory since in reality there have been or there are non-democratic states that recognize the freedom of individual better than those democracies that selectively crush human rights and freedoms.

Third, there are religion-oriented states both monarchial[18] and republican, like, Islamic Republic of Afghanistan or Islamic Republic of Pakistan. However, religion as a base for constitutional organization is since adoption of 1948 Universal Declaration of Human Rights and the two 1966 Covenants on Economic and Civil Rights stands discredited and is regarded to be an archaic concept. Still, there are a number of States which constitutionally

17. Also, Cuba and North Korea.

18. For example, Saudi Arabia or Thailand.

sponsor particular religions, like, Islam, Hinduism,[19] Buddhism[20] or Catholicism.[21] Such states also profess to give equal treatment to other religions and try to maintain equality before law and social justice.

Constitution of USA started the cult of 'religious freedom and equality' in state politics. This ideal is set out in the First Amendment: "Congress shall make no law respecting an establishment of religion or prohibiting the free exercise thereof" by its citizens. America was constituted of Catholics, Jews, Anglican Church followers, Presbyterians and atheists. Madison had in 1780s asserted[22] that religion was a divine matter and every government must give freedom to its people to embrace, to profess and to observe the religion; that rulers who wished to subvert the public liberty, found in religion a convenient oppressive auxiliary; that the government cannot deny an equal freedom to those who do not believe in that God that has convinced the rulers; and, that freedom of religion is in its nature an unalienable right. The philosophy of *Remonstrance* of USA is, since the Charter of UNO (1945), widely reflected in constitutions.[23] Indian Constitution (1949) established India as a secular democratic State. The Marxist States deny religion and regard it as a vice that corrupts individual thought against Marxism.

Fourth, there are Marxist States called communist States. These follow the constitutional principles of 1936 Constitution of

---

19. For example, Nepal: Article 4 of 1990 Constitution, "Nepal is a multiethnic, multilingual, democratic, independent, indivisible, sovereign Hindu and Monarchial Kingdom."
20. For example, Sri Lanka and Myanmar. Interestingly, Article 3 of the Constitution of Bhutan declares that "1. Buddhism is the spriritual heritage of Bhutan, which promotes among others the principles and values of peace, non-violence, compassion and tolerance. 2. The Druk Gyalpo (Majesty the King) is the protector of all religions in Bhutan".
21. For example, Italy and most of other states of Central Europe and Americas.
22. Vide *Memorial and Remonstrance against Religious Assessments.*
23. Interestingly, the Swiss Federation Constitution (1874) by Articles 49 and 50 guarantees liberty of conscience and creed, and free exercise of religion, but by Articles 51 and 52 makes exception against Jesuits and founding of new religious houses or religious orders within the state.

USSR. They do not distinguish between Communist Party, State Constitution and Law. These believe in the "People's democratic dictatorship" which means that the Communist Party and the State act on behalf of the people, but can and do use dictatorial methods in order to maintain the Constitution by remaining in power in the face of hostile forces. It is implicit in the concept of the people's democratic dictatorship that dictatorial means are not evil and that dictatorship is necessary for a Socialist State. The communist movement is mainstay of Constitution of a State; the dictatorship of proletariat for achievement of 'Socialist State' is the end to be achieved by the Constitution.

Unitary and Federal Constitutions: For administrative and democratic efficiency the states have been divided into zones, areas, provinces or states. Accordingly when there is one set of government, the Constitution for all the territories it is unitary but when there are two sets of government one for whole and other for units it is a federal Constitution. In simple terms a federal Constitution has one central capital city and several other capital cities depending on the number of units.

(1) *Unitary Constitutions*: As a general feature all the monarchies have had unitary state with centralized government for the territory forming their kingdom but often divided into dominions for administrative convenience. Most of them have now developed into constitutional monarchies with parliamentary democratic form of government of British pattern. Nepal[24] and Bhutan[25] have been fluctuating between absolute monarchy and constitutional monarchy and now Nepal is poised to be a

24. Article 27 (2) of 1990 Constitution of Nepal: "His Majesty is the symbol of Nepalese nationality and the unity of the Nepalese people." Part 5 of the Constitution fixes constitutional parameters of King's powers, expenditures, privileges, resources of income, inheritance or succession, among King's other attributes.
25. Article 2 of the 2005 Constitution of Bhutan, Clauses 1 to 26, in detail define the "Institution of Monarchy" while under Article 1(9) "This Constitution is the Supreme Law of the State". Article 10 (1) states: "There shall be a Parliament for Bhutan in which all legislative powers under the Constitution are vested and which shall consist of the King, the National Council and the National Assembly."

republic under a new constitution (2007-08), but it is to have unitary Constitution. Bhutan State is to have an elected National Assembly and a Prime Minister on British pattern for its Constitution. A unitary state has single government for whole country though it may be divided into provinces for administrative reasons maintaining direct control of central government; there is an absence of subsidiary autonomous bodies sharing sovereignty or absolute powers of the state in a unitary Constitution. England, France, China, Japan, Singapore are examples of states possessing unitary character.[26] The subsidiary bodies are creation of central government and can be scrapped by it. In empire system[27] the Colonies or Dominions were ruled under the unitary constitution for Mainland. However, in other marks of constitutionalism, the unitary Constitutions might differ. The Constitution of Japan (1946) is unitary, has kingship[28] and parliamentary form of government of British pattern but unlike the British Constitution the Japanese Constitution is rigid. The amendments unlike as in England require special majority in the two houses of the Diet (Parliament) followed by referendum requiring majority of votes cast thereon (Article 96). While in monarchial England, Parliament is supreme, in monarchial Japan the unitary Constitution is "the supreme law of the nation and no law, ordinance, imperial rescript or other act of government, or part thereof, contrary to the provisions hereof, shall have legal force or validity (Article 98).

26. Indian Constitution is regarded to be federal with strong unitary features. It is a unique Constitution on this aspect of constitutionalism.
27. Britain, France, Holland, Belgium, Portugal or Spain were main imperial States in 1945 at the beginning of UNO.
28. Chapter 1 of the Constitution of Japan: "Article 1. The Emperor shall be the symbol of the State and of the unity of the people, deriving his position from the will of the people with whom resides sovereign power. Article 2. The imperial throne shall be dynastic and succeeded to in accordance with the Imperial House Law passed by the Diet. Article 3. The advice and approval of the Cabinet shall be required for all acts of the Emperor in matters of State, and the Cabinet shall be responsible therefor."

The People's Republic of China has a notable unitary character, it has one party democracy but here the Communist Party is supreme. The administration of all the territories of the Republic China is done from the capital.

(2) *Federal Form Constitutions*: Two or more monarchies combined for common interest or under pressure integrated to form a 'confederation' or 'federal state'; out of Austria, Croatia, Czechoslovakia, Germany, Hungary, Serbs and Slovenes or in contemporary Middle East confederations were occasionally[29] formed. Similar has been the case with republics. In confederations the constituents are loosely integrated and all of them maintain international identity, generally in some agreed matters the constituents act together viz. Federation of Malaysia and Singapore (1963-65).[30] Often, when the confederation is loose the units maintain their international personality. Soviet Russia under the Charter of United Nations Organization had a character of confederation, its units were members of UNO and Soviet Russia had three votes in UN General Assembly. British Empire had like confederations several votes in UN General Assembly till its Dominions and Colonies became real independent states.

By theory in all 'federal' states there is a division of sovereignty, legislative and administrative powers between the federal authority and the integrated states, normally external sovereignty dealing with foreign relations, war and peace or diplomatic relations has been exercised by the federal wing of the state. In early times Greeks and Romans had at times formed federation. The Swiss Confederation is the oldest federal state since 1291 originally formed by three Forest Cantons. However, the United States of America where thirteen colonies of England first declared their independence from

---

29. United Arab Republic united Egypt and Syria while Iraq and Jordan formed monarchial counter-federation. These were temporary alignments lasting few years.
30. These separated in 1965 to again become independent states.

British Empire and thereafter formed a union as an independent country is taken to be the prototype of modern federal state system. Germany as Prussian Empire had been a federal state since 1815 with common monarchial government till the end of First World War. Afghanistan, Australia, Bangladesh, Canada, Germany, Pakistan, Switzerland and the USA are having federal Constitution with division of power between Central Government on one hand and provincial unit or constituent state governments on the other. Obviously there are and have been variations within the type of union desired or achieved by the federation. There is national sovereignty and also international sovereignty of the federated state that rests in federal part of state. The details of variation are conditions of conciliation or peace between federal authority and its units. Accordingly, the Constitution becomes superior both to the federation and the federated units. The Constitution has a degree of permanence and it cannot be changed without participation of the federated units when it is truly a federation.

Some Constitutions like those of United States of America and Commonwealth of Australia comparatively keep the powers of federal authority under check as against federated units by giving only specific powers to the former and leaving other powers, called residuary powers, of the sovereign with the latter. The Swiss Constitution is prototype of this kind of division of powers. The Constitution of Commonwealth of Australia narrates the powers of Commonwealth Government and leaves others for the units called 'States'. The Constitution of Canada is federal on reverse lines: the Constitution strengthens the Dominion Government as against the units of federation, called 'Provinces' and not 'States'. Most of the federal states[31] are of Canadian type, e.g. Afghanistan, Bangladesh and Pakistan.

The federalism in Constitution of India is more flexible in the matter of distribution of powers between Union Government

31. India is another important example but it terms the units of federation as 'states'.

and federal units called States, with residuary powers given to Union, like Canada.[32] The Constitution of India gives guided powers and procedure to the Union Government to change the boundaries of State units. The units are based on administrative convenience, language or cultural affinity of the area.

The Swiss Confederation is a federal state of unique type. It started as a confederation of several Roman Catholic cantons. After a Civil War in which seven cantons unsuccessfully attempted to secede, in 1848 a new Constitution of Swiss Confederation was adopted with federal government more powerful without 'annihilating state identity' of cantons with three national languages, German, French and Italian, are recognized. The residuary powers (Article 3) are with units; all the units have same form of democratic government; and federal authority is to guarantee the cantonal constitutions.[33] The Swiss Constitution is rigid in order to make secure both federal and cantonal rights; it can be amended only through referendum of people in cantons. Further in bicameral federal legislature the canton decide and not the constitution the manner of selecting or electing the cantonal members representing them in Council of States, the federal Upper House.

Effect on Federalism of National Emergencies: As history has been, the federal constitutions are compromises between different cultural and socially distinguishable communes living on the territory of the state but politically united for common good. The basic idea has been that all those people that can be identified as separate on linguistic or cultural basis should have equal opportunity of developing themselves by a limited self-

32. India is a federal state with division of powers between Union and States which are creation of the Constitution under its Seventh Schedule. The sovereign power is with Union and the administrative officers for enforcement of laws enacted by either are the same. There is a Concurrent List also.

    Constitution of Federation of Russia (1993) has federal structure much on the lines of US Constitution.

33. The Constitution of India has adopted this pattern for federal units.

government within the framework of the federation. In other words in a unitary political state all people are likely get regimented despite right to equality available to different areas of the state. In United Kingdom the catholic Eire preferred to separate identifying its distinct traditions and culture.[34] However when there is a national emergency like a war or internal strife, all federal Constitutions in national interest become unitary in character fully or in parts, for example,[35] the Switzerland or Pakistan. The federal government is given full powers to deal with the cause of emergency by curtailing autonomy of the federal units. This aspect has been further introduced subsequently.

Rigid or Flexible Constitution: Comparative study of various Constitutions gives importance to the question whether a Constitution is rigid or flexible. It is an enquiry into the stability of the constitutional organization of the state. An unstable Constitution leads to uncertainty of durability of the government and uncertainty of law when these can be changed by new administration.

(1) *Constitutional Flexibility*: A documented Constitution is like a deed that sets the rights and duties of the parties that they execute for future reference. Politically, the Constitution is a deed between the ruler and the subjects that sets the method of governance and the rights of people. Normally, there is a break in continuity or a change in political organization of the country, may be involving separation, split or unification and the Constitution represents the new accepted order. However, political change is law of nature; it may be peaceful, brought about war, by a revolution or by renovation. Change from monarchies to republicanism has been generally by assassination of monarchs or by coups. The famous French Revolution of

34. It was given independence by Britain in 1937. The Eire Constitution has not been incorporated in this book.
35. Indian Constitution is also an example where during an emergency the unitary character fast develops under its chapter XVIII. This takes place at the expense of autonomy of federal units.

1789 and the Russian Revolution of 1917 saw systematic massacres of King and associates. In England in 1688, James II escaped death by escaping from the country and the important constitutional Acts, namely, Bill of Rights 1689 and Act of Settlement 1701 had followed which after a brief interlude created a contractual or constitutional monarchy.

Much in the same manner republican constitutions have undergone political upheavals in which one dictator has replaced another or democratic President has been replaced by military junta, administrative council or dictator or else one State has broken down into several states. The flexible Constitution of India (1950) has been amended often in order to deal with new situations or new ideals not contemplated in 1950. In the context of this book, the fluctuations in the constitutional settings in the State of Federal Republic of Germany and the State of Pakistan show such fluctuations that have been of political nature.

(a) *Flexible Constitution of Germany*: Germany was known as Prussian Empire till 1919 when after defeat in First World War it became Weimar Republic (1919) which Hitler overthrew. The Constitution (1946) for West Germany was produced by Allies England, France and USA, after II World War. Later in 1990 German Democratic Republic (East Germany) under Soviet Russia united with West Germany and the Basic Law of 1949 remained the Constitution of united Germany with necessary minor changes to give effect to the reunion and the name of the country remained Federal Republic of Germany.

(b) *Constitutional Flexibility in Pakistan*: The form of government in Pakistan has alternated between civilian democracy and military dictatorship that enforced martial law in the country. In Pakistan a Constituent Assembly had framed a Democratic, Federal and Islamic Republic Constitution that came into operation in 1956. A military dictatorship was established after a coup in 1957; the Constitution was abrogated and martial law was imposed in the country. Under a new Constitution of 1962 a civilian democratic government under military patronage was installed in 1962. It provided for the election of President, national and provincial assemblies by a restricted electoral college composed of members of local councils. In 1969 there was again a military takeover that lasted till 1973 and another new (third) Constitution was adopted. This Constitution provided for a parliamentary system with a President as Head of State and popularly with elected Prime Minister as Head of Government. The 1973 Constitution was suspended when there was a military coup in July 1977 and martial law was imposed. Under a makeshift Provisional Constitution, the Chief Administrator of Martial Law proclaimed himself as President of Pakistan in 1978. In March 1981 a Provisional Constitutional Order was promulgated by the President, which provided a framework for civilian government under martial law followed by a national referendum. This was eighth amendment of the Constitution that gave to the President extraordinary discretionary powers to be exercised in supreme national interest – to dismiss the elected Prime Minister and to dissolve the National Assembly. In 1985 a process for reinstating the Constitution of 1973 by President was initiated under this, in October 1985 a newly elected National Assembly had passed an amended Constitution, giving extraordinary powers to the President, including the authority to appoint any member of the National Assembly as Prime Minister.

The Constitution was again amended in 1988 for a semi-presidential system; it provided for a President as head of state and a Prime Minister as head of government; both must be Muslims. The National Assembly, the Senate, and the four provincial assemblies were to elect the President for a term of five years. The Prime Minister is to be elected by the National Assembly. The President is to act on the advice of the Prime Minister whom he can dismiss and form another government. It made mandatory for the President to seek the advice of Prime Minister in matters relating to the dissolution of National Assembly. Under this Constitution before being scrapped by the Thirteenth Amendment in 1997 the power to dismiss the elected governments was exercised four times.

Pakistan currently has no identifiable Constitution, every thing being in form of Presidential Orders. The 1973 document was suspended for the third time in its history in November 2007 by the President by Proclamation of Emergency Order 2007. A number of amendments that have followed have secured the pre-eminent position of President, particularly the Constitution (Second Amendment) Order 2007 of 14 December 2007, and have revived to some extent the Constitution cautiously. Pakistan Constitution unlike as in England depends on presidential supremacy for its substance. Hence the flexibility quotient is very high in constitutional power politics of Pakistan.

In Bangladesh the Constitution has been flexible intrinsically to allow military takeover of government in certain eventualities. Constitution of Bangladesh has been amended fourteen times since 1972. The Constitution of Bangladesh is since 2006 inoperative.[36]

(2) *Rigidity of Constitutions—Forms and Patterns*: It has been mentioned that rigid Constitution is one that has a permanency and cannot be changed or amended by exercise of normal executive, legislative or judicial powers. The Constitution is source of all powers including its own amendment. As such the rigidity of any Constitution is to be adjudged by the process of its amendment. The requirements of special majority for enactment of the amendment, referendum, that is, political acceptance by majority of people or the state or in case of federal state approval of the amendment by majority or all of the constituent units determine the form of rigidity.

The British Constitution is least rigid since it is in form of Acts of Parliament that do not require any special majority in Parliament or referendum.

---

36. The 2006 election to Bangladesh Parliament was postponed indefinitely and a caretaker government was formed. It works to revise the voter list and to end corruption. The government declared to hold new elections by 2008 but national recent activities have created uncertainty about elections. Meanwhile the Bangladesh Military has interfered and plans to have an "own brand of democracy" by making changes in the constitution to allow military participation in politics. The military has also imposed censorship of the national media.

The Constitution of People's Republic of China is a Communist Party product. It does not have a formal procedure for its amendment at all. The 1982 Constitution rather provides a legal basis for the broad changes in China's social and economic institutions which significantly revise government structure and procedures that are to take place as required from time to time initiated by National People's Congress (NPC). The 1982 State Constitution is lengthy, unclear documents cover 138 articles. Most of sections have been adapted directly from the earlier 1954 and the 1978 State Constitution. Four major revisions have been made by the 1982 Constitution. The Constitution stipulates the NPC as the highest organ of state authority and power under which the State Council, the Supreme People's Court and the Supreme Peoples Procuratorate are elected and are responsible to the NPC. Thus there is unilateral rigidity that depends on policy decisions of the National People's Congress in Constitution of Chinese People's Republic.

The Constitution of Swiss Confederation, 1874 as amended in 1891 provides a rigid method for maintaining its character of a confederation and participation of people by process of referendum in national decision making. This shows in the methods adopted for making amendments in its Constitution. In substance there are two pathways for effecting amendment: (1) by National Assembly proposals and (2) by people's initiative directly. Under the first method, the Swiss 'supreme power of the Confederation' including the power of amendment called 'Revision' of the Constitution, vide Article 85 (14), is exercised by the Federal Assembly. For 'total revision' is effected only through the forms required for passing Federal Laws[37] while a 'partial revision' can be undertaken 'by means of popular initiative' or through the forms required for passing Federal Laws. The process of popular initiative for revision is laid down by Federal Legislation. In either process the amendment is completed 'when it has been accepted by a majority of the Swiss citizens taking part in the voting thereon

37. Article 119: Swiss Constitution.

and by a majority of the states'.[38] The rigidity of Swiss Constitution is to be reckoned in referendum and the acceptance of the referendum by majority of constituent states of the Confederation.

Japanese Constitution on the other hand has been constitutionally stable and is in the category of rigid Constitutions. Here under the provisions of its Article 96 amendments to the Constitution are initiated by the Diet (Parliament) through a concurring vote of two-thirds or more of the members of each House and are thereupon submitted to the people for ratification that requires the affirmative vote of all votes caste thereon, at a special referendum or at such election as the Diet would so specify. Emperor has no power of withholding the amendment and this becomes an integral part of the Constitution of Japan. The requirement of referendum confirms the role of people in the acceptance of the Constitution.

The 1958 Fifth Constitution of France has its own form of rigidity. Its Article 89 prohibits (1) pursuing or initiating of any revision (amendment) procedure when the integrity of the territory is under attack, (2) the Republican form of government. Further, the right to propose amendments to the Constitution belongs concurrently (1) to the President of the Republic, on the proposal of Prime Minister, and (2) members of Parliament; besides passing of the proposal by the two assemblies in identical terms it has to be approved by referendum. However, the referendum requirement is waived when the President in his discretion decides to submit the amending proposal to a meeting of the two Houses in a Congress where it is passed by a majority of three-fifth of the votes cast by members. It is to be mentioned here that the Fifth French Constitution was adopted to solve the problem of overseas territories of France, Algeria particularly, which were to become independent states eventually under international developments but rigidity of the Fourth Constitution was coming in the way.

The Constitution of United States of America (1787) adopted rigidity in favour of the constituent State units of the federation

38. Article 123: Swiss Constitution.

(Article V). The Senate of the Congress is composed of two Senators from each state chosen by the Legislatures of the states, and by amendment of the Constitution equal suffrage for the states in the Senate cannot be denied. The amendments to the Constitution can be initiated in two ways: (1) By the Congress when two-third majority in each House propose amendments, (2) On application of the Legislatures of two-thirds of the several States to call a Convention for proposing amendments on certain items. *In either case* the proposal for amendment has to be ratified either by the Legislatures of three-fourths of several states or by three-fourth states meeting in Convention before it becomes part of the US Constitution. There is no condition for reference to people for referendum for effecting an amendment.

The Constitution of Sri Lanka is quite amendable but the procedure is elaborate and depends on referendum in many circumstances. Utmost rigidity is directed both in provisions dealing with legislators and executive. The Constitution by Article 82 (7) defines that "amendment" includes repeal, alteration and addition. The Constitution can also be replaced by another by the set procedure for amendment. A Bill that amends any existing provisions or which repeals or replaces the Constitution and a Bill that is inconsistent with or violates the provisions of the Constitution are specifically and separately dealt with by the Constitution. Referendum is the ultimate tool of rigidity for maintaining the original division of powers and functions.

First, under Article 80 of the Constitution of Sri Lanka a Bill including a Bill that amends the Constitution becomes law when the Bill is passed by Parliament and when the certificate of the Speaker is endorsed thereon. However, where the Cabinet of Ministers has certified that any Bill or any provision thereof is intended to be submitted for approval by the People at a Referendum or where the Supreme Court has determined that a Bill or any provision thereof requires the approval of the People at a Referendum or where any Bill is submitted to the People by Referendum under paragraph (2) of Article 85, such Bill or such provision shall become law upon being approved by the People at a Referendum in accordance with paragraph (3) of Article 85 that too only when the President certifies that the Bill or provision thereof has been so approved and the period of challenging the validity of Referendum in Supreme Court has expired or the Supreme Court has held the referendum to be valid.

Second, the Bill for repeal or amendment of Constitution under Article 82 must specifically express this purpose. The passing of such a Bill requires special majority, vide Article 82(4). Under this requirement the Bill for the amendment of any provision of the Constitution or for the repeal and replacement of the Constitution, shall become law only when the number of votes cast in favour thereof amounts to not less than two-thirds of the whole number of Members (including those not present) and upon a certificate by the President or the Speaker, as the case may be, being endorsed thereon in accordance with the provisions of Article 80 or 79. However, amendment of certain specified provisions of the Constitution mentioned in Article 83 require submission of the Bill for Referendum compulsorily.

Third, any Bill for amendment of an Act which is inconsistent with any provision of the Constitution is to be placed on the 'Order Paper of Parliament'. Thereafter, either the Cabinet of Ministers has to certify that the Bill is intended to be passed by the special majority required by Article 84 or where the Supreme Court has determined that a Bill requires to be passed by such special majority, such Bill shall become law only if the number of votes cast in favour thereof amounts to not less than two-thirds of the whole number of Members (including those not present). But, such an Act does not, and is not deemed to, amend, repeal or replace the Constitution or any provision thereof. The Constitution of Sri Lanka is thus rigid in an exceptional way.

Referendum for Rigidity: Referendum is a constitutional device for maintaining public or people's control over existing constitutional principles. It implies reference of a new constitution, amendment or change in constitution, or any enactment to people for approval by a vote. In **modern** constitutionalism people assert themselves in their political setup by (i) Referendum, (ii) Popular Initiative for amendment of Constitution or enactment of a law, and (iii) by Recall of their elected representatives. These are recurrent processes for maintaining supremacy of people over the government and the Constitution.

Referendum may be direct or indirect. It is direct when it is obligatory that the new Constitution or amendment of the existing Constitution be put to a popular approval by vote. Currently, the new Constitution for a republican Nepal (2007) would replace the existing monarchial Constitution of 1990 after an election in April 2008. Similarly, in Bhutan the general election to be held in April 2008 is to adopt a Constitution establishing a National Assembly for the Kingdom. Referendum as integral part for rigidity and stability of political organization of the State is incorporated in the Constitutions of Japan (Article 96), Switzerland (Article 123), Australia (Article 70), Republics of France (Title XIV), Eire (Article 47), or Sri Lanka (Articles 80 to 85) among several others. The 2005 Constitution of Bhutan under its Article 32 provides the elaborated conditions for holding of "National Referendum".[39] As already introduced under the Constitution of Sri Lanka both constitutional provisions and enactments by legislature can be placed for referendum in a variety of ways. The demand for Referendum by 'Popular Initiative' can be made at any time in Switzerland when a demand for this is made by fifty thousand voter citizens.

Indirect referendum is resorted to by many states on British pattern. Under the British 'Conventions of Constitution' when a law is desired which is opposed by other political party and which requires a basic change in the pattern of liberties or established parliamentary system details, the party forming the government seeks a vote of people by going for a fresh mandate at a general election to the House of Commons after premature dissolution. Only after the Party forming the government returns to power, it undertakes to adopt the law. In a classic

39. Nagatively, Clause (3) of Article 32 lays down: "A referendum shall not be held on the question of imposition, variation or repeal of taxes".

illustration, Prime Minister Atlee of England contested and won the election for Labour Party on the issue of nationalization of steel industry; this concept of nationalization of a private industry was contrary to established economic policy of England.[40] This constitutional principle is followed by most of the states that were part of British Empire. In India, for instance, a two third majority in House of People is required for making any Constitution Amendment Act. Several times the Prime Ministers have sought two-third majority in House of People at fresh elections for implementing amendments to Constitution for achievement of their policies. The elections held after dissolution of House of People in 1971, 1977 and 1980 were in nature of referendum, seeking approval of people for or against the policies of the Political Party forming the Government. In first of these, the ruling Prime Minister was returned with two-third majority and proceeded with more than five amendments in the Constitution; in the second and third of these elections, the ruling Party was defeated and the opposition Parties came to power and these also made sweeping amendments to the Constitution.

Indirect referendum is also conducted by Joint Sitting of the two Houses of the national Legislature which is required to adopt the Bill or resolution by special majority on matters of amendment of the Constitution or passing of controversial Bills, viz. Article V of the US Constitution or Article 368 of the Constitution of India. In Japan the two Houses have to pass an amendment bill by two-third majority in each before the amendment is put for referendum. The idea is that the two Houses of the legislature represent a cross section of all or different views and opinions held by the people.

A partial referendum aspect is the 'right to recall' an elected representative when the latter no longer represents the views of the people that elected him; it is a principle which regards the elected representative as trustee of the 'will' of the constituency which elected him. However, this 'right to recall' is not found at

40. However, after forming the Government he did not nationalize the steel industry.

national level accept in Stalinist Constitutions. It is marginally adopted in India where under anti-defection constitutional provision a political party can disown a person who was elected as its nominee; but there is no sequential re-election.

Constitutions and Sovereignty of States: Supremacy of Constitution is an intrinsic idea which depends on the location of internal sovereignty of the state. By the accepted common sense now, those who lay down the Constitution and those who can amend it are sovereigns. Even now in twenty-first century there are autocracies and dictators who significantly exercise sovereign power of their state; these amend, scrape or restructure a new constitution at will. Pakistan State is a contemporary example of this characteristic. The Constitutions are in the nature of legal documents instead of being orders, edicts or law which are not above the powerful individuals who or oligarchies which issue or lay them down. Constitutions deal with hierarchy of norms and political organization of people. Some old States have been prototypes, in the sense that these have provided basics of constitutional forms that have been copied, adopted or adapted by other States.

Normally the modern constitutions declare that these derive their validity from the wishes or consent of people of that State:

The Constitution of USA (1787) proclaims in its preamble "We, the people of United States ..." as its source;

The Swiss Constitution (1874) has the Cantons, Federal Powers and the People as its source; same is the position of Constitution Act of Australia (1900) but the status of Crown of United Kingdom as nominal constitutional head was maintained as in England;

The Constitution of former USSR (1936) rested sovereignty on "the working people of town and country as represented by the Soviets of Working People's Deputies";

The Constitution of Eire (1937) structures its origin on "We, the People of Eire ...";

The Constitution of Japan (1946) "We, the Japanese people" expressly proclaimed that "the sovereign power resides with the people" and who "do firmly establish this Constitution ...".

The Constitution of Fifth French Republic (1956) originated in the resolve of French people, "The French people hereby solemnly proclaim their attachment to the Rights of Man and to the principles of national sovereignty as defined by Declaration of 1789 ..." and the declaration[41] that "National sovereignty belongs to the people ...."

In the Constitution of India (1950), there is a declaration "We, the people of India ... do hereby adopt, enact and give to ourselves this Constitution ...."

Most of the former colonies of British Empire which have now become independent give validity to their Constitutions, following the tradition of unwritten British Constitution, through their legislature and characterize their Constitution as the "Supreme Law of the Land". For example, the Constitution of South Africa (1996) declares Constitution as 'Supreme Law of the Land' but is now independent of Britain. Similar is the position in Constitutions of Bangladesh and Singapore.

The Constitution of Sri Lanka of 1978 expressly lays down by its Article 3 that "In the Republic of Sri Lanka sovereignty is in the people and is inalienable. Sovereignty includes the powers of government, fundamental rights and the franchise".

In Republic of China (Constitution of 1982 and earlier), in accordance with Marxist idea of the dictatorship of the proletariat the Constitution asserts that the People's Democratic Dictatorship would be necessary until the Communist Party of China achieves a true socialist society. The premise of the "People's democratic dictatorship" is that the Communist Party of China and the state act on behalf of the people, but can and do use dictatorial methods in order to maintain the supremacy of the Constitution by remaining in power in the face of hostile forces. It is implicit in the concept of the people's democratic dictatorship that dictatorial means are not evil and that dictatorship is necessary for the Constitution of a Socialist State.

41. Article 3: Constitution of French Republic.

In all these Constitutions the amending power is not given to legislature or executive alone but is dispersed in order to give the elements of rigidity, superiority and sacred characters to the constitution. The above mentioned constitutions are adapted and adopted by other democratic states of modern-world States.

Separation of Constitutional Powers: The Doctrine

Absolutism or all powers concentrated in one constitutional organ lead to tyranny of state over its subjects. Breaking of absolute powers of State so that it may be exercised by several organs of state is regarded to be good for the people and for the progress of a country. Tyranny is opposed to public welfare and public interest. Separation in powers of the state also ensures better management of democratic government. As once professed by Spencer, greater the diversity of elements or components and greater their unity then greater is progress through evolutionary process. In simple but modern terms, split of government into legislative, executive and judicial organs and with greater the number of Ministries under a government working for welfare of country and people under a common unifying planning system provided by the Constitution would lead to better progress or prosperity of the country. Similarly, separation between prosecutor and judge would lead to better administration of justice. Politically the division or separation of state functions and assignment of these functions to different autonomous organs, with the Constitution being the unifying force, leads to better management of the state affairs.

Constitutional theory and Constitutions now consider it wise or expedient to divide state functions of the state in between President, Legislatures, Election Commissions, Ministries, Executive, Audit of Accountants, Judiciary, Administrative Tribunals, Ombudsman, Constitutional Councils and the People. All are to perform their constitutionally assigned functions separately with a clearly discernible separation from each other and should be autonomous or 'equal and mutually independent of each other'. These should exercise or perform their allocated functions without delegating these to others. The doctrine of separation of powers is a system of 'check and balance' operating within the four walls of the Constitution.

All modern Constitutions have their distinct margins in laying down separation of powers. Historically, this doctrine was propounded by Locke (d. 1704)[42] of England while appreciating and justifying the results of Glorious Revolution 1688, Bill of Rights, 1689 and the Act of Succession 1701 of England which made kingship contractual, separated judiciary and Parliament from King's influence and ensured the people of their basic rights. His ideas were picked by rationalist European thinkers of eighteenth century, mainly Montesquieu (d. 1755)[43] and Rousseau (d. 1788)[44] and who advocated similar government setup for their and other European countries and called the British achievement a natural 'social contract'. The European thinkers were more concerned with the influence of Kings on judiciary which denied justice to people, hence these found an answer to King's tyranny in the doctrine of separation of powers and theory of social contract. The separation of the concepts of natural rights and fundamental liberties from the jurisdiction of state powers was a significant contribution to constitutional theories of the age of rationalism of eighteenth and nineteenth centuries. Hume, Thomas Paine and other subsequent influential political thinkers have prevailed in forming Constitutions based on these principles in Europe and in Americas. It is observed that the Constitutions of USA (1783) and of France after Revolution of 1789 alongwith British

42. Locke, *Second Treatise of Civil Government*, Chapter XII.

43. A Frenchman, he had lectured in Austria, Hungary, Italy, Germany, Switzerland and England. He believed in uniformity of human conduct; that Governments are not to exist in isolation but be related to human aspirations and behaviour; and that humans are social beings and state-made laws should in spirit reflect universal naturalism.

44. An Austrian, he propounded the theory of popular sovereignty and separation of governmental powers accordingly. He was opposed to 'inequality' prevailing in European States. Liberty, equality and fraternity were part of his theory of social contract. His theories contributed to American Declaration of Independence (1776) and French Revolution (1788).

parliamentary system variants are behind all Constitutions framed in nineteenth century onwards for the reason that the modern political world existed as colonies or empires of European States till 1945. It is the breaking of these empires and colonies that has given rise to about one hundred new states since 1945 and these states have followed the constitutional pattern if their metropolitan state.

The salient details of the application of constitutionalism reflecting the doctrine of separation of powers followed in modern Constitutions under reference in the book are as under:

(1) *Separation of Executive from Legislature*: Historically, separation of governmental powers began with separation between King, the chief executive, on one hand and legislatures on the other.

Opposition to concentration of all powers in the King has been at the origin of modern States since the Glorious Revolution of 1688 in England. In constitutional terms since ancient times the king was world over the chief executive, law-giver to the people and was the fountain of justice. This Glorious Revolution made the kingship contractual in the sense that he was subject to the powers of British Parliament; there was a separation of executive and legislative powers and the King was to act on the advice of Prime Minister while the Prime Minister was dependant on majority in elected House of Commons. Earlier in 1607 Chief Justice Coke of England had held that interpretation of a law and justice according to established law was the function of Courts and not of the King. These developments are taken to be the origin of doctrine of separation of governmental powers. The British and European political thinkers of late seventeenth and of eighteenth century extolled the achievements of British politicians under which there was a separation between legislative and executive functions; they recommended to other states to go for separation of kingship from law-making. Normally the doctrine of separation of powers as developed by European thinkers envisages that executive and judiciary should be separated, that is, the executive should not decide disputes and the judiciary should not make law. The delegated legislation and judicial activism both examined in details afterward are tolerated vices from the point of view of this doctrine. The legislature should not directly enforce laws enacted by it or decide controversies but only make laws as and when these might be necessary according to policies it deems necessary or good for the people while executive should enforce laws made by legislature. When there is a dispute or necessity of interpreting the existing law of the land this is to be done by judiciary. In Ireland while examining the constitutionality of State (Amendment Bill), 1940, it was observed that in the three great departments of State—the Oirachtas (Legislature), the Executive and the Judiciary, for the harmonies working of the machinery of State it is essential that each Department should confine itself its own constitutional functions.[45] The delegation of legislative powers by the Legislature to Executive to frame rules is a controversial matter in this context but it does take place within certain parameters.

(2) *Separation of Executive and Judicial Functions*: There is a wise dictum of natural justice that a person should not be a judge in his own cause. When there is dispute between two individuals the King's courts were natural attribute of kingship as everywhere king was regarded as fountain of justice. But where the issue or dispute is between people and the King or State, the judiciary must be neutral and unbiased. A separation between executive powers and judiciary is needed for justice. In England, this had been achieved by a series of steps, beginning with famous decision of Chief Justice Coke in 1607,[46] that were prelude to Glorious Revolution of 1688 also. In the next

45. [1940] Ir. R. 481.

46. Case: *Prohibitions del Roy* (1607): All cases "ought to be determined and adjudged in some court of justice according to the law and custom of England. God had endowed His Majesty with excellent science and great endowments of nature, but His Majesty was not learned in the laws of his realm of England, and causes which concern the life, or inheritance, or goods or fortunes of his subjects, are not to be decided by natural reason, but by artificial reason and judgment of law, which law is an art which requires long study and experience, before that a man can attain to the cognizance of it."

century the Continental political thinkers, viz. Montesquieu, Rousseau, Hume or Thomas Paine including American Madison had extended the concept of separation of powers to judiciary and executive branches of government also. This principle is now an accepted part of constitutionalism and is followed practically in all constitutional states. However, in some states like India, Canada, Australia, Federal Republic of South Africa, Japan or Republic if Sri Lanka, the judiciary is also given a definitive supervisory role over exercise of administrative and legislative powers by the organs of government.

(3) *Separate Identity of Judiciary and Law*: The constitutional status of judiciary with reference to the doctrine of separation of powers has several facets and patterns.

First, it is appropriate that the "judges should not only be independent of the Government, but also free from liability to vexatious actions for acts done in exercise of duty. ... These considerations apply to judges of any country, but they apply with greater force to the judges of a country in which individual rights and constitutional liberties depend upon the decisions "of the courts whether formally guaranteed by a Constitution or not."[47]

The basic function of judiciary is to decide impartially the disputes between subjects of law and also between subjects and the state. However, under French constitutional system followed by several republic states in the world, administrative tribunals and not judiciary determine the disputes between State and subjects.

Second, in autocracies, the judiciary is not independent of policy movements or considerations of the government which it does not dare to ignore. The judges stand the risk of removal and imprisonment for giving a verdict against government. Position of judiciary under Constitution of Pakistan in first decade of this century was of this kind. Independence of

---

47. Wade and Phillips, *Constitutional Law*, Part V, 'The Judiciary': Chapter on 'The Judicial Function'; C.F. Strong, *Modern Political Constitutions*.

judiciary entails their method of appointment, removal or dismissal, salaries, separation from executive in the matters of internal organization including promotion and assignment of functional duties, and judicial immunity from civil actions and criminal liability for things done officially. The judges once appointed, they are not "subject to fluctuations of the electoral results as are the two other branches of government". The judicial power of giving punishment for 'Contempt of Court' is an important ingredient of judicial independence.

Third, the judicial process in democracy depends on rule or supremacy of law and Constitution while the law is laid down by Legislature of the state. In this scenario the judiciary applies the existing law or constitutional rights to individual cases. In England and other states which have followed British pattern, the doctrine of precedent implies that any interpretation given to Constitution or law becomes part of the Constitution or law until it is overruled by the court itself or else the Constitution or the law is appropriately amended by Constituent Authority or Legislature as the case might be. The Constitutions of USA, Australia, South Africa, Japan, Sri Lanka and of India among others follow this pattern.

Fourth, the European continental States and Ireland have separation of powers concept limited to chief legislator and chief executive with judiciary having defined powers. The *Droit Administratif* (administrative law) system of France followed by Continental and other states, gives a limited importance to judiciary. But, the federal constitutions of USA, India, Canada, Australia and others have wider or different dimensions for separation of powers and judiciary has singular status.

Fifth, the 'Separation of Powers' doctrine in democracies has also maintained a distance between people, law, justice entailing judiciary and the state; this relativity is contemporaneously determined and fixed by the Constitutions of different states differently. This aspect is taken up separately subsequently.

Forms of Governments

The most definitive function of the Constitution is to define the pattern of Government for the country. The Executive and Legislature are most important or leading part of Governments

Historically, the parliamentary and presidential forms of government are the two primary methods by which the governments by elected representatives are being made functional in the politics of the world. In both of them executive function extends to direction of general policy and includes initiation of legislation by formulating a bill, maintenance of public order and in a welfare state it embraces social and economic development of the people. The presidential form of constitution involves both elected president and the legislature since it exists only in republican state. In democratic republics people matter and so the legislative function extends to converting a bill proposed by the executive into law after taking into account the interests of the people rather than of the government alone. The French model of democracy took into account both British and American constitutionalism and so government of France is an admixture of both: Presidentship of USA is combined with parliamentary and judicial systems of England. The balance is maintained differently in different Constitutions of the States of the world taking into account the domestic socio-political environment and that turns out to be the characteristic of a Constitution. For example, in Indian Constitution the President is nominal head of the state as the King is in England but parliamentary system of England has been coupled with guarantee of fundamental liberties and with judiciary functioning as in USA.

Thus, contemporary constitutional theory brings out three or four prototypes of democratic governments: the US, British, and French models. The Constitutions of democratic States follow one or other models and are distinct only in matters of details. The US Constitution is benchmark for presidential form of government with stringent separation of powers and a dominant judiciary; French pattern of President and Parliament relationship is preferred now over US pattern of pure

Presidentship. England is example for parliamentary form of constitution with parliamentary supremacy concept; while European States have generally followed French or Swiss form of constitutionalism with referendum as necessary part of constitutional set up. Following Swiss and Eire Constitutions many Constitutions provide directive principles of state policy for guidance of their legislatures and governments.

First, British Constitution has provided the format for parliamentary form of government since eighteenth century with typical separation of powers of executive and legislature. Parliamentary supremacy, bicameral national legislature called Parliament, Diet or National Assembly and all knit together with 'rule of law' are solid contributions of British constitutionalism to constitutional theory. Further, the executive generally called Council of Ministers or Cabinet headed by a Prime Minister that has to have continued support of majority of elected members of the legislature and that the legislature has additional function or power of censoring the Prime Minister are constitutional elements that have their origin in British Constitution. These aspects now integral part of constitutional theory have worldwide application except in absolute dictatorships.

The Chief executive in parliamentary form of government may be hereditary monarch or elected president. This pattern is generally followed in several of states that were once a part of British Empire and is compromised when the State has federal structure. Separation of powers in parliamentary form of government mainly means that law is to be finally made by the legislature only but the legislature cannot enforce the laws made by it. The British parliamentary system is based on supremacy of Parliament which in turn means supremacy of enacted law and in general the 'rule of law'. Accordingly, the judicial powers are limited to interpretation of enacted law and not the intrinsic worth of the law. The rights of people also flow out of the enacted law but by a system of political checks – the Parliament does not take away the established rights of the people. The Members of House of Commons of England can by defeating a government sponsored Bill or by passing a 'motion of no-confidence' in the Ministry or Prime Minister at any time topple the government for fresh election have to follow even when the term has not been completed. This is an important tool of parliamentary form of government, analysed below. The executive has some prerogatives over the affairs of the State subject to the Ministry retaining majority in House of Commons. Many of the monarchial States, like Japan, or Sweden, and republican states like India, Sri Lanka, Republic of South Africa, follow this pattern.

No-Confidence Motion: The parliamentarian check on policies and functioning of the government takes place through 'motions' moved by the opposition parties. The function[48] of opposition parties in democracy is to criticize the Government and to expose its incompetence to the people; it is not to obstruct or hinder the Government. The policies of government may be of foreign relations or affairs, financial or on any domestic matter of national importance. Every Bill for enactment is a policy matter and if it is rejected in elected House of Parliament or National Assembly it amounts to a no-confidence motion adopted against the government. But, more significant are 'adjournment motion' and 'regular motion' on a particular matter: former is meant for urgent or immediate consideration of objectionable emergent issues but when the Speaker rules that there is no urgency it becomes a regular motion to be moved in accordance with rules.[49] In either case when adopted it is a censor leading to downfall of the government. Apart from these, there are regular motions against particular Minister or the Council of Ministers.[50] When a motion of censor is moved discussions 'for' and 'against' the motion take place and it is for

48. See: Jennings, *The British Constitution,* pp. 86-94.
49. Adjournment Motion: In India: *House of People, Rules of Procedure and Conduct of Business, Chapter IX, Rules 338-347*;
    Regular Motions: *Ibid.*, Chapter XIV Rules 186-192 and Chapter XXVII Rules 338-347.
50. In India: *House of People, Rules of Procedure and Conduct of Business, Chapter XXVII, Rules 362-367AA.*

government to move for 'closure' of debate, if it is challenged by opposition there is division or voting (there are four procedures of deciding the matter by voting at this stage) when vote is for opposition demand it amounts to 'no-confidence' vote and the Council of Ministers has to resign.

The right to move the adjournment motion or raising no-confidence motion of the House for the purpose of discussing a definite matter of urgent public importance may be subject to the various restrictions,[51] viz.:

(i) Not more than one such motion might be made at the same sitting;

(ii) Not more than one matter might be discussed on the same motion;

(iii) The motion might be restricted to a specific matter of recent occurrence involving responsibility of the Government;

(iv) The motion might not raise a question of privilege of the House;

(v) The motion is not to revive discussion on a matter which has been discussed in the same session;

(vi) The motion shall not anticipate a matter, which has been previously appointed for consideration. Further, in determining whether a discussion is out of order on the ground of anticipation, regard is to be given by the Speaker to the probability of the anticipated matter being in regular course brought before the House within a reasonable time;

(vii) The motion is postponed and is not to deal with a matter which is under adjudication by a court of law having jurisdiction or statutory tribunal or statutory authority performing any judicial or quasi-judicial functions or any commission or court of enquiry appointed to enquire into or to investigate into the matter.

---

51. The narration of these restrictions is based on Indian law, procedure and practice.

After ample discussions have taken place on the matters of motion, the Speaker at the appointed hour on the allotted day or to the last of the allotted days, as the case may be, forthwith puts to vote alongwith every question necessary to determine the decision of the House on the original question raised in the motion. The 'effectiveness' of the motion depends on relative member-strength of opposition in elected Chamber of Parliament or National Assembly. When in danger the Government can in order to avoid no-confidence motion:

(a) make compromise or understanding with the Opposition Parties;

(b) withdraw a Bill or cancel the matter of objected policy; or

(c) make a revised stand on the matter of policy.

There is nothing like 'no-confidence motion' in the US kind of presidential system of Constitution.

Further, as mentioned the British parliamentary system has been incorporated in most of the democratic States. It very much suits unitary Constitutions and those countries where general public is politically enlightened and takes active interests in the fulfilment of popular aspirations by the government. Otherwise, Presidential form of government of US pattern or an admixture of the two models on French pattern is preferred.

Second, the US Constitution is the prototype of presidential form of government and is marked for extreme separation between legislative and executive powers and judiciary having the final powers of interpreting the Constitution and enacted laws. This is made possible by having elected president and also elected legislature both for fixed terms. Their tenure of both President and of Congress, composed of Senate and House of Representatives, is fixed by the Constitution, unlike British parliamentary system in which Prime Minister, the de facto chief executive can dissolve the elected House and the elected House of the legislature can at any time rubbish Prime Minister by withdrawing support necessary for majority. Like in parliamentary government the legislations under US Constitution are initiated by the government which may be adopted as such or with modifications. There are some matters[52] mentioned in the US Constitution like treaties, appointment of ambassadors, judges of Supreme Court, and other federal appointments, when the presidential functions involving these require confirmation by special majority in the Senate of the Congress. But as in England the executive of which President is the Head, must exercise powers within the parameters of enacted law and the enacted law can be amended only by the procedure prescribed by the Constitution. The US Congress and President cannot be toppled by defeat of a Bill or passing of a no-confidence motion in Congress; either a Bill is passed or is rejected by the Congress. The President can function without majority in House of Representatives.

Basis of Presidential Government Concepts of USA: For elucidating and critically appreciating presidential form of government under constitutional theory reference to some background precepts is called for since these principles are sought to be followed and are being followed in new or other Constitutions worldwide.

The prevailing eighteenth century concept of doctrine of separation of powers found its first application in the first ever written Constitution drafted in 1783. It had been recognized by democrats in USA in 1780s that 'power is a heady thing'. Power feeds the ego of a person and he works for more power; be the person a king, president or dictator. It is also true for a legislature, a court or administrative office. Generally power is more satisfying than wealth. In political forms of the monarchy, fascist autocracy or communist regimes there is direct or indirect concentration of legislative or executive power in the ruler. At the beginning of American experiment on separation of powers in 1780s it was emphasized by James Madison that security 'against' gradual concentration of power in one department of government was necessary; the tyranny of any government should be resisted. In the political organization provided by a Constitution, 'a legislative, an executive and a

---

52. US Constitution: Article II, Section 2 (2).

judicial power comprehend the whole of what is meant and understood by government. It is by balancing each of these powers against the other two that the efforts in human nature against tyranny can alone be checked and restrained, and any freedom preserved in the Constitution. The legislature and executive are the proactive part of government and judiciary is the shield for people against any tyranny by any of these. He had further elucidated that "In the United States ... the People, not the government, possess the absolute sovereignty. The Legislature, no less than the Executive, is under the limitations of power. Encroachments are regarded as possible from one as well as from the other. Hence, in the United States the great and essential rights of people are secured against legislative as well as against executive ambition. They are secured, not by laws paramount to prerogative, but by Constitutions paramount to laws".

Thus the presidential form of USA shifts the sovereignty from rulers to people and makes exercise of powers and laws made by legislature subordinate to the Constitution. In constitutional format the concept of constitutional paramountcy is at variance with concept of parliamentary supremacy. In Indian, French, Irish, Swiss or Australian or Japanese constitutions, the US concept of constitutional supremacy is followed directly or indirectly though a presidential form of governmental setup is not adopted.

Direct constitutional paramountcy means that express provisions are included in the Constitution that in effect declare that the Constitution of the country is supreme and all legislative and executive powers are derived from the Constitution and people are the source of the Constitution.

Third, the French Constitution, now the Constitution of Fifth French Republic (1958), incorporates the basic formulations of Fourth French Republic of 1946. As mentioned, it is the third model Constitution which has been widely copied by new states since the end of Second World War. It is based on the constitutional theories propounded by both British and US Constitutions. It has following distinctive features:

(1) It is based on constitutional supremacy but the constitutional supremacy is maintained by (i) a Constitutional Council[53] which is composed of nine wise, experienced and legal persons, (ii) a system of organic laws[54] and (iii) direct participation of people through the process of referendum.[55]

(2) It combines republican and presidential systems. President is elected for seven years by a special electoral college.[56] President is both the Head of the State and Head of the elected government. He presides over the meetings of Council of Ministers. He appoints Prime Minister who appoints other members of Council of Ministers, but both President and Prime Minister are responsible to National Assembly of French Parliament. Passing of a vote of censor motion is against Prime Minister is accepted part. By Article 50, on passing of such motion of censure the President can dissolve the National Assembly as he is 'to ensure respect for the Constitution' and to ensure the 'regular functioning of the public authorities and continuity of the state'. On rejection of a Government's programme or a general statement of Government's policy, the Prime Minister must tender the resignation of the Government to the President of the French Republic. The President can dissolve the National Assembly.[57] If the President also wants to resign, the procedure thereafter is provided by Article 7 of the Constitution.

(3) The Constitution of France pays obeisance to the 'Rights of Man and to the principles of national sovereignty as defined by the Declaration of 1789' in its Preamble. Article 2 ensures the 'equality before the law of all citizens, without distinction of origin, race or relgion'. For details by Article 34 the laws made by Parliament are to determine the rules 'concerning civic rights and the fundamental guarantees of the public liberties of the citizen.

53. Constitution of Fifth French Republic (1958): Title VII.
54. Articles 45, 46, etc.
55. Articles 89 and 7.
56. Article 6.
57. Articles 5 and 12; The President can dissolve the "National Assembly after consulting the Prime Minister and the Presidents of the Assemblies".

At the same time Article 3 declares that: "National sovereignty belongs to the people, which shall be exercised through its representatives and through referendum". The States following French system make a constitutional promise or declaration of liberties of people.

(4) France has a multiple system of judicial organization: (a) the Constitutional Council is quasi-judicial authority to decide the constitutionality of any law or action; (b) court of appeal finally decides the civil disputes between people; (c) the administrative tribunals decide any dispute between administration and the people. This system of separating judicial organ from determining constitutionality of laws and administrative actions is followed by several States now, like, Republic of South Africa.

This French judicial system is more like that obtainable in England and obviously different from US wide ranging judicial process. Several countries, including India are diversifying adjudicating process by introducing industrial or administrative tribunals.

What makes French Constitution attractive is the fixed tenure of President of Republic coupled with the Council of Ministers made dependent on majority in National Assembly, like as in England, but the National Assembly itself can be dissolved on the Government losing majority support as in England but unlike as in US. Further the liberties of people are assured by Constitution and law but the remedies for aggrieved citizen are different both from US and British constitutional law. The system of referendum taken from Swiss and Irish Constitutions gives weight to the participation of people in operation of the Constitution unlike as in USA or India.

Constitutional Governments in Other States: **Canada:** The Constitution of Dominion of Canada is the British North America Act, 1867, enacted by British Parliament. Canada is a federal state comprising three former Provinces of Canada, Nova Scotia and New Brunswick with a Constitution similar in principle to that of the United Kingdom. The Province of Canada is now divided into two Provinces: Ontario and Quebec.

The Crown of England continues to be executive Head of Canada under Part III of the Constitution. The Federal Legislature is called Parliament of Canada with the Queen of England, Upper House called Senate and House of Commons as its components. Parliament has legislative and executive powers for Canada. Part VI of the Constitution distributes legislative powers between Parliament and Provinces. The judiciary for Canada and Provinces is provided by federal government, with powers of interpretation and enforcement of laws as in England.

Canada is a sovereign independent State recognized as such by the UNO irrespective of its political continuity with England.

Switzerland: The Constitution of Swiss Federation 1874, creates a federal welfare state wherein the legislative and executive powers and duties of Confederation and Cantons (federal units) alongwith the liberties of the people are clearly in detail demarcated and defined.[58] However for matters not visualized the powers on such residuary matters are to be exercised by Cantons. The supreme power of the Confederation is exercised by Federal Assembly[59] which is bicameral: The National Council, an elected body representing people, and the Council of States with 44 deputies representing the Cantons. The Federal Council is an important constitutional body, like Council of Ministers in other Constitutions, since the 'supreme directing and executive power of the Confederation' is exercised by it. It is composed of seven members elected by joint sessions of the two Chambers of Federal Assembly for a term of four years out of all citizens of Switzerland who are qualified to be elected to National Council. After every general election of National Council the Federal Assembly renewed. Like as under French Constitution, the President of Confederation presides over the Federal Council. Its powers are defined by Article 102 of the Swiss Constitution. The Constitution creates a Federal Tribunal. Its jurisdiction is defined essentially by Articles 110 to 114. The disputes of administrative nature are under the

58. Articles 5 to 70.

59. Article 71.

jurisdiction of Federal Administrative Court, unlike US Constitution but like French Constitution.

Australia: Britain while maintaining unitary form of Government in mainland preferred federal form of Government for its Colonies and Dominions. The Constitutions of Australia and Canada are combination of US federalism and British parliamentary system with Prime Minister from Parliament is the working head of the executive. Australia has several provinces called states and a federal government, all states have parliamentary government. However, the judiciary in Australia is of US pattern both for upholding primacy of Constitution and keeping administrative actions under rule of law.

The Commonwealth of Australia Constitution Act, (1900), enacted by British Parliament, maintained the status of British King or Queen as constitutional Head of Australia. Parliament of Australia composed of Queen of England, Senate representing the States and the House of Representatives representing the people by direct election, as in USA.

There is no Part of the Constitution dealing with sanctified fundamental liberties of people, except for freedom of religion and no discrimination of people in a State against those normally resident of other States.[60] Australia maintains the British policy of liberties being protected subject to law and keeping Australia reserved as far as possible for immigrants from Britain only. Australia does not practice racial discrimination in the form Union of South Africa or Rhodesia did in the past. Australia is extreme devotee of British politico-socio-culture. Australia is a sovereign independent State under the 'Crown' of the United Kingdom of Great Britain and Ireland and is a member of UNO.

Germany: The Basic Law (Constitution) of 1949 established West Germany as a liberal parliamentary republic committed to a "social market economy". For the nature of Government Germany is a federal, parliamentary, representative democratic Republic. It is based by Article 20 of the Basic Law on the

60. Articles 116 and 117.

principle of separation of powers into executive, legislative and judicial branches for German Government.

The German *Bundespräsident* (federal president) is non-partisan Head of German State with a ceremonial position who like the King of England or President of India represents politics of the cabinet and the parliament. The President of Germany, is elected by the electoral college, *Bundesversammlung* (federal convention), which is constituted of the members of the *Bundestag* (popularly elected Chamber of German Parliament) and an equal number of delegates from federal units

The Federal legislative branch of the German Parliament consists of lower House *Bundestag* with popularly elected members and the upper House of parliament, called the *Bundesrat.* in which the sixteen German *Länder (States)* are represented; the members of the *Bundesrat* and are members of the sixteen State cabinets, which appoint them and can remove them at any time. The lower chamber, the *Bundestag* is elected through a set of proportional representation and direct mandate of people.

The executive head of government is called the Chancellor of Germany; he is normally the leader of the largest grouping in the *Bundestag.* Chancellor is nominated by the President of Germany after being elected by the *Bundestag.* His role is similar to that of Prime Minister of England or of India. The Chancellor can be removed by a constructive motion of no-confidence by the *Bundestag.*

The articles that guarantee fundamental rights, a democratic State, and the right to resist attempts to overthrow the Constitution are permanent basic features and cannot be amended.

The Federal Constitutional Court of Germany is a special Court established by the German Basic Law in addition to regular judiciary under Supreme Court. The main task of the Constitutional Court is judicial review of legislative and executive powers under Article 20. As such it has jurisdiction to declare public acts unconstitutional and thus render them ineffective. As such, it is similar to the US Supreme Court. The Constitutional

Court, however, is not an integral part of the regular judicial system except for the enforcement of constitutional law and public international law It can declare statutes as null and void if they are in violation of the Basic Law, as such, it oversees the constitutionality of laws and it is protector of Basic Law and its judgments have are binding like any ordinary law. Violation of election laws including prohibiting of a political party, impeachment cases against President of Republic or Judges of Supreme Court are decided by the Constitutional Court.

Japan: The Preamble to the Constitution of Japan (1946) states that Japanese people proclaim that: "sovereign power resides with the people and (they) do firmly establish this Constitution". Chapter I of the Constitution lays down that the "Emperor shall be the symbol of the state" and Article 4 enacts that "The Emperor shall perform only such acts in matters of State as are provided by the Constitution, and he shall not have powers related to the government".[61] It is noted that while in British Constitution the powers and functions of King are basically regulated by conventions of Constitution, in Japan the Constitution being written the constitutional powers of monarch have been spelled out. At the same time he is formal appointing authority for various constitutional offices and performs various acts in matters of State on behalf of people.

The supreme Legislature in Japan is Diet composed of directly elected House of Representatives and the upper House of Councillors elected by procedure laid down by law. The Executive power of the state is vested in Cabinet.[62] The Prime Minister and Ministers must be civilians and at all times majority of members of Cabinet should be from this catagory. The principle of collective responsibility of Cabinet apply and when a motion of no-confidence is adopted in House of Representatives, the Cabinet en masse resigns and fresh election of House of Representatives follows.

---

61. Article 4.
62. Chapter V.

The Rights and Duties of the People are guaranteed and regulated by Constitution. The fundamental human rights guaranteed by the Constitution cannot be taken away by amendment.

The judicial power of state is vested in the Supreme Court and in such inferior courts as are established by law. The Supreme Court is the court of last resort with powers to determine the constitutionality of any law, regulation or official act.[63] Further, Article 98 declares that the "Constitution shall be the supreme law of the nation and no law, ordinance, imperial rescript or other act of government, or part thereof, contrary to provisions hereof, shall have legal force or validity".

Any amendment of the Japanese Constitution requires a referendum before being effective.

Thus the Japanese Constitution has adopted US system of wide powers of judicial review, British pattern of monarchial system and Cabinet System of Government, and French system for amendment of the Constitution.

Pakistan: The constitutional system in Pakistan has been grossly unstable and defies generalization. It has been all through a federal state but the government has been parliamentary democratic or military dictatorship with martial law which is military rule without fixed Constitution.

Pakistan began as a federal state with a civilian parliamentary government under a first Constitution adapted from the Government of India Act of 1935. After military coup of 1957 martial law rule was imposed in the country and first Constitution was abrogated. In 1967, again a make-shift civilian democratic government was installed under the second Constitution of 1962 laid down by Constitutional Order of military dictator Ayub Khan. In 1969 there was again a military coup and martial law regime became Constitution of Pakistan. The third Constitution of Pakistan was adopted in April 1973. This third Constitution continues to provide constitutional framework after frequent suspensions and administratively made

63. Article 81.

amendments by military administrators. It was reinstated in 1985 with revamped extraordinary powers for President.

By the amendment of 1988, another (fifth) Constitution came into operation. Under this the President is the Head of State and Prime Minister is Head of the Government and both must be Muslims. The President is elected for a term of five years by the National Assembly, the Senate and the four provincial Assemblies. The Prime Minister is elected by National Assembly. The President acts on the advice of the Prime Minister, but he has special powers to dismiss the Prime Minister and provide another government. However, the National Assembly can be dismissed by President only on the advice of Prime Minister. Martial Law was again imposed in October 1999. Since then several Constitutional Orders have been adopted to adjust the status of President and after elections held in February 2008 a civilian Government is to be formed.

Basically, the latest 2008 Constitution of Pakistan entrenches itself in the third Constitution of 1973. Pakistan has the constitutional peculiarity that the frequent Constitutional Orders alter the status of President and of Prime Minister but maintain a federal structure for the country.

The powers and status of Supreme Court of Pakistan have been fluctuating since President of Pakistan has the powers to dismiss the Chief Justice at his discretion and to appoint others and has exercised this power. Otherwise the Supreme Court of Pakistan is very much like the Supreme Court of USA in constitutional matters. It is also court of final appeal in other matters

China: The Chinese People's Republic Constitution is strongly opposed to the western system or constitutional theory of separation of executive, legislature and judicial powers of Government. In keeping with Stalinist Marxist political organization the Constitution of People's Republic of China, the current[64] version of 1982, has one-party elected totalitarian

64. Four previous Constitutions of 1954, 1962, 1975 and 1978 were superseded in 1982.

or dictatorial government that does not allow political opposition and places natural freedoms of the people as a condition of loyalty to Communist Party of China. The state fiat is part of the rule under the Marxist dogma that there is no distinction between state, law, government and people. The Communist Party is supposed to express and further fundamental development of whole people of the state since it represents the 'democratic will of the people'. The integral class struggle stage of Marxism was over in communist China by end of 1970s and so the 1982 Constitution puts into background the Marxist theory of 'class struggle' and gives top priority to 'development'. Further, the new Constitution accepts the contributions and interests of non-party groups in economic modernization of country. This has helped China to shed isolation in world comity. The Chinese 1982 Constitution formally creates a 'unitary' but multinational State.

To comprehend, at the helm of the Constitution of China is the National People's Congress (NPC) led by the Communist Party, the only political party of China, In practice the Constitution of People's Republic of China concentrates more on explaining the manifesto of Communist Party of China (CPC) on 'what is aspired and how to achieve' theme. China is to become a perfect Socialist State. The form of government is not a prominent part of the Constitution since the Government under the Constitution is an agency working under the "people's democratic dictatorship". The premise of the "People's democratic dictatorship" is that the Communist Party of China and the state act on behalf of the people, but these can and do use dictatorial methods in order to maintain the Constitution and remain in power in the face of hostile forces. Also implicit in the concept of the people's democratic dictatorship is the notion that dictatorial means are a necessary evil, and that without a dictatorship, the government may collapse and create a situation which is worse than the dictatorship.

The 'socialist law' of the Constitution is accepted as the regulator of the behaviour both of state and people this perspective the Constitution defines citizen's rights and duties.

For the Government, the National People's Congress (NPC) is the highest organ of State authority and power. It functions through State Council (NPCSC) and its Committees (SCC). The NPC elects members of State Council, the Supreme People's Court and the Supreme People's Procurator. All these authorities are responsible to NPC. As the CPC is the only recognized and operative political party, all nominated bodies are constituted of members nominated by the Communist Party of China.

After the acceptance of globalization of world economy, the Constitution of People's Republic of China was amended in March 2004 to recognize 'private property' and 'human rights' of citizens: The "legally obtained private property of the citizens shall not be violated".

The Constitution stipulates that the National People's Congress and its Standing Committee have the power to review whether laws or activities violate the Constitution.

Since 2002, there has been a special committee of the Standing Committee of the National People's Congress (NPCSC) which has reviewed laws and regulations for constitutionality

Sri Lanka: The form of Government in Sri Lanka has been drifting with the change in pattern of Constitution. Briefly, the Ceylon Independence Act, 1947 of British Parliament conferred dominion status on the Colony, and on 4 February 1948 it became an independent state The Governor General was Head of State and represented the British monarch in government system. Ceylon had a bicameral Legislature; and, on matters on which the Constitution was silent, the conventions of the United Kingdom were to be followed. The Constitution in general followed British parliamentary government system.

Proceeding under this constitutional set-up, a new Constitution of 1972 was proclaimed by the Sri Lanka Freedom Party (SLFP) forming the Government. Ceylon was renamed as the Republic of Sri Lanka, with a President as Head of State. Democracy of British model was envisaged but all legislative powers were to be exercised by a unicameral elected legislature. The executive power of the State was vested in the Prime Minister and his Cabinet.

Before the 1977 General Election the United National Party (UNP) sought a mandate from the people to adopt a new Constitution. After success in election a Select Committee was appointed to consider the revision of the Constitution. The new Constitution was promulgated in 7 September 1978, but this much revised Constitution of Sri Lanka was installed in February 1978. It changed the name of country to the Democratic Socialist Republic of Sri Lanka and it introduced a government system very much based on the French model. The Constitution of 1978 created Executive Presidency and the then Prime Minister, took over as the first elected Executive President. Parliament was made unicameral and the term of both President and Parliament was set to six years. President appoints Cabinet of Ministers composed of elected members of Parliament on the basis of proportional representation of the Districts. The Prime Minister, who leads the ruling in parliament is President's deputy and shares many executive responsibilities particularly in domestic affairs.

The government of Sri Lanka under this Constitution of 1978 is composite of the presidential and parliamentary systems. The President of Sri Lanka is the Head of State, the Commander-in-Chief of armed forces, and is Head of Council of Ministers which is the real executive. In the exercise of duties, the President along with Prime Minister is responsible to the Parliament of Sri Lanka where he must command support of majority of its 225-members. The President and Prime Minister are subject to no-confidence vote in Parliament.

The President can summon, suspend, or end a legislative session and dissolve Parliament any time after it has served for one year. The Parliament has the exclusive power to make laws.

The Constitution of Sri Lanka has provided for an independent Judiciary and guaranteed Fundamental Rights that are protected by the Supreme Court against any violation. The Constitution also provides a Parliamentary Commissioner for Administration (Ombudsman) who is to investigate public grievances against Government Institutions and State officers and give redress; for Proportional Representation system, anti-defection laws, Directive Principle of State Policy for Parliament and process for referendums on certain Bills and Amendment of Constitution.

Republic of South Africa: The Republic of South Africa has had a variegated history as a Colony and Dominion of British Empire. It was hated by Africans and Asians for its racist pro-white discriminatory constitutional and legal policies till 1996 when it adopted non-racist Constitution with constitutional equality to all of its citizens.

The Constitution of the Republic of South Africa was adopted after a long racist political turmoil ending with an agreement among White, Coloured, Asians and African nationals in 1996 and it came into effect in February 1997. It enacted a new beginning when under section 2 of chapter 1 of this Constitution, all statutes and laws that conflict with the Constitution and the Bill of Rights in Chapter 2 are of no force or effect. This overriding principle is against the government of South Africa, including its executive, legislative and judicial branches. The new pattern of government is non-racist marking a civilizational adjustment of importance.

The Constitution of 1996 makes Republic of South Africa is a constitutional democracy with a three-tier system of government functioning on the British parliamentary pattern and with an independent judicial system composed of Constitutional Court and Supreme Court of appeals.

It is a novel type of federal State not based on autonomy of territorial segments but a federation of several languages, African tribes, white settlers from England, Asians and colored people. There are national, provincial and local levels of government with all having legislative and executive authority in their own spheres, and are defined in the Constitution of South Africa as "distinctive, interdependent and interrelated". All bodies of the South African government are subject to the Constitution, which is the supreme law in South Africa.

The national government has the usual three interconnected arms of government:

(1) The Legislature composed of the National Assembly with a five-year term and the National Council of Provinces.

(2) Executive of which the President of Republic of South Africa is both 'Head of State' and 'Head of Government' at the same time.

(3) Judiciary: It consists of the Constitutional Court for all matters pertaining to enforcement of Constitution, the Supreme Court of Appeal, and the High Courts of Provinces.

The President of the Republic of South Africa is elected by members of the National Assembly, the elected lower house of Parliament and he is the leader of the largest party in National Assembly after an election. He appoints Ministers and is the leader of the Cabinet but as President he must approve all bills, legislations and amendments of the Constitution. The Section 88 of the Constitution limits the President's tenure to two terms. Presidents are elected after each parliamentary election.

The South African Constitutional Court was established in 1994 under earlier Constitution. The Judges are independent. and are duty bound to uphold the law and the Constitution. The Constitutional Court is the highest court in the land for all constitutional matters, while the Supreme Court of Appeal is the final court for all matters which do not involve the interpretation of the Constitution. For this the Constitutional Court has final authority to determine which issues are constitutional matters and which are not. The Constitutional Court has a special adjudicating responsibility for any dispute between the Parliament and Provincial Legislatures.

Nepal: The form of constitutional government in Nepal is not yet finalized and monarchy is having fluctuating fortunes. Political stability necessary for democratic Constitution is wanting in Nepal. People and politicians are not tuned to one another.

From absolute monarchy in 1990 Nepal had become constitutional monarchy[65] with King as the Head of State and

65. Part 5 of the 1990 Constitution had provided the status of "His Majesty" to the King of Nepal. The King has been replaced by an elected President.

with a Prime Minister heading a Council of Ministers as chief executive. There was a *Raj Parishad* (State Council) to aid and advise the King in matters referred to it by the King.[66] The Parliament, Nepal's National Legislature[67] was bicameral consisting of directly elected House of Representative called the *Pratinidhi Sabha* and a sixty-member National Council called the *Rastriya Sabha*. The House of Representatives consisted of 205 members directly elected by the people. The National Council had ten members nominated by the King, thirty-five elected by the House of Representatives and the remaining fifteen elected by an electoral college constituted from village and town *panchayats*. The legislature had a five-year term, but could be dissolved by the King before expiry of its term. The Supreme Court headed the judiciary with jurisdiction to interpret Constitution, exercise of powers according to Constitution and appellate powers.[68]

The representative Governments under this Constitution were highly unstable as no government could survive for more than two years since 1991, affected either by internal collapse or parliamentary dissolution by the King on the recommendation of Prime Minister according to the Constitution. The National Assembly was in dissolved condition in early 2006, and the King was regarded to be responsible for this instability by the political parties. Following a democratic movement after a turmoil,[69] the King agreed to relinquish the sovereign power in favour of the people and reinstated the dissolved House of Representatives on 24 April 2006. Using its newly acquired sovereign authority, on 18 May 2006, the resumed House of Representatives unanimously passed a motion to constitutionally

66. Part 6, *ibid.*
67. Part 8, *ibid.*
68. Part 11, *ibid.*, Article 88.
69. The movement in April 2006, brought about a change in the national politics when an interim Constitution was promulgated with the King proposing to give up power as Head of State, and an interim House of Representatives was formed alongwith Maoist members after the new government held peace talks with the Maoist rebels.

curtail the powers of the King and to declare Nepal a secular State. An interim Constitution was adopted with a new interim Parliament. It was not elected by people but nominated by seven political parties according to the provisions of the interim Constitution. The 1990 Constitution was drastically amended for final Constitution and the latest Parliament acting as constituent body voted to abolish the monarchy in Nepal on 28 December 2007. For this the Interim Government has proposed to amend Article 159 of the 1990 Constitution and declare Nepal a federal republic thereby abolishing the monarchy. Under this amendment in Article 159 of the interim Constitution the phrase "Provisions of the Head of the State" replace the "Provisions regarding the King". The Constitution amendment bill, however, will come into force only after the forthcoming elections scheduled for April 2008 which are to be in the nature of referendum. The election for referendum has faced postponements since the people, politicians apart, have special regard for monarchy; the politicians are not sure of the verdict of referendum.

Bhutan: The State was a protectorate of British India till 1947 with princely monarchy for Government. Its sovereign independence was recognized thereafter. It is a member of UNO. Now under the 2005 Constitution Bhutan is democratic constitutional monarchy, a sovereign Kingdom with sovereign power belonging to people of Bhutan.[70] The Institution of Monarchy is constitutionally controlled and defined.[71] Buddhism is State professed religion but with utmost religious freedom for others. Fundamental rights and duties of people are defined and the Legislature is to endeavor to follow "Principles of State Policy" laid down by the Constitution.

The Parliament is the ruler for the country following the British pattern of democracy: the hereditary King, the nominated National Council and the elected National Assembly are its members. The Prime Minster heads the executive composed of

70. Article 1: Constitution of Bhutan.
71. Article 2.

Ministers "to protect and strengthen the sovereignty of the Kingdom, provide good governance, and ensure peace, security, well being and happiness of the people" with collective responsibility.[72] Constitution provides for Interim Government to be appointed by the King when the Prime Minister and ministers resign. Also, the Prime Minister is to resign when elections are to be held and Interim Government takes over.[73]

Judiciary of Bhutan is called Royal Court of Justice and comprises Supreme Court, the High Court and District Courts. The Supreme Court interprets Constitution, decides all matters under the Constitution and is final court of appeal in all matters.[74]

Singapore: Under British Empire Malaya included Singapore as an important sea route controlling point. After the Japanese World War II occupation of Malaya ended in 1945, the British rulers had separated administration with two Governors one each for Malaya and Singapore though both were designated as Crown Colonies. Gradually as British had to make all non-self-governing territories independent under its UNO obligations, local governments were established on British parliamentary system. Singapore had been a British Crown Colony under "Rendel Constitution" of 1955 enacted by British Parliament. The Singapore (Constitution) Order-in-Council 1958 was enacted and Singapore became a state instead of Crown Colony; it also created the position of a constitutional Head of state, a Prime Minister, his Cabinet and a 51-elected member State Legislative Assembly.

Later when State of Malayasia was created by British on 16 September 1963, Singapore was included in its federal structure. Further later, by the three Constitution of Malaysia (Singapore Amendment) Act, the Constitution of Singapore (Amendment) Act and the Republic of Singapore Independence Act of 1965. Singapore and Malaysia became two separate

---

72. Article 29.

73. Article 19; this provision for Interim Government follows the Constitution of Bangladesh.

74. Article 21.

independent sovereign republics with parliamentary form of Government. The Constitution Act of Singapore was amended in 1991 to provide for a popularly elected President and the National Assembly became Parliament.

The Constitution of Singapore is republican, unitary, codified and is the supreme law of Singapore. There is a Supreme Court. The President can seek opinion on constitutional issues from a Bench consisting of not less than three judges of the Supreme Court.

Afghanistan: Afghanistan an Islamic State has had several successive Constitutions. The Third Afghan Constitution of 1964 established a constitutional monarchy while the Fourth Afghan Constitution of 1976 made the country a republic with National Assembly and constitutional judiciary. However, in 1980 this third Constitution was superseded and a temporary Constitution "Fundamental Principles of the Democratic Republic of Afghanistan" was adopted. Again there was turmoil and Soviet intervention resulted in another Constitution Afghanistan Republic was enforced in 1987 on Marxist pattern. Anarchy and civil war had followed and on intervention of United Nations Organization the present Sixth Constitution of Afghanistan of 2003 is in operation. The present Afghanistan State is federal republic with federal and provincial governments. It has a popularly elected President and National Assembly. The Government is organized on a US presidential government format.

Bangladesh: People's Republic of Bangladesh was established in the 1947 as East Pakistan of the then newly formed Pakistan after partition of British India. Bangladesh had declared independence in 1971 after India-Pakistan War of 1971. Bangladesh had its Constitution in 1972.

Bangladesh is a republic with parliamentary system of democracy. President functions under a unicameral Parliament with Islam as the state religion. Direct elections for Parliament are held every five years. The President acts on the advice of Prime Minister who forms his Cabinet, as chief executive of the Government of Bangladesh. The President formally appoints the Prime Minister who must be an elected member of Parliament and should always command a majority in Parliament. Parliament elects the President. Political turmoil since 1972 in Bangladesh, led to about fourteen changes in the government and at least four military coups.

However, the powers of President are substantially increased during the tenure of a caretaker government, which has the important responsibility of conducting of elections and transfer of power. The incumbents of the caretaker government must be non-partisan and are normally given three months to complete their task. This transitional arrangement is an innovation that was institutionalized in 1996 through its 13th constitutional amendment. The 2006 election was postponed indefinitely since the constitutional 'caretaker government' of decided to revise the voter list and crack down on corruption before elections were held. The 'caretaker government' plans to hold now elections by 2008 but there is lack of coordination between Election Commission and the Government. Ostensibly convicts on criminal charges are to be prevented from contesting elections. In this context it is noted that:

Khaleda Zia and Sheikh Hasina two prominent former Prime Ministers are facing criminal charges in court.

Meanwhile the Bangladesh military commanders have expressed their interest in controlling the country with intentions of making changes in the Constitution to allow participation of military in politics or in order to synchronize democracy with military trappings.

The highest judicial body of Bangladesh is the Supreme Court. The Judges are appointed by the President. It interprets the Constitution and it is final court of appeal also.

Constitutions and Liberties of People

Since the American Declaration of Independence (1776) and French Revolution (1789) all republican constitutions and constitutional monarchies profess to be champions or protectors of civil liberties of people. Sovereignty of State has shifted to people and justification of all constitutional governments is now to achieve of a working rule for benefit of the people. Most of the contemporary Constitutions boldly declare and list the fundamental liberties of their citizens and give some of these the status of being immutable.

The value of any constitutional declaration of the liberties of the people is to be read

1. in the enforcement process, and

2. in the capacity of the system to change the content and scope of liberties for the better since written Constitutions and declarations have an element of rigidity.

In India, for example, the property and economic rights of people had both increased or decreased while personal liberty and social equality and freedom of expression have increased with maturity of nation. Along with this in order to accommodate these fluctuations the Constitution has to be amenable for amendment with the change of times. This is to observe that such a declaration of fundamental liberties is to be both expandable and to be eternal and immutable at the same time. It is also to be emphasized that states have some rudimentary notions and politico-philosophical base and the contents of liberties become dependent accordingly. For example, the Fifth Constitution of France (1946) reiterates the 1789 Declaration on Rights of Man as the rational basis of the Constitution and constitutional values. Similarly, the Constitution of People's Republic of China reiterates everywhere that its political system has to achieve the Marxist manifesto of the Communist Party and all liberties and duties of people are subject to this project. In India both amendments to the Chapter on Fundamental Rights can be made by Parliament[75] and the Supreme Court can by interpretation extend the scope of liberties as it has done by giving enlarged contents to protection of 'personal liberty'.

Liberties and Form of Governments

As at present there are three prominent democratic systems that correlate the form of government with protection of civil

75. Article 368 of the Constitution of India provides for special majority in Parliament for a bill making amendment but such bill does not require ratification by State units of federation.

liberties, viz. the US, British and French. Most of the states follow either of these with some variations of their own.

Under the impact of contemporary constitutional morality put forth by the 1948 Universal Declaration of Human Rights, the member States of the United Nations are to orient the government organization or Constitution from the point of view of democracy and the political, civil and economic liberties of their people. The importance given to civil liberties by any Constitution is directly linked with the proposition whether the Constitution is *flexible* or *rigid*. The latter identifies the importance of civil liberties with the sanctity of the Constitution itself; this aspect was separately examined earlier with reference to various Constitutions.

There exists a delicate balance between the powers of different organs of the government and the liberties of the people defined on the basis of the socio-economic culture and the political philosophy preferred by the makers and leaders of a State. There is no ambiguity and the form and the purpose of the governments have now come to be focused on the achievement of maximum welfare of the people through the medium of the government. The government of a State is no longer concerned with maintaining hegemony of few or administering law and order among the people.

The modern Constitutions now profess to be democratic in the sense that these derive their power and sanction from the wishes of the people and, therefore it is presumed that the end of the State is to provide maximum possible welfare of the people by taking initiatives also for this and by proactive participation in regulation of socio-economic life of the community. Even the totalitarian governments make a compromise in favour of welfare of people. For example, the State of Bhutan has politically absolute or totalitarian monarchial system. Bhutan is a member of UNO. It is predominantly Buddhist State but there is a harmony between religious ideals of Buddhist society and the rule of the King. Buddhism as a religion is non-aggressive, peaceful, tolerant of others and has basically a cooperative culture.[76] The

---

76. Buddhism correlates peace of mind with individual's own and social life.

State of Bhutan has a professional executive and judiciary, all are regulated by the edicts of the monarch and not by laws made by popularly elected representatives of people, yet Bhutan is not despotic but a welfare state.[77]

Where the democratic form of government has penetrated into the monarchial form of Constitution as in England or Japan,[78] the basic rights of people excel the status of kings and law regulates the latter: *lex* is *rex* and not the reverse is the rule. In England the Bill of Rights 1689 declares the rights and liberties of the people and the Act of Settlement (1701) and other enactments considered as constitutional documents provide and regulate the position and status of the King.[79] In Japan the documentary 1946 Constitution defines both aspects. In constitutional monarchies the income of State is not personal income of the monarch.

As mentioned earlier republican states might be autocratic or democratic. Here again there is anomaly contrary to commonsense. Historically, as mentioned earlier republicans reject monarchs as head of government yet constitutional theory accepts that a republic may be autocracy. Normally, republican states now as a result of UNO are not immune from autocracy; these develop into military dictatorship with a formal constitution provided by the dictator that depends on the will of ruling commanders, for example, contemporary Pakistan and Afghanistan have such a history. The Charter of UNO is neutral on the form of government in a State but where democracy is subverted, its Organs censor the development as retrogressive. Usually the military dictators begin with a

77. The status and form of government are elsewhere incorporated in this book.

78. Norway and Sweden are other examples.

79. Likewise, the Constitution of Sweden 1809 regulates the status of kingship and guarantees the basic freedoms of the people, which cannot be taken away without amendment of the Constitution.

Also the Constitution of Thai Kingdom 1952, the Constitution of Norway 1814 as amended and the Constitution of Denmark 1953 likewise provide controlled kingship with guarantee of fundamental liberties of people.

revolutionary military council, which is in course of time replaced by a showpiece Constitution. The military dictatorships generally profess to be transitional till an efficient civilian government capable of carrying out the obligations towards the nation responsibly can be developed; but complete democracy is rarely revived. The dictatorships are known for arbitrariness and suppression of liberties of the people and not for the promotion of the latter.

During the years of Cold War (1945-1991) communist party of the new states, normally forming governments following a civil war, would enforce party dictatorship based on 1936 Soviet Russia Constitution, viz. in Communist China, Cuba, North Korea or Viet Nam.[80] A communist-party dictatorship[81] is in first step democratic for the structure of party organization but beyond this the government formed tends to be uncompromisingly autocratic. For the people the liberties are curtailed, censored are conditioned and existed or exist only to the extent these are consistent with the survival, continuance and programmes of the communist party.

In republics with true democratic principles, the government professes to derive its powers from the people, tolerates different shades of religious, political or socio-economic thoughts, treats equals equally, abstains from interfering with the declared basic rights of people and actively participates in the plans for the progress of the community extending to the country. Following the political theory, the modern states including both monarchies and republics regard people as the real sovereign and project the people as the sanction behind or the legitimacy of the government and of the Constitution.

Paramountcy of Civil Liberties: Within the democratic organization of governments by formal written Constitutions,

---

80. Only the Constitution of People's Republic of China is cited in the book.
81. During the period of two world wars, Nazi Germany of Hitler and Fascist Italy of Mussolini were party dictatorships that had come to power after elections under a Constitution for the country and not after a civil war.

as mentioned earlier, there are three different methods for maintaining the supremacy and effective protection of civil liberties.

First, following the traditions of British Constitution as benchmark the sanctity of fundamental liberties is maintained through elected Parliament. There is the basic principle that 'rule of law' is supreme, law is that which the legislature lays down and it is for elected legislature to supervise the enforcement of laws relating to civil liberties. The executive is functionally subordinate to and not equal to legislature. In England, the jurist Halsbury[82] has remarked that only that Constitution can be acceptable to the people which protects the rights and liberties of the people as are defined through the "four great Charters or Statutes which regulate the relations between Crown and the people", namely, Magna Carta, Petition of Rights, Bill of Rights and the Act of Settlement.[83] In principle, these four sacrosanct political Charters prescribe the basic freedoms as injunctions against the government and are maintained by a correlation between the 'rule of law' that prevents executive arbitrariness and the constitutional supremacy of British Parliament while the latter is the supreme and exclusive law-making body. Judiciary in England has also recognized in the leading case *Liversidge vs Anderson*[84] that the executive cannot act or subvert established rights of people without the sanction of law. The power of judicial review operates to censor executive or administrative actions taken without backing of law. By the established British thinking the legislative functions are controlled in favour of the rights of people by the vigilant public opinion that asserts at time of elections to the House of Commons of British Parliament as well as by the respect which the people of England have for the traditions and 'Conventions of the Constitution'. Parliamentary

82. Halsbury, *Laws of England,* Ed. 2, pp. 389-99.
83. Other constitutional Acts of England are mentioned in Part III of the Book, entitled *Important Constitutional Documents* (*UK*).
84. (1941) All E.R. 336.

control of Chief Executive, the Prime Minister, through 'no-confidence motion' is partly through Conventions of British Constitution.

As was mentioned, England does not have a documented Constitution. It is unwritten but there are Acts of Parliament and 'Conventions of Constitution that are regarded to be sacrosanct and form the base of the political organization of the country. Many States have copied the British system of parliamentary government but have documented their Constitutions codifying the basic British Acts and 'Conventions'.[85] The basic feature emanating from the 'Conventions' is that there is a House of Legislature which is directly elected by the people, it provides ministers called a Cabinet or Council of Ministers with a Prime Minister at its head to aid and advise the executive, the ministers have a tenure till the party forming the government retains majority in this elected House and there are periodic elections to elect the members to this House on multiparty system basis. The Speaker of the House has privileged status immune from political party wrangles. The Constitutions of Australia, Bangladesh, Canada, republican India and monarchial Japan among other states follow their own pattern of codified British parliamentary system. The system is coordinated for protection of civil liberties by political will expressed in British Charters and in respect for documented Constitutions.

It is part of the constitutional theory adopted in England that the political party forming the government has unlimited field for operating the government through Parliament and the laws framed by it; at the same time the government is bound to receive severe censor from the opposition political parties and the people if it legislates to restrict the established rights of the people. In England the politically uncommitted public opinion is powerful and vigilant enough to keep the government in check against making any affront to the cherished liberties. As

85. For example, the Constitutions of India, Japan, Germany, Bangladesh among many others have codified British Conventions of Constitution.

British parliamentary system is almost universal with variations of type, it is to be mentioned that the dependence of the people on the elected national legislature for protection of their basic civil or fundamental liberties can be constitutionally successful where people are keenly conscious of the heritage of their liberties and take intimate or proactive interest in the working of their political institutions operating under the Constitution. In England the parliamentary democracy has thrived safely since by incidence of history there have been only two effective political parties; and these two political parties have adhered to or shared common national interest or imperial aspirations and their programmes have not been diametrically opposed to each other's. But, when there is a plethora of political parties in a State with different ideologies and no individual political party has absolute majority necessary for forming the government, as in France, India or Sri Lanka, coalition governments have to be formed. Under these circumstances of ideological variations the parliamentary democracy has needed additional safeguards for protecting the fundamental liberties of people.

In practice the parliamentary system, as was mentioned, refers to the control of people over government in power. It proceeds through the mechanism of 'no-confidence motion', which might lead to general elections. This is the most important tool of parliamentary democracy.

The French and US models of Constitutions provide alternate mechanisms for protection of documented civil liberties.

The French System, particularly since the 1958 Constitution of Fifth Republic, has provided another popular system for maintaining the primacy of civil liberties. In France, there was a frequent change in the political parties forming the government and safeguards were regarded to be necessary for sustaining the fundamentals of the Constitution including declaration of fundamental liberties of the people. The danger was feared from the chance possibility of a party coming into power that did not share the existing constitutional values. The rigidity of the French Constitution requires that the 'organic laws', which included the one for civil liberties, can be amended or taken away only on the recommendation of 'Constitutional Council'.[86] This Constitutional Council, composed of senior and experienced persons, has supervisory-cum-advisory constitutional role and is an independent body. When any law or administrative order which is impugned for violating fundamental liberty or any other constitutional provisions is placed before the Constitutional Council, the latter can declare it unconstitutional and thereafter it comes to an end (Articles 61 and 62). President of France, President of National Assembly and the President of Senate nominate its members for one term only of nine years, the ex-Presidents are life members of this body (Article 56). Many States apart from States of Europe, have followed French system of creating Constitutional Council in one form or other, for maintaining primacy of civil liberties and for sanctity of constitutional provisions, viz. Sri Lanka or Republic of South Africa that provide a Constitutional Court. This system basically disfavors exclusive power of judiciary to interpret and maintain supremacy of constitution over the executive and legislative wings of the Government. Of course, the executive and administrative actions have to follow the enacted law and both French and British systems accomplish this by their own set of judicial system. France has administrative courts with exclusive jurisdiction in such matters.[87] The French system of separation of civil and administrative litigation jurisdictions is followed by most of the European Constitutions

The *third* method for maintaining paramountcy of Constitution and the civil liberties alongwith is by vesting power in judiciary for examining constitutional validity of all actions of executive and legislature. This power extends to examining whether any legislative or executive action violates the liberties guaranteed by the Constitution. This is a function exercised by the courts in addition to their normal function of interpreting laws and enforcing them and of being final appellate

---

86. *Conseil constitutionnel.*

87. Under its system of separation of powers, India has also adopted the system of administrative tribunals for dealing with intra-administration disputes but regular judiciary deals with disputes between people and administrative actions.

court. The Constitution of USA and the practices developed by its Supreme Court are forerunner of this method. Those states that have not adopted French method of creating an independent Constitutional Council and British method of depending on elected Parliament for maintaining sanctity of fundamental liberties follow the US method in varying degrees. Japan, Bangladesh, Republic of South Africa and Pakistan among other States have adopted the exclusive power for judiciary for interpreting their Constitutions.[88] British sovereign in British Colonies and Dominions adopted the US pattern of judiciary and the Acts of British Parliament creating the Government of the Dominion and Colony was treated as basic Constitution, viz. Canada, Australia or British India.

This third method from USA proceeds on two concepts of constitutional theory: First that Constitution is supreme, inviolable and immutable. It is superior to executive and legislative organs and other authorities created by it and none of these can assume powers not assigned to them by the Constitution. Second, that the judiciary is the guardian of the Constitution and can declare unconstitutional and inoperative both legislative enactments and executive actions which exceed the powers assigned to them by the Constitution.[89] The fundamental liberties of people as defined under the US Constitution are regarded to be reservations both from legislative and executive powers and so neither of them can circumvent. These are technically controversies between State and the people arising out of laws made by the government, Federal or State, with reference to Article III of the US Constitution. The Supreme Court here examines whether a liberty protected by Constitution is available against State legislations or not since the Constitution of USA was supposed to define only federal

---

88. The Constitution of India is the best adopter of US system for protecting liberties of people and the powers or *vires*, of executive and legislative actions or measures.

89. This principle of 'legal realism' was elaborately examined and enunciated by the US Supreme Court in the case West Coast Hotel vs Parrish, (1937) 300 US 379.

powers and jurisdiction. Further, the US Supreme Court regards Constitution is supreme law and its interpretation as exclusive judicial function and, therefore regards itself as real and final authority for interpreting and fixing the meanings of terms and phrases that define the powers of the organs of the Government under the Constitution.

Unlike as in unitary Constitution of England, the US Constitution is federal and so the judiciary has the additional function of deciding the constitutionality of respective jurisdiction of States and the Federal Government as part of its function of interpreting the Constitution. The judicial function of this nature has been highly significant in US in the tussle between liberalism, social change in favor of liberties of the people on one hand and capitalist conservatism on the other.[90] However, a majority of the Constitutions, whether federal or unitary, accord the function of protection of liberties if people to the judiciary, viz. Constitutions of Australia, Canada, Eire, India, Japan, Nepal, Pakistan, Republic of South Africa or Russian Federation (1993). Further, many Constitutions regard that power of amendment does not extend to amending basic features of the Constitution and some or many liberties,[91] viz. equality, freedom of religion, freedom of speech and expression, are intrinsic or basic features of the Constitution. The judicial powers extend to protecting such liberties of people against being taken away by amendment of the Constitution as well.

The status and importance of Fundamental Liberties in some key Constitutions can be mentioned here as introduction.

In the Constitution of Swiss Confederation, Article 113, the Federal Tribunal has explicit jurisdiction in regard to "complaints

---

90. During the years 1890 to 1938, the conservative Supreme Court of USA had held over 225 legislations as unconstitutional for violating a negative interpretation of 'liberty' under the XIV Amendment of the Constitution: Jackson, *The Struggle for Judicial Supremacy*, p. 3.

91. In various Constitutions, the Constitutional Councils or equivalents do the same function, viz. France, People's Republic of South Africa or Sri Lanka.

of violation of constitutional rights of citizens and complaints by individuals of violation of concordats and treaties".

In Australia, the Commonwealth of Australia Constitution Act (1900) by its Articles 75 and 76 grants jurisdiction to the Supreme Court called High Court of Australia in all matters coming under the Constitutional Act that include mandamus against executive for protecting the rights of people in law and equity and in matters arising out of laws made by Parliament or by federal units.

In the Constitution of Eire (Ireland) (1937) all "powers of government are exercisable only by or on the authority of the organs of state established by this Constitution"; under Article 34 (3)(b) "jurisdiction of the High Court shall extend to the question of validity of any law having regard to the provision of this Constitution and in all cases in which any such matter shall come into question"; and the 'Fundamental Rights' of citizens are defined in substance in Articles 40 to 44 of the Eire Constitution. Thus powers of judiciary are behind the validity of liberties of people.

The Constitution of Japan in Chapter III (Articles 10 to 40) in utmost details defines the 'Rights and Duties of the People'. Under Article 97 these are "for all time inviolate" while the "Constitution shall be the supreme law of the nation and no law, ordinance, imperial rescript or other act of government, or part thereof, contrary to the provision hereof, shall have legal force or validity". In this context through Articles 81 and 82 the Supreme Court of Japan is the court of last resort with "power to determine the constitutionality of any law, order, regulation or official act"; further, the trial of cases involving the rights of people guaranteed by Chapter III of the Constitution are to be always conducted publicly.

The Constitution of Russian Federation (1993) also secures the liberties of people through the powers of judiciary quite on US pattern. Article 15 provides that the "Constitution of the Russian Federation shall have supreme legal force and direct effect, and shall be applicable throughout the entire territory of the Russian Federation. Laws and other legal acts adopted by the Russian Federation may not contravene the Constitution of the Russian Federation". Chapter 2 of the Constitution through Articles 17 to 64 guarantees the 'Rights and Liberties of Man and Citizen' with obligation of mutuality; these liberties "shall be secured by the judiciary" since the rights and liberties of man and citizen have direct constitutional link. The judiciary is to determine "the meaning, content and application of the laws, and the activities of the legislative and executive branches and local self-government".

The Constitution of India (1950) is more forthright on this score. Its Part III defining the Fundamental Rights, by its Article 13 makes any law that violates Fundamental Rights as void; Article 32 gives to the Supreme Court of India judicial powers of declaring any law or administrative action taken under it as unconstitutional and so void; Article 226 gives the same jurisdiction to the High Courts of the States with additional jurisdiction to be exercised 'for any other purpose' for protection of constitutional rights other than Fundamental Rights.

The Constitution of Sri Lanka follows an admixture of French and British constitutional systems for protection of Fundamental Rights of people. The constitutionality of all laws including Fundamental Rights is determined by an elaborate constitutional procedure by Article 84, otherwise than by powers of judicial review of laws. Only executive actions are subject to judicial scrutiny for violation of fundamental rights guaranteed by Chapter II Article 10 to 15 of the Constitution. Article 17 provides the remedy for the infringement of fundamental rights by executive: "Every person shall be entitled to apply to the Supreme Court, as provided by Article 126, in respect of the infringement or imminent infringement, by executive or administrative action, of a fundamental right to which such person is entitled under the provisions of this Chapter."

The 1996 Constitution of the Republic of South Africa is the supreme law of South Africa. The Constitution, as mentioned, is quasi-federal in the sense that it unites four distinct communities living on the same soil. It defines fundamental liberties of the people both in generic and details: Chapter 1 defines that the Republic is based on the principles of protecting dignity, human rights and the rule of law, while Chapter 2 entitled Bill of Rights, part of the Constitution, contains detailed provisions concerning civil, political, social and economic rights. These rights are subject to legislated limitations set out in section 36, but these must be reasonable and must have an important objective. The limitations should be "less restrictive" and should not annul as such the rights in the Bill of Rights. The South African Constitutional Court has the duty to uphold the law and the constitution including liberties of people, which they must apply impartially maintaining right to equality. The Constitutional Court has final authority to determine which matters are constitutional matters, like US or Indian Supreme Court. All bodies of the South African government are subject to the rule of the Constitution, which is the supreme law. In interpreting the Constitution, the court is by Constitution required to consider international law on human rights and may also consider the law of other democratic countries.

The Constitution of People's Republic of Bangladesh by Part III guarantees Fundamental Rights of the people. Laws inconsistent with fundamental rights are to be void. It is laid down that:

"(1) All existing law inconsistent with the provisions of this Part shall, to the extent of such inconsistency, become void on the commencement of this Constitution.

"(2) The state shall not make any law inconsistent with any provisions of this Part, and any law so made shall, to the extent of such inconsistency, be void." Judiciary is thus given the power of reviewing the constitutionality of laws.

The Constitution of Republic of Afghanistan provides for enforcement of constitutional rights of people by its highest court '*Stera Mahkama*' (Supreme Court). Constitution guarantees some basic inviolable freedoms subject to law but no law is to contradict the beliefs and provisions of Islam. The Supreme Court is to protect the freedoms and use Hanafi Jurisprudence of Islam in situations where the Constitution lacks provisions.

The Constitution of Singapore, termed as Republic of Singapore Independence Act of 1965, is the supreme law of Singapore and it is codified, unitary and flexible like the British Constitution. Part IV of the Constitution guarantees the 'Fundamental Liberties' of citizens and others, by Part IV subject to laws made by Singapore Parliament but which both Parliament and government should respect. The Constitution follows British pattern of powers for judiciary accordingly.

Constitution of United Kingdom

1

{ICL Document Status: 1992}

{Information Source: This document is not a written Constitution (cf. Section 1), but rather a compilation of information material originally provided by the British Embassy for purposes of publication. Most of the information has not been updated since the date mentioned in the ICL Document Status. However, some amendments have been included whenever information about changes of the law was provided to ICL.}

Chapter 1

Human Rights

Part 1

Legal Framework

Section 1 Overview

There is no written constitution or comprehensive Bill of Rights; Britain's constitution is to be found partly in conventions and customs and partly in statute. The Act known as the Bill of Rights 1689 deals with the exercise of the royal prerogative and succession to the Crown.

The British legal system provides some remedies to deal with human rights abuses. For instance, the remedy of 'habeas corpus' secures the individual's right to freedom from any unlawful or arbitrary detention.

Parliament, however, has power to enact any law and change any previous law.

There is no fundamental distinction between 'public law' and 'private law'. Any person can take proceedings against the

Government or a local government authority to protect his or her legal rights and to obtain a remedy for any injury suffered.

Britain has not generally codified its law and courts adopt a relatively strict and literal approach to the interpretation of statutes. The ratification of a treaty or international convention does not make it automatically part of the domestic law. Where necessary, the Government amends domestic law to bring it in line with the convention. Because of Britain's membership of the European Community, Community law is part of British law and takes precedence in the event of conflict between the two.

Part 2

International Human Rights

Section 2 International Arrangements

Since the Universal Declaration of Human Rights is not a legally binding document, the UN General Assembly adopted, in 1966, the 'International Covenant on Economic, Social and Political Rights' and the 'International Covenant on Civil and Political Rights'. Britain ratified both covenants in 1976.

Britain is bound by the Council of Europe's 1953 'European Convention for the Protection of Human Rights and Fundamental Freedoms'. The Convention allows individual petitions against governments to the European Commission on Human Rights, if all possible domestic remedies have been exhausted. Since 1966 Britain has accepted the right of individual petition under the Convention and the compulsory jurisdiction of the European Court of Human Rights. The outcome of some cases has led to changes in British law to improve human rights, for example the abolition of corporal punishment in state schools and improved rights for prisoners. Britain is not a party to the Convention's Fourth Protocol (Freedom of Movement) because of inconsistency with some aspects of the United Kingdom immigration control system nor the Sixth Protocol (abolition of the death penalty).

Part 3

General Provisions

Section 3 Human Dignity

All human beings are born free and equal in dignity and rights, endowed with reason and conscience, and should act towards one another in a spirit of brotherhood.

Section 4 Equality

Everyone is equally entitled to all rights and freedoms without distinction of any kind, such as race, color, sex, language, religion, political or other opinion, national or social origin, property, birth, or other status.

(1) Sex Discrimination: It is unlawful to treat one person less favorably than another on grounds of sex when offering employment. This also applies to education courses and the provision to the public of housing, goods, facilities and services such as insurance. Advertisements indicating an intention to discriminate in this way are also illegal.

(2) Equal Pay: Women employed by the same employer can claim the same pay as men for work of equal value. This right also applies to work which is the same or broadly similar or work which is judged equal by a job evaluation scheme. The same rights apply to men.

(3) European Community Legislation: States are obliged to eliminate discrimination in state social security schemes providing protection against sickness, unemployment, invalidity, old age, accidents at work or occupational diseases.

(4) Racial Equality: It is unlawful to treat one person less favorably than another on grounds of race, color, nationality or ethnic or national origins. This applies to employment (including training), education, and the provision to the public of housing, goods, facilities and services, and premises. Discriminatory advertisements are also unlawful.

Part 4

Integrity

Section 5 Personal Integrity

Everyone has the right to life, Liberty, and the security of person.

(1) Taking of Life: The mandatory penalty for murder is imprisonment for life. Anyone sent to prison for murder is liable to be detained for the rest of his or her life but may be released on license.

(2) Control of Firearms: There is strict licensing and control over the sale of firearms and their possession. Private ownership of highly dangerous weapons is banned.

(3) Victims of violent crime, including foreign nationals, may apply for compensation under the Criminal Injuries Compensation Scheme. In 1990 the Government published its Victims' Charter setting out for the first time the rights and expectations of victims of violent and other crime. There are more than 350 victim support schemes with over 6,000 trained volunteers which help well over 500,000 people a year.

(4) In Northern Ireland the security forces have special powers to search, question and arrest suspected terrorists. Throughout Britain the maximum period for which the police can hold a suspected terrorist is 48 hours. This period can be extended for up to five days with the consent of the appropriate Secretary of State. The Government has powers to ban terrorist organizations in Northern Ireland and in the rest of Britain.

(5) Incitement to racial hatred is a criminal offence. It is against the law to use threatening, abusive, or insulting words or to display, publish or distribute such material. It is also an offence to possess racially inflammatory material, the police having powers of search, seizure and forfeiture.

Section 6 Abolishment of Slavery

No one may be held in slavery or servitude; slavery and the slave trade are prohibited.

Section 7 Punishment

No one shall be subjected to torture or to cruel, inhuman, or degrading treatment or punishment.

(1) If a police officer fails to comply with this provision, he or she can be disciplined and the courts may reject any evidence so obtained.

(2) Custody: Under the Criminal Justice Act 1991, the offence must be so serious that it merits custody. Longer custodial sentences – within the statutory maxima – will be given to persistent violent and sexual offenders in order to protect the public from serious harm.

(3) Most prisoners are eligible for remission of one-third of their sentence. Release is unconditional and does not involve any official supervision in the community. It may be forfeited for serious misconduct in prison.

(4) Parole: Prisoners serving more than 12 months can be released conditionally on parole when they have served one-third of the sentence or six months, whichever expires the later. Three quarters of prisoners serving sentences of less than two years receive parole. The parole license remains in force until the date on which the prisoner would otherwise have been released from prison.

(5) Life Sentence Prisoners: People serving life sentences for the murder of police and prison officers, terrorist murders, murder by firearms in the course of crime or the sexual or sadistic murder of children are normally detained for at least 20 years. Life sentence prisoners are released on life license and are subject to recall should their behavior suggest that they might again be a danger to the public.

Section 8 Marriage and Family

(1) Men and women of full age, without any limitation due to race, nationality or religion, have the right to marry and to found a family. They are entitled to equal rights as to marriage, during marriage and at its dissolution.

(2) Marriage shall be entered into only with the free and full consent of the intending spouses.

(3) The family is the natural and fundamental group unit of society and is entitled to protection by society and the state.

(4) All marriages are registered by the state. It is unlawful to force anyone to marry against his or her will or to bring about a marriage by fraudulent means.

(5) Members of the family are in an advantageous position in matters of succession. If death occurs without a valid will, the spouse and children of the deceased have priority. Children have equal rights of inheritance from parents whether the parents are married or unmarried.

Section 9 Property

(1) Everyone has the right to own property alone as well as in association with others.

(2) No one shall be arbitrarily deprived of his property.

(3) Compensation is paid for any losses suffered through compulsory purchase or the deterioration of property as a result of activities by public authorities.

Part 5

Legal Protection

Section 10 Dignity before Courts

Everyone has the right to recognition everywhere as a person before the law.

Section 11 Equality before the Law

All are equal before the law and are entitled without any discrimination to equal protection of the law.

Section 12 Redress and Remedies

Everyone has the right to an effective remedy by the competent national tribunals for acts violating the fundamental rights granted him by the constitution or by law.

(1) Redress and Remedies: Everyone has the right of access to the courts and to the legal remedies available there.

(2) Legal aid schemes help people with limited resources to meet the cost of work done by a lawyer. Solicitors give legal advice and assistance to suspects at police stations.

(3) All state authorities are subject to judicial control. Government departments and public authorities can be sued for compensation for wrongful acts or breach of contract in the same way as individuals.

Seciton 13 Fair Trial

Everyone is entitled in full equality to a fair and public hearing by an independent and impartial tribunal in the determination of his rights and obligations and of any criminal charge against him.

(1) Civil and criminal cases are heard by an independent judiciary.

(2) In criminal cases the prosecution must prove guilt beyond reasonable doubt. Following a series of miscarriages of justice which took place in the mid 1970s, the Government has set up a Royal Commission to examine the effectiveness of the criminal justice system.

(3) In jury trials the judge decides questions of law, sums up the evidence for the jury, and discharges the accused or passes sentence. A jury is independent of the judiciary. Any attempt to interfere with the jury once it is sworn in is a criminal offence.

(4) Publicity: Court proceedings are normally held in public and reporters from the media are admitted. In rape cases, the identity of the complainant cannot be reported.

Section 14 Presumption of Innocence

(1) Everyone charged with a penal offence has the right to be presumed innocent until proved guilty according to law in a public trial at which he has had all the guarantees necessary for his defence.

(2) No one shall be held guilty of any penal offence on account of any act or omission which did not constitute a penal offence, under national or international law, at the time when it was committed. Nor shall a heavier penalty be imposed than the one that was applicable at the time the penal offence was committed.

Part 6

Liberties

Section 15 Personal Liberty

No one shall be subjected to arbitrary arrest, detention, or exile. Everyone has a legal right to personal liberty. No one can be arrested with the exception of those suspected of committing a crime, those failing to comply with certain civil court orders, or individuals in contempt of a superior court or of Parliament. An arrest to enforce a court order in civil proceedings can only be made under a warrant issued by a court or by a power of arrest granted by the court in cases of domestic violence.

(1) Arrests in Criminal Proceedings: The police have power to arrest a suspect without a warrant if he or she is reasonably suspected of involvement in an arrestable offence, that is, one where the maximum penalty is five years imprisonment or more. They must normally obtain a warrant before arresting someone for other offenses; an immediate arrest without a warrant may, however, take place if the police believe it is not possible or appropriate to issue a summons to appear in court, for instance where a suspect refuses to give a name and address.

(2) An arrested person has the right to:

- consult a solicitor;
- ask the police to notify a relative or other named person likely to take an interest in his or her welfare; and
- consult the code of practice regarding treatment in police custody.

The police may delay the exercise of the first two of these rights for up to 36 hours.

(3) Consultation: Solicitors are available on a 2-hour basis to offer free legal advice for people being questioned at police stations. The police must caution a suspect before any questions are put for the purpose of obtaining evidence. The caution informs the suspect that he or she is entitled to refuse to answer questions – the so-called 'right of silence'.

(4) The suspect may not normally be detained for more than 24 hours without charge. In the case of a suspect arrested in connection with a serious arrestable offence, however, he or she may be detained for up to 36 hours without charge on the authority of a senior police officer; if the police wish to detain the suspect for longer than 36 hours, they must obtain authority from a court, which may not grant authority for a period beyond 96 hours from first detention. Reviews must be made of a person's detention at regular intervals to check whether the criteria for detention are still satisfied. If they are not, the person must be released immediately.

(5) Tape recording of interviews with suspected offenders at police stations is a universal practice.

(6) Habeas Corpus: Anyone who thinks that his or her detention is illegal may apply to the High Court for a writ of habeas corpus against the person detaining him or her. If no lawful cause can be shown, the prisoner must be released immediately. A habeas corpus case has priority over other cases in the order of court business.

(7) Bail: Most accused people are released on bail pending trial. They are not remanded in custody except where strictly necessary.

Section 16 Right to Privacy

No one shall be subjected to arbitrary interference with his privacy, family, home or correspondence, nor to attacks upon his honor and reputation. Everyone has the right to the protection of the law against such interference or attacks.

(1) The common law allows people to speak and act in their own homes as they please and to carry on their daily business, provided that they do not infringe the rights of others or commit an offence.

(2) Parents are free to bring up their children as they so wish, provided that they do not infringe laws against cruelty and exposure to moral and physical danger. Parents also have to observe the law regarding compulsory education of their children.

(3) Is a criminal offence for a man to commit a homosexual act with a person under the age of 18. The age was changed from 21 to 18 with a vote of 336 to 129. A 1999 bill to further reduce that age to 16 has failed.

(4) Privacy and the Press: Action is being taken by the Government to deal with media intrusion into the privacy of individuals. The law against libel gives protection against attacks on a person's honor and reputation.

(5) Some other forms of intrusion are criminal offenses, for example, the use of unlicensed radio transmitters for bugging, the harassment of tenants to make them quit, or the sending of unsolicited obscene material through the post. Other attempts to obtain private information may involve offenses of criminal trespass.

(6) Interception of Communications: Legislation authorizes governmental interception of postal and telephone services but only on certain limited grounds. Any interception outside these procedures is a criminal offence.

(7) Computers: Under the Data Protection Act 1984, which gives effect to a Council of Europe Convention, data users are required to register a description of the personal data they hold, the purposes for which they use it, the sources from which they obtain it and the categories of person to whom they may disclose it. They must also provide an address to which data subjects may write for access to the data. Individuals have the legal right to know about the data held on them and the right to ask a court to have factually wrong or misleading data corrected or deleted. In addition they have the right to claim compensation for damages if the data are lost, inaccurate, or disclosed without authority.

Section 17 Freedom of Movement

(1) Everyone has the right to freedom of movement and residence within the borders of each state.

(2) Everyone has the right to leave any country, including his own, and to return to his country.

Section 18 Freedom of Religion

Everyone has the right to freedom of thought, conscience and religion; this right includes freedom to change his religion or belief, and freedom, either alone or in community with others and in public or private, to manifest his religion or belief in teaching, practice, worship and observance.

(1) Worship and religious teaching take place without any interference from the state. There is complete freedom of thought, conscience or form of worship and no restriction on the right of any citizen to change his or her religion. Atheists and agnostics are also free to propagate their views.

(2) A person may, however, be held guilty of blasphemous libel if he or she publishes scurrilous and offensive references to Christianity that go beyond the limits of proper controversy. This does not apply to debate and discussion about the truth of Christian doctrines.

(3) Churches and religious societies of all kinds own property, run schools and propagate their beliefs in speech and writing. Inquiries are not made about religion in population censuses or other official returns.

(4) There is no religious bar to the holding of public office except in the case of the Sovereign who must by law be a Protestant. The Church of England and the Church of Scotland are the established 'official' churches for state ceremonies of a religious nature. Their members, however, do not obtain any advantages from being members of an established church rather than of any other church.

(5) Religious education has to be provided in all schools financed from public funds and is part of the national curriculum. Parents have the right to ask for their children to be withdrawn from such classes. Some publicly maintained schools are provided by religious denominations and receive varying amounts of public finance, according to type.

(6) Television and radio programs are broadcast on religious topics; these include religious services as well as programs in which adherents of the main religions and non-believers discuss

their views. Advertising aiming to promote religious ends is not permitted on television or radio.

Section 19 Freedom of Expression

Everyone has the right to freedom of opinion and expression; this right includes freedom to hold opinions without interference and to seek, receive, and impart information and ideas through any media and regardless of frontiers.

(1) Restrictions include the official secrets, civil defamation, criminal libel, obscenity, sedition, incitement to racial hatred, and contempt of court.

(2) There are legal remedies against defamation. Fair comment on matters of public interest may be a defence. Proof that the alleged defamatory matter is true is also a defence. In the same way, frank discussion of sexual problems is not considered to be an infringement of the law on obscenity.

(3) There is no state control or censorship of the press. Foreign language papers are freely imported.

(4) British broadcasting is based on the tradition that it is a public service accountable to the people through Parliament. Television and radio services are provided by the British Broadcasting Corporation (BBC). Other operators are licensed individually by the Independent Television Commission (ITC) and the Radio Authority. The responsibilities of these public bodies are set out in legislation. The Government itself is not responsible for program content or broadcasters' day-to-day conduct of business.

(5) The independence of the broadcasters requires them to maintain certain standards regarding programs and program content. Under the relevant legislation and the codes of practice applied by the broadcasting authorities, programs must display, as far as possible, a proper balance and wide range of subject matter, and impartiality in matters of controversy. There are also rules relating to violence and standards of taste and decency in television programs, particularly during hours when large numbers of children are likely to be watching. Broadcasters must also comply with the general law relating to obscenity and incitement to racial hatred.

(6) According to 1991 European agreements on cross-border broadcasting, programs may not be indecent, contain pornography, give undue emphasis to violence, or be likely to incite racial hatred. Nor should programs unsuitable for children be broadcast when they can be expected to be watching.

(7) Theater: There is no censorship of plays. It is, however, a criminal offence to present or direct an obscene performance of a play in public or private. Such a performance is defined as one which, taken as a whole, tends to 'deprave and corrupt persons who are likely to attend it'. There is a defence against an obscenity charge on the grounds that the performance is for the public good in the interest of drama, opera or literature.

(8) Films and Video: Government has no power to censor films. Cinemas are licensed by local government authorities, which have a legal duty to prohibit the admission of children under 16 to unsuitable films, and may prevent the showing of any film, although this particular power is hardly ever exercised. In assessing the suitability of films, authorities rely on the British Board for Film Classification, an independent non-statutory body to which films offered to the public must be submitted.

Part 7

Political Rights

Section 20 General Political Rights

(1) Everyone has the right to take part in the government of his country, directly or through freely chosen representatives.

(2) Everyone has the right of equal access to public service in his country.

(3) The will of the people shall be the basis of the authority of government; this will shall be expressed in periodic and genuine elections which shall be by universal and equal suffrage and shall be held by secret vote or by equivalent free voting procedures.

(4) Britain is a parliamentary democracy, the Government being responsible to the people through the elected House of

Commons, which has the power to force a government to resign on a vote of no-confidence. The other House in the British Parliament is the non-elected House of Lords, which is normally a chamber of discussion and revision of proposals and not a rival to the Commons. Its powers to delay legislation are limited by law.

(5) Candidature for parliamentary elections is open to anyone aged 21 and over who is eligible to vote.

(6) The secret ballot is used in all British elections. The electoral system is the 'simple majority' system. The candidate with the largest number of votes is elected.

(7) Officials working in central and local government have a long tradition of political neutrality. A change of minister therefore does not involve a change of departmental staff, whose functions remain the same whichever political party is in office.

Public offices are open to men and women, without distinction on grounds of sex, religion, race or color. Staff are recruited to the Civil Service and its executive agencies through fair and open competition solely on the basis of merit.

Section 21 Political Asylum

(1) Everyone has the right to seek and to enjoy in other countries asylum from persecution.

(2) This right may not be invoked in the case of prosecutions genuinely arising from non-political crimes or from acts contrary to the purposes and principles of the United Nations.

(3) Britain is a signatory of the 1951 United Nations Convention Relating to the Status of Refugees and its 1967 Protocol and continues to meet its obligations to refugees under these instruments. The Convention defines a refugee 'as a person who has a well-founded fear of being persecuted for reasons of race, religion, nationality, membership of a particular social group or political opinion'.

(4) Britain and the other European Community members have signed the Dublin Convention, which defines when a member state is responsible for dealing with an asylum

application. Applicants may no longer lodge successive claims in different countries.

(5) Under recent legislation people are not extradited to face trial or imprisonment if they face persecution on grounds of race, religion, nationality or political opinion. British extradition law prevents extradition for political offenses.

Section 22 Nationality

(1) Everyone has the right to a nationality.

(2) No one shall be arbitrarily deprived of his nationality nor denied the right to change his nationality.

(3) British citizenship is acquired automatically at birth by a child born in Britain if the father (in cases of legitimate birth) or mother is a British citizen or is settled in Britain.

(4) British Dependent Territories citizens, British Nationals (Overseas), British overseas citizens, British subjects under the Citizenship Act and British protected persons are entitled to be registered as British citizens after five years' residence in Britain. British Dependent Territories citizens from Gibraltar have an absolute right to be registered as British citizens without needing to reside in Britain.

(5) Commonwealth citizens, citizens of the Irish Republic and foreign nationals can acquire British citizenship by naturalization.

(6) British citizenship can be renounced by a person if he or she possesses, or is about to acquire, the nationality or citizenship of another country.

(7) Under the Hong Kong Act 1985 citizens are entitled to acquire a new form of nationality, that of British National (Overseas), together with a passport showing that an entry clearance is not required to visit Britain. In April 1990 legislation was passed to give British citizenship to 50,000 key people in Hong Kong and their dependents without their having to leave the territory to qualify. Its purpose is to persuade these people – selected under a points system – to remain in Hong Kong so that the territory can remain stable and prosperous up to the change to Chinese sovereignty in 1997 and beyond.

Section 23 Assemblies and Associations

(1) Everyone has the right to freedom of peaceful assembly and association.

(2) No one may be compelled to belong to an association.

Part 8

Social Rights

Section 24 General Social Rights

Everyone, as a member of society, has the right to social security and is entitled to the realization, through national effort and international cooperation and in accordance with the organization and resources of each state, of the economic, social and cultural rights indispensable for his dignity and the free development of his personality.

Section 25 Work

(1) Everyone has the right to work, to free choice of employment, to just and favourable conditions of work and to protection against unemployment.

(2) Everyone, without any discrimination, has the right to equal pay for equal work.

(3) Everyone who works has the right to just and favourable remuneration ensuring for himself and his family an existence worthy of human dignity, and supplemented, if necessary, by other means of social protection.

(4) Everyone has the right to form and to join trade unions for the protection of his interests.

(5) The Employment Service, an executive agency of the Department of Employment, helps unemployed people to find work through its job placement and other services and pays benefits and allowances to those entitled to them.

(6) A fundamental reform of the vocational qualifications system is being undertaken by the National Council for Vocational Qualifications. It aims to develop a system of nationally recognized vocational qualifications based on standards of workplace competence set by employers. Equal

esteem for academic and vocational qualifications is being promoted with clearer and more accessible paths between them.

(7) In most industries the pay and conditions of workers are settled by national and/or plant bargaining between employers and trade unions.

(8) Laws impose duties on employers and others to ensure the health, safety and welfare of their employees in factories offices, mines, building sites and all other work activities.

(9) People may join trade unions, which have members in virtually every occupation and some 10 million members in all. Dismissals for union membership or non-membership are automatically unfair. It is also unlawful for an employer to refuse to employ an individual on the grounds of that individual's membership or non-membership of a trade union.

Section 26 Working Hours

Everyone has the right to rest and leisure, including reasonable limitation of working hours and periodic holidays with pay.

The basic working week in Great Britain is about 37.5 to 40 hours for manual work and 35 to 38 for non-manual work. A five-day week is usually worked. Overtime is paid at higher rates.

Section 27 Home

(1) Everyone has the right to a standard of living adequate for the health and well-being of himself and of his family, including food, clothing, housing and medical care and necessary social services, and the right to security in the event of unemployment, sickness, disability, widowhood, old age or other lack of livelihood in circumstances beyond his control.

(2) Motherhood and childhood are entitled to special care and assistance. All children, whether born in or out of wedlock, shall enjoy the same social protection.

(3) The National Health Service (NHS) provides comprehensive health care to all residents. Treatment is based on medical priority regardless of patients' income and is

financed mainly out of general taxation. Patients pay charges for prescriptions although in practice some 75 per cent are supplied free, since charges do not apply to people on low incomes, children, expectant mothers, pensioners and other groups.

(4) Patients are free to seek private medical treatment and doctors, dentists, opticians and pharmacists are able to practice privately. NHS hospital doctors, too, can practice privately, subject to certain rules. There is limited provision for them to treat their private patients in NHS hospitals. NHS patients are sometimes treated at public expense in private hospitals. Some 7.5 million people are covered by private medical insurance.

(5) A local authority may apply to the court for a child care order. This can only be made by the court if it is satisfied that the child is suffering, or is likely to suffer, significant harm.

(6) Children who break the criminal law are brought before youth courts.

(7) The social security system aims to provide financial help to people who are elderly, sick, disabled, unemployed, widowed or bringing up children. The system includes contributory national insurance benefits covering sickness, invalidity, unemployment, widowhood, and retirement. There is also statutory sick pay and maternity pay paid for their employees by employers. Another part of the system consists of non-contributory benefits such as child benefit paid for every child in a family and a range of benefits for severely disabled people and those looking after them.

(8) Preventive services are designed to safeguard the health of pregnant women and mothers with young children. Pregnant working women have the right to visit clinics during working hours. Nearly all women have their babies in hospital, returning home shortly after to be attended by a midwife or health visitor and, where necessary, the family doctor. Child health centers check the physical and mental health of pre-school children. There are voluntary programs of immunization against diphtheria, measles, rubella (women of child-bearing age and girls only), poliomyelitis, tetanus, tuberculosis, and whooping

cough. There is a combined vaccination against measles, mumps and rubella for children in the second year of life.

(9) Statutory maternity pay is available for up to 18 weeks when a women is away from work because of her pregnancy. The pay is 90 per cent of earnings for six weeks followed by a flat rate payment for a further 12 weeks. To qualify, a woman must have worked for the same employer for at least two years; where a woman has been employed for between six months and two years, she is entitled to payments for the full 18 weeks at the flat rate only. If a woman does not qualify for maternity pay, she may receive a maternity allowance if she has worked for an employer or as a self-employed person and paid a specified number of national insurance contributions. The allowance is paid for 18 weeks.

(10) Britain is a party to the Council of Europe's convention on the legal status of children born to unmarried parents. This provides for common rules under which the legal status of such children is the same as for those born to a married couple. Legislation has been passed to remove former legal disadvantages suffered by children of unmarried parents.

(11) Under the Abortion Act 1967, as amended in 1990, a pregnancy may only be terminated if two registered doctors consider that this step is justified in terms of one or more of the grounds specified in the Act. The Act does not apply in Northern Ireland.

(12) The birth of the world's first 'test tube baby' took place in Britain in 1978, using the technique of in vitro fertilization. The social, ethical, and legal implications were examined by a committee of enquiry under Baroness Warnock, which concluded that certain specialized forms of infertility treatment, including artificial insemination by donor and in vitro fertilization, were ethically acceptable. The committee also considered that research on human embryos could take place under certain conditions.

(13) About two-thirds of the housing stock in Britain is owner-occupied. With a few exceptions, secure public sector tenants have the right to buy their house or flat at a discount if they have been public sector tenants for at least two years.

Under legislation passed in 1988 a Housing Action Trust can be proposed for an area of public sector housing in England and Wales. If the majority of tenants vote in support of a proposal to set up a Trust in their area, the Trust, which is a public body, takes over the ownership of the housing in order to undertake major physical, social, and economic regeneration. Once the work is completed, the tenants decide on the future of their homes, such as a transfer to a housing association, formation of a tenants' cooperative, or a return to the local government authority. Additional low-cost housing is provided by non-profit-making housing associations.

(14) Local government authorities have a statutory duty to ensure that accommodation is provided for people who are or are about to become unintentionally homeless.

(15) It is a criminal offence for a landlord to harass tenants. If tenants are driven out by harassment or illegally evicted, they must he compensated. If a landlord harasses or evicts a tenant in order to re-let at market rent, the courts may award damages to the tenant based on the profit made by the landlord. As a general principle, tenants and most other residential occupiers cannot be evicted without a court order.

Section 28 Education, Science, and the Arts

(1) Everyone has the right to education. Education shall be free, at least in the elementary and fundamental stages. Elementary education shall be compulsory. Technical and professional education shall be made generally available and higher education shall be equally accessible to all on the basis of merit.

(2) Education shall be directed to the full development of the human personality and to the strengthening of respect for human rights and fundamental freedoms. It shall promote understanding, tolerance and friendship among all nations, racial or religious groups, and shall further the activities of the United Nations for the maintenance of peace.

(3) Parents have a prior right to choose the kind of education that shall be given to their children.

(4) The state education system is free, but a small proportion of children attend private fee-paying schools. Local education authorities have to meet the parents' wishes unless the school is full or, if selective, the child does not meet required academic standards. Secondary schools – those catering for 11- to 16-year-olds – in England and Wales are required to admit pupils up to the limit of their available physical capacity if there is sufficient demand on behalf of eligible children by parents.

(5) Children whose learning difficulties are severe or complex, wherever possible, are educated in ordinary schools.

Section 29 Culture

(1) Everyone has the right freely to participate in the cultural life of the community, to enjoy the arts, and to share in scientific advancement and its benefits.

(2) Everyone has the right to the protection of the moral and material interests resulting from any scientific, literary, or artistic production of which he is the author.

(3) The Government and local government authorities give financial support to the arts. The preservation of the artistic heritage is encouraged by tax relief and other measures including certain controls on the export of works of art. The Arts Council allocates funds to the major opera, dance, and drama companies, symphony orchestras, small touring theaters, experimental groups, and creative artists.

(4) Original literary, dramatic, musical, or artistic works, films, and sound recordings are automatically protected. The copyright owner has rights against unauthorized reproduction, public performance, and broadcasting of his or her work. In most cases the author is the first owner of the copyright, its term being the life of the author and a period of 50 years after his or her death (50 years from the date of release for films and sound recordings). Under legislation passed in 1988 authors have the right to be identified on their works and to object to any unjustified modifications of them. The law also protects performers against the trading in unauthorized recordings of live performance, the term of protection being 50 years from the

year in which the performance is given. A copyright work first published in Britain has automatic copyright in all other countries which are members of the Berne Copyright Convention and the Universal Copyright Convention. The law secures the rights of the originators of inventions, new industrial designs, and trade marks. Protection is also available under the European Patent Convention and the Patent Cooperation Treaty; benefits may be claimed in other countries under the International Convention for the Protection of Industrial Property.

(5) The Government has taken steps to protect the ownership of ideas by means of patents, registered designs, trade marks, and copyright. Measures include the extension of copyright protection to computer software owners, the extension of trade marks to cover services, and powers to enable customs authorities to prevent the entry of counterfeit goods. Legislation passed in 1988 made provision for a new form of protection for designs and made litigation regarding patents simpler and cheaper.

Part 9

Restrictions

Section 30 Restrictions

(1) Everyone has duties to the community in which alone the free and full development of his personality is possible.

(2) In the exercise of his rights and freedoms, everyone shall be subject only to such limitations as are determined by law solely for the purpose of securing due recognition and respect for the rights and freedoms of others and of meeting the just requirements of morality, public order, and the general welfare in a democratic society.

(3) These rights and freedoms may in no case be exercised contrary to the purposes and principles of the United Nations.

Chapter 2
State Organization

Part 1
Overview

Section 31 Basic Structure

(1) The British constitution is made up of statute law, common law, and conventions. Conventions are rules and practices which are not legally enforceable but which are regarded as indispensable to the working of government; many are derived from the historical events through which the British system of government has evolved.

(2) The Queen is head of State and an important symbol of national unity. She is:

- head of the executive;
- an integral part of the legislature;
- head of the judiciary;
- commander-in-chief of all the Armed Forces of the Crown; and
- the 'supreme governor' of the established Church of England.

The Queen acts on the advice of her ministers. Britain is governed by Her Majesty's Government in the name of the Queen. In international affairs the Queen, as head of State, has the power to declare war and make peace, to recognize foreign states and governments, to conclude treaties and to annex or cede territory.

(3) Three elements make up Parliament – the Queen, the House of Lords and the elected House of Commons. The agreement of all three is normally required for legislation. As there are no legal restraints imposed by a written constitution, Parliament can make or change any law. It can even prolong its own life beyond the normal period without consulting the electorate. In practice, however, Parliament does not assert its supremacy in this way.

(4) The validity of an Act of Parliament, once passed, cannot be disputed in the law courts. The House of Commons is directly responsible to the electorate, and in this century the House of Lords has recognized the supremacy of the elected chamber. The system of party government helps to ensure that Parliament legislates with its responsibility to the electorate in mind.

(5) A Parliament has a maximum duration of five years, but in practice general elections are usually held before the end of this term. The maximum life has been prolonged by legislation in rare circumstances such as the two world wars.

Part 2

Parliament

Section 32 House of Commons

(1) Officers: The officers of the House of Commons are the Speaker, three Deputy Speakers and other permanent officers and staff (Clerks, Sergeants, Library, Official Report, Finance and Administration, and Refreshment).

(2) Electorate: British citizens, together with citizens of other Commonwealth countries and citizens of the Irish Republic resident in Britain, may vote provided they are aged 18 or over, included in the annual register of electors for the constituency, and not subject to any disqualification.

(3) Elections: For electoral purposes Britain is divided into 651 constituencies, each of which returns one member to the House of Commons. Each elector may cast one vote, normally in person at a polling station. Voting is not compulsory; 76.9 per cent of a total electorate of 43.3 million people voted in the general election in April 1992. The simple majority system of voting is used. Candidates are elected if they have more votes than any of the other candidates, although not necessarily an absolute majority over all other candidates.

(4) Candidates: British citizens and citizens of other Commonwealth countries, together with citizens of the Irish Republic, may stand for election as MPs provided they are aged 21 or over and are not disqualified. A candidate must also

deposit 500 pounds, which is returned if he or she receives 5 per cent or more of the votes cast. The maximum sum a candidate may spend on a general election campaign is 4,330 pounds plus 3.7 pence for each elector in a borough constituency or 4.9 pence for each elector in a county constituency. All election expenses, apart from the candidate's personal expenses, are subject to the statutory limit.

Section 33 Parties

(1) Parties are not registered or formally recognized in law, but in practice most candidates in elections, and almost all winning candidates, belong to one of the main parties. In 1992 General Elections, the Conservative Party reached 42%, Labour Party 35%, and the Liberal Democrats 18% of votes.

(2) Since 1945 either the Conservative Party, whose origins go back to the eighteenth century, or the Labour Party, which emerged in the last decade of the nineteenth century, has held power. A new party – the Liberal Democrats – was formed in 1988 when the Liberal Party, which could trace its origins to the eighteenth century, merged with the Social Democratic Party, which was formed in 1981.

(3) Leaders of the Government and Opposition sit on the front benches on either side of the Commons chamber with their supporters – the backbenchers – sitting behind them. Inside Parliament, party control is exercised by the Chief Whips and their assistants, who are chosen within the party.

(4) Annual assistance from public funds helps opposition parties carry out their parliamentary work at Westminster. It is limited to parties which had at least two members elected at the previous general election or one member elected and a minimum of 150,000 votes cast. The amount is 2,550 pounds for every seat won, plus 5.10 pounds for every 200 votes.

Section 34 Procedure

(1) Each subject starts off as a proposal or 'motion' by a member. At the end of each debate the question may be decided without voting, or by a simple majority vote. The Speaker has discretion on whether to allow a motion to end discussion so

that a matter may be put to the vote and has powers to put a stop to irrelevance and repetition in debate, and to save time in other ways.

(2) In a tied vote the Speaker gives a casting vote, without expressing an opinion on the merits of the question.

(3) Members with a financial interest in a debate in the House must declare it when speaking. To act as a disqualification from voting the interest must be direct, immediate and personal.

(4) Proceedings of both Houses are normally public and visitors can watch the proceedings from the galleries of both chambers. The minutes and speeches are published daily. The records of the Lords from 1497 and of the Commons from 1547, together with the parliamentary and political papers of a number of former members of both Houses, are available to the public through the House of Lords Record Office. The proceedings of both Houses of Parliament may be broadcast on television and radio, either live or, more usually, in recorded or edited form.

Section 35 Legislation

(1) Bills: Draft laws take the form of parliamentary Bills. Most are public Bills involving measures relating to public policy. Private Bills deal with matters of individual, corporate or local interest. Proposals for legislative changes are sometimes set out in government 'White Papers'. Consultation papers, sometimes called 'Green Papers', set out government proposals which are still taking shape and seek comments from the public.

(2) A draft law is given a first reading in the House of Commons without debate; this is followed by a thorough debate on general principles at second reading. It is then given detailed consideration, clause by clause, by a Commons committee before report stage in the whole House, and a third and final reading.

(3) Bills must normally be passed by both Houses. They must then receive the Royal Assent before becoming Acts. In practice this is a formality.

Section 36 Committees

(1) Standing committees debate and consider amendments to public Bills at the committee stage and, in certain cases, discuss them at the second reading stage. Ordinary standing committees do not have names but are referred to simply as Standing Committee A, B, C, and so on; a new set of members are appointed to them to consider each Bill. Each committee has between 16 and 50 members, with a party balance reflecting as far as possible that in the House as a whole.

(2) Select committees are appointed, normally for the duration of a Parliament, to examine subjects by taking written and oral evidence. After private discussion they report their conclusions and recommendations. Committees include those on European Legislation, Science and Technology, Public Accounts, Members' Interests, and the Parliamentary Commissioner for Administration.

(3) Party Committees: In addition to the official committees of the two Houses there are several unofficial party organizations or committees. The Conservative and Unionist Members' Committee (the 1922 Committee) consists of the backbench membership of the party in the House of Commons. When the Conservative Party is in office, ministers attend its meetings by invitation and not by right. When the party is in opposition, the whole membership of the party may attend meetings. The leader appoints a consultative committee, which acts as the party's 'shadow cabinet'.

Section 37 House of Lords

There are opportunities for criticism and examination of government policy in the House of Lords at daily question time and during debates on general motions. Other opportunities include 'unstarred' questions, which can be debated at the end of the day's business, and debates on proposed legislation.

Section 38 Finances

The Finance Act is the most important of the annual statutes, and authorizes the raising of revenue. The legislation is based on the Chancellor of the Exchequer's Budget statement, normally made in March or April each year. It includes a review of the public finances of the previous year, and proposals for the estimated expenditure of the coming year. Scrutiny of public expenditure is carried out by House of Commons select committees.

Section 39 European Community Affairs

To keep the two Houses informed of European Community developments, and to enable them to scrutinise and debate Community policies and proposals, there is a select committee in each House and two standing committees debate specific European legislative proposals in the House of Commons. Ministers also make regular statements about Community business.

Section 40 Members of Parliament

(1) Members of Parliament represent all their constituents, including those who voted for other parties.

(2) The privileges of the members of the Commons include freedom of speech; freedom from arrest in civil actions; exemption from serving on juries, or being compelled to attend court as witnesses; and the right of access to the Crown, which is a collective privilege of the House.

Section 41 Parliamentary Ombudsman

The Parliamentary Commissioner for Administration investigates, independently, complaints of maladministration when asked to do so by MPs on behalf of members of the public. The Commissioner must report annually to Parliament. He or she also publishes details of selected investigations at quarterly intervals and may submit other reports where necessary.

Part 3

Government

Section 42 Composition

(1) The Prime Minister is appointed by the Queen, and all other ministers are appointed by the Queen on the recommendation of the Prime Minister. Most ministers are members of the Commons, although the Government is also

fully represented by ministers in the Lords. The Lord Chancellor is always a member of the House of Lords.

(2) The composition of governments can vary both in the number of ministers and in the titles of some offices.

(3) The Prime Minister is, by tradition, First Lord of the Treasury and Minister for the Civil Service. The Prime Minister's office is located at 10 Downing Street in central London.

(4) Ministers in charge of government departments are usually in the Cabinet; they are known as 'Secretary of State' or 'Minister', or may have a special title, as in the case of the Chancellor of the Exchequer.

(5) To keep the workload of the Cabinet within manageable limits, a great deal of work is carried on through the committee system. The membership of all ministerial Cabinet committees is published.

(6) The doctrine of collective responsibility means that the Cabinet acts unanimously even when Cabinet ministers do not all agree on a subject.

Section 43 Lobby

As press adviser to the Prime Minister, the Prime Minister's Press Secretary and other staff in the Prime Minister's Press Office have direct contact with the parliamentary press through regular meetings with the Lobby correspondents. The Lobby correspondents are a group of political correspondents who have the special privilege of access to the Lobby of the House of Commons where they can talk privately to government ministers and other members of the House. The Prime Minister's Press Office is the accepted channel through which information about parliamentary business is passed to the media.

Section 44 Privy Council

The main function of the Privy Council is to advise the Queen to approve Orders in Council – those made under prerogative powers and those made under statutory powers. Cabinet ministers must be Privy Counsellors and are sworn in on first assuming office.

Part 4

Local Government

Section 45 Local authority councils

(1) Local authority councils consist of elected councillors, elected on a similar basis to parliamentary elections. They serve for four years.

(2) In the metropolitan counties, district councils are responsible for all services apart from the police, the fire service and public transport and, in some areas, waste regulation and disposal. In Greater London the boroughs and the City Corporation have similar functions but London's metropolitan police force is directly responsible to the Home Secretary.

(3) Local authorities in Great Britain raise revenue through a council tax. Each household receives a single bill based on the market value of property and the number of adults living in it. Couples on low incomes will be entitled to rebates of up to 100 per cent on their council tax bills.

Part 5

Judiciary

Section 46 Legal System in General

(1) Although Britain is a unitary state, England and Wales, Scotland and Northern Ireland all have their own legal systems, with considerable differences in law, organization and practice. However, a large amount of modern legislation applies throughout Britain. The law is divided into criminal law and civil law; the latter regulates the conduct of people in ordinary relations with one another. The distinction between the two is reflected in the procedures used, the courts in which cases may be heard and the sanctions which may be applied.

(2) The legal system of England and Wales comprises both an historic body of conventions known as common law and equity, and parliamentary and European Community legislation. Common law, which is based on custom and interpreted in court cases by judges, has never been precisely defined or codified. It forms the basis of the law except when superseded

by legislation. Equity law consists of a body of historic rules and principles which are applied by the courts. The English legal system is therefore distinct from many of those of Western Europe, which have codes derived from Roman law.

(3) European Community law, which applies throughout Britain, is confined mainly to economic and social matters; in certain circumstances it takes precedence over domestic law. It is normally applied by the domestic courts, but the most authoritative rulings are given by the Community's Court of Justice.

Section 47 Judiciary in General

(1) The judiciary is independent of the executive; its judgments are not subject to ministerial direction or control. The Prime Minister recommends the highest judicial appointments to the Crown.

(2) The Lord Chancellor is head of the judiciary, except in Scotland. His responsibilities include court procedure and the administration of courts.

Section 48 Criminal Courts

(1) Summary or less serious offenses, which make up the vast majority of criminal cases, are tried in England and Wales by unpaid lay magistrates – justices of the peace (JPs), although in areas with a heavy workload there are a number of full-time, stipendiary magistrates. More serious offenses are tried by the Crown Court, presided over by a judge sitting with a jury. The Crown Court sits at about 90 centers and is presided over by High Court judges, full-time 'circuit judges' and part-time recorders.

(2) Appeals from the magistrates' courts go before the Crown Court or the High Court. Appeals from the Crown Court are made to the Court of Appeal (Criminal Division). The House of Lords is the final appeal court in all cases.

Section 49 Civil Courts

(1) Magistrates' courts have limited civil jurisdiction. The 286 county courts have a wider jurisdiction; cases are normally tried by judges sitting alone. The 80 or so judges in the High

Court cover civil cases and some criminal cases, and also deal with the appeals. The High Court sits at the Royal Courts of Justice in London or at 26 district registries. Appeals from the High Court are heard in the Court of Appeal (Civil Division), and may go on to the House of Lords, the final court of appeal.

Section 50 Tribunals

(1) Tribunals are a specialized group of judicial bodies, akin to courts of law. They are normally set up under statutory powers which also govern their constitution, functions and procedure. Tribunals often consist of laypeople, but they are generally chaired by someone who is legally qualified. They tend to be less expensive, and less formal, than courts of law.

(2) Independently of the executive, tribunals decide the rights and obligations of private citizens towards one another or towards a government department or other public authority. Important examples are industrial tribunals, rent tribunals and social security appeal tribunals.

(3) In many cases there is a right of appeal to a higher tribunal and, on points of law, to the courts. Tribunals do not normally employ staff or spend money themselves, but their expenses are paid by the government departments concerned. An independent Council on Tribunals exercises general supervision over many tribunals.

Section 51 European Courts

(1) The Court of Justice consists of 13 judges. It interprets and adjudicates on the meaning of the treaties and on measures taken by the Council of Ministers and the Commission. It also hears complaints and appeals brought by or against Community institutions, member states or individuals and gives preliminary rulings on cases referred by courts in member states. It represents the final authority on all aspects of Community law.

(2) The Single European Act of 1986 provided for a Court of First Instance to relieve the Court of Justice of a substantial part of its workload. The new court began working in 1989.

Constitution of the United States of America

2

We the People of the United States, in Order to form a more perfect Union, establish Justice, insure domestic Tranquility, provide for the common defence, promote the general Welfare, and secure the Blessings of Liberty to ourselves and our Posterity, do ordain and establish this Constitution for the United States of America.

Article I

Section 1. All legislative Powers herein granted shall be vested in a Congress of the United States, which shall consist of a Senate and House of Representatives.

Section 2. The House of Representatives shall be composed of Members chosen every second Year by the People of the several States, and the Electors in each State shall have the Qualifications requisite for Electors of the most numerous Branch of the State Legislature.

No Person shall be a Representative who shall not have attained to the Age of twenty-five Years, and been seven Years a Citizen of the United States, and who shall not, when elected, be an Inhabitant of that State in which he shall be chosen.

Representatives and direct Taxes shall be apportioned among the several States which may be included within this Union, according to their respective Numbers, which shall be determined by adding to the whole Number of free Persons, including those bound to Service for a Term of Years, and excluding Indians not taxed, three fifths of all other Persons [Modified by Amendment XIV]. The actual Enumeration shall be made within three Years after the first Meeting of the Congress of the United States, and within every subsequent

Term of ten Years, in such Manner as they shall by Law direct. The Number of Representatives shall not exceed one for every thirty Thousand, but each State shall have at Least one Representative; and until such enumeration shall be made, the State of New Hampshire shall be entitled to choose three, Massachusetts eight, Rhode Island and Providence Plantations one, Connecticut five, New York six, New Jersey four, Pennsylvania eight, Delaware one, Maryland six, Virginia ten, North Carolina five, South Carolina five, and Georgia three.

When vacancies happen in the Representation from any State, the Executive Authority thereof shall issue Writs of Election to fill such Vacancies.

The House of Representatives shall choose their Speaker and other Officers; and shall have the sole Power of Impeachment.

Section 3. The Senate of the United States shall be composed of two Senators from each State, chosen by the Legislature thereof [Modified by Amendment XVII], for six Years; and each Senator shall have one Vote.

Immediately after they shall be assembled in Consequence of the first Election, they shall be divided as equally as may be into three Classes. The Seats of the Senators of the first Class shall be vacated at the Expiration of the second Year, of the second Class at the Expiration of the fourth Year, and of the third Class at the Expiration of the sixth Year, so that one third may be chosen every second Year; and if Vacancies happen by Resignation, or otherwise, during the Recess of the Legislature of any State, the Executive thereof may make temporary Appointments until the next Meeting of the Legislature, which shall then fill such Vacancies [Modified by Amendment XVII].

No Person shall be a Senator who shall not have attained to the Age of thirty Years, and been nine Years a Citizen of the United States, and who shall not, when elected, be an Inhabitant of that State for which he shall be chosen.

The Vice President of the United States shall be President of the Senate, but shall have no Vote, unless they be equally divided.

The Senate shall choose their other Officers, and also a President pro tempore, in the Absence of the Vice President, or when he shall exercise the Office of President of the United States.

The Senate shall have the sole Power to try all Impeachments. When sitting for that Purpose, they shall be on Oath or Affirmation. When the President of the United States is tried, the Chief Justice shall preside: And no Person shall be convicted without the Concurrence of two thirds of the Members present.

Judgment in Cases of Impeachment shall not extend further than to removal from Office, and disqualification to hold and enjoy any Office of honor, Trust or Profit under the United States: but the Party convicted shall nevertheless be liable and subject to Indictment, Trial, Judgement and Punishment, according to Law.

Section 4. The Times, Places and Manner of holding Elections for Senators and Representatives, shall be prescribed in each State by the Legislature thereof; but the Congress may at any time by Law make or alter such Regulations, except as to the Places of choosing Senators.

The Congress shall assemble at least once every Year, and such Meeting shall be on the first Monday in December [Modified by Amendment XX], unless they shall by Law appoint a different Day.

Section 5. Each House shall be the Judge of the Elections, Returns and Qualifications of its own Members, and a Majority of each shall constitute a Quorum to do Business; but a smaller Number may adjourn from day to day, and may be authorized to compel the Attendance of absent Members, in such Manner, and under such Penalties as each House may provide.

Each House may determine the Rules of its Proceedings, punish its Members for disorderly Behaviour, and, with the Concurrence of two thirds, expel a Member.

Each House shall keep a Journal of its Proceedings, and from time to time publish the same, excepting such Parts as may in their Judgment require Secrecy; and the Yeas and Nays of the

Members of either House on any question shall, at the Desire of one fifth of those Present, be entered on the Journal.

Neither House, during the Session of Congress, shall, without the Consent of the other, adjourn for more than three days, nor to any other Place than that in which the two Houses shall be sitting.

Section 6. The Senators and Representatives shall receive a Compensation for their Services, to be ascertained by Law, and paid out of the Treasury of the United States. They shall in all Cases, except Treason, Felony and Breach of the Peace, be privileged from Arrest during their Attendance at the Session of their respective Houses, and in going to and returning from the same; and for any Speech or Debate in either House, they shall not be questioned in any other Place.

No Senator or Representative shall, during the Time for which he was elected, be appointed to any civil Office under the Authority of the United States, which shall have been created, or the Emoluments whereof shall have been encreased during such time; and no Person holding any Office under the United States, shall be a Member of either House during his Continuance in Office.

Section 7. All Bills for raising Revenue shall originate in the House of Representatives; but the Senate may propose or concur with Amendments as on other Bills.

Every Bill which shall have passed the House of Representatives and the Senate, shall, before it become a Law, be presented to the President of the United States;[2] If he approve he shall sign it, but if not he shall return it, with his Objections to that House in which it shall have originated, who shall enter the Objections at large on their Journal, and proceed to reconsider it. If after such Reconsideration two thirds of that House shall agree to pass the Bill, it shall be sent, together with the Objections, to the other House, by which it shall likewise be reconsidered, and if approved by two thirds of that House, it shall become a Law. But in all such Cases the Votes of both Houses shall be determined by Yeas and Nays, and the Names of the Persons voting for and against the Bill shall be entered on the Journal of each House respectively. If any Bill shall not be returned by the President within ten Days (Sundays excepted) after it shall have been presented to him, the Same shall be a Law, in like Manner as if he had signed it, unless the Congress by their Adjournment prevent its Return, in which Case it shall not be a Law.

Every Order, Resolution, or Vote to which the Concurrence of the Senate and House of Representatives may be necessary (except on a question of Adjournment) shall be presented to the President of the United States; and before the Same shall take Effect, shall be approved by him, or being disapproved by him, shall be repassed by two thirds of the Senate and House of Representatives, according to the Rules and Limitations prescribed in the Case of a Bill.

Section 8. The Congress shall have Power to lay and collect Taxes, Duties, Imposts and Excises, to pay the Debts and provide for the common Defence and general Welfare of the United States; but all Duties, Imposts and Excises shall be uniform throughout the United States;

To borrow Money on the credit of the United States;

To regulate Commerce with foreign Nations, and among the several States, and with the Indian Tribes;

To establish an uniform Rule of Naturalization, and uniform Laws on the subject of Bankruptcies throughout the United States;

To coin Money, regulate the Value thereof, and of foreign Coin, and fix the Standard of Weights and Measures;

To provide for the Punishment of counterfeiting the Securities and current Coin of the United States;

To establish Post Offices and post Roads;

To promote the Progress of Science and useful Arts, by securing for limited Times to Authors and Inventors the exclusive Right to their respective Writings and Discoveries;

To constitute Tribunals inferior to the supreme Court;

To define and punish Piracies and Felonies committed on the high Seas, and Offences against the Law of Nations;

To declare War, grant Letters of Marque and Reprisal, and make Rules concerning Captures on Land and Water;

To raise and support Armies, but no Appropriation of Money to that Use shall be for a longer Term than two Years;

To provide and maintain a Navy;

To make Rules for the Government and Regulation of the land and naval Forces;

To provide for calling forth the Militia to execute the Laws of the Union, suppress Insurrections and repel Invasions;

To provide for organizing, arming, and disciplining, the Militia, and for governing such Part of them as may be employed in the Service of the United States, reserving to the States respectively, the Appointment of the Officers, and the Authority of training the Militia according to the discipline prescribed by Congress;

To exercise exclusive Legislation in all Cases whatsoever, over such District (not exceeding ten Miles square) as may, by Cession of particular States, and the Acceptance of Congress, become the Seat of the Government of the United States, and to exercise like Authority over all Places purchased by the Consent of the Legislature of the State in which the Same shall be, for the Erection of Forts, Magazines, Arsenals, Dockyards, and other needful Buildings; – And

To make all Laws which shall be necessary and proper for carrying into Execution the foregoing Powers, and all other Powers vested by this Constitution in the Government of the United States, or in any Department or Officer thereof.

Section 9. The Migration or Importation of such Persons as any of the States now existing shall think proper to admit, shall not be prohibited by the Congress prior to the Year one thousand eight hundred and eight, but a Tax or duty may be imposed on such Importation, not exceeding ten dollars for each Person.

The Privilege of the Writ of Habeas Corpus shall not be suspended, unless when in Cases of Rebellion or Invasion the public Safety may require it.

No Bill of Attainder or ex post facto Law shall be passed.

No Capitation, or other direct, Tax shall be laid, unless in Proportion to the Census or Enumeration herein before directed to be taken.

No Tax or Duty shall be laid on Articles exported from any State.

No Preference shall be given by any Regulation of Commerce or Revenue to the Ports of one State over those of another; nor shall Vessels bound to, or from, one State, be obliged to enter, clear, or pay Duties in another.

No Money shall be drawn from the Treasury, but in Consequence of Appropriations made by Law; and a regular Statement and Account of the Receipts and Expenditures of all public Money shall be published from time to time.

No Title of Nobility shall be granted by the United States: And no Person holding any Office of Profit or Trust under them, shall, without the Consent of the Congress, accept of any present, Emolument, Office, or Title, of any kind whatever, from any King, Prince, or foreign State.

Section 10. No State shall enter into any Treaty, Alliance, or Confederation; grant Letters of Marque and Reprisal; coin Money; emit Bills of Credit; make any Thing but gold and silver Coin a Tender in Payment of Debts; pass any Bill of Attainder, ex post facto Law, or Law impairing the Obligation of Contracts, or grant any Title of Nobility.

No State shall, without the Consent of the Congress, lay any Imposts or Duties on Imports or Exports, except what may be absolutely necessary for executing its inspection Laws; and the net Produce of all Duties and Imposts, laid by any State on Imports or Exports, shall be for the Use of the Treasury of the United States; and all such Laws shall be subject to the Revision and Control of the Congress.

No State shall, without the Consent of Congress, lay any Duty of Tonnage, keep Troops, or Ships of War in time of Peace, enter into any Agreement or Compact with another State, or with a foreign Power, or engage in War, unless actually invaded, or in such imminent Danger as will not admit of delay.

Article II

Section 1. The executive Power shall be vested in a President of the United States of America. He shall hold his Office during the Term of four Years, and, together with the Vice-President, chosen for the same Term, be elected, as follows:

Each State shall appoint, in such Manner as the Legislature thereof may direct, a Number of Electors, equal to the whole Number of Senators and Representatives to which the State may be entitled in the Congress: but no Senator or Representative, or Person holding an Office of Trust or Profit under the United States, shall be appointed an Elector.

The Electors shall meet in their respective States, and vote by Ballot for two Persons, of whom one at least shall not be an Inhabitant of the same State with themselves. And they shall make a List of all the Persons voted for, and of the Number of Votes for each; which List they shall sign and certify, and transmit sealed to the Seat of the Government of the United States, directed to the President of the Senate. The President of the Senate shall, in the Presence of the Senate and House of Representatives, open all the Certificates, and the Votes shall then be counted. The Person having the greatest Number of Votes shall be the President, if such Number be a Majority of the whole Number of Electors appointed; and if there be more than one who have such Majority, and have an equal Number of Votes, then the House of Representatives shall immediately choose by Ballot one of them for President; and if no Person have a Majority, then from the five highest on the List the said House shall in like Manner choose the President. But in choosing the President, the Votes shall be taken by States, the Representation from each State having one Vote; a quorum for this Purpose shall consist of a Member or Members from two-thirds of the States, and a Majority of all the States shall be necessary to a Choice. In every Case, after the Choice of the President, the Person having the greatest Number of Votes of the Electors shall be the Vice-President. But if there should remain two or more who have equal Votes, the Senate shall choose from them by Ballot the Vice-President [Modified by Amendment XII].

The Congress may determine the Time of choosing the Electors, and the Day on which they shall give their Votes; which Day shall be the same throughout the United States.

No Person except a natural born Citizen, or a Citizen of the United States, at the time of the Adoption of this Constitution, shall be eligible to the Office of President; neither shall any Person be eligible to that Office who shall not have attained to the Age of thirty five Years, and been fourteen Years a Resident within the United States.

In Case of the Removal of the President from Office, or of his Death, Resignation, or Inability to discharge the Powers and Duties of the said Office, the Same shall devolve on the Vice President, and the Congress may by Law provide for the Case of Removal, Death, Resignation or Inability, both of the President and Vice President, declaring what Officer shall then act as President, and such Officer shall act accordingly, until the Disability be removed, or a President shall be elected [Modified by Amendment XXV].

The President shall, at stated Times, receive for his Services, a Compensation, which shall neither be increased nor diminished during the Period for which he shall have been elected, and he shall not receive within that Period any other Emolument from the United States, or any of them.

Before he enter on the Execution of his Office, he shall take the following Oath or Affirmation: "I do solemnly swear (or affirm) that I will faithfully execute the Office of President of the United States, and will to the best of my Ability, preserve, protect and defend the Constitution of the United States."

Section 2. The President shall be Commander in Chief of the Army and Navy of the United States, and of the Militia of the several States, when called into the actual Service of the United States; he may require the Opinion, in writing, of the principal Officer in each of the executive Departments, upon any Subject relating to the Duties of their respective Offices, and he shall have Power to grant Reprieves and Pardons for Offences against the United States, except in Cases of Impeachment.

He shall have Power, by and with the Advice and Consent of the Senate, to make Treaties, provided two thirds of the Senators present concur; and he shall nominate, and by and with the Advice and Consent of the Senate, shall appoint Ambassadors, other public Ministers and Consuls, Judges of the supreme Court, and all other Officers of the United States, whose Appointments are not herein otherwise provided for, and which shall be established by Law: but the Congress may by Law vest the Appointment of such inferior Officers, as they think proper, in the President alone, in the Courts of Law, or in the Heads of Departments.

The President shall have Power to fill up all Vacancies that may happen during the Recess of the Senate, by granting Commissions which shall expire at the End of their next Session.

Section 3. He shall from time to time give to the Congress Information of the State of the Union, and recommend to their Consideration such Measures as he shall judge necessary and expedient; he may, on extraordinary Occasions, convene both Houses, or either of them, and in Case of Disagreement between them, with Respect to the Time of Adjournment, he may adjourn them to such Time as he shall think proper; he shall receive Ambassadors and other public Ministers; he shall take Care that the Laws be faithfully executed, and shall Commission all the Officers of the United States.

Section 4. The President, Vice-President and all civil Officers of the United States, shall be removed from Office on Impeachment for, and Conviction of, Treason, Bribery, or other high Crimes and Misdemeanors.

Article III

Section 1. The judicial Power of the United States shall be vested in one supreme Court, and in such inferior Courts as the Congress may from time to time ordain and establish. The Judges, both of the supreme and inferior Courts, shall hold their Offices during good Behaviour, and shall, at stated Times, receive for their Services a Compensation, which shall not be diminished during their Continuance in Office.

Section 2. The judicial Power shall extend to all Cases, in Law and Equity, arising under this Constitution, the Laws of the United States, and Treaties made, or which shall be made, under their Authority; – to all Cases affecting Ambassadors, other public Ministers and Consuls; – to all Cases of admiralty and maritime Jurisdiction; – to Controversies to which the United States shall be a Party; – to Controversies between two or more States; – between a State and Citizens of another State [Modified by Amendment XI]; between Citizens of different States; – between Citizens of the same State claiming Lands under Grants of different States, and between a State, or the Citizens thereof, and foreign States, Citizens or Subjects.

In all Cases affecting Ambassadors, other public Ministers and Consuls, and those in which a State shall be Party, the supreme Court shall have original Jurisdiction. In all the other Cases before mentioned, the supreme Court shall have appellate Jurisdiction, both as to Law and Fact, with such Exceptions, and under such Regulations as the Congress shall make.

The Trial of all Crimes, except in Cases of Impeachment, shall be by Jury; and such Trial shall be held in the State where the said Crimes shall have been committed; but when not committed within any State, the Trial shall be at such Place or Places as the Congress may by Law have directed.

Section 3. Treason against the United States shall consist only in levying War against them, or in adhering to their Enemies, giving them Aid and Comfort. No Person shall be convicted of Treason unless on the Testimony of two Witnesses to the same overt Act, or on Confession in open Court.

The Congress shall have Power to declare the Punishment of Treason, but no Attainder of Treason shall work Corruption of Blood, or Forfeiture except during the Life of the Person attainted.

Article IV

Section 1. Full Faith and Credit shall be given in each State to the public Acts, Records, and judicial Proceedings of every other State. And the Congress may by general Laws prescribe the Manner in which such Acts, Records and Proceedings shall be proved, and the Effect thereof.

Section 2. The Citizens of each State shall be entitled to all Privileges and Immunities of Citizens in the several States.

A Person charged in any State with Treason, Felony, or other Crime, who shall flee from Justice, and be found in another State, shall on Demand of the executive Authority of the State from which he fled, be delivered up, to be removed to the State having Jurisdiction of the Crime.

No Person held to Service or Labour in one State, under the Laws thereof, escaping into another, shall, in Consequence of any Law or Regulation therein, be discharged from such Service or Labour, but shall be delivered up on Claim of the Party to whom such Service or Labour may be due [Modified by Amendment XIII].

Section 3. New States may be admitted by the Congress into this Union; but no new State shall be formed or erected within the Jurisdiction of any other State; nor any State be formed by the Junction of two or more States, or Parts of States, without the Consent of the Legislatures of the States concerned as well as of the Congress.

The Congress shall have Power to dispose of and make all needful Rules and Regulations respecting the Territory or other Property belonging to the United States; and nothing in this Constitution shall be so construed as to Prejudice any Claims of the United States, or of any particular State.

Section 4. The United States shall guarantee to every State in this Union a Republican Form of Government, and shall protect each of them against Invasion; and on Application of the Legislature, or of the Executive (when the Legislature cannot be convened), against domestic Violence.

Article V

The Congress, whenever two thirds of both Houses shall deem it necessary, shall propose Amendments to this Constitution, or, on the Application of the Legislatures of two thirds of the several States, shall call a Convention for proposing

Amendments, which, in either Case, shall be valid to all Intents and Purposes, as Part of this Constitution, when ratified by the Legislatures of three fourths of the several States, or by Conventions in three fourths thereof, as the one or the other Mode of Ratification may be proposed by the Congress; Provided that no Amendment which may be made prior to the Year One thousand eight hundred and eight shall in any Manner affect the first and fourth Clauses in the Ninth Section of the first Article; and that no State, without its Consent, shall be deprived of its equal Suffrage in the Senate.

Article VI

All Debts contracted and Engagements entered into, before the Adoption of this Constitution, shall be as valid against the United States under this Constitution, as under the Confederation.

This Constitution, and the Laws of the United States which shall be made in Pursuance thereof; and all Treaties made, or which shall be made, under the Authority of the United States, shall be the supreme Law of the Land; and the Judges in every State shall be bound thereby, any Thing in the Constitution or Laws of any State to the Contrary notwithstanding.

The Senators and Representatives before mentioned, and the Members of the several State Legislatures, and all executive and judicial Officers, both of the United States and of the several States, shall be bound by Oath or Affirmation, to support this Constitution; but no religious Test shall ever be required as a Qualification to any Office or public Trust under the United States.

Article VII

The Ratification of the Conventions of nine States, shall be sufficient for the Establishment of this Constitution between the States so ratifying the Same.

The Word, "the," being interlined between the seventh and eighth Lines of the first Page, The Word "Thirty" being partly written on an Erazure in the fifteenth Line of the first Page, The Words "is tried" being interlined between the thirty second and thirty third Lines of the first Page and the Word "the" being interlined between the forty third and forty fourth Lines of the second Page.

Attest William Jackson

Secretary done in Convention by the Unanimous Consent of the States present the Seventeenth Day of September in the Year of our Lord one thousand seven hundred and Eighty seven and of the Independence of the United States of America the Twelfth In witness whereof We have hereunto subscribed our Names,

GO. WASHINGTON – President.

and deputy from Virginia

New Hampshire

JOHN LANGDON

NICHOLAS GILMAN

Massachusetts

NATHANIEL GORHAM

RUFUS KING

Connecticut

WM. SAML. JOHNSON

ROGER SHERMAN

New York

ALEXANDER HAMILTON

New Jersey

WIL. LIVINGSTON

DAVID BREARLEY

WM. PATERSON

JONA. DAYTON

Pennsylvania

B FRANKLIN

THOMAS MIFFLIN

ROBT MORRIS

GEO. CLYMER

THOS. FITZ SIMONS

JARED INGERSOLL
JAMES WILSON
GOUV MORRIS
Delaware
GEO. READ
GUNNING BEDFORD jun
JOHN DICKINSON
RICHARD BASSETT
JACO. BROOM
Maryland
JAMES MCHENRY
DAN OF ST THOS. JENIFER
DANL CARROLL
Virginia
JOHN BLAIR
JAMES MADISON
North Carolina
WM. BLOUNT
RICHD. DOBBS SPAIGHT
HU WILLIAMSON
South Carolina
J. RUTLEDGE
CHARLES COTESWORTH PINCKNEY
CHARLES PINCKNEY
PIERCE BUTLER
Georgia
WILLIAM FEW
ABR BALDWIN
In Convention Monday, September 17th, 1787
Present
The States of

New Hampshire, Massachusetts, Connecticut, Hamilton from New York, New Jersey, Pennsylvania, Delaware, Maryland, Virginia, North Carolina, South Carolina and Georgia.

Resolved,

That the preceeding Constitution be laid before the United States in Congress assembled, and that it is the Opinion of this Convention, that it should afterwards be submitted to a Convention of Delegates, chosen in each State by the People thereof, under the Recommendation of its Legislature, for their Assent and Ratification; and that each Convention assenting to, and ratifying the Same, should give Notice thereof to the United States in Congress assembled. Resolved, That it is the Opinion of this Convention, that as soon as the Conventions of nine States shall have ratified this Constitution, the United States in Congress assembled should fix a Day on which Electors should be appointed by the States which have ratified the same, and a Day on which the Electors should assemble to vote for the President, and the Time and Place for commencing Proceedings under this Constitution. That after such Publication the Electors should be appointed, and the Senators and Representatives elected: That the Electors should meet on the Day fixed for the Election of the President, and should transmit their Votes certified, signed, sealed and directed, as the Constitution requires, to the Secretary of the United States in Congress assembled, that the Senators and Representatives should convene at the Time and Place assigned; that the Senators should appoint a President of the Senate, for the sole purpose of receiving, opening and counting the Votes for President; and, that after he shall be chosen, the Congress, together with the President, should, without Delay, proceed to execute this Constitution.

By the Unanimous Order of the Convention

GO. WASHINGTON – President.

W. JACKSON Secretary

[Bill of Rights]

The conventions of a number of the States having at the time of their adopting the Constitution, expressed a desire, in order to prevent misconstruction or abuse of its powers, that further declaratory and restrictive clauses should be added.

Article the first [Not Ratified]

After the first enumeration required by the first article of the Constitution, there shall be one Representative for every thirty thousand, until the number shall amount to one hundred, after which the proportion shall be so regulated by Congress, that there shall be not less than one hundred Representatives, nor less than one Representative for every forty thousand persons, until the number of Representatives shall amount to two hundred; after which the proportion shall be so regulated by Congress, that there shall not be less than two hundred Representatives, nor more than one Representative for every fifty thousand persons.

Article the second [Amendment XXVII - Ratified 1992]

No law, varying the compensation for the services of the Senators and Representatives, shall take effect, until an election of Representatives shall have intervened.

Article the third [Amendment I]

Congress shall make no law respecting an establishment of religion, or prohibiting the free exercise thereof; or abridging the freedom of speech, or of the press; or the right of the people peaceably to assemble, and to petition the Government for a redress of grievances.

Article the fourth [Amendment II][3]

A well regulated Militia, being necessary to the security of a free State, the right of the people to keep and bear Arms, shall not be infringed.

Article the fifth [Amendment III]

No Soldier shall, in time of peace be quartered in any house, without the consent of the Owner, nor in time of war, but in a manner to be prescribed by law.

Article the sixth [Amendment IV]

The right of the people to be secure in their persons, houses, papers, and effects, against unreasonable searches and seizures, shall not be violated, and no Warrants shall issue, but upon probable cause, supported by Oath or affirmation, and particularly describing the place to be searched, and the persons or things to be seized.

Article the seventh [Amendment V]

No person shall be held to answer for a capital, or otherwise infamous crime, unless on a presentment or indictment of a Grand Jury, except in cases arising in the land or naval forces, or in the Militia, when in actual service in time of War or public danger; nor shall any person be subject for the same offence to be twice put in jeopardy of life or limb; nor shall be compelled in any criminal case to be a witness against himself, nor be deprived of life, liberty, or property, without due process of law; nor shall private property be taken for public use, without just compensation.

Article the eighth [Amendment VI]

In all criminal prosecutions, the accused shall enjoy the right to a speedy and public trial, by an impartial jury of the State and district wherein the crime shall have been committed, which district shall have been previously ascertained by law, and to be informed of the nature and cause of the accusation; to be confronted with the witnesses against him; to have compulsory process for obtaining witnesses in his favor, and to have the Assistance of Counsel for his defence.

Article the ninth [Amendment VII]

In Suits at common law, where the value in controversy shall exceed twenty dollars, the right of trial by jury shall be preserved, and no fact tried by a jury, shall be otherwise re-examined in any Court of the United States, than according to the rules of the common law.

Article the tenth [Amendment VIII]

Excessive bail shall not be required, nor excessive fines imposed, nor cruel and unusual punishments inflicted.

Article the eleventh [Amendment IX]

The enumeration in the Constitution, of certain rights, shall not be construed to deny or disparage others retained by the people.

Article the twelfth [Amendment X]

The powers not delegated to the United States by the Constitution, nor prohibited by it to the States, are reserved to the States respectively, or to the people.

[Additional Amendments to the Constitution]

ARTICLES in addition to, and Amendment of, the Constitution of the United States of America, proposed by Congress, and ratified by the Legislatures of the several States, pursuant to the fifth Article of the original Constitution

Article XI

[Proposed 1794; Ratified 1798]

The Judicial power of the United States shall not be construed to extend to any suit in law or equity, commenced or prosecuted against one of the United States by Citizens of another State, or by Citizens or Subjects of any Foreign State.

Article XII

[Proposed 1803; Ratified 1804]

The Electors shall meet in their respective states, and vote by ballot for President and Vice President, one of whom, at least, shall not be an inhabitant of the same state with themselves; they shall name in their ballots the person voted for as President, and in distinct ballots the person voted for as Vice-President, and they shall make distinct lists of all persons voted for as President, and of all persons voted for as Vice-President, and of the number of votes for each, which lists they shall sign and certify, and transmit sealed to the seat of the government of the United States, directed to the President of the Senate; – The President of the Senate shall, in the presence of the Senate and House of Representatives, open all the certificates and the votes shall then be counted; – The person having the greatest number of votes for President, shall be the President, if such number be a majority of the whole number of Electors appointed; and if no person have such majority, then from the persons having the highest numbers not exceeding three on the list of those voted for as President, the House of Representatives shall choose immediately, by ballot, the President. But in choosing the President, the votes shall be taken by states, the representation from each state having one vote; a quorum for this purpose shall consist of a member or members from two-thirds of the states, and a majority of all the states shall be necessary to a choice. And if the House of Representatives shall not choose a President whenever the right of choice shall devolve upon them, before the fourth day of March next following, then the Vice-President shall act as President, as in the case of the death or other constitutional disability of the President. The person having the greatest number of votes as Vice-President, shall be the Vice-President, if such number be a majority of the whole number of Electors appointed, and if no person have a majority, then from the two highest numbers on the list, the Senate shall choose the Vice-President; a quorum for the purpose shall consist of two-thirds of the whole number of Senators, and a majority of the whole number shall be necessary to a choice. But no person constitutionally ineligible to the office of President shall be eligible to that of Vice-President of the United States.

Contested Article

[Proposed 1810; Probably Ratified 1819]

If any Citizen of the United States shall accept, claim, receive or retain any Title of Nobility or Honour, or shall, without the Consent of Congress, accept and retain any present, Pension, Office or Emolument of any kind whatever, from any Emperor, King, Prince or foreign Power, such Person shall cease to be a Citizen of the United States, and shall be incapable of holding any Office of Trust or Profit under them, or either of them.

Unratified Article

[Proposed 1861; Signed by President Lincoln; Unratified]

Article Thirteen

No amendment shall be made to the Constitution which will authorize or give to Congress the power to abolish or interfere, within any State, with the domestic institutions thereof, including that of persons held to labor or service by the laws of said State.

Article XIII

[Proposed 1865; Ratified 1865]

Section. 1. Neither slavery nor involuntary servitude, except as a punishment for crime whereof the party shall have been duly convicted, shall exist within the United States, or any place subject to their jurisdiction.

Section. 2. Congress shall have power to enforce this article by appropriate legislation.

Article XIV

[Proposed 1866; Ratified Under Duress 1868]

Section 1. All persons born or naturalized in the United States, and subject to the jurisdiction thereof, are citizens of the United States and of the State wherein they reside. No State shall make or enforce any law which shall abridge the privileges or immunities of citizens of the United States; nor shall any State deprive any person of life, liberty, or property, without due process of law; nor deny to any person within its jurisdiction the equal protection of the laws.

Section 2. Representatives shall be apportioned among the several States according to their respective numbers, counting the whole number of persons in each State, excluding Indians not taxed. But when the right to vote at any election for the choice of electors for President and Vice-President of the United States, Representatives in Congress, the Executive and Judicial officers of a State, or the members of the Legislature thereof, is denied to any of the male inhabitants of such State, being twenty-one years of age, and citizens of the United States, or in any way abridged, except for participation in rebellion, or other crime, the basis of representation therein shall be reduced in the proportion which the number of such male citizens shall bear to the whole number of male citizens twenty-one years of age in such State.

Section 3. No person shall be a Senator or Representative in Congress, or elector of President and Vice President, or hold any office, civil or military, under the United States, or under any State, who, having previously taken an oath, as a member of Congress, or as an officer of the United States, or as a member of any State legislature, or as an executive or judicial officer of any State, to support the Constitution of the United States, shall have engaged in insurrection or rebellion against the same, or given aid or comfort to the enemies thereof. But Congress may by a vote of two-thirds of each House, remove such disability.

Section 4. The validity of the public debt of the United States, authorized by law, including debts incurred for payment of pensions and bounties for services in suppressing insurrection or rebellion, shall not be questioned. But neither the United States nor any State shall assume or pay any debt or obligation incurred in aid of insurrection or rebellion against the United States, or any claim for the loss or emancipation of any slave; but all such debts, obligations and claims shall be held illegal and void.

Section 5. The Congress shall have power to enforce, by appropriate legislation, the provisions of this article.

Article XV

[Proposed 1869; Ratified 1870]

Section 1. The right of citizens of the United States to vote shall not be denied or abridged by the United States or by any State on account of race, color, or previous condition of servitude.

Section 2. The Congress shall have power to enforce this article by appropriate legislation.

Article XVI

[Proposed 1909; Questionably Ratified 1913]

The Congress shall have power to lay and collect taxes on incomes, from whatever source derived, without apportionment among the several States, and without regard to any census or enumeration.

Article XVII

[Proposed 1912; Ratified 1913; Possibly Unconstitutional (See Article V, Clause 3 of the Constitution)]

The Senate of the United States shall be composed of two Senators from each State, elected by the people thereof, for six years; and each Senator shall have one vote. The electors in each State shall have the qualifications requisite for electors of the most numerous branch of the State legislatures.

When vacancies happen in the representation of any State in the Senate, the executive authority of such State shall issue writs of election to fill such vacancies: Provided, That the legislature of any State may empower the executive thereof to make temporary appointments until the people fill the vacancies by election as the legislature may direct.

This amendment shall not be so construed as to affect the election or term of any Senator chosen before it becomes valid as part of the Constitution.

Article XVIII

[Proposed 1917; Ratified 1919; Repealed 1933] (See Amendment XXI, Section 1)

Section 1. After one year from the ratification of this article the manufacture, sale, or transportation of intoxicating liquors within, the importation thereof into, or the exportation thereof from the United States and all territory subject to the jurisdiction thereof for beverage purposes is hereby prohibited.

Section 2. The Congress and the several States shall have concurrent power to enforce this article by appropriate legislation.

Section 3. This article shall be inoperative unless it shall have been ratified as an amendment to the Constitution by the legislatures of the several States, as provided in the Constitution, within seven years from the date of the submission hereof to the States by the Congress.

Article XIX

[Proposed 1919; Ratified 1920]

The right of citizens of the United States to vote shall not be denied or abridged by the United States or by any State on account of sex.

Congress shall have power to enforce this article by appropriate legislation.

Unratified Article

[Proposed 1926; Unratified]

Article

Section. 1. The Congress shall have power to limit, regulate, and prohibit the labor of persons under eighteen years of age.

Section. 2. The power of the several States is unimpaired by this article except that the operation of State laws shall be suspended to the extent necessary to give effect to legislation enacted by the Congress.

Article XX

[Proposed 1932; Ratified 1933]

Section 1. The terms of the President and Vice-President shall end at noon on the 20th day of January, and the terms of Senators and Representatives at noon on the 3rd day of January of the years in which such terms would have ended if this article had not been ratified; and the terms of their successors shall then begin.

Section 2. The Congress shall assemble at least once in every year, and such meeting shall begin at noon on the 3rd day of January, unless they shall by law appoint a different day.

Section 3. If, at the time fixed for the beginning of the term of the President, the President elect shall have died, the

Vice-President elect shall become President. If a President shall not have been chosen before the time fixed for the beginning of his term, or if the President elect shall have failed to qualify, then the Vice-President elect shall act as President until a President shall have qualified; and the Congress may by law provide for the case wherein neither a President elect nor a Vice-President elect shall have qualified, declaring who shall then act as President, or the manner in which one who is to act shall be selected, and such person shall act accordingly until a President or Vice President shall have qualified.

Section 4. The Congress may by law provide for the case of the death of any of the persons from whom the House of Representatives may choose a President whenever the right of choice shall have devolved upon them, and for the case of the death of any of the persons from whom the Senate may choose a Vice President whenever the right of choice shall have devolved upon them.

Section 5. Sections 1 and 2 shall take effect on the 15th day of October following the ratification of this article.

Section 6. This article shall be inoperative unless it shall have been ratified as an amendment to the Constitution by the legislatures of three-fourths of the several States within seven years from the date of its submission.

Article XXI

[Proposed 1933; Ratified 1933]

Section 1. The eighteenth article of amendment to the Constitution of the United States is hereby repealed.

Section 2. The transportation or importation into any State, Territory, or possession of the United States for delivery or use therein of intoxicating liquors, in violation of the laws thereof, is hereby prohibited.

Section 3. This article shall be inoperative unless it shall have been ratified as an amendment to the Constitution by conventions in the several States, as provided in the Constitution, within seven years from the date of the submission hereof to the States by the Congress.

Article XXII

[Proposed 1947; Ratified 1951]

Section 1. No person shall be elected to the office of the President more than twice, and no person who has held the office of President, or acted as President, for more than two years of a term to which some other person was elected President shall be elected to the office of the President more than once. But this Article shall not apply to any person holding the office of President when this Article was proposed by the Congress, and shall not prevent any person who may be holding the office of President, or acting as President, during the term within which this Article becomes operative from holding the office of President or acting as President during the remainder of such term.

Section 2. This article shall be inoperative unless it shall have been ratified as an amendment to the Constitution by the legislatures of three-fourths of the several States within seven years from the date of its submission to the States by the Congress.

Article XXIII

[Proposed 1960; Ratified 1961]

Section 1. The District constituting the seat of Government of the United States shall appoint in such manner as the Congress may direct:

A number of electors of President and Vice-President equal to the whole number of Senators and Representatives in Congress to which the District would be entitled if it were a state, but in no event more than the least populous state; they shall be in addition to those appointed by the states, but they shall be considered, for the purposes of the election of President and Vice-President, to be electors appointed by a state; and they shall meet in the District and perform such duties as provided by the twelfth article of amendment.

Section 2. The Congress shall have power to enforce this article by appropriate legislation.

Article XXIV

[Proposed 1962; Ratified 1964]

Section 1. The right of citizens of the United States to vote in any primary or other election for President or Vice-President, for electors for President or Vice-President, or for Senator or Representative in Congress, shall not be denied or abridged by the United States or any State by reason of failure to pay any poll tax or other tax.

Section 2. The Congress shall have power to enforce this article by appropriate legislation.

Article XXV

[Proposed 1965; Ratified 1967]

Section 1. In case of the removal of the President from office or of his death or resignation, the Vice-President shall become President.

Section 2. Whenever there is a vacancy in the office of the Vice-President, the President shall nominate a Vice-President who shall take office upon confirmation by a majority vote of both Houses of Congress.

Section 3. Whenever the President transmits to the President pro tempore of the Senate and the Speaker of the House of Representatives his written declaration that he is unable to discharge the powers and duties of his office, and until he transmits to them a written declaration to the contrary, such powers and duties shall be discharged by the Vice-President as Acting President.

Section 4. Whenever the Vice-President and a majority of either the principal officers of the executive departments or of such other body as Congress may by law provide, transmit to the President pro tempore of the Senate and the Speaker of the House of Representatives their written declaration that the President is unable to discharge the powers and duties of his office, the Vice-President shall immediately assume the powers and duties of the office as Acting President.

Thereafter, when the President transmits to the President pro tempore of the Senate and the Speaker of the House of Representatives his written declaration that no inability exists, he shall resume the powers and duties of his office unless the Vice-President and a majority of either the principal officers of the executive department or of such other body as Congress may by law provide, transmit within four days to the President pro tempore of the Senate and the Speaker of the House of Representatives their written declaration that the President is unable to discharge the powers and duties of his office. Thereupon Congress shall decide the issue, assembling within forty-eight hours for that purpose if not in session. If the Congress, within twenty-one days after receipt of the latter written declaration, or, if Congress is not in session, within twenty-one days after Congress is required to assemble, determines by two-thirds vote of both Houses that the President is unable to discharge the powers and duties of his office, the Vice-President shall continue to discharge the same as Acting President; otherwise, the President shall resume the powers and duties of his office.

Article XXVI

[Proposed 1971; Ratified 1971]

Section 1. The right of citizens of the United States, who are eighteen years of age or older, to vote shall not be denied or abridged by the United States or by any state on account of age.

Section 2. The Congress shall have power to enforce this article by appropriate legislation.

Inoperative Article

[Proposed 1972; Expired Unratified 1982]

Article

Section 1. Equality of rights under the law shall not be denied or abridged by the United States or by any state on account of sex.

Section 2. The Congress shall have the power to enforce, by appropriate legislation, the provisions of this article.

Section 3. This amendment shall take effect two years after the date of ratification.

Inoperative Article

[Proposed 1978; Expired Unratified 1985]

Article

Section 1. For purposes of representation in the Congress, election of the President and Vice President, and article V of this Constitution, the District constituting the seat of government of the United States shall be treated as though it were a State.

Section 2. The exercise of the rights and powers conferred under this article shall be by the people of the District constituting the seat of government, and as shall be provided by the Congress.

Section 3. The twenty-third article of amendment to the Constitution of the United States is hereby repealed.

Section 4. This article shall be inoperative, unless it shall have been ratified as an amendment to the Constitution by the legislatures of three-fourths of the several States within seven years from the date of its submission.

Article XXVII

[Proposed 1789; Ratified 1992; Second of twelve Articles comprising the Bill of Rights]

No law, varying the compensation for the services of the Senators and Representatives, shall take effect, until an election of Representatives shall have intervened.

A well regulated Militia being necessary to the security of a free state, the right of the people to keep and bear Arms shall not be infringed.

The question remains open of where those additional, and grammatically spurious, commas came from, but they do not change the legal meaning of the provision, and it would not be erroneous to omit them.

Constitution of Australia

3

Commonwealth of Australia Constitution Act

[9th July 1900]

Preamble

An Act to constitute the Commonwealth of Australia.

Whereas the people of New South Wales, Victoria, South Australia, Queensland, and

Tasmania, humbly relying on the blessing of Almighty God, have agreed to unite in one indissoluble Federal Commonwealth under the Crown of the United Kingdom of Great Britain and Ireland, and under the Constitution hereby established:

And whereas it is expedient to provide for the admission into the Commonwealth of other Australasian Colonies and possessions of the Queen:

Be it therefore enacted by the Queen's most Excellent Majesty, by and with the advice and consent of the Lords Spiritual and Temporal, and Commons, in this present Parliament assembled, and by the authority of the same, as follows:

1. Short title [see Note 1]

This Act may be cited as the Commonwealth of Australia Constitution Act.

2. Act to extend to the Queen's successors

The provisions of this Act referring to the Queen shall extend to Her Majesty's heirs and successors in the sovereignty of the United Kingdom.

3. Proclamation of Commonwealth [see Note 2]

It shall be lawful for the Queen, with the advice of the Privy Council, to declare by proclamation that, on and after a day therein appointed, not being later than one year after the passing of this Act, the people of New South Wales, Victoria, South Australia, Queensland, and Tasmania, and also, if Her Majesty is satisfied that the people of Western Australia have agreed thereto, of Western Australia, shall be united in a Federal Commonwealth under the name of the Commonwealth of Australia. But the Queen may, at any time after the proclamation, appoint a Governor General for the Commonwealth.

Clause 4

4. Commencement of Act

The Commonwealth shall be established, and the Constitution of the Commonwealth shall take effect, on and after the day so appointed. But the Parliaments of the several colonies may at any time after the passing of this Act make any such laws, to come into operation on the day so appointed, as they might have made if the Constitution had taken effect at the passing of this Act.

5. Operation of the Constitution and laws [see Note 3]

This Act, and all laws made by the Parliament of the Commonwealth under the Constitution, shall be binding on the courts, judges, and people of every state and of every part of the Commonwealth, notwithstanding anything in the laws of any state; and the laws of the Commonwealth shall be in force on all British ships, the Queen's ships of war excepted, whose first port of clearance and whose port of destination are in the Commonwealth.

6. Definitions

The Commonwealth shall mean the Commonwealth of Australia as established under this Act.

The states shall mean such of the colonies of New South Wales, New Zealand, Queensland, Tasmania, Victoria, Western

Australia, and South Australia, including the northern territory of South Australia, as for the time being are parts of the Commonwealth, and such colonies or territories as may be admitted into or established by the Commonwealth as States; and each of such parts of the Commonwealth shall be called *a State.*

Original States shall mean such states as are parts of the Commonwealth at its establishment.

7. Repeal of Federal Council Act [see Note 4]

The Federal Council of Australasia Act, 1885, is hereby repealed, but so as not to affect any laws passed by the Federal Council of Australasia and in force at the establishment of the Commonwealth.

Clause 8

Any such law may be repealed as to any state by the Parliament of the Commonwealth, or as to any colony not being a State by the Parliament thereof.

8. Application of Colonial Boundaries Act

After the passing of this Act the Colonial Boundaries Act, 1895, shall not apply to any colony which becomes a State of the Commonwealth; but the Commonwealth shall be taken to be a self-governing colony for the purposes of that Act.

9. Constitution [see Note 1]

The Constitution of the Commonwealth shall be as follows:

The Constitution

This Constitution is divided as follows:

Chapter I

The Parliament

Part I

General

1. Legislative power

The legislative power of the Commonwealth shall be vested in a Federal Parliament, which shall consist of the Queen, a Senate, and a House of Representatives, and which is hereinafter called *The Parliament*, or *The Parliament of the Commonwealth*.

2. Governor General

A Governor General appointed by the Queen shall be Her Majesty's representative in the Commonwealth, and shall have and may exercise in the Commonwealth during the Queen's pleasure, but subject to this Constitution, such powers and functions of the Queen as Her Majesty may be pleased to assign to him.

3. Salary of Governor General

There shall be payable to the Queen out of the Consolidated Revenue fund of the Commonwealth, for the salary of the Governor General, an annual sum which, until the Parliament otherwise provides, shall be ten thousand pounds.

The salary of a Governor General shall not be altered during his continuance in office.

4. Provisions relating to Governor General

The provisions of this Constitution relating to the Governor-General extend and apply to the Governor General for the time being, or such person as the Queen may appoint to administer the Government of the Commonwealth; but no such person shall be entitled to receive any salary from the Commonwealth in respect of any other office during his administration of the Government of the Commonwealth.

5. Sessions of Parliament: Prorogation and dissolution

The Governor General may appoint such times for holding the sessions of the Parliament as he thinks fit, and may also from time to time, by Proclamation or otherwise, prorogue the Parliament, and may in like manner dissolve the House of Representatives.

Summoning Parliament

After any general election the Parliament shall be summoned to meet not later than thirty days after the day appointed for the return of the writs.

First session

The Parliament shall be summoned to meet not later than six months after the establishment of the Commonwealth.

6. Yearly session of Parliament

There shall be a session of the Parliament once at least in every year, so that twelve months shall not intervene between the last sitting of the Parliament in one session and its first sitting in the next session.

Part II

The Senate

7. The Senate [see Note 5]

The Senate shall be composed of senators for each State, directly chosen by the people of the state, voting, until the Parliament otherwise provides, as one electorate.

But until the Parliament of the Commonwealth otherwise provides, the Parliament of the state of Queensland, if that state be an Original State, may make laws dividing the state into divisions and determining the number of senators to be chosen for each division, and in the absence of such provision the state shall be one electorate.

Until the Parliament otherwise provides there shall be six senators for each Original State. The Parliament may make laws increasing or diminishing the number of senators for each state, but so that equal representation of the several Original States shall be maintained and that no Original State shall have less than six senators.

The senators shall be chosen for a term of six years, and the names of the senators chosen for each state shall be certified by the Governor to the Governor General.

8. Qualification of electors

The qualification of electors of senators shall be in each state that which is prescribed by this Constitution, or by the Parliament, as the qualification for electors of members of the House of Representatives; but in the choosing of senators each elector shall vote only once.

9. Method of election of senators [see Note 6]

The Parliament of the Commonwealth may make laws prescribing the method of choosing senators, but so that the method shall be uniform for all the states. Subject to any such law, the Parliament of each state may make laws prescribing the method of choosing the senators for that state.

Times and places *[see Note 6]*

The Parliament of a state may make laws for determining the times and places of elections of senators for the State.

10. Application of State laws

Until the Parliament otherwise provides, but subject to this Constitution, the laws in force in each state, for the time being, relating to elections for the more numerous House of the Parliament of the state shall, as nearly as practicable, apply to elections of senators for the state.

11. Failure to choose senators

The Senate may proceed to the despatch of business, notwithstanding the failure of any state to provide for its representation in the Senate.

12. Issue of writs

The Governor of any state may cause writs to be issued for elections of senators for the state. In case of the dissolution of the Senate the writs shall be issued within ten days from the proclamation of such dissolution.

13. Rotation of senators

As soon as may be after the Senate first meets, and after each first meeting of the Senate following a dissolution thereof, the Senate shall divide the senators chosen for each state into two classes, as nearly equal in number as practicable; and the places of the senators of the first class shall become vacant at the expiration of three years, and the places of those of the second class at the expiration of six years, from the beginning of their term of service; and afterwards the places of senators shall become vacant at the expiration of six years from the beginning of their term of service.

The election to fill vacant places shall be made within one year before the places are to become vacant.

For the purposes of this section the term of service of a senator shall be taken to begin on the first day of January/July following the day of his election, except in the cases of the first election and of the election next after any dissolution of the Senate, when it shall be taken to begin on the first day of January/July preceding the day of his election.

14. Further provision for rotation [see Note 7]

Whenever the number of senators for a State is increased or diminished, the Parliament of the Commonwealth may make such provision for the vacating of the places of senators for the state as it deems necessary to maintain regularity in the rotation.

15. Casual vacancies [see Note 8]

If the place of a senator becomes vacant before the expiration of his term of service, the Houses of Parliament of the state for which he was chosen, sitting and voting together, or, if there is only one House of that Parliament, that House, shall choose a person to hold the place until the expiration of the term. But if the Parliament of the state is not in session when the vacancy is notified, the Governor of the state, with the advice of the Executive Council thereof, may appoint a person to hold the place until the expiration of fourteen days from the beginning of the next session of the Parliament of the State or the expiration of the term, whichever first happens.

Where a vacancy has at any time occurred in the place of a senator chosen by the people of a state and, at the time when he was so chosen, he was publicly recognized by a particular political party as being an endorsed candidate of that party and publicly represented himself to be such a candidate, a person chosen or appointed under this section in consequence of that vacancy, or in consequence of that vacancy and a subsequent vacancy or vacancies, shall, unless there is no member of that party available to be chosen or appointed, be a member of that party.

Where:

(a) in accordance with the last preceding paragraph, a member of a particular political party is chosen or appointed to hold the place of a senator whose place had become vacant; and

(b) before taking his seat he ceases to be a member of that party (otherwise than by reason of the party having ceased to exist);

he shall be deemed not to have been so chosen or appointed and the vacancy shall be again notified in accordance with section twenty-one of this Constitution.

The name of any senator chosen or appointed under this section shall be certified by the Governor of the state to the Governor General.

If the place of a senator chosen by the people of the State at the election of senators last held before the commencement of the *Constitution Alteration (Senate Casual Vacancies) 1977* became vacant before that commencement and, at that commencement, no person chosen by the House or Houses of Parliament of the state, or appointed by the Governor of the state, in consequence of that vacancy, or in consequence of that vacancy and a subsequent vacancy or vacancies, held office, this section applies as if the place of the senator chosen by the people of the state had become vacant after that commencement.

A senator holding office at the commencement of the *Constitution Alteration (Senate Casual Vacancies) 1977*, being a senator appointed by the Governor of a state in consequence of a vacancy that had at any time occurred in the place of a senator chosen by the people of the state, shall be deemed to have been appointed to hold the place until the expiration of fourteen days after the beginning of the next session of the Parliament of the state that commenced or commences after he was appointed and further action under this section shall be taken as if the vacancy in the place of the senator chosen by the people of the state had occurred after that commencement.

Subject to the next succeeding paragraph, a senator holding office at the commencement of the *Constitution Alteration (Senate Casual Vacancies) 1977* who was chosen by the House or Houses of Parliament of a state in consequence of a vacancy that had at any time occurred in the place of a senator chosen by the people of the state shall be deemed to have been chosen to hold office until the expiration of the term of service of the senator elected by the people of the state.

If, at or before the commencement of the *Constitution Alteration (Senate Casual Vacancies) 1977*, a law to alter the Constitution entitled "*Constitution Alteration (Simultaneous Elections) 1977*" came into operation, a senator holding office at the commencement of that law who was chosen by the House or Houses of Parliament of a state in consequence of a vacancy that had at any time occurred in the place of a senator chosen by the people of the state shall be deemed to have been chosen to hold office:

(a) if the senator elected by the people of the State had a term of service expiring on the thirtieth day of June, One thousand nine hundred and seventy-eight—until the expiration or dissolution of the first House of Representatives to expire or be dissolved after that law came into operation; or

(b) if the senator elected by the people of the state had a term of service expiring on the thirtieth day of June, One thousand nine hundred and eighty-one—until the expiration or dissolution of the second House of Representatives to expire or be dissolved after that law came into operation or, if there is an earlier dissolution of the Senate, until that dissolution.

16. Qualifications of senator

The qualifications of a senator shall be the same as those of a member of the House of Representatives.

17. Election of President

The Senate shall, before proceeding to the despatch of any other business, choose a senator to be the President of the Senate; and as often as the office of President becomes vacant the Senate shall again choose a senator to be the President.

The President shall cease to hold his office if he ceases to be a senator. He may be removed from office by a vote of the Senate, or he may resign his office or his seat by writing addressed to the Governor General.

18. Absence of President

Before or during any absence of the President, the Senate may choose a senator to perform his duties in his absence.

19. Resignation of senator

A senator may, by writing addressed to the President, or to the Governor General if there is no President or if the President is absent from the Commonwealth, resign his place, which thereupon shall become vacant.

20. Vacancy by absence

The place of a senator shall become vacant if for two consecutive months of any session of the Parliament he, without the permission of the Senate, fails to attend the Senate.

21. Vacancy to be notified

Whenever a vacancy happens in the Senate, the President, or if there is no President or if the President is absent from the

Commonwealth the Governor General, shall notify the same to the Governor of the state in the representation of which the vacancy has happened.

22. Quorum

Until the Parliament otherwise provides, the presence of at least one-third of the whole number of the senators shall be necessary to constitute a meeting of the Senate for the exercise of its powers.

23. Voting in the Senate

Questions arising in the Senate shall be determined by a majority of votes, and each senator shall have one vote. The President shall in all cases be entitled to a vote; and when the votes are equal the question shall pass in the negative.

Part III

The House of Representatives

24. Constitution of House of Representatives

The House of Representatives shall be composed of members directly chosen by the people of the Commonwealth, and the number of such members shall be, as nearly as practicable, twice the number of the senators.

The number of members chosen in the several States shall be in proportion to the respective numbers of their people, and shall, until the Parliament otherwise provides, be determined, whenever necessary, in the following manner:

(i) a quota shall be ascertained by dividing the number of the people of the Commonwealth, as shown by the latest statistics of the Commonwealth, by twice the number of the senators;

(ii) the number of members to be chosen in each State shall be determined by dividing the number of the people of the State, as shown by the latest statistics of the Commonwealth, by the quota; and if on such division there is a remainder greater than one-half of the quota, one more member shall be chosen in the State.

But notwithstanding anything in this section, five members at least shall be chosen in each Original State.

25. Provision as to races disqualified from voting

For the purposes of the last section, if by the law of any state all persons of any race are disqualified from voting at elections for the more numerous House of the Parliament of the state, then, in reckoning the number of the people of the state or of the Commonwealth, persons of that race resident in that state shall not be counted.

26. Representatives in first Parliament

Notwithstanding anything in section twenty-four, the number of members to be chosen in each state at the first election shall be as follows:

New South Wales .... twenty-three;
Victoria.. twenty;
Queensland .... eight;
South Australia .... six;
Tasmania .... five;

Provided that if Western Australia is an Original State, the numbers shall be as follows:

New South Wales .... twenty-six;
Victoria.. twenty-three;
Queensland .... nine;
South Australia .... seven;
Western Australia .... five;
Tasmania .... five.

27. Alteration of number of members

Subject to this Constitution, the Parliament may make laws for increasing or diminishing the number of the members of the House of Representatives.

28. Duration of House of Representatives

Every House of Representatives shall continue for three years from the first meeting of the House, and no longer, but may be sooner dissolved by the Governor General.

29. Electoral divisions [see Note 9]

Until the Parliament of the Commonwealth otherwise provides, the Parliament of any state may make laws for determining the divisions in each state for which members of the House of Representatives may be chosen, and the number of members to be chosen for each division. A division shall not be formed out of parts of different States.

In the absence of other provision, each state shall be one electorate.

30. Qualification of electors

Until the Parliament otherwise provides, the qualification of electors of members of the House of Representatives shall be in each state that which is prescribed by the law of the state as the qualification of electors of the more numerous House of Parliament of the state; but in the choosing of members each elector shall vote only once.

31. Application of State laws

Until the Parliament otherwise provides, but subject to this Constitution, the laws in force in each state for the time being relating to elections for the more numerous House of the Parliament of the state shall, as nearly as practicable, apply to elections in the state of members of the House of Representatives.

32. Writs for general election

The Governor General in Council may cause writs to be issued for general elections of members of the House of Representatives.

After the first general election, the writs shall be issued within ten days from the expiry of a House of Representatives or from the proclamation of a dissolution thereof.

33. Writs for vacancies

Whenever a vacancy happens in the House of Representatives, the Speaker shall issue his writ for the election of a new member, or if there is no Speaker or if he is absent from the Commonwealth the Governor General in Council may issue the writ.

34. Qualifications of members

Until the Parliament otherwise provides, the qualifications of a member of the House of Representatives shall be as follows:

(i) he must be of the full age of twenty-one years, and must be an elector entitled to vote at the election of members of the House of Representatives, or a person qualified to become such elector, and must have been for three years at the least a resident within the limits of the Commonwealth as existing at the time when he is chosen;

(ii) he must be a subject of the Queen, either natural-born or for at least five years naturalized under a law of the United Kingdom, or of a Colony which has become or becomes a State, or of the Commonwealth, or of a state.

35. Election of Speaker

The House of Representatives shall, before proceeding to the despatch of any other business, choose a member to be the Speaker of the House, and as often as the office of Speaker becomes vacant the House shall again choose a member to be the Speaker.

The Speaker shall cease to hold his office if he ceases to be a member. He may be removed from office by a vote of the House, or he may resign his office or his seat by writing addressed to the Governor General.

36. Absence of Speaker

Before or during any absence of the Speaker, the House of Representatives may choose a member to perform his duties in his absence.

37. Resignation of member

A member may by writing addressed to the Speaker, or to the Governor General if there is no Speaker or if the Speaker is absent from the Commonwealth, resign his place, which thereupon shall become vacant.

38. Vacancy by absence

The place of a member shall become vacant if for two consecutive months of any session of the Parliament he, without the permission of the House, fails to attend the House.

39. Quorum

Until the Parliament otherwise provides, the presence of at least one-third of the whole number of the members of the House of Representatives shall be necessary to constitute a meeting of the House for the exercise of its powers.

40. Voting in House of Representatives

Questions arising in the House of Representatives shall be determined by a majority of votes other than that of the Speaker. The Speaker shall not vote unless the numbers are equal, and then he shall have a casting vote.

Part IV

Both Houses of the Parliament

41. Right of electors of States

No adult person who has or acquires a right to vote at elections for the more numerous House of the Parliament of a State shall, while the right continues, be prevented by any law of the Commonwealth from voting at elections for either House of the Parliament of the Commonwealth.

42. Oath or affirmation of allegiance

Every senator and every member of the House of Representatives shall before taking his seat make and subscribe before the Governor General, or some person authorised by him, an oath or affirmation of allegiance in the form set forth in the schedule to this Constitution.

43. Member of one House ineligible for other

A member of either House of the Parliament shall be incapable of being chosen or of sitting as a member of the other House.

44. Disqualification

Any person who:

(i) is under any acknowledgment of allegiance, obedience, or adherence to a foreign power, or is a subject or a citizen or entitled to the rights or privileges of a subject or a citizen of a foreign power; or

(ii) is attainted of treason, or has been convicted and is under sentence, or subject to be sentenced, for any offence punishable under the law of the Commonwealth or of a State by imprisonment for one year or longer; or

(iii) is an undischarged bankrupt or insolvent; or

(iv) holds any office of profit under the Crown, or any pension payable during the pleasure of the Crown out of any of the revenues of the Commonwealth; or

(v) has any direct or indirect pecuniary interest in any agreement with the Public Service of the Commonwealth otherwise than as a member and in common with the other members of an incorporated company consisting of more than twenty-five persons;

shall be incapable of being chosen or of sitting as a senator or a member of the House of Representatives.

But subsection (iv) does not apply to the office of any of the Queen's Ministers of State for the Commonwealth, or of any of the Queen's Ministers for a state, or to the receipt of pay, half pay, or a pension, by any person as an officer or member of the Queen's navy or army, or to the receipt of pay as an officer or member of the naval or military forces of the Commonwealth by any person whose services are not wholly employed by the Commonwealth.

45. Vacancy on happening of disqualification

If a senator or member of the House of Representatives:

(i) becomes subject to any of the disabilities mentioned in the last preceding section; or

(ii) takes the benefit, whether by assignment, composition, or otherwise, of any law relating to bankrupt or insolvent debtors; or

(iii) directly or indirectly takes or agrees to take any fee or honorarium for services rendered to the

Commonwealth, or for services rendered in the Parliament to any person or state; his place shall thereupon become vacant.

46. Penalty for sitting when disqualified

Until the Parliament otherwise provides, any person declared by this Constitution to be incapable of sitting as a senator or as a member of the House of Representatives shall, for every day on which he so sits, be liable to pay the sum of one hundred pounds to any person who sues for it in any court of competent jurisdiction.

47. Disputed elections

Until the Parliament otherwise provides, any question respecting the qualification of a senator or of a member of the House of Representatives, or respecting a vacancy in either House of the Parliament, and any question of a disputed election to either House, shall be determined by the House in which the question arises.

48. Allowance to members

Until the Parliament otherwise provides, each senator and each member of the House of Representatives shall receive an allowance of four hundred pounds a year, to be reckoned from the day on which he takes his seat.

49. Privileges, etc. of Houses

The powers, privileges, and immunities of the Senate and of the House of Representatives, and of the members and the committees of each House, shall be such as are declared by the Parliament, and until declared shall be those of the Commons House of Parliament of the United Kingdom, and of its members and committees, at the establishment of the Commonwealth.

50. Rules and orders

Each House of the Parliament may make rules and orders with respect to:

(i) the mode in which its powers, privileges, and immunities may be exercised and upheld;

(ii) the order and conduct of its business and proceedings either separately or jointly with the other House.

Part V

Powers of the Parliament

51. Legislative powers of the Parliament [see Notes 10 and 11]

The Parliament shall, subject to this Constitution, have power to make laws for the peace, order, and good government of the Commonwealth with respect to:

(i) trade and commerce with other countries, and among the states;

(ii) taxation; but so as not to discriminate between states or parts of states;

(iii) bounties on the production or export of goods, but so that such bounties shall be uniform throughout the Commonwealth;

(iv) borrowing money on the public credit of the Commonwealth;

(v) postal, telegraphic, telephonic, and other like services;

(vi) the naval and military defence of the Commonwealth and of the several states, and the control of the forces to execute and maintain the laws of the Commonwealth;

(vii) lighthouses, lightships, beacons and buoys;

(viii) astronomical and meteorological observations;

(ix) quarantine;

(x) fisheries in Australian waters beyond territorial limits;

(xi) census and statistics;

(xii) currency, coinage, and legal tender;

(xiii) banking, other than state banking; also state banking extending beyond the limits of the state concerned, the incorporation of banks, and the issue of paper money;

(xiv) insurance, other than state insurance; also State insurance extending beyond the limits of the State concerned;

(xv) weights and measures;

(xvi) bills of exchange and promissory notes;

(xvii) bankruptcy and insolvency;

(xviii) copyrights, patents of inventions and designs, and trade marks;

(xix) naturalization and aliens;

(xx) foreign corporations, and trading or financial corporations formed within the limits of the Commonwealth;

(xxi) marriage;

(xxii) divorce and matrimonial causes; and in relation thereto, parental rights, and the custody and guardianship of infants;

(xxiii) invalid and old-age pensions;

(xxiiiA) the provision of maternity allowances, widows' pensions, child endowment, unemployment, pharmaceutical, sickness and hospital benefits, medical and dental services (but not so as to authorize any form of civil conscription), benefits to students and family allowances;

(xxiv) the service and execution throughout the Commonwealth of the civil and criminal process and the judgments of the courts of the states;

(xxv) the recognition throughout the Commonwealth of the laws, the public Acts and records, and the judicial proceedings of the states;

(xxvi) the people of any race for whom it is deemed necessary to make special laws;

(xxvii) immigration and emigration;

(xxviii) the influx of criminals;

(xxix) external affairs;

(xxx) the relations of the Commonwealth with the islands of the Pacific;

(xxxi) the acquisition of property on just terms from any state or person for any purpose in respect of which the Parliament has power to make laws;

(xxxii) the control of railways with respect to transport for the naval and military purposes of the Commonwealth;

(xxxiii) the acquisition, with the consent of a state, of any railways of the state on terms arranged between the Commonwealth and the state;

(xxxiv) railway construction and extension in any State with the consent of that state;

(xxxv) conciliation and arbitration for the prevention and settlement of industrial disputes extending beyond the limits of any one state;

(xxxvi) matters in respect of which this Constitution makes provision until the Parliament otherwise provides;

(xxxvii) matters referred to the Parliament of the Commonwealth by the Parliament or Parliaments of any state or states, but so that the law shall extend only to states by whose Parliaments the matter is referred, or which afterwards adopt the law;

(xxxviii) the exercise within the Commonwealth, at the request or with the concurrence of the Parliaments of all the States directly concerned, of any power which can at the establishment of this Constitution be exercised only by the Parliament of the United Kingdom or by the Federal Council of Australasia;

(xxxix) matters incidental to the execution of any power vested by this Constitution in the Parliament or in either House thereof, or in the Government of the Commonwealth, or in the Federal Judicature, or in any department or officer of the Commonwealth.

52. Exclusive powers of the Parliament

The Parliament shall, subject to this Constitution, have exclusive power to make laws for the peace, order, and good government of the Commonwealth with respect to:

(i) the seat of government of the Commonwealth, and all places acquired by the Commonwealth for public purposes;

(ii) matters relating to any department of the public service the control of which is by this Constitution transferred to the Executive Government of the Commonwealth;

(iii) other matters declared by this Constitution to be within the exclusive power of the Parliament.

53. Powers of the Houses in respect of legislation

Proposed laws appropriating revenue or moneys, or imposing taxation, shall not originate in the Senate. But a proposed law shall not be taken to appropriate revenue or moneys, or to impose taxation, by reason only of its containing provisions for the imposition or appropriation of fines or other pecuniary penalties, or for the demand or payment or appropriation of fees for licences, or fees for services under the proposed law.

The Senate may not amend proposed laws imposing taxation, or proposed laws appropriating revenue or moneys for the ordinary annual services of the Government.

The Senate may not amend any proposed law so as to increase any proposed charge or burden on the people.

The Senate may at any stage return to the House of Representatives any proposed law which the Senate may not amend, requesting, by message, the omission or amendment of any items or provisions therein. And the House of Representatives may, if it thinks fit, make any of such omissions or amendments, with or without modifications.

Except as provided in this section, the Senate shall have equal power with the House of Representatives in respect of all proposed laws.

54. Appropriation Bills

The proposed law which appropriates revenue or moneys for the ordinary annual services of the Government shall deal only with such appropriation.

55. Tax Bill

Laws imposing taxation shall deal only with the imposition of taxation, and any provision therein dealing with any other matter shall be of no effect.

Laws imposing taxation, except laws imposing duties of customs or of excise, shall deal with one subject of taxation only; but laws imposing duties of customs shall deal with duties of customs only, and laws imposing duties of excise shall deal with duties of excise only.

56. Recommendation of money votes

A vote, resolution, or proposed law for the appropriation of revenue or moneys shall not be passed unless the purpose of the appropriation has in the same session been recommended by message of the Governor General to the House in which the proposal originated.

57. Disagreement between the Houses

If the House of Representatives passes any proposed law, and the Senate rejects or fails to pass it, or passes it with amendments to which the House of Representatives will not agree, and if after an interval of three months the House of Representatives, in the same or the next session, again passes the proposed law with or without any amendments which have been made, suggested, or agreed to by the Senate, and the Senate rejects or fails to pass it, or passes it with amendments to which the House of Representatives will not agree, the Governor General may dissolve the Senate and the House of Representatives simultaneously. But such dissolution shall not take place within six months before the date of the expiry of the House of Representatives by effluxion of time.

If after such dissolution the House of Representatives again passes the proposed law, with or without any amendments which have been made, suggested, or agreed to by the Senate, and the Senate rejects or fails to pass it, or passes it with amendments to which the House of Representatives will not agree, the Governor General may convene a joint sitting of the members of the Senate and of the House of Representatives.

The members present at the joint sitting may deliberate and shall vote together upon the proposed law as last proposed by the House of Representatives, and upon amendments, if any, which have been made therein by one House and not agreed to by the other, and any such amendments which are affirmed by an absolute majority of the total number of the members of the Senate and House of Representatives shall be taken to have been carried, and if the proposed law, with the amendments, if any, so carried is affirmed by an absolute majority of the total number of the members of the Senate and House of Representatives, it shall be taken to have been duly passed by both Houses of the Parliament, and shall be presented to the Governor General for the Queen's assent.

58. Royal assent to Bills

When a proposed law passed by both Houses of the Parliament is presented to the Governor General for the Queen's assent, he shall declare, according to his discretion, but subject to this Constitution, that he assents in the Queen's name, or that he withholds assent, or that he reserves the law for the Queen's pleasure.

Recommendations by Governor General

The Governor General may return to the house in which it originated any proposed law so presented to him, and may transmit therewith any amendments which he may recommend, and the Houses may deal with the recommendation.

59. Disallowance by the Queen

The Queen may disallow any law within one year from the Governor General's assent, and such disallowance on being made known by the Governor General by speech or message to each of the Houses of the Parliament, or by Proclamation, shall annul the law from the day when the disallowance is so made known.

60. Signification of Queen's pleasure on Bills reserved

A proposed law reserved for the Queen's pleasure shall not have any force unless and until within two years from the day on which it was presented to the Governor General for the Queen's assent the Governor General makes known, by speech or message to each of the Houses of the Parliament, or by Proclamation, that it has received the Queen's assent.

Chapter II

The Executive Government

61. Executive power

The executive power of the Commonwealth is vested in the Queen and is exercisable by the Governor General as the Queen's representative, and extends to the execution and maintenance of this Constitution, and of the laws of the Commonwealth.

62. Federal Executive Council

There shall be a Federal Executive Council to advise the Governor General in the government of the Commonwealth, and the members of the Council shall be chosen and summoned by the Governor General and sworn as Executive Councillors, and shall hold office during his pleasure.

63. Provisions referring to Governor General

The provisions of this Constitution referring to the Governor General in Council shall be construed as referring to the Governor General acting with the advice of the Federal Executive Council.

64. Ministers of State

The Governor General may appoint officers to administer such departments of state of the Commonwealth as the Governor General in Council may establish.

Such officers shall hold office during the pleasure of the Governor General. They shall be members of the Federal Executive Council, and shall be the Queen's Ministers of State for the Commonwealth.

Ministers to sit in Parliament

After the first general election no Minister of State shall hold office for a longer period than three months unless he is or becomes a senator or a member of the House of Representatives.

65. Number of Ministers

Until the Parliament otherwise provides, the Ministers of State shall not exceed seven in number, and shall hold such offices as the Parliament prescribes, or, in the absence of provision, as the Governor General directs.

66. Salaries of Ministers

There shall be payable to the Queen, out of the Consolidated Revenue Fund of the Commonwealth, for the salaries of the Ministers of State, an annual sum which, until the Parliament otherwise provides, shall not exceed twelve thousand pounds a year.

67. Appointment of civil servants

Until the Parliament otherwise provides, the appointment and removal of all other officers of the Executive Government of the Commonwealth shall be vested in the Governor General in Council, unless the appointment is delegated by the Governor General in Council or by a law of the Commonwealth to some other authority.

68. Command of naval and military forces

The command in chief of the naval and military forces of the Commonwealth is vested in the Governor General as the Queen's representative.

69. Transfer of certain departments

On a date or dates to be proclaimed by the Governor General after the establishment of the Commonwealth the following departments of the public service in each state shall become transferred to the Commonwealth: posts, telegraphs, and telephones; naval and military defence; lighthouses, lightships, beacons, and buoys; quarantine.

But the departments of customs and of excise in each state shall become transferred to the Commonwealth on its establishment.

70. Certain powers of Governors to vest in Governor General

In respect of matters which, under this Constitution, pass to the Executive Government of the Commonwealth, all powers and functions which at the establishment of the Commonwealth are vested in the Governor of a Colony, or in the Governor of a Colony with the advice of his Executive Council, or in any authority of a Colony, shall vest in the Governor General, or in the Governor General in Council, or in the authority exercising similar powers under the Commonwealth, as the case requires.

Chapter III

The Judicature

71. Judicial power and courts

The judicial power of the Commonwealth shall be vested in a Federal Supreme Court, to be called the High Court of Australia, and in such other federal courts as the Parliament creates, and in such other courts as it invests with federal jurisdiction. The High Court shall consist of a Chief Justice, and so many other Justices, not less than two, as the Parliament prescribes.

72. Judges' appointment, tenure, and remuneration

The Justices of the High Court and of the other courts created by the Parliament:

(i) shall be appointed by the Governor General in Council;

(ii) shall not be removed except by the Governor General in Council, on an address from both Houses of the Parliament in the same session, praying for such removal on the ground of proved misbehaviour or incapacity;

(iii) shall receive such remuneration as the Parliament may fix; but the remuneration shall not be diminished during their continuance in office.

The appointment of a Justice of the High Court shall be for a term expiring upon his attaining the age of seventy years, and a person shall not be appointed as a Justice of the High Court if he has attained that age.

The appointment of a Justice of a court created by the Parliament shall be for a term expiring upon his attaining the age that is, at the time of his appointment, the maximum age for Justices of that court and a person shall not be appointed as a Justice of such a court if he has attained the age that is for the time being the maximum age for Justices of that court.

Subject to this section, the maximum age for Justices of any court created by the Parliament is seventy years.

The Parliament may make a law fixing an age that is less than seventy years as the maximum age for Justices of a court created by the Parliament and may at any time repeal or amend such a law, but any such repeal or amendment does not affect the term of office of a Justice under an appointment made before the repeal or amendment.

A Justice of the High Court or of a court created by the Parliament may resign his office by writing under his hand delivered to the Governor General.

Nothing in the provisions added to this section by the *Constitution Alteration (Retirement of Judges) 1977* affects the continuance of a person in office as a Justice of a court under an appointment made before the commencement of those provisions.

A reference in this section to the appointment of a Justice of the High Court or of a court created by the Parliament shall be read as including a reference to the appointment of a person who holds office as a Justice of the High Court or of a court created by the Parliament to another office of Justice of the same court having a different status or designation.

73. Appellate jurisdiction of High Court

The High Court shall have jurisdiction, with such exceptions and subject to such regulations as the Parliament prescribes, to hear and determine appeals from all judgements, decrees, orders, and sentences:

(i) of any Justice or Justices exercising the original jurisdiction of the High Court;

(ii) of any other federal court, or court exercising federal jurisdiction; or of the Supreme Court of any State, or of any other court of any state from which at the establishment of the Commonwealth an appeal lies to the Queen in Council;

(iii) of the Inter-State Commission, but as to questions of law only; and the judgment of the High Court in all such cases shall be final and conclusive.

But no exception or regulation prescribed by the Parliament shall prevent the High Court from hearing and determining any appeal from the Supreme Court of a state in any matter in which at the establishment of the Commonwealth an appeal lies from such Supreme Court to the Queen in Council.

Until the Parliament otherwise provides, the conditions of and restrictions on appeals to the Queen in Council from the Supreme Courts of the several states shall be applicable to appeals from them to the High Court.

74. Appeal to Queen in Council [see Note 12]

No appeal shall be permitted to the Queen in Council from a decision of the High Court upon any question, howsoever arising, as to the limits inter se of the Constitutional powers of the Commonwealth and those of any state or states, or as to the limits inter se of the Constitutional powers of any two or more States, unless the High Court shall certify that the question is one which ought to be determined by Her Majesty in Council.

The High Court may so certify if satisfied that for any special reason the certificate should be granted, and thereupon an appeal shall lie to Her Majesty in Council on the question without further leave.

Except as provided in this section, this Constitution shall not impair any right which the Queen may be pleased to exercise by virtue of Her Royal prerogative to grant special leave of appeal from the High Court to Her Majesty in Council. The Parliament may make laws limiting the matters in which such leave may be asked, but proposed laws containing any such limitation shall be reserved by the Governor General for Her Majesty's pleasure.

75. Original jurisdiction of High Court

In all matters:

(i) arising under any treaty;

(ii) affecting consuls or other representatives of other countries;

(iii) in which the Commonwealth, or a person suing or being sued on behalf of the Commonwealth, is a party;

(iv) between States, or between residents of different states, or between a state and a resident of another state;

(v) in which a writ of mandamus or prohibition or an injunction is sought against an officer of the Commonwealth; the High Court shall have original jurisdiction.

76. Additional original jurisdiction

The Parliament may make laws conferring original jurisdiction on the High Court in any matter:

(i) arising under this Constitution, or involving its interpretation;

(ii) arising under any laws made by the Parliament;

(iii) of Admiralty and maritime jurisdiction;

(iv) relating to the same subject-matter claimed under the laws of different States.

77. Power to define jurisdiction

With respect to any of the matters mentioned in the last two sections the Parliament may make laws:

(i) defining the jurisdiction of any federal court other than the High Court;

(ii) defining the extent to which the jurisdiction of any federal court shall be exclusive of that which belongs to or is invested in the courts of the states;

(iii) investing any court of a state with federal jurisdiction.

78. Proceedings against Commonwealth or State

The Parliament may make laws conferring rights to proceed against the Commonwealth or a state in respect of matters within the limits of the judicial power.

79. Number of judges

The federal jurisdiction of any court may be exercised by such number of judges as the Parliament prescribes.

80. Trial by jury

The trial on indictment of any offence against any law of the Commonwealth shall be by jury, and every such trial shall be held in the state where the offence was committed, and if the offence was not committed within any state the trial shall be held at such place or places as the Parliament prescribes.

Chapter IV

Finance and Trade

81. Consolidated Revenue Fund

All revenues or moneys raised or received by the Executive Government of the Commonwealth shall form one Consolidated Revenue Fund, to be appropriated for the purposes of the Commonwealth in the manner and subject to the charges and liabilities imposed by this Constitution.

82. Expenditure charged thereon

The costs, charges, and expenses incident to the collection, management, and receipt of the Consolidated Revenue Fund shall form the first charge thereon; and the revenue of the Commonwealth shall in the first instance be applied to the payment of the expenditure of the Commonwealth.

83. Money to be appropriated by law

No money shall be drawn from the Treasury of the Commonwealth except under appropriation made by law.

But until the expiration of one month after the first meeting of the Parliament the Governor General in Council may draw from the Treasury and expend such moneys as may be necessary for the maintenance of any department transferred to the

Commonwealth and for the holding of the first elections for the Parliament.

84. Transfer of officers

When any department of the public service of a State becomes transferred to the Commonwealth, all officers of the department shall become subject to the control of the Executive Government of the Commonwealth.

Any such officer who is not retained in the service of the Commonwealth shall, unless he is appointed to some other office of equal emolument in the public service of the state, be entitled to receive from the state any pension, gratuity, or other compensation, payable under the law of the state on the abolition of his office.

Any such officer who is retained in the service of the Commonwealth shall preserve all his existing and accruing rights, and shall be entitled to retire from office at the time, and on the pension or retiring allowance, which would be permitted by the law of the state if his service with the Commonwealth were a continuation of his service with the state. Such pension or retiring allowance shall be paid to him by the Commonwealth; but the state shall pay to the Commonwealth a part thereof, to be calculated on the proportion which his term of service with the state bears to his whole term of service, and for the purpose of the calculation his salary shall be taken to be that paid to him by the state at the time of the transfer.

Any officer who is, at the establishment of the Commonwealth, in the public service of a state, and who is, by consent of the Governor of the state with the advice of the Executive Council thereof, transferred to the public service of the Commonwealth, shall have the same rights as if he had been an officer of a department transferred to the Commonwealth and were retained in the service of the Commonwealth.

85. Transfer of property of State

When any department of the public service of a state is transferred to the Commonwealth:

(i) all property of the state of any kind, used exclusively in connection with the department, shall become vested in the Commonwealth; but, in the case of the departments controlling customs and excise and bounties, for such time only as the Governor General in Council may declare to be necessary;

(ii) the Commonwealth may acquire any property of the State, of any kind used, but not exclusively used in connection with the department; the value thereof shall, if no agreement can be made, be ascertained in, as nearly as may be, the manner in which the value of land, or of an interest in land, taken by the State for public purposes is ascertained under the law of the State in force at the establishment of the Commonwealth;

(iii) the Commonwealth shall compensate the state for the value of any property passing to the Commonwealth under this section; if no agreement can be made as to the mode of compensation, it shall be determined under laws to be made by the Parliament;

(iv) the Commonwealth shall, at the date of the transfer, assume the current obligations of the state in respect of the department transferred.

86. Customs, excise, and bounties [see Note 13]

On the establishment of the Commonwealth, the collection and control of duties of customs and of excise, and the control of the payment of bounties, shall pass to the Executive Government of the Commonwealth.

87. Revenue from customs and excise duties [see Note 13]

During a period of ten years after the establishment of the Commonwealth and thereafter until the Parliament otherwise provides, of the net revenue of the Commonwealth from duties of customs and of excise not more than one-fourth shall be applied annually by the Commonwealth towards its expenditure.

The balance shall, in accordance with this Constitution, be paid to the several states, or applied towards the payment of interest on debts of the several states taken over by the Commonwealth.

88. Uniform duties of customs

Uniform duties of customs shall be imposed within two years after the establishment of the Commonwealth.

89. Payment to States before uniform duties

Until the imposition of uniform duties of customs:

(i) the Commonwealth shall credit to each state the revenues collected therein by the Commonwealth;

(ii) the Commonwealth shall debit to each state:

(a) the expenditure therein of the Commonwealth incurred solely for the maintenance or continuance, as at the time of transfer, of any department transferred from the state to the Commonwealth;

(b) the proportion of the state, according to the number of its people, in the other expenditure of the Commonwealth;

(iii) the Commonwealth shall pay to each state month by month the balance (if any) in favour of the state.

90. Exclusive power over customs, excise, and bounties

On the imposition of uniform duties of customs the power of the Parliament to impose duties of customs and of excise, and to grant bounties on the production or export of goods, shall become exclusive.

On the imposition of uniform duties of customs all laws of the several states imposing duties of customs or of excise, or offering bounties on the production or export of goods, shall cease to have effect, but any grant of or agreement for any such bounty lawfully made by or under the authority of the Government of any state shall be taken to be good if made before the thirtieth day of June, one thousand eight hundred and ninety-eight, and not otherwise.

91. Exceptions as to bounties

Nothing in this Constitution prohibits a state from granting any aid to or bounty on mining for gold, silver, or other metals, nor from granting, with the consent of both Houses of the

Parliament of the Commonwealth expressed by resolution, any aid to or bounty on the production or export of goods.

92. Trade within the Commonwealth to be free

On the imposition of uniform duties of customs, trade, commerce, and intercourse among the states, whether by means of internal carriage or ocean navigation, shall be absolutely free.

But notwithstanding anything in this Constitution, goods imported before the imposition of uniform duties of customs into any state, or into any Colony which, whilst the goods remain therein, becomes a state, shall, on thence passing into another state within two years after the imposition of such duties, be liable to any duty chargeable on the importation of such goods into the Commonwealth, less any duty paid in respect of the goods on their importation.

93. Payment to States for five years after uniform tariffs

During the first five years after the imposition of uniform duties of customs, and thereafter until the Parliament otherwise provides:

(i) the duties of customs chargeable on goods imported into a state and afterwards passing into another State for consumption, and the duties of excise paid on goods produced or manufactured in a state and afterwards passing into another state for consumption, shall be taken to have been collected not in the former but in the latter state;

(ii) subject to the last subsection, the Commonwealth shall credit revenue, debit expenditure, and pay balances to the several states as prescribed for the period preceding the imposition of uniform duties of customs.

94. Distribution of surplus

After five years from the imposition of uniform duties of customs, the Parliament may provide, on such basis as it deems fair, for the monthly payment to the several states of all surplus revenue of the Commonwealth.

95. Customs duties of Western Australia

Notwithstanding anything in this Constitution, the Parliament of the State of Western Australia, if that state be an Original State, may, during the first five years after the imposition of uniform duties of customs, impose duties of customs on goods passing into that state and not originally imported from beyond the limits of the Commonwealth; and such duties shall be collected by the Commonwealth.

But any duty so imposed on any goods shall not exceed during the first of such years the duty chargeable on the goods under the law of Western Australia in force at the imposition of uniform duties, and shall not exceed during the second, third, fourth, and fifth of such years respectively, four-fifths, three-fifths, two-fifths, and one-fifth of such latter duty, and all duties imposed under this section shall cease at the expiration of the fifth year after the imposition of uniform duties.

If at any time during the five years the duty on any goods under this section is higher than the duty imposed by the Commonwealth on the importation of the like goods, then such higher duty shall be collected on the goods when imported into Western Australia from beyond the limits of the Commonwealth.

96. Financial assistance to States

During a period of ten years after the establishment of the Commonwealth and thereafter until the Parliament otherwise provides, the Parliament may grant financial assistance to any state on such terms and conditions as the Parliament thinks fit.

97. Audit

Until the Parliament otherwise provides, the laws in force in any Colony which has become or becomes a state with respect to the receipt of revenue and the expenditure of money on account of the Government of the Colony, and the review and audit of such receipt and expenditure, shall apply to the receipt of revenue and the expenditure of money on account of the Commonwealth in the state in the same manner as if the Commonwealth, or the Government or an officer of the Commonwealth, were mentioned whenever the Colony, or the Government or an officer of the Colony, is mentioned.

98. Trade and commerce includes navigation and State railways

The power of the Parliament to make laws with respect to trade and commerce extends to navigation and shipping, and to railways the property of any state.

99. Commonwealth not to give preference

The Commonwealth shall not, by any law or regulation of trade, commerce, or revenue, give preference to one State or any part thereof over another state or any part thereof.

100. Nor abridge right to use water

The Commonwealth shall not, by any law or regulation of trade or commerce, abridge the right of a state or of the residents therein to the reasonable use of the waters of rivers for conservation or irrigation.

101. Inter-State Commission

There shall be an Inter-State Commission, with such powers of adjudication and administration as the Parliament deems necessary for the execution and maintenance, within the Commonwealth, of the provisions of this Constitution relating to trade and commerce, and of all laws made thereunder.

102. Parliament may forbid preferences by State

The Parliament may by any law with respect to trade or commerce forbid, as to railways, any preference or discrimination by any State, or by any authority constituted under a state, if such preference or discrimination is undue and unreasonable, or unjust to any state; due regard being had to the financial responsibilities incurred by any State in connection with the construction and maintenance of its railways. But no preference or discrimination shall, within the meaning of this section, be taken to be undue and unreasonable, or unjust to any state, unless so adjudged by the Inter-State Commission.

103. Commissioners' appointment, tenure, and remuneration

The members of the Inter-State Commission:

(i) shall be appointed by the Governor-General in Council;

(ii) shall hold office for seven years, but may be removed within that time by the Governor General in Council, on an address from both Houses of the Parliament in the same session praying for such removal on the ground of proved misbehaviour or incapacity;

(iii) shall receive such remuneration as the Parliament may fix; but such remuneration shall not be diminished during their continuance in office.

104. Saving of certain rates

Nothing in this Constitution shall render unlawful any rate for the carriage of goods upon a railway, the property of a state, if the rate is deemed by the Inter-State Commission to be necessary for the development of the territory of the state, and if the rate applies equally to goods within the state and to goods passing into the state from other states.

105. Taking over public debts of States

The Parliament may take over from the states their public debts or a proportion thereof according to the respective numbers of their people as shown by the latest statistics of the Commonwealth, and may convert, renew, or consolidate such debts, or any part thereof; and the states shall indemnify the Commonwealth in respect of the debts taken over, and thereafter the interest payable in respect of the debts shall be deducted and retained from the portions of the surplus revenue of the Commonwealth payable to the several states, or if such surplus is insufficient, or if there is no surplus, then the deficiency or the whole amount shall be paid by the several states.

105A. Agreements with respect to State debts

(1) The Commonwealth may make agreements with the States with respect to the public debts of the states, including:

(a) the taking over of such debts by the Commonwealth;

(b) the management of such debts;

(c) the payment of interest and the provision and management of sinking funds in respect of such debts;

(d) the consolidation, renewal, conversion, and redemption of such debts;

(e) the indemnification of the Commonwealth by the states in respect of debts taken over by the Commonwealth; and

(f) the borrowing of money by the states or by the Commonwealth, or by the Commonwealth for the states.

(2) The Parliament may make laws for validating any such agreement made before the commencement of this section.

(3) The Parliament may make laws for the carrying out by the parties thereto of any such agreement.

(4) Any such agreement may be varied or rescinded by the parties thereto.

(5) Every such agreement and any such variation thereof shall be binding upon the Commonwealth and the states parties thereto notwithstanding anything contained in this Constitution or the Constitution of the several states or in any law of the Parliament of the Commonwealth or of any state.

(6) The powers conferred by this section shall not be construed as being limited in any way by the provisions of section one hundred and five of this Constitution.

Chapter V

The States

106. Saving of Constitutions

The Constitution of each State of the Commonwealth shall, subject to this Constitution, continue as at the establishment of the Commonwealth, or as at the admission or establishment of the state, as the case may be, until altered in accordance with the Constitution of the state.

107. Saving of Power of State Parliaments

Every power of the Parliament of a Colony which has become or becomes a state, shall, unless it is by this Constitution exclusively vested in the Parliament of the Commonwealth or withdrawn from the Parliament of the state, continue as at the establishment of the Commonwealth, or as at the admission or establishment of the state, as the case may be.

108. Saving of State laws

Every law in force in a Colony which has become or becomes a state, and relating to any matter within the powers of the Parliament of the Commonwealth, shall, subject to this Constitution, continue in force in the state; and, until provision is made in that behalf by the Parliament of the Commonwealth, the Parliament of the state shall have such powers of alteration and of repeal in respect of any such law as the Parliament of the Colony had until the Colony became a state.

109. Inconsistency of laws

When a law of a state is inconsistent with a law of the Commonwealth, the latter shall prevail, and the former shall, to the extent of the inconsistency, be invalid.

110. Provisions referring to Governor

The provisions of this Constitution relating to the Governor of a state extend and apply to the Governor for the time being of the state, or other chief executive officer or administrator of the government of the state.

111. States may surrender territory

The Parliament of a state may surrender any part of the state to the Commonwealth; and upon such surrender, and the acceptance thereof by the Commonwealth, such part of the state shall become subject to the exclusive jurisdiction of the Commonwealth.

112. States may levy charges for inspection laws

After uniform duties of customs have been imposed, a State may levy on imports or exports, or on goods passing into or out of the state, such charges as may be necessary for executing the inspection laws of the state; but the net produce of all charges so levied shall be for the use of the Commonwealth; and any such inspection laws may be annulled by the Parliament of the Commonwealth.

113. Intoxicating liquids

All fermented, distilled, or other intoxicating liquids passing into any state or remaining therein for use, consumption, sale, or storage, shall be subject to the laws of the state as if such liquids had been produced in the state.

114. States may not raise forces. Taxation of property of Commonwealth or State

A State shall not, without the consent of the Parliament of the Commonwealth, raise or maintain any naval or military force, or impose any tax on property of any kind belonging to the Commonwealth, nor shall the Commonwealth impose any tax on property of any kind belonging to a state.

115. States not to coin money

A state shall not coin money, nor make anything but gold and silver coin a legal tender in payment of debts.

116. Commonwealth not to legislate in respect of religion

The Commonwealth shall not make any law for establishing any religion, or for imposing any religious observance, or for prohibiting the free exercise of any religion, and no religious test shall be required as a qualification for any office or public trust under the Commonwealth.

117. Rights of residents in States

A subject of the Queen, resident in any State, shall not be subject in any other state to any disability or discrimination which would not be equally applicable to him if he were a subject of the Queen resident in such other state.

118. Recognition of laws etc. of States

Full faith and credit shall be given, throughout the Commonwealth to the laws, the public Acts and records, and the judicial proceedings of every state.

119. Protection of States from invasion and violence

The Commonwealth shall protect every state against invasion and, on the application of the Executive Government of the State, against domestic violence.

120. Custody of offenders against laws of the Commonwealth

Every state shall make provision for the detention in its prisons of persons accused or convicted of offences against the laws of the Commonwealth, and for the punishment of persons convicted of such offences, and the Parliament of the Commonwealth may make laws to give effect to this provision.

Chapter VI

New States

121. New States may be admitted or established

The Parliament may admit to the Commonwealth or establish new states, and may upon such admission or establishment make or impose such terms and conditions, including the extent of representation in either House of the Parliament, as it thinks fit.

122. Government of territories

The Parliament may make laws for the government of any territory surrendered by any state to and accepted by the Commonwealth, or of any territory placed by the Queen under the authority of and accepted by the Commonwealth, or otherwise acquired by the Commonwealth, and may allow the representation of such territory in either House of the Parliament to the extent and on the terms which it thinks fit.

123. Alteration of limits of States

The Parliament of the Commonwealth may, with the consent of the Parliament of a state, and the approval of the majority of the electors of the state voting upon the question, increase, diminish, or otherwise alter the limits of the state, upon such terms and conditions as may be agreed on, and may, with the like consent, make provision respecting the effect and operation of any increase or diminution or alteration of territory in relation to any state affected.

124. Formation of new States

A new state may be formed by separation of territory from a state, but only with the consent of the Parliament thereof, and a new state may be formed by the union of two or more States or parts of states, but only with the consent of the Parliaments of the states affected.

Chapter VII

Miscellaneous

125. Seat of Government

The seat of Government of the Commonwealth shall be determined by the Parliament, and shall be within territory which shall have been granted to or acquired by the Commonwealth, and shall be vested in and belong to the Commonwealth, and shall be in the State of New South Wales, and be distant not less than one hundred miles from Sydney.

Such territory shall contain an area of not less than one hundred square miles, and such portion thereof as shall consist of Crown lands shall be granted to the Commonwealth without any payment therefor.

The Parliament shall sit at Melbourne until it meets at the seat of Government.

126. Power to Her Majesty to authorise Governor General to appoint deputies [see Note 14]

The Queen may authorise the Governor General to appoint any person, or any persons jointly or severally, to be his deputy or deputies within any part of the Commonwealth, and in that capacity to exercise during the pleasure of the Governor General such powers and functions of the Governor General as he thinks fit to assign to such deputy or deputies, subject to any limitations expressed or directions given by the Queen; but the appointment of such deputy or deputies shall not affect the exercise by the Governor General himself of any power or function.

...

Chapter VIII

Alteration of the Constitution

127. Mode of altering the Constitution [see Note 1]

This Constitution shall not be altered except in the following manner:

The proposed law for the alteration thereof must be passed by an absolute majority of each House of the Parliament, and not less than two or more than six months after its passage through both Houses the proposed law shall be submitted in each state and Territory to the electors qualified to vote for the election of members of the House of Representatives.

But if either House passes any such proposed law by an absolute majority, and the other House rejects or fails to pass it, or passes it with any amendment to which the first-mentioned House will not agree, and if after an interval of three months the first-mentioned House in the same or the next session again passes the proposed law by an absolute majority with or without any amendment which has been made or agreed to by the other House, and such other House rejects or fails to pass it or passes it with any amendment to which the first-mentioned House will not agree, the Governor General may submit the proposed law as last proposed by the first-mentioned House, and either with or without any amendments subsequently agreed to by both Houses, to the electors in each state and Territory qualified to vote for the election of the House of Representatives.

When a proposed law is submitted to the electors the vote shall be taken in such manner as the Parliament prescribes. But until the qualification of electors of members of the House of Representatives becomes uniform throughout the Commonwealth, only one-half of the electors voting for and against the proposed law shall be counted in any State in which adult suffrage prevails.

And if in a majority of the states a majority of the electors voting approve the proposed law, and if a majority of all the electors voting also approve the proposed law, it shall be presented to the Governor General for the Queen's assent.

No alteration diminishing the proportionate representation of any state in either House of the Parliament, or the minimum number of representatives of a state in the House of Representatives, or increasing, diminishing, or otherwise altering the limits of the state, or in any manner affecting the provisions of the Constitution in relation thereto, shall become law unless the majority of the electors voting in that state approve the proposed law.

In this section, *Territory* means any territory referred to in section one hundred and twenty-two of this Constitution in respect of which there is in force a law allowing its representation in the House of Representatives.

Schedule

OATH

I, *A.B.*, do swear that I will be faithful and bear true allegiance to Her Majesty Queen Victoria, Her heirs and successors according to law. SO HELP ME GOD!

AFFIRMATION

I, *A.B.*, do solemnly and sincerely affirm and declare that I will be faithful and bear true allegiance to Her Majesty Queen Victoria, Her heirs and successors according to law.

(NOTE: *The name of the King or Queen of the United Kingdom of Great Britain and Ireland for the time being is to be substituted from time to time.*)

Table of Acts

Notes to the Commonwealth of Australia Constitution Act

Note 1

The Commonwealth of Australia Constitution Act (the Constitution) as shown in this compilation comprises the Constitution amended as indicated in the Tables below.

Act	Number and year	Date of Assent
Constitution Alteration (Senate Elections) 1906	1, 1907	3 Apr 1907
Constitution Alteration (State Debts) 1909	3, 1910	6 Aug 1910
Constitution Alteration (State Debts) 1928	1, 1929	13 Feb 1929
Constitution Alteration (Social Services) 1946	81, 1946	19 Dec 1946
Constitution Alteration (Aboriginals) 1967	55, 1967	10 Aug 1967
Constitution Alteration (Senate Casual Vacancies) 1977	82, 1977	29 July 1977
Constitution Alteration (Retirement of Judges) 1977	83, 1977	29 July 1977
Constitution Alteration (Referendums) 1977	84, 1977	29 July 1977

Table of Amendments

ad. = added or inserted am. = amended rep. = repealed
rs. = repealed and substituted

Provision affected	How affected
S. 13	am. No. 1, 1907
S 15	rs. No. 82, 1977
S. 51	am. No. 81, 1946; No. 55, 1967
S. 72	am. No. 83, 1977
S. 105	am. No. 3, 1910
S. 105A	ad. No. 1, 1929
S. 127	rep. No. 55, 1967
S. 128	am. No. 84, 1977

Note 2

Covering Clause 3—The Proclamation under covering clause 3 was made on 17 September 1900 and published in Gazette 1901.

Note 3

Covering Clause 5—*see also* the *Statute of Westminster Adoption Act 1942.*

Note 4

Covering Clause 7—The following Acts have repealed Acts passed by the Federal Council of Australasia:

Defence Act 1903 (No. 20, 1903), s. 6

Pearl Fisheries Act 1952 (No. 8, 1952), s. 3 (*Pearl Fisheries Act 1952* repealed by *Continental Shelf (Living Natural Resources) Act 1968*, s. 3)

Service and Execution of Process Act 1901 (No. 11, 1901), s. 2 (subsequently repealed by *Service and Execution of Process Act 1963*, s. 3).

Note 5

Section 7—The number of senators for each State was increased to 12 by the *Representation Act 1983*, s. 3.

Note 6

Section 9—The following State Acts have been passed in pursuance of the powers conferred by s. 9:

State	Number	Short title	How affected
New South Wales	No. 73, 1900	*Federal Elections Act 1900*	Ss. 2, 3, 4, 5 and 6 and the Schedule repealed by No. 9, 1903; wholly repealed by No. 41, 1912
	No. 9, 1903	*Senators' Elections Act 1903*	(still in force)
Victoria	No. 1715	*Federal Elections Act 1900*	Repealed by No. 1860
	No. 1860	*Senate Elections (Times and Places) Act 1903*	Repealed by No. 2723

Note 7

State	Number	Short title	How affected
	No. 2399	*Senate Elections (Times and Places) Act 1912*	Repealed by No. 2723
	No. 2723	*Senate Elections (Times and Places) Act 1915*	Repealed by No. 3769
	No. 3769	*Senate Elections (Times and Places) Act 1928*	Repealed by No. 6365
	No. 6365	*Senate Elections Act 1958*	(still in force)
Queensland	64 Vic. No. 25	*The Parliament of the Commonwealth Elections Act* and *the Elections Acts 1885 to 1898 Amendment Act of 1900*	Operation exhausted
	3 Edw. VII.	*The Election of Senators*	Repealed by 9 Eliz
	No. 6	*Act of 1903*	II. No. 20
	9 Eliz. II.	*The Senate Elections Act*	(still in force)
	No. 20	*of 1960*	
South Australia	No. 834	*The Election of Senators Act 1903*	(still in force)

Western Australia	No. 11, 1903	*Election of Senators Act 1903*	(still in force)
Tasmania	64 Vic. No. 59	*The Federal Elections Act 1900*	Repealed by 26 Geo. V. No. 3
	3 Edw. VII.	*The Election of Senators*	Repealed by 26
	No. 5	*Act 1903*	Geo. V. No. 3
	26 Geo. V.	*Senate Elections Act 1935*	(still in force)
	No. 3		

Note 7

Section 14—For the provisions applicable upon the increase in the number of senators to 12 made by the *Representation Act 1983*, *see* s. 3 of that Act.

Note 8

Section 15—The proposed law to alter the Constitution entitled "*Constitution Alteration (Simultaneous Elections) 1977*" was submitted to the electors in each State of the Commonwealth on 21 May 1977: it was not approved by a majority of all the electors voting in a majority of the states. See Gazette 1977, No. S100.

Note 9

Section 29—The following State Acts were passed in pursuance of the powers conferred by s. 29, but ceased to be in force upon the enactment of the *Commonwealth Electoral Act 1902*:

State	Number	Short title
New South Wales	No. 73, 1900	*Federal Elections Act 1900*
Victoria	No. 1667	*Federal House of Representatives Victorian Electorates Act 1900*
Queensland	64 Vic. No. 25	*The Parliament of the Commonwealth Elections Act* and *The Elections Acts 1885 to 1898 Amendment Act of 1900*
Western Australia	64 Vic. No. 6	*Federal House of Representatives Western Australian Electorates Act 1900*

Note 10

Section 51—The following Imperial Acts extended the legislative powers of the Parliament:

Whaling Industry (Regulations) Act 1934, s. 15

Geneva Convention Act, 1937, s. 2

Emergency Powers (Defence) Act 1939, s. 5

Army and Air Force (Annual) Act 1940, s. 3.

Note 11

Section 51 (xxxvii)—The following Acts have been passed by the Parliaments of the States to refer matters to the Parliament under section 51 (xxxvii):

State	Number	Short title	How affected
New South Wales	No. 65, 1915	*Commonwealth Powers (War) Act 1915*	Expired 9 Jan 1921; *see* s. 5
	No. 33, 1942	*Commonwealth Powers Act 1942*	Expired; *see* s. 4
	No. 18, 1943	*Commonwealth Powers Act 1943*	Expired; *see* s. 4
	No. 48, 1983	*Commonwealth Powers (Meat Inspection) Act 1983*	(still in force)
	No. 182, 1986	*Commonwealth Powers (Family Law–Children) Act 1986*	(still in force)
	No. 61, 1992	*Mutual Recognition (New South Wales) Act 1992*	(still in force)
	No. 104, 1992	*Commonwealth Powers (State Banking) Act 1992*	(still in force)
	No. 100, 1993	*Commonwealth Powers (Poultry Processing) Act 1993*	(still in force)
	No. 1, 2001	*Corporations (Commonwealth Powers) Act 2001*	(still in force)
	No. 114, 2002	*Terrorism (Commonwealth Powers) Act 2002*	(still in force)
Victoria	No. 3108	*Commonwealth Powers (Air Navigation) Act 1920*	Repealed by No. 4502

(Continued)

	No. 3658	*Commonwealth Arrangements Act 1928 (Part III)*	Part III Repealed by No. 4502: Parts I & II Repealed by No. 6223
	No. 4009	*Debt Conversion Agreement Act 1931 (No. 2)*	(still in force)
	No. 4950	*Commonwealth Powers Act 1943*	Not proclaimed to come into operation and cannot now be so proclaimed
	No. 92, 1986	*Commonwealth Powers (Family Law–Children) Act 1986*	(still in force)
	No. 2, 1993	*Mutual Recognition (Victoria) Act 1993*	(still in force)
	No. 59, 1996	*Commonwealth Powers (Industrial Relations) Act 1996*	(still in force)
	No. 6, 2001	*Corporations (Commonwealth Powers) Act 2001*	(still in force)
	No. 14, 2003	*Terrorism (Commonwealth Powers) Act 2003*	(still in force)
Queensland	12 Geo. V. No. 30	*The Commonwealth Powers (Air Navigation) Act 1921*	Repealed by 1 Geo. VI. No. 8
	22 Geo. V. No. 30	*The Commonwealth Legislative Power Act 1931*	Repealed by No. 46, 1983
	7 Geo. VI. No. 19	*Commonwealth Powers Act 1943*	Expired; *see* s. 4
	14 Geo. VI. No. 2	*The Commonwealth Powers (Air Transport) Act 1950*	(still in force)
	No. 37, 1990	*Commonwealth Powers (Family Law–Children) Act 1990*	(still in force)
	No. 67, 1992	*Mutual Recognition (Queensland) Act 1992*	(still in force)
	No. 43, 2001	*Corporations (Commonwealth Powers) Act 2001*	(still in force)
	No. 79, 2002	*Terrorism (Commonwealth Powers) Act 2002*	(still in force)
South Australia	No. 1469, 1921	*Commonwealth Powers (Air Navigation) Act 1921*	Repealed by No. 2352, 1937

	No. 2061, 1931	*Commonwealth Legislative Power Act 1931*	(still in force)
	No. 3, 1943	*Commonwealth Powers Act 1943*	Expired; *see* s. 5
	No. 89, 1986	*Commonwealth Powers (Family Law) Act 1986*	(still in force)
	No. 72, 1993	*Mutual Recognition (South Australia) Act 1993*	(still in force)
	No. 21, 2001	*Corporations (Commonwealth Powers) Act 2001*	(still in force)
	No. 50, 2002	*Terrorism (Commonwealth Powers) Act 2002*	(still in force)
Western Australia	No. 4, 1943	*Commonwealth Powers Act 1943*	Repealed by No. 58, 1965
	No. 57, 1945	*Commonwealth Powers Act 1945*	Repealed by No. 58, 1965
	No. 30, 1947	*Commonwealth Powers Act 1943, Amendment Act 1947*	Repealed by No. 58, 1965
	No. 31, 1947	*Commonwealth Powers Act 1945, Amendment Act 1947*	Repealed by No. 58, 1965
	No. 73, 1947	*Commonwealth Powers Act 1945, Amendment Act (No. 2), 1947*	Repealed by No. 58, 1965
	No. 81, 1947	*Commonwealth Powers Act 1945-1947, Amendment (Continuance) Act 1947*	Repealed by No. 58, 1965
	No. 53, 1995	*Mutual Recognition (Western Australia) Act 1995*	(still in force)
	No. 7, 2001	*Corporations (Commonwealth Powers) Act 2001*	(still in force)
	No. 53, 2002	*Terrorism (Commonwealth Powers) Act 2002*	(still in force)
Tasmania	11 Geo. V. No. 42	*Commonwealth Powers (Air Navigation) Act 1920*	Repealed by 1 Geo. VI. No. 14
	No. 46, 1952	*Commonwealth Powers (Air Transport) Act 1952*	(still in force)

Note 12

State	Number	Short title	How affected
	No. 62, 1966	*Commonwealth Powers (Trade Practices) Act 1966*	Expired; *see* s. 2
	No. 5, 1987	*Commonwealth Powers (Family Law) Act 1987*	(still in force)
	No. 33, 1993	*Mutual Recognition (Tasmania) Act 1993*	(still in force)
	No. 20, 1994	*Commonwealth Powers (Family Law) Amendment Act 1994*	(still in force)
	No. 39, 2001	*Corporations (Commonwealth Powers) Act 2001*	(still in force)
	No. 68, 2002	*Terrorism (Commonwealth Powers) Act 2002*	(still in force)

Note 12

Section 74—*See Privy Council (Limitation of Appeals) Act 1968*, *Privy Council (Appeals from the High Court) Act 1975* and Kirmani vs Captain Cook Cruises (P) Ltd [No. 2] (1985) 159 CLR 461.

Note 13

Sections 86 and 87—the headings for these sections have been added for compilation purposes.

Note 14

S. 126—*See* clause IV of the Letters Patent relating to the Office of Governor General, published in Gazette 1984, S334.

Basic Law for Federal Republic of Germany

4

The Federal Republic of Germany Basic Law, 1949

The following is a letter from President Richard von Weizsäcker concerning the Basic Law for the Federal Republic of Germany. It is not part of the Basic Law but is interesting reading:

Foreword by the Federal President

For more than forty years, the Basic Law has determined the development of the polity of the Federal Republic of Germany. In its area of application, it has bestowed on the citizens a life in liberty, democratic self-determination and personal responsibility, protected by law and justice.

This political order is the freest the Germans have enjoyed in their history to date. For decades, the division of Germany prevented the entire German people from living in such freedom.

On 3 October 1990, we accomplished the unity and liberty of Germany in free self-determination. Thus all Germans now live under a constitution which protects the dignity and basic rights of man, regulates public life and facilitates peaceful change. No Constitution, of course, can endow us with the ability to achieve such things. We ourselves must give life to it. We are the ones who must recognize and address new challenges, not least when it comes to forging human links between east and west in a united land.

For the first time in centuries, we Germans are no longer a source of strife on the agenda of Europe. Our unification was not forced on Europe; rather, it was achieved in peaceful agreement. It is part of a common historical development, one which assures nations their liberty and which can overcome the division of our continent. We Germans in particular want to contribute resolutely to this process and have a special obligation to do so. Our unity is dedicated to it. In doing so, we fulfil the mandate of our constitution together.

Richard von Weizsäcker

Basic Law for Federal Republic of Germany

(Promulgated by the Parliamentary Council on 23 May 1949)

(as Amended by the Unification Treaty of 31 August 1990 and

Federal Statute of 23 September 1990)

Preamble

(Amended by Unification Treaty, 31 August 1990 and federal statute of 23 September 1990, Federal Law Gazette II p. 885).

Conscious of their responsibility before God and Men, Animated by the resolve to serve world peace as an equal partner in a united Europe, the German people have adopted, by virtue of their constituent power, this Basic Law.

The Germans in the Länder of Baden-Wuerttemberg, Bavaria, Berlin, Brandenburg, Bremen, Hamburg, Hesse, Lower Saxony, Mecklenburg-Western Pomerania, North-Rhine-Weststphalia, Rhineland-Paltinate, Saarland, Saxony, Saxony-Anhalt, Schleswig-Holstein, and Thuringia have achieved the unity and freedom of Germany in free self-determination. This Basic Law is thus valid for the entire German People.

I. Basic Rights

Article 1

(Protection of human dignity)

(1) The dignity of man is inviolable. To respect and protect it is the duty of all state authority.

(2) The German people therefore acknowledge inviolable and inalienable human rights as the basis of every community, of peace and of justice in the world.

(3) The following basic rights bind the legislature, the executive and the judiciary as directly enforceable law.

Article 2

(Rights of liberty)

(1) Everyone has the right to the free development of his personality insofar as he does not violate the rights of others or offend against the constitutional order or the moral code.

(2) Everyone has the right to life and to inviolability of his person. The freedom of the individual is inviolable. These rights may only be encroached upon pursuant to a law.

Article 3

(Equality before the law)

(1) All persons are equal before the law.

(2) Men and women have equal rights.

(3) No one may be prejudiced or favored because of his sex, his parentage, his race, his language, his homeland and origin, his faith or his religious or political opinions.

Article 4

(Freedom of faith, of conscience and of creed)

(1) Freedom of faith and of conscience, and freedom of creed, religious or ideological, are inviolable.

(2) The undisturbed practice of religion is guaranteed.

(3) No one may be compelled against his conscience to render war service as an armed combatant. Details will be regulated by a Federal law.

Article 5

(Freedom of expression)

(1) Everyone has the right freely to express and to disseminate his opinion by speech, writing and pictures and freely to inform himself from generally accessible sources. Freedom of the press and freedom of reporting by radio and motion pictures are guaranteed. There shall be no censorship.

(2) These rights are limited by the provisions of the general laws, the provisions of law for the protection of youth and by the right to inviolability of personal honor.

(3) Art and science, research and teaching are free. Freedom of teaching does not absolve from loyalty to the Constitution.

Article 6

(Freedom of expression)

(1) Marriage and family enjoy the special protection of the state.

(2) Care and upbringing of children are the natural right of the parents and a duty primarily incumbent on them. The state watches over the performance of this duty.

(3) Separation of children from the family against the will of the persons entitled to bring them up may take place only pursuant to a law, if those so entitled fail in their duty or if the children are otherwise threatened with neglect.

(4) Every mother is entitled to the protection and care of the community.

(5) Illegitimate children shall be provided by legislation with the same opportunities for their physical and spiritual development and their position in society as are enjoyed by legitimate children.

Article 7

(Education)

(1) The entire education system is under the supervision of the state.

(2) The persons entitled to bring up a child have the right to decide whether they shall receive religious instruction.

(3) Religious instruction forms part of the ordinary curriculum in state and municipal schools, excepting secular schools. Without prejudice to the state's right of supervision, religious instruction is given in accordance with the tenets of the religious communities. No teacher may be obliged against his will to give religious instruction.

(4) The right to establish private schools is guaranteed. Private schools as a substitute for state or municipal schools, require the approval of the state and are subject to the laws of the Laender. This approval must be given if private schools are not inferior to the state or municipal schools in their educational aims, their facilities and the professional training of their teaching staff, and if a segregation of the pupils according to the means of the parents is not promoted. This approval must be withheld if the economic and legal position of the teaching staff is not sufficiently assured.

(5) A private elementary school shall be admitted only if the educational authority finds that it serves a special pedagogic interest or if, on the application of persons entitled to bring up children, it is to be established as an interdenominational or denominational or ideological school and a state or municipal elementary school of this type does not exist in the community

(6) Preparatory schools remain abolished.

Article 8

(Freedom of assembly)

(1) All Germans have the right to assemble peacefully and unarmed without prior notification or permission.

(2) With regard to open-air meetings this right may be restricted by or pursuant to a law.

Article 9

(Freedom of association)

(1) All Germans have the right to form associations and societies.

(2) Associations, the objects or activities of which conflict with the criminal laws or which are directed against the constitutional order or the concept of international understanding, are prohibited.

(3) The right to form associations to safeguard and improve working and economic conditions is guaranteed to everyone and to all trades and professions. Agreements which restrict or seek to hinder this right are null and void; measures directed to this end are illegal.

Article 10

(Privacy of letters, posts, and telecommunications) amended 24 June 1968

(1) Privacy of letters, posts, and telecommunications shall be inviolable.

(2) Restrictions may only be ordered pursuant to a statute. Where a restriction serves to protect the free democratic basic order or the existence or security of the Federation, the statute may stipulate that the person affected shall not be informed of such restriction and that recourse to the courts shall be replaced by a review of the case by bodies and auxiliary bodies appointed by Parliament.

Article 11

(Freedom of movement)

(1) All Germans enjoy freedom of movement throughout the Federal territory.

(2) This right may be restricted only by or pursuant to a statute, and only in cases in which an adequate basis of existence is lacking and special burdens would arise to the community, or in which the restriction is necessary to avert an imminent danger to the existence or the free democratic basic order of the Federation or a Land, to combat the danger of epidemics, to deal with natural disasters or particularly grave accidents, to protect young people from neglect or to prevent crime.

Article 12

(Right to choose an occupation, prohibition of forced work) amended 19 March 1956

(1) All Germans have the right freely to choose their trade or profession their place of work and their place of training. The practice of trades and professions may be regulated by law.

(2) No one may be compelled to perform a particular work except within the framework of a traditional compulsory public service which applies generally and equally to all. Anyone who refuses on conscientious grounds to render war service involving

the use of arms may be required to render an alternative service. The duration of this alternative service shall not exceed the duration of military service. Details shall be regulated by a law which shall not prejudice freedom of conscience and shall provide also for the possibility of an alternative service having no connection with any unit of the Armed Forces.

(3) Women shall not be required by law to render service in any unit of the Armed Forces. On no account shall they be employed in any service involving the use of arms.

(4) Forced labor may be imposed only in the event that a person is deprived of his freedom by the sentence of a court.

Article 12a

(Liability to military and other service) added 24 June 1968

(1) Men who have attained the age of 18 years may be required to serve in the Armed Forces, in the Federal Border Guard, or in a civil defense organization.

(2) A person who refuses, on grounds of conscience, to render war service involving the use of arms may be required to render a substitute service. The duration of such substitute service shall not exceed the duration of military service. Details shall be regulated by a statute which shall not interfere with freedom to take a decision based on conscience and shall also provide for the possibility of a substitute service not connected with units of the Armed Forces or of the Federal Border Guard.

(3) Persons liable to military service who are not required to render service pursuant to paragraph (1) or (2) of this Article may, during a state of defense (Verteidigungsfall), be assigned by or pursuant to a statute to an employment involving civilian services for defense purposes, including the protection of the civilian population; it shall, however, not be permissible to assign persons to an employment subject to public law except for the purpose of discharging police functions or such other functions of public administration as can only be discharged by persons employed under public law. Persons may be assigned to an employment – as referred to in the first sentence of this paragraph – with the Armed forces, including the supplying and

servicing of the latter, or with public administrative authorities; assignments to employment connected with supplying and servicing the civilian population shall not be permissible except in order to meet their vital requirements or to guarantee their safety.

(4) Where, during a state of defense, civilian service requirements in the civilian health system or in the stationary military hospital organization cannot be met on a voluntary basis, women between eighteen and fifty-five years of age may be assigned to such services by or pursuant to a statute. They may on no account render service involving the use of arms.

(5) Prior to the existence of a state of defense, assignments, under paragraph 3 of this Article may only be made where the requirements of paragraph 1 of Article 80a are satisfied. It shall be admissible to require persons by or pursuant to a statute to attend training courses in order to prepare them for the performance of such services in accordance with paragraph 3 of this Article as require special knowledge or skills. To this extent, the first sentence of this paragraph shall not apply.

(6) Where, during a state of defense, staffing requirements for the purposes referred to in the second sentence of paragraph 3 of this Article cannot be met on a voluntary basis, the right of a German to quit the pursuit of his occupation or quit his place of work may be restricted by or pursuant to a statute in order to meet these requirements. The first sentence of paragraph 5 of this Article shall apply mutatis mutandis prior to the existence of a state of defense.

Article 13

(Inviolability of the home)

(1) The home is inviolable.

(2) Searches may be ordered only by a judge or, in the event of danger in delay, by other organs as provided by law and may be carried out only in the form prescribed by law.

(3) Otherwise, this inviolability may be encroached upon or restricted only to avert a common danger or a mortal danger to individuals, or, pursuant to a law, to prevent imminent danger

to public security and order, especially to alleviate the housing shortage, to combat the danger of epidemics or to protect endangered juveniles.

Article 14

(Property, right of inheritance, taking of property)

(1) Property and the rights of inheritance are guaranteed. Their content and limits are determined by the laws.

(2) Property imposes duties. Its use should also serve the public weal.

(3) Expropriation is permitted only in the public weal. It may take place only by or pursuant to law which provides for kind and extent of the compensation. The compensation shall be determined upon just consideration of the public interest and of the interests of the persons affected. In case of dispute regarding the amount of compensation, recourse may be had to the ordinary courts.

Article 15

(Socialization)

Land, natural resources and means of production may for the purpose of socialization be transferred into public ownership or other forms of publicly-controlled economy by a law which provides for kind and extent of the compensation. With respect to such compensation Article 14, para 3, sentences 3 and 4, apply mutatis mutandis.

Article 16

(Deprivation of citizenship, extradition, right of asylum)

(1) No one may be deprived of his German citizenship. Loss of citizenship may arise only pursuant to a law, and against the will of the person affected it may arise only if such person does not thereby become stateless.

(2) No German may be extradited to a foreign country. Persons persecuted for political reasons enjoy the right of asylum

Article 17

(Right of petition)

Everyone has the right individually or jointly with others to address written requests or complaints to the competent authorities and to the representative assemblies.

Article 17a

(Restriction of individual basic rights through legislation enacted for defense purposes and concerning substitute service) amended 19 March 1956

(1) Laws concerning military services and alternative service may by provisions applying to members of the Armed Forces and of alternative services during their period of military or alternative service, restrict the basic right freely to express and to disseminate opinions by speech, writing, and pictures (Article 5, paragraph (1) first half-sentence), the basic right of assembly (Article 9), and the right of petition Article 17) insofar as it permits to address requests or complaints jointly with others.

(2) Laws for defense purposes, including the protection of the civilian population may provide for the restriction of the basic rights of freedom of movement (Article 11) and inviolability of the home (Article 13).

Article 18

(Forfeiture of basic rights)

Whoever abuses freedom of opinion, in particular freedom of the press (Article 5, paragraph 1) freedom of teaching (Article 5, paragraph 3), freedom of assembly (Article 8), freedom of association (Article 9), the secrecy of mail posts and telecommunications (Article 10), property (Article 14), or the right of asylum (Article 16, paragraph 2) in order to attack the free democratic basic order, forfeits these basic rights. The forfeiture and its extent are pronounced by the Federal Constitutional Court.

Article 19

(Restriction of Basic Rights)

(1) Insofar as under this Basic Law a basic right may be restricted by or pursuant to a law, the law must apply generally and not solely to an individual case. Furthermore the law must name the basic right, indicating the Article.

(2) In no case may a basic right be infringed upon in its essential content.

(3) The basic rights apply also to corporations established under German Public law to the extent that the nature of such rights permits.

(4) Should any person's right be violated by public authority, recourse to the court shall be open to him. If no other court has jurisdiction, recourse shall be to the ordinary courts.

II. THE FEDERATION AND THE LÄNDER

Article 20

(Basic principles of state order, right to resist)

(1) The Federal Republic of Germany is a democratic and social Federal state.

(2) All state authority emanates from the people. It is exercised by the people by means of elections and voting and by separate legislative, executive and judicial organs.

(3) Legislation is subject to the constitutional order; the executive and the judiciary are bound by the law.

(4) All Germans shall have the right to resist any person seeking to abolish this constitutional order, should no other remedy be possible. (inserted 24 June 1968)

Article 21

(Political Parties) amended 21 December 1983

(1) The political parties participate in the forming of the political will of the people. They may be freely established. Their internal organization shall conform to democratic principles. They shall publicly account for the sources of their funds and for their assets.

(2) Parties which, by reason of their aims or the behavior of their adherents, seek or impair or destroy the free democratic basic order or to endanger the existence of the Federal Republic of Germany shall be unconstitutional. The Federal Constitutional Court decides on the question of unconstitutionality.

(3) Details will be regulated by Federal legislation.

Article 22

The Federal flag is black-red-gold.

Article 23

(Repealed 31 August 1990, Unification Treaty and Federal Statute of 23 September 1990)

Article 24

(Entry into a collective security system)

(1) The Federation may, by legislation, transfer sovereign powers to international institutions.

(2) For the maintenance of peace, the Federation may join a system of mutual collective security; in doing so it will consent to such limitations upon its sovereign powers as will bring about and secure a peaceful and lasting order in Europe and among the nations of the world.

(3) For the settlement of disputes between nations, the Federation will accede to agreements concerning a general, comprehensive and obligatory system of international arbitration.

Article 25

(Public international law and federal law)

The general rules of public international law form part of the Federal law. They take precedence over the laws and directly create rights and duties for the inhabitants of the Federal territory.

Article 26

(Ban on preparing a war of aggression)

(1) Activities tending and undertaken with the intent to disturb peaceful relations between nations, especially to prepare

for aggressive war, are unconstitutional. They shall be made a punishable offense.

(2) Weapons designed for warfare may be manufactured, transported or marketed only with the permission of the Federal Government. Details will be regulated by a Federal Law.

Article 27

(Merchant fleet)

All German merchant vessels form one merchant fleet.

Article 28

(Federal guarantee concerning Länder Constitution, guarantee of self-government for local authorities)

(1) The constitutional order in the Länder must conform to the principles of republican, democratic, and social government based on the rule of law, within the meaning of this Basic Law. In each of the Länder counties and communities, the people must be represented by a body chosen in universal, direct, free, equal and secret elections. In the communities the assembly of the community may take the place of an elected body.

(2) The communities must be guaranteed the right to regulate on their own responsibility all the affairs of the local community within the limits set by law. The associations of communities also have the right of self-government in accordance with the law within the limits of the functions given them by law.

(3) The Federation guarantees that the constitutional order of the Länder conforms to the basic rights and to the provisions of paragraphs (1) and (2).

Article 29

(New delimitation of Länder boundaries) amended 19 August 1969 and 23 August 1976

(1) A new delimitation of federal territory may be made to ensure that the Länder by the size and capacity are able effectively to fulfil the functions incumbent upon them. Due regard shall be given to regional, historical and cultural ties, economic expediency, and the requirements of regional policy and planning.

(2) Measures for a new delimitation of federal territory shall be effected by federal statutes which shall require confirmation by referendum. The Länder thus affected shall be consulted.

(3) A referendum shall be held in the Länder from whose territories or partial territories a new Land or a Land which redefined boundaries is to be formed (affecting Länder). The referendum shall be held on the question whether the affected Länder are to remain within their existing boundaries or whether the new Land or Land with redefined boundaries should be formed. The referendum shall be deemed to be in favor of the formation of a new Land or of a Land with redefined boundaries where approval is given to the change by a majority in all the territories or partial territories of an affected Land whose assignment to a Land is to be changed in the same sense. The referendum shall be deemed not to be in favor of change; such rejection shall, however, be of no consequence where in one part of the territory whose assignment of the affected Land is to be changed a majority of two-thirds approve of the change, unless in the entire territory of the affected Land a majority of two-thirds reject the change.

(4) Where in a clearly definable area of interconnected population and economic settlement, the parts of which lie in several Länder and which has a population of at least one million, one tenth of those of its population entitled to vote in Bundestag elections petition by popular initiative for the assignment of that area to one Land, provision shall be made within two years in a federal statute determining whether the delimitation of the affected Länder shall be changed pursuant to paragraph 2 of this Article or determining that a plebiscite shall be held in the affected Länder.

(5) The plebiscite shall establish whether approval is given to a change of Länder delimitation to be proposed in the statute. The statute may put forward different proposals, not exceeding two in number, for the plebiscite. Where approval is given by a majority to a proposed change of Länder delimitation, provision shall be made within two years in a federal statute determining

whether the delimitation of the Länder concerned shall be changed pursuant to paragraph 2 of this Article. Where approval is given, in accordance with the third and fourth sentences of paragraph 3 of this Article, to a proposal put forward for the plebiscite, a federal statute providing for the formation of the proposed Land shall be enacted within two years of the plebiscite and shall no longer require confirmation by referendum.

(6) A majority in a referendum or in a plebiscite shall consist of a majority of the votes cast, provided that they amount to at least one quarter of the population entitled to vote in Bundestag elections. Other detailed provisions concerning referendums, popular petitions and plebiscites (Volksentscheide, Volksbefragungen) shall be made in a federal statute; such statute may also provide that popular petitions may not be repeated within a period of five years.

(7) Other changes concerning the territory of the Länder may be effected by state agreements between the Länder concerned or by a federal statute with the approval of the Bundesrat where the territory which is to be the subject of a new delimitation does not have more than 10,000 inhabitants. Detailed provision shall be made in a federal statute requiring the approval of the Bundesrat and the majority of the members of the Bundestag. It shall make provision for the affected communes and districts to be heard.

Article 30

(Distribution of competence between the Federation and the Länder)

The exercise of governmental powers and the discharge of governmental functions is incumbent on the Länder insofar as this Basic Law does not otherwise prescribe or permit.

Article 31

Federal law overrides Land law.

Article 32

(Foreign Relations)

(1) The conduct of relations with foreign states is the concern of the Federation.

(2) Before the conclusion of a treaty affecting the special interests of a Land, this Land must be consulted in sufficient time.

(3) Insofar as the Länder have power to legislate, they may, with the consent of the Federal Government, conclude treaties with foreign states.

Article 33

(Equal political status of all Germans, professional, civil service)

(1) Every German has in every Land the same civil rights and duties.

(2) Every German is equally eligible for any public office according to his aptitude, qualifications and professional achievements.

(3) Enjoyment of civil and civic rights, eligibility for public office, and rights acquired in the public service are independent of religious denomination. No one may suffer disadvantage by reason of his adherence or non-adherence to a denomination or ideology.

(4) The exercise of state authority as a permanent function shall as a rule be entrusted to members of the public service whose status, service and loyalty are governed by public law.

(5) The law of the public service shall be regulated with due regard to the traditional principles of the permanent civil service.

Article 34

(Liability in the event of a breach of official duty)

If any person, in the exercise of a public office entrusted to him, violates his official obligations to a third party, liability rests in principle on the state or the public authority which employs him. In the case of wilful intent or gross carelessness the right of recourse is reserved. With respect to the claim for compensation or the right of recourse, the jurisdiction of the ordinary courts must not be excluded.

Article 35

(Legal and administrative assistance, assistance during disasters)

(1) All Federal and Land authorities render each other mutual legal and administrative assistance.

(2) In order to maintain or to restore public security or order, a Land may, in cases of particular importance, call upon forces and facilities of the Federal Border Guard to assist its police where without this assistance the police could not, or only with considerable difficulty, fulfil a task. In order to deal with a natural disaster or as especially grave accident, a Land may request the assistance of the police forces of other Länder or of forces and facilities of other administrative authorities or of the Federal Border Guard or the Armed Forces. (amended 28 July 1972)

(3) Where the natural disaster or the accident endangers a region larger than a Land, the Federal Government may, insofar as this is necessary to effectively deal with such danger, instruct the Land governments to place their police forces at the disposal of other Länder, and may use units of the Federal Border Guard or the Armed Forces to support the first sentence of this paragraph shall be revoked at any time on demand of the Bundesrat, and otherwise immediately upon removal of the danger.

Article 36

(Personnel of the federal authorities) amended 19 March 1956

(1) Civil servants employed in the highest Federal authorities shall be drawn from all Länder in appropriate proportion. Persons employed in other Federal authorities should, as a rule be drawn from the Land in which they serve.

(2) Military laws shall take into account the division of the Federal Länder and the latter's particular ethnic conditions.

Article 37

(Federal coercion)

(1) If a Land fails to comply with its obligations of a Federal character imposed by the Basic Law or another Federal law, the Federal Government may, with the consent of the Bundesrat, take necessary measures to enforce such compliance by the Land by way of Federal compulsion.

(2) To carry out such Federal compulsion the Federal Government or its commissioner has the right to give instructions to all Länder and their authorities.

III. THE LOWER HOUSE OF PARLIAMENT (BUNDESTAG)

Article 38

(Elections)

(1) The deputies to the German Bundestag are elected in universal, direct, free, equal and secret elections. They are representatives of the whole people, are not bound by orders and instructions and are subject only to their conscience.

(2) Anyone who has attained the age of twenty-one is entitled to vote; anyone who has attained the age of twenty-five is eligible for election.

(3) Details will be regulated by a Federal law.

Article 39

(Assembly and legislative term) amended 23 August 1976

(1) The Bundestag is elected for a four-year term. Its legislative term ends with the assembly of a new Bundestag. The new election shall be held forty-five months at the earliest, and forty-seven months at the latest after the beginning of the legislative term. Where the Bundestag is dissolved, the new election shall be held within sixty days.

(2) The Bundestag shall assemble, at the latest, on the thirtieth day after the election.

(3) The Bundestag determines the termination and resumption of its meetings. The President of the Bundestag may convene it at an earlier date. He must do so if one-third of the

members, the Federal President or the Federal Chancellor so demand.

Article 40

(President, rules of procedure)

(1) The Bundestag elects its President, Vice-Presidents and Secretaries. It draws up its rules of procedure.

(2) The President exercises the proprietary and police powers in the Bundestag building. No search or seizure may take place in the premises of the Bundestag without his permission.

Article 41

(Scrutiny of elections)

(1) The scrutiny of elections is the responsibility of the Bundestag. It also decides whether a deputy has lost his seat in the Bundestag.

(2) Against the decision of the Bundestag an appeal can be made to the Federal Constitutional Court.

(3) Details will be regulated by a Federal law.

Article 42

(Proceedings, voting)

(1) The meetings of the Bundestag are public. Upon a motion of one-tenth of its members, or upon a motion of the Federal Government, the public may, by a two-thirds majority vote, be excluded. The decision on the motion is taken at a meeting not open to the public.

(2) Decisions of the Bundestag require a majority of votes cast unless this Basic Law provides otherwise. For the elections to be made by the Bundestag the rules of procedure may provide exemptions.

(3) True and accurate reports of the public meetings of the Bundestag and of its committees shall not give rise to any liability.

Article 43

(Presence of members of the Federal Government and of the Bundesrat)

(1) The Bundestag and its committees may demand the presence of any member of the Federal Government.

(2) The members of the Bundesrat and of the Federal Government as well as persons commissioned by them have access to all meetings of the Bundestag and its committees. They must be heard at any time.

Article 44

(Committees of investigation)

(1) The Bundestag has the right, and upon the motion of one-fourth of its members the duty, to set up a committee of investigation which shall take the requisite evidence at public hearings. The public may be excluded.

(2) The rules of criminal procedure shall apply mutatis mutandis to the taking of evidence. The secrecy of the mail, posts and telecommunications remains unaffected.

(3) Courts and administrative authorities are bound to render legal and administrative assistance.

(4) The decisions of the committees of investigation are not subject to judicial consideration. The courts are free to evaluate and judge the facts on which the investigation is based

Article 45

(Repealed, 23 August 1976)

Article 45a

(Committees on Foreign Affairs and Defense) added 19 March 1956

(1) The Bundestag shall appoint a Committee on Foreign Affairs and a Committee on Defense. (**2nd sentence deleted, 23 Aug 1976)

(2) The Committee on Defense shall also have the rights of a committee on investigation. Upon the motion of one-fourth of its members it shall have the duty to make a specific matter the subject of investigation.

(3) Article 44 paragraph (1) shall not be applied in matters of defense.

Article 45b

(Defense Commissioner of the Bundestag) inserted 17 July 1975

A Defense Commissioner of the Bundestag shall be appointed to safeguard the basic rights and to assist the Bundestag in exercising parliamentary control. Details shall be regulated by a federal statute.

Article 45c

(Petitions Committee) inserted 17 July 1975

(1) The Bundestag shall appoint a Petitions Committee to deal with requests and complaints addressed to the Bundestag pursuant to Article 17.

(2) The powers of the Committee to consider complaints shall be regulated by federal statute.

Article 46

(Indemnity and immunity of deputies)

(1) A deputy may not at any time be prosecuted in the courts or subjected to disciplinary action or otherwise called to account outside the Bundestag on account of a vote cast or an utterance made by him in the Bundestag or one of its committees. This does not apply to defamatory insults.

(2) A deputy may be called to account or arrested for a punishable offense only by permission of the Bundestag, unless he is apprehended in the commission of the offense or during the course of the following day.

(3) The permission of the Bundestag is also necessary for any other restriction of the personal freedom of a duty or for the initiation of proceedings against a deputy under Article 18.

(4) Any criminal proceedings and any proceedings under Article 18 against a deputy, any detention and any other restriction of his personal freedom shall be suspended upon the request of the Bundestag.

Article 47

(Right of deputies to refuse to give evidence)

Deputies may refuse to give evidence concerning persons who have confided facts to them in their capacity as deputies or to whom they have confided facts in such capacity, as well a concerning these facts themselves. To the extent that this right to refuse to give evidence exists, no seizure of documents may take place.

Article 48

(Entitlements of deputies)

(1) Any person seeking election to the Bundestag is entitled to the leave necessary for his election campaign.

(2) No one may be prevented from accepting and exercising the office of deputy. He may not be dismissed from employment, with or without notice, on this ground.

(3) Deputies are entitled to compensation adequate to ensure their independence. They are entitled to the free use of all state owned transport. Details will be regulated by a Federal Law.

Article 49

(Repealed, 23 August 1976)

IV. THE UPPER HOUSE OF PARLIAMENT (BUNDESRAT)

Article 50

(Functions)

The Länder participate through the Bundesrat in the legislation and administration of the Federation.

Article 51

(Composition)

(1) The Bundesrat consists of members of the Länder governments which appoint and recall them. Other members of such governments may act as substitutes.

(2) Each Land has at least three votes; Länder with more than two million inhabitants have four, Länder with more than

seven million inhabitants, six votes (amended Unification Treaty of 31 August 1990).

(3) Each Land may delegate as many members as it has votes. The votes of each Land may be cast only as a block vote and only by members present or their substitutes.

Article 52

(President, rules of procedure)

(1) The Bundesrat elects its President for one year.

(2) The President convenes the Bundesrat. He must convene it if the members for at least two Länder or the Federal Government so demand.

(3) The Bundesrat takes its decisions by at least a majority of its votes It draws up its rules of procedure. Its meetings are public. The public may be excluded.

(4) Other members of, or persons Commissioned by, Länder governments may serve on the committees of the Bundesrat.

Article 53

(Presence of members of the Federal Government)

The members of the Federal Government have the right, and on demand the duty to take part in the debates of the Bundesrat and of its Committees. They must be heard at any time. The Bundesrat must be currently kept informed by the Federal Government of the conduct of affairs.

IVa. THE JOINT COMMITTEE

(Inserted by Federal Statute of 24 June 1968)

Article 53a

(Composition, rules of procedure, right to information)

(1) Two-thirds of the members of the Joint Committee shall be deputies of the Bundestag and one-third shall be members of the Bundesrat. The Bundestag shall delegate its deputies in proportion to the relative strength of its parliamentary groups; deputies shall not be members of the Federal Government. Each

Land shall be represented by a Bundesrat member of its choice; these members shall not be bound by instructions. The establishment of the Joint Committee and its procedures shall be regulated by rules of procedure to be adopted by the Bundestag and requiring the consent of the Bundesrat.

(2) The Federal Government shall inform the Joint Committee about its plans in respect of a state of Defense. The rights of the Bundestag and its committees under paragraph 1 of Article 43 shall remain unaffected by the provision of this paragraph.

V. THE FEDERAL PRESIDENT

Article 54

(Election)

(1) The Federal President is elected, without debate, by the Federal Convention. Every German is eligible who is entitled to vote for the Bundestag and who has attained the age of forty.

(2) The term of office of the Federal President is five years. Re-election for a consecutive term is permitted only once.

(3) The Federal Convention consists of the members of the Bundestag and an equal number of members elected by the representative assemblies of the Länder according to the rules of proportional representation.

(4) The Federal Convention meets not later than thirty days before the expiration of the term of office of the Federal President or in the case of premature termination, not later than thirty days after this date. It is convened by the President of the Bundestag.

(5) After expiration of the legislative term the period specified in paragraph 4, first sentence, begins with the first meeting of the Bundestag.

(6) The person receiving the votes of the majority of the members of the Federal Convention is elected. If such majority is not obtained by any candidate in two ballots, the candidate who receives the largest number of votes in a further ballot is elected.

(7) Details will be regulated by a Federal law.

Article 55

(Incompatibilities)

(1) The Federal President may not be a member of the Government or of a legislative body of the Federation or of a Land.

(2) The Federal President may not hold any other salaried office, nor engage in a trade, nor practice a profession, nor belong to the management or ends in any event on the first meeting of a new Bundestag, the tenure of office of a Federal Minister ends also on any other termination of the tenure of office of the Federal Chancellor.

(3) At the request of the Federal President, the Federal Chancellor, or at the request of the Federal Chancellor or of the Federal President, a Federal Minister is bound to continue to transact the business of his office until the appointment of a successor.

Article 56

(Oath of office)

On assuming his office the Federal President takes the following oath before the assembled members of the Bundestag and the Bundesrat:

"I swear that I will dedicate my efforts to the well-being of the German people, enhance its benefits, ward harm from it, uphold and defend the Basic Law and the laws of the Federation, fulfil my duties conscientiously, and do justice to all. So help me God." The oath may also be taken without religious affirmation.

Article 57

(Representation)

If the Federal President is prevented from exercising his powers or if his office falls prematurely vacant his powers will be exercised by the President of the Bundesrat.

Article 58

(Countersignature)

Orders and decrees of the Federal President require for their validity the countersignature of the Federal Chancellor or the appropriate Federal minister. This does not apply to the appointment and dismissal of the Federal Chancellor, the dissolution of the Bundestag under Article 63 and the request under Article 69, paragraph 3.

Article 59

(Authority to represent the Federation in its international relations)

(1) The Federal President represents the Federation in its international relations. He concludes treaties with foreign states on behalf of the Federation. He accredits and receives envoys.

(2) Treaties which regulate the political relations of the Federation or relate to matters of Federal legislation require the consent or participation, in the form of a Federal law, of the bodies competent in any specific case for such Federal legislation. For administrative agreements the provisions concerning the Federal administration apply mutatis mutandis.

Article 59a

(Repealed)

Article 60 (Appointment and dismissal of federal judges, federal civil servants and soldiers; right of pardon) – As amended 19 March 1956.

(1) The Federal President appoints and dismisses the Federal judges the Federal civil servants, the officers and non-commissioned officers, unless otherwise provided for by law.

(2) He exercises the power of pardon on behalf of the Federation in individual cases.

(3) He may delegate these powers to other authorities.

(4) Paragraphs 2 to 4 of Article 46 apply mutatis mutandis to the Federal President.

Article 61

(Impeachment before the Federal Constitutional Court)

(1) The Bundestag or the Bundesrat may impeach the Federal President before the Federal Constitutional Court for wilful violation of the Basic Law or any other Federal Law. The motion for impeachment must be brought forward by at least one-fourth of the members of the Bundestag or one-fourth of the votes of the Bundesrat. The decision to impeach requires a majority of two-thirds of the members of the Bundestag or of two-thirds of the votes of the Bundesrat. The prosecution is conducted by a person commission by the impeaching body.

(2) If the Federal Constitutional Court finds the Federal President guilty of a wilful violation of the Basic Law or of another Federal Law it may declare him to have forfeited his office. After impeachment, it may issue an interim order preventing the Federal President from exercising the powers of his office.

VI. THE FEDERAL GOVERNMENT

Article 62

The Federal Government consists of the Federal Chancellor and the Federal Ministers.

Article 63

(Election and appointment of the Federal Chancellor)

(1) The Federal Chancellor is elected, without debate, by the Bundestag on the proposal of the Federal President.

(2) The person obtaining the votes of the majority of the members of the Bundestag is elected. The persons elected must be appointed by the Federal President.

(3) If the person proposed is not elected, the Bundestag may elect within fourteen days of the ballot a Federal Chancellor by more than one-half of its members.

(4) If there is no election within this period, a new ballot shall take place without delay in which the person obtaining the largest number of votes is elected. If the person elected obtained the votes of the majority of the members of the Bundestag the

Federal President must appoint him within seven days of the election. If the person elected did not receive this majority, the Federal President must within seven days either appoint him or dissolve the Bundestag.

Article 64

(Appointment of Federal Ministers)

(1) The Federal Ministers are appointed and dismissed by the Federal President upon the proposal of the Federal Chancellor.

(2) The Federal Chancellor and the Federal Ministers, on assuming office, take before the Bundestag the oath provided in Article 56.

Article 65

(Powers exercised in the Federal Government)

The Federal Chancellor determines and is responsible for general policy. Within the limits of this general policy, each Federal Minister conducts the business of his department autonomously and on his own responsibility. The Federal Government decides on differences of opinion between the Federal Ministers. The Federal Chancellor conducts the business of the Federal Government in accordance with rules of procedure adopted by it and approved by the Federal President.

Article 65a

(Power of command over the Armed Forces) amended 24 June 1968

Power of command in respect of the Armed Forces shall be vested in the Federal Minister of Defense.

Article 66

(Incompatibilities)

The Federal Chancellor and the Federal Ministers may not hold any other salaried office, nor engage in a trade, nor practice a profession, nor belong to the management or, without the consent of the Bundestag, to the board of directors of an enterprise carried on for profit.

Article 67

(Constructive vote of no confidence)

(1) The Bundestag can express its lack of confidence in the Federal Chancellor only by electing a successor by the majority of its members and by requesting the Federal President to dismiss the Federal Chancellor. The Federal President must comply with the request and appoint the person elected.

(2) Forty-eight hours must elapse between the motion and the election.

Article 68

(Vote of confidence, dissolution of the Bundestag)

(1) If a motion of the Federal Chancellor for a vote of no confidence is not assented to by the majority of the members of the Bundestag, the Federal President may, upon the proposal of the Federal Chancellor, dissolve the Bundestag within twenty-one days. The right to dissolve lapses as soon as the Bundestag by the majority of its members elects another Federal Chancellor.

(2) Forty-eight hours must elapse between the motion and the vote thereon.

Article 69

(Deputy Federal Chancellor, tenure of office of members of the Federal Government)

(1) The Federal Chancellor appoints a Federal Minister as his deputy.

(2) The tenure of office of the Federal Chancellor or a Federal Minister.

VII. LEGISLATIVE POWERS OF THE FEDERATION

Article 70

(Legislation of the Federation and the Länder)

(1) The Länder have the power to legislate insofar as this Basic Law does not confer legislative powers on the Federation.

(2) The division of competence between the Federation and the Länder is determined by the provisions of this Basic Law concerning exclusive and concurrent legislative powers.

Article 71

(Exclusive legislative power of the Federation, concept)

On matters within the exclusive legislative powers of the Federation the Länder have authority to legislate only if, and to the extent that, a Federal law explicitly so authorizes them.

Article 72

(Concurrent legislative power of the Federation, concept)

(1) On matters within the concurrent legislative powers the Länder have authority to legislate as long as, and to the extent that the Federation does not use its legislative power.

(2) The Federation has the right to legislate on these matters to the extent that a need for a Federal rule exists because (1) a matter cannot be effectively dealt with by the legislation of individual Länder, or (2) dealing with a matter by Land law might prejudice the interests of other Länder or of the entire community, or (3) the maintenance of legal or economic unity, especially the maintenance of uniformity of living conditions beyond the territory of a Land necessitates it.

Article 73

(Exclusive legislative power, catalogue) as amended 24 June 1968

The Federation has the exclusive power to legislate on:

1. foreign affairs and defense, including the protection of the civilian population;

2. citizenship in the Federation;

3. freedom of movement, passports, immigration and emigration, and extradition;

4. currency, money and coinage, weights and measures, as well as computation of time;

5. the unity of the customs and commercial territory, commercial and navigation agreements, the freedom of movement of goods, and the exchange of goods and payment with foreign countries, including customs and frontier protection;

6. Federal railroads and air traffic;

7. postal and telecommunication services;

8. the legal status of persons employed by the Federation and by Federal bodies-corporate under public law;

9. industrial property rights, copyrights and publication rights;

10. cooperation of the Federation and the Länder in matters of

(a) criminal police,

(b) protection of the free democratic basic order, of the existence and the security of the Federation or a Land (protection of the constitution) and

(c) protection against activities in the federal territory which, through the use of force or actions in preparation for the use of force, endanger the foreign interests of the Federal Republic of Germany, as well as the establishment of a Federal Criminal Police Office and the international control of crime.

11. statistics for Federal purposes.

Article 74

(Concurrent legislation, catalogue)

Concurrent legislative powers extend to the following matters:

1. civil law, criminal law and execution of sentences, the system of judicature, the procedure of the courts, the legal profession, notaries and legal advice;

2. registration of births, deaths, and marriages;

3. the law of association and assembly;

4. the law relating to residence and establishment of aliens;

4a. the law relating to weapons and explosives (inserted 28 July 1972 and amended 23 August 1972);

5. the protection of German cultural treasures against removal abroad;

6. the affairs of refugees and expellees;

7. public welfare;

8. citizenship in the Länder;

9. war damage and reparations;

10. benefits to war-disabled persons and to dependents of those killed in the war, assistance to former prisoners of war, and care of war graves;

10a. war graves of soldiers, graves of other victims of war and of the victims of despotism (inserted 16 June 1965);

11. the law relating to economic matters (mining, industry, supply of power. crafts. trades, commerce, banking and stock exchanges, private insurance);

11a. the production and utilization of nuclear energy for peaceful purposes, the construction and operation of installations serving these purposes, protection against dangers arising from the release of nuclear energy or from ionizing rays, and removal of radioactive material;

12. Labor law, including the legal organization of enterprises; protection of workers, employment exchanges and agencies, as well as social insurance, including unemployment insurance;

13. the regulation of educational and training grants and the promotion of scientific research (as amended 12 May 1969);

14. the law regarding expropriation, to the extent that matters enumerated in Articles 73 and 74 are concerned;

15. transfer of land, natural resources and means of production into public ownership or other forms of publicly controlled economy;

16. prevention of the abuse of economic power;

17. promotion of agricultural and forest production, safeguarding of the supply of food, the import and export of agricultural and forest products, deep sea and coastal fishing, and preservation of the coasts;

18. dealings in real estate, land law and matters concerning agricultural leases, housing, settlements and homesteads;

19. measures against epidemic and infectious diseases of humans and animals, admission to medical and other professions and practices in the field of healing, traffic in drugs, medicines, narcotics, and poisons;

19a. the economic viability of hospitals and the regulation of hospitalization fees (inserted 12 May 1969);

20. protection with regard to traffic in food and stimulants as well as in necessities of life, in fodder, in agricultural and forest seeds and seedlings, and protection of trees and plants against diseases and pests;

21. ocean and coastal shipping as well as aids to navigation, inland shipping, meteorological services, sea waterways and inland waterways used for general traffic;

22. road traffic, motor transport, construction and maintenance of long distance highways, as well as the collection of charges for the use of public highways by vehicles and the allocation of revenue therefrom (amended 12 May 1969);

23. railroads other than Federal railroads, except mountain railroads;

24. waste disposal, air pollution control and noise abatement. (amended 12 May 1969).

Article 74a+

(Concurrent legislative power of the Federation, remuneration and pensions of members of public service)

(1) Concurrent legislative power shall further extend to the remuneration and pensions of members of the public service whose service and loyalty are governed by public law, insofar as the Federation does not have exclusive power to legislate pursuant to item 8 of Article 73.

(2) Federal statutes enacted pursuant to paragraph (1) of this Article shall require the consent of the Bundesrat.

(3) Federal statutes enacted pursuant to item 8 of Article 73 shall likewise require the consent of the Bundesrat, insofar as for the structure and assessment of remuneration and pensions, including the rating of posts, provision is made for criteria or minimum or maximum rates other than those provided for in federal statutes enacted pursuant to paragraph (1) of this Article.

(4) Paragraphs (1) and (2) of this Article shall apply mutatis mutandis to the remuneration and pensions of judges in the Länder. Paragraph (3) of this Article shall apply mutatis mutandis to statutes enacted pursuant to paragraph (1) of Article 98.

Article 75

(Power of the Federation to pass framework legislation catalogue) amended 18 March 1969

Subject to the conditions of Article 72 the Federation has the right to enact general rules concerning:

1. the legal status of persons in the public service of the Länder, communities other corporate bodies of public law, insofar as Article 74a does not provide otherwise;

1a. the general principles governing higher education (inserted 12 May 1969);

2. the general rules of law concerning the status of the press and motion pictures;

3. hunting, protection of nature and care of the countryside;

4. land distribution, regional planning and water conservation;

5. matters relating to registration and identity cards.

Article 76

(Bills) amended 15 November 1968 and 12 May 1969

(1) Bills are introduced in the Bundestag by the Federal Government, by members of the Bundestag or by the Bundesrat.

(2) Bills of the Federal Government shall be submitted first to the Bundesrat. The Bundesrat is entitled to state its position on these bills within six weeks.

(3) Bills of the Bundesrat shall be submitted to the Bundestag by the Federal Government within 3 months. In doing so the Federal Government shall state its own views.

Article 77

(Legislative procedure) amended 15 Nov 1968

(1) Federal laws are adopted by the Bundestag. Upon their adoption, they shall, without delay, be transmitted to the Bundesrat by the President of the Bundestag.

(2) The Bundesrat may, within three weeks of the receipt of the adopted bill, demand that a committee for joint consideration of bills, composed of members of the Bundestag and the Bundesrat, be convened. The composition and the procedure of this committee are regulated by rules of procedure adopted by the Bundestag and requiring the consent of the Bundesrat. The members of the Bundesrat on this committee are not bound by instructions. Where the consent of the Bundesrat is required for a law, the demand for convening this committee may also be made by the Bundestag or the Federal Government. Should the committee propose any amendment to the adopted bill, the Bundestag must again vote on the bill.

(3) Insofar as the consent of the Bundesrat is not required for a law, the Bundesrat may, if the proceedings under paragraph 2 are completed, enter a protest within two weeks against a law adopted by the Bundestag. This period begins, in the case of paragraph 2, last sentence, on the receipt of the bill as re-adopted by the Bundestag, in all other cases on the receipt of a communication from the chairman of the committee provided for in paragraph (2) of this Article to the effect that the committee's proceedings have been concluded.

(4) If the protest is adopted by a majority of the votes of the Bundesrat, it can be rejected by a decision of the majority of the members of the Bundestag. If the Bundesrat adopted the protest by a majority of at least two-thirds of its votes, the rejection by the Bundestag requires a majority of two-thirds, including at least the majority of the members of the Bundestag.

Article 78

(Passage of federal statutes)

A bill adopted by the Bundestag is deemed to have been passed if the Bundesrat consents to it, does not make a demand pursuant to Article 77, paragraph 2, does not enter a protest within the time limited by Article 77 paragraph 3, or withdraws such protest, or if the protest is overridden by the Bundestag.

Article 79

(Amendment of the Basic Law) as amended 27 March 1954

(1) The Basic Law can be amended only by a law which expressly amends or supplements the text thereof. With respect to international treaties the subject of which is a peace settlement, the preparation of a peace settlement or the abolition of an occupation regime, or which are designed to serve the defense of the Federal Republic, it shall be sufficient, for the purpose of a clarifying interpretation to the effect that the provisions of the Basic Law are not contrary to the conclusion and entry into force of such treaties, to effect a supplementation of the Basic Law confined to this clarifying interpretation.

(2) Such a law requires the affirmative vote of two-thirds of the members of the Bundestag and two-thirds of the votes of the Bundesrat.

(3) An amendment of this Basic Law affecting the division of the Federation into Länder, the participation in principle of the Länder in legislation, or the basic principles laid down in Articles 1 and 20, is inadmissible.

Article 80

(Issue of ordinances)

(1) The Federal Government, a Federal Minister or the Land Governments may be authorized by a law to issue ordinances having the force of law. The content, purpose and scope of the powers conferred must be set forth in the law. The legal basis must be stated in the ordinance. If a law provides that a power may be further delegated, an ordinance having the force of law is necessary in order to delegate the power.

(2) The consent of the Bundesrat is required unless otherwise provided by Federal legislation, for ordinances having the force of law issued by the Federal Government or a Federal Minister concerning basic rules for the use of facilities of the Federal

railroads and of postal and telecommunication services, or charges therefore, or concerning the construction and operation of railroads, as well as for ordinances having the force of law issued on the basis of Federal laws that require the consent of the Bundesrat or that are executed by the Länder as agents of the Federation or as masters of their own concern.

Article 80a*

(Application of legal provisions in a state of tension)

(1) Where this Basic Law or a federal statute on Defense, including the protection of the civilian population, stipulates that legal provisions may only be applied in accordance with this Article, their application shall, except in a state of Defense, be admissible only after the Bundestag has determined that a state of tension (Spannungsfall) exists or where it has specifically approved such application. In respect of the cases mentioned in the first sentence of paragraph (5) and the second sentence of paragraph (6) of Article 12a, such determination of a state of tension and such specific approval shall require a two-thirds majority of the votes cast.

(2) Any measures taken by virtue of legal provisions enacted under paragraph (1) of this Article shall be revoked whenever the Bundestag so demands.

(3) In derogation of paragraph (1) of this Article, the application of such legal provisions shall also be admissible by virtue of and in accordance with a decision taken with the consent of the Federal Government by an international body within the framework of a treaty of alliance. Any measures taken pursuant to this paragraph shall be revoked whenever the Bundestag so demands with the majority of its members.

Article 81

(State of legislative emergency)

(1) Should in the circumstances of Article 68 the Bundestag not be dissolved, the Federal President may, at the request of the Federal Government and with the consent of the Bundesrat,

* Inserted by federal statute of 24 June 1968 (Federal Law Gazette I p. 711).

declare a state of legislative emergency with respect to a bill, if the Bundestag rejects the bill although the Federal Government has declared it to be urgent. The same applies if a bill has been rejected although the Federal Chancellor had combined with it the motion under Article 68.

(2) If, after a state of legislative emergency has been declared, the Bundestag again rejects the bill or adopts it in a version declared to be unacceptable to the Federal Government the bill is deemed to have been passed insofar as the Bundesrat consents to it. The same applies if the bill is not adopted by the Bundestag within four weeks of its reintroduction.

(3) During the term of office of a Federal Chancellor, any other bill rejected by the Bundestag may be passed in accordance with paragraphs 1 and 2 within a period of six months after the first declaration of a state of legislative emergency. After expiration of this period, a further declaration of a state of legislative emergency is inadmissible during the term of office of the same Federal Chancellor.

(4) The Basic Law may not be amended nor be repealed nor suspended in whole or in part by a law passed pursuant to paragraph 2.

Article 82

(Promulgation and effective date of legal provisions)

(1) Laws passed in accordance with the provisions of this Basic Law will, after countersignature, be signed by the Federal President and promulgated in the Federal Gazette. Ordinances having the force of law will be signed by the agency which issues them, and unless otherwise provided by law, will be promulgated in the Federal Gazette.

(2) Every law and every ordinance having the force of law should specify its effective date. In the absence of such a provision, it becomes effective on the fourteenth day after the end of the day on which the Federal Gazette was published.

VIII. THE EXECUTION OF FEDERAL LAWS AND THE FEDERAL ADMINISTRATION

Article 83

(Distribution of competence between the Federation and the Länder)

The Länder execute Federal Laws as matters of their own concern insofar as this Basic Law does not otherwise provide or permit.

Article 84

(Land execution and Federal Government supervision)

(1) If the Länder execute Federal Laws as matters of their own concern, they provide for the establishment of authorities and the regulation of administrative procedures insofar as Federal Laws consented to by the Bundesrat do not otherwise provide.

(2) The Federal Government may, with the consent of the Bundesrat, issue general administrative rules.

(3) The Federal Government exercises supervision to ensure that the Länder execute Federal Laws in accordance with applicable law. For this purpose the Federal Government may send commissioners to the highest Land authorities and, with their consent or, if this consent is refused, with the consent of the Bundesrat, also to subordinate authorities.

(4) Should any shortcomings which the Federal Government has found to exist in the execution of Federal Laws in the Länder not be corrected, the Bundesrat decides, on the application of the Federal Government or the Land whether the Land has acted unlawfully. The decision of the Bundesrat may be challenged in the Federal Constitutional Court.

(5) For the execution of Federal Laws, the Federal Government may, by Federal Law requiring the consent of the Bundesrat, be authorized to issue individual instructions for particular cases. They must be addressed to the highest Land authorities unless the Federal Government considers the matter urgent.

Article 85

(Execution by the Länder as agents of the Federation)

(1) Where the Länder execute Federal laws as agents of the Federation, the establishment of the authorities remains the concern of the Länder insofar as Federal laws consented to by the Bundesrat do not otherwise provide.

(2) The Federal Government may with the consent of the Bundesrat, issue general administrative rules. It may regulate the uniform training of civil servants and salaried government employees The heads of authorities at intermediate level shall be appointed with its agreement.

(3) The Land authorities are subject to the instructions of the appropriate highest Federal authorities. The instructions shall be addressed to the highest Land authorities unless the Federal Government considers the matter urgent. Execution of the instructions shall be ensured by the highest Land authorities.

(4) Federal supervision extends to the conformity with law and appropriateness of the execution. The Federal Government may, for this purpose, require the submission of reports and documents and send commissioners to all authorities.

Article 86

(Direct federal administration)

Where the Federation executes laws by Federal administrative agencies or by Federal bodies-corporate or institutions under public law, the Federal Government issues, insofar as the law contains no special provision, the general administrative rules. It provides for the establishment of authorities insofar as the law does not otherwise provide.

Article 87

(Matters for direct federal administration)

(1) The foreign service the Federal finance administration, the Federal railroads, the Federal postal service and, in accordance with the provisions of Article 89, the administration of the Federal waterways and of shipping are conducted as matters of Federal administration with their own subordinate

administrative structure, Federal frontier protection authorities and central offices for police information and communications, for the compilation of data for the purpose of protecting the Constitution and for the criminal police may be established by Federal legislation.

(2) Social insurance institutions whose sphere of competence extends beyond the territory of one Land are conducted as Federal bodies-corporate under public law.

(3) In addition, independent Federal higher authorities and Federal bodies- corporate and institutions under public law may be established by Federal law for matters on which the Federation has the power to legislate. If new functions arise for the Federation in matters on which it has the power to legislate, Federal authorities at intermediate and lower level may be established in case of urgent need, with the consent of the Bundesrat and of the majority of the members of the Bundestag.

Article 87a

Added 19 March 1956

Article 87a

(Establishment and powers of the Armed Forces)

(1) The Federation shall establish Armed Forces for Defense purposes. Their numerical strength and general organizational structure shall be shown in the budget.

(2) Apart from Defense, the Armed Forces may only be used insofar as explicitly permitted by this Basic Law.

(3) While a state of Defense or a state of tension exists, the Armed Forces shall have the power to protect civilian property and discharge functions of traffic control insofar as this is necessary for the performance of their Defense mission. Moreover, the Armed Forces may, when a state of Defense or a state of tension exists, be entrusted with the protection of civilian property also in support of police measures; in this event the Armed Forces shall cooperate with the competent authorities.

(4) In order to avert any imminent danger to the existence or to the free democratic basic order of the Federation or a Land, the Federal Government may, should conditions as envisaged in paragraph (2) of Article 91 obtain and the police forces and the Federal Border Guard be inadequate, use the Armed Forces to support the police and the Federal Border Guard in the protection of civilian property and in combating organized and militantly armed insurgents. Any such use of the Armed Forces shall be discontinued whenever the Bundestag or the Bundesrat so demands.

Article 87b

(Administration of the Federal Armed Forces) added 19 March 1956

(1) The administration of the Federal defense Forces shall be conducted as a Federal administration with its own administrative substructure. Its function shall be to administer matters pertaining to personnel and to the immediate supply of the material requirements of the Armed Forces. Tasks connected with benefits to invalids or construction work shall not be assigned to the administration of the Federal Defense Forces except by Federal legislation which shall require the consent of the Bundesrat. Such consent shall also be required for any legislative provisions empowering the administration of the Federal Defense Forces to interfere with rights of third parties: this shall, however, not apply in the case of laws concerning personnel.

(2) Moreover, Federal laws concerning defense including recruitment for military service and protection of the civilian population may, with the consent of the Bundesrat, stipulate that they shall be carried out, wholly or in part, either under Federal administration with its own administrative substructure or by the Länder acting as agents of the Federation. If such laws are executed by the Länder acting as agents of the Federation, they may, with the consent of the Bundesrat, stipulate that the powers vested by virtue of Article 85 in thc Federal Government and appropriate highest Federal authorities shall be transferred wholly or partly to higher Federal authorities in such an event it

may be enacted that these authorities shall not require the consent of the Bundesrat in issuing general administrative rules as referred to in Article 85 paragraph (2) first sentence.

Article 87c

inserted 23 December 1959

Laws enacted under item 11a of Article 74 may, with the consent of the Bundesrat stipulate that they shall be executed by the Länder acting as agents of the Federation.

Article 87d

Added 6 Feb 1961

(1) The Aviation Administration shall be administered by the Federation.

(2) By Federal Law requiring the consent of the Bundesrat, the functions of the Aviation Administration may be assigned to the Länder as agents of the Federation.

Article 88

The Federation establishes a note-issuing and currency bank as the Federal Bank.

Article 89

(Federal waterways)

(1) The Federation is the owner of the former Reich waterways.

(2) The Federation administers the Federal waterways through its own authorities. It exercises the public functions relating to inland shipping which extend beyond the territory of one Land and those relating to maritime shipping which are conferred on it by law. Upon request, the Federation may transfer the administration of Federal waterways insofar as they lie within the territory of one Land, to this Land as an agent. If a waterway touches the territories of several Länder the Federation may designate as its agent one Land if so requested by the Länder concerned.

(3) In the administration, development and new construction of waterways the needs of soil cultivation and of regulating

water supply shall be safeguarded in agreement with the Länder.

Article 90

(Federal highways)

(1) The Federation is the owner of the former Reich motor roads and Reich highways.

(2) The Länder, or such self-governing bodies-corporate as are competent under Land law, administer as agents of the Federation the Federal motor roads and other Federal highways used for long-distance traffic.

(3) At the request of a Land, the Federation may take under direct Federal administration Federal motor roads and other Federal highways used for long-distance traffic, insofar as they lie within the territory of the Land.

Article 91

(Internal emergency) amended 24 June 1968

(1) In order to avert any imminent danger to the existence or to the free democratic basic order of the Federation or of a Land, a Land may request the services of the police forces of other Länder or of the forces and facilities of other administrative authorities and the Federal Border Guard.

(2) If the Land in which the danger is imminent is not itself willing or able to fight the danger, the Federal Government may place the police in that Land and the police forces of other Länder under its own instructions and use units of the Federal Border Guard. The order for this shall be rescinded after the danger is past, or else at any time on the demand of the Bundesrat. Where the danger extends to a region larger than a Land, the Federal Government may, insofar as is necessary for effectively combating such danger, issue instructions to the Land governments; the first and second sentences of this paragraph shall not be affected by this provision.

VIIIa. JOINT TASKS*

Article 91a*

(Participation of the Federation by virtue of federal legislation)

(1) The Federation shall participate in the following sectors, in the discharge of responsibilities of the Länder, provided that such responsibilities are important to society as a whole and that federal participation is necessary for the improvement of living conditions (joint tasks):

1.** extension and construction of institutions of higher education, including university clinics;

2. improvement of regional economic structures;

3. improvement of the agrarian structure and of coast preservation.

(2) Joint tasks shall be defined in detail by a federal statute requiring the consent of the Bundesrat. Such legislation should include general principles governing the discharge of joint tasks.

(3) Such legislation shall provide for the procedure and the institutions required for joint overall planning. The inclusion of a project in the overall planning shall require the consent of the Land in which it is to be carried out.

(4) In cases to which items 1 and 2 of paragraph (1) of this Article apply, the Federation shall meet one half of the expenditure in each Land. In cases to which item 3 of paragraph (1) of this Article applies, the Federation shall meet at least one half of the expenditure, and such proportion shall be the same for all the Länder. Details shall be regulated by statute. Provision of funds shall be subject to appropriation in the budgets of the Federation and the Länder.

(5) The Federal Government and the Bundesrat shall be informed about the execution of joint tasks, should they so demand.

---

* Inserted by federal statute of 12 May 1969 (Federal Law Gazette I, p. 359).

** As amended by federal statute of 31 July 1970 (Federal Law Gazette I, p. 1161).

IX. THE ADMINISTRATION OF JUSTICE

Article 92

(Court Organization)

The judicial authority is vested in the judges; it is exercised by the Federal Constitutional Court, by the Supreme Federal Court, by the Federal courts provided for in this Basic Law and by the courts of the Länder.

Article 93

(Federal Constitutional Court, jurisdiction)

(1) The Federal Constitutional Court decides:

1. on the interpretation of this Basic Law in the event of disputes concerning the extent of the rights and duties of a supreme Federal organ or of other parties concerned who have been endowed with independent rights by this Basic Law or by rules of procedure of a supreme Federal organ;

2. in case of differences of opinion or doubts on the formal and material compatibility of Federal law or Land law with this Basic Law, or on the compatibility of Land law with other Federal law, at the request of the Federal Government, of a Land government or of one-third of the Bundestag members;

3. in case of differences of opinion on the rights and duties of the Federation and the Länder, particularly in the execution of Federal law by the Länder and in the exercise of Federal supervision;

4. on other disputes of public law between the Federation and the Länder between different Länder or within a Land, unless recourse to another court exists;

4a. on complaints of unconstitutionality, which may be entered by any person who claims that one of his basic rights or one of his rights under paragraph (4) of Article 20 or under Articles 33, 38, 101, 103, or 104 has been violated by public authority;

4b. on complaints of unconstitutionality entered by communes or associations of communes on the ground that their right to self-government under Article 28 has been violated by a statute other than a Land statute open to complaint to the respective Land constitutional court;

5. in the other cases provided for in this Basic Law.

(2) The Federal Constitutional Court shall also act in such cases as are otherwise assigned to it by Federal law.

Article 94

(Federal Constitutional Court, composition)

(1) The Federal Constitutional Court consists of Federal judges and other members. Half of the members of the Federal Constitutional Court are elected by the Bundestag and half by the Bundesrat. They may not belong to the Bundestag, the Bundesrat, the Federal Government or the corresponding organs of a Land.

(2) Its constitution and procedures will be regulated by a Federal law, which will specify in what cases its decisions shall have the force of law.

Article 95

(Highest courts of justice of the Federation, Joint Panel) amended 18 June 1968

(1) To preserve the uniformity of application of Federal law, a Supreme Federal Court will be established.

(2) The Supreme Federal Court decides cases in which the decision is of fundamental importance for the uniformity of the administration of justice by the higher Federal courts.

(3) The judges of the Supreme Federal Court are selected jointly by the Federal Minister of justice and a committee for the selection of judges consisting of the Land Ministers of justice and an equal number of members elected by the Bundestag.

(4) In other respects the constitution of the Supreme Federal Court and is procedure will be regulated by Federal legislation.

Article 96

(Other federal courts, exercise of federal jurisdiction by courts of the Länder) amended 26 August 1969

(1) The Federation may establish a federal court for matters concerning industrial property rights.

(2) The Federation may establish military criminal courts for the Armed Forces as federal courts. They may only exercise criminal jurisdiction while a state of defence exists, and otherwise only over members of the Armed Forces serving abroad or on board warships. Details shall be regulated by federal statute. These courts shall be within the competence of the Federal Minister of Justice. Their full-time judges shall be persons qualified to hold judicial office.

(3) The highest court of justice for appeals from the courts mentioned in paragraphs (1) and (2) of this Article shall be the Federal Court of Justice.

(4) The Federation may establish federal courts for disciplinary proceedings against, and for proceedings in pursuance of complaints by, persons in the federal public service.

(5) In respect of criminal proceedings under paragraph (1) of Article 26 or involving the protection of the state, a federal statute requiring the consent of the Bundesrat may provide that Land courts shall exercise federal jurisdiction.

Article 97

(Independence of the judges)

(1) The judges are independent and subject only to the law.

(2) Judges appointed permanently on a full-time basis to an established post can, against their will, be dismissed, or permanently or temporarily suspended from office or transferred to another post or retired before expiration of their term of office only under authority of a judicial decision and only on grounds and in the form provided by law. Legislation may set age limits for the retirement of judges appointed for life. In the event of changes in the structure of the courts or their areas of

jurisdiction, judges may be transferred to another court or removed from their office, provided they retain their full salary.

Article 98

amended 18 March 1971

(1) The legal status of the Federal judges shall be regulated by a Special Federal law.

(2) If a Federal judge, in his official capacity or unofficially, infringes upon the principle of the Basic Law or the constitutional order of a Land, the Federal Constitutional Court may decide by a two-thirds majority, upon the request of the Bundestag, that the judge be transferred to another office or placed on the retired list. In a case of an intentional infringement, his dismissal may be ordered.

(3) The legal status of the judges in the Länder shall be regulated by special Land laws. The Federation may enact outline provisions, insofar as paragraph (4) of Article 74a does not provide otherwise.

(4) The Länder may provide that the Land Minister of Justice together with a committee for the selection of judges shall decide on the appointment of judges in the Länder.

(5) The Länder may, with respect to Land judges, enact provisions corresponding with paragraph 2. Existing Land constitutional law remains unaffected. The decision in a case of impeachment of a judge rests with the Federal Constitutional Court.

Article 99

(as amended 18 June 1968)

The decision on constitutional disputes within a Land may be assigned by a Land law to the Federal Constitutional Court, and the decision of last instance in matters involving the application of Land law, to the higher Federal courts of justice referred to in paragraph (1) of Article 95.

Article 100

amended 18 June 1968

(1) Where a court considers a law unconstitutional, the validity of which is relevant to its decision, the proceedings shall be stayed, and a decision shall be obtained from the Land court competent for constitutional disputes if the matter concerns the violation of the constitution of a Land, or from the Federal Constitutional Court if the matter concerns the violation of the Basic Law. This also applies if the matter concerns the violation of this Basic Law by Land law or the incompatibility of a Land law with a Federal law.

(2) If, in the course of litigation doubt exists whether a rule of public international law forms part of the Federal law and whether such rule directly creates rights and duties for the individual (Article 25), the court shall obtain the decision of the Federal Constitutional Court.

(3) Where the constitutional court of a Land, in interpreting the Basic Law, intends to deviate from a decision of the Federal Constitutional Court or of the constitutional court of another Land, it must obtain the decision of the Federal Constitutional Court.

Article 101

(1) Extraordinary courts are inadmissible. No one may be removed from the jurisdiction of his lawful judge.

(2) Courts for special fields may be established only by law.

Article 102

Capital punishment is abolished.

Article 103

(1) In the courts everyone is entitled to a hearing in accordance with the law.

(2) An act can be punished only if it was a punishable offense by law before the act was committed.

(3) No one may be punished for the same act more than once in pursuance of general penal legislation.

Article 104

(1) The freedom of the individual may be restricted only on the basis of a formal law and only with due regard to the forms prescribed therein. Detained persons may be subjected neither to mental nor to physical ill-treatment.

(2) Only judges may decide on admissibility or extension of a deprivation of liberty. Where such deprivation is not based on the order of a judge, a judicial decision must be obtained without delay. The police may hold no one on their own authority in their own custody longer than the end of the day after the arrest. Details shall be regulated by legislation.

(3) Any person provisionally detained on-suspicion of having committed a punishable offense must be brought before a judge at the latest on the day following the arrest; the judge shall inform him of the reasons for detention, examine him and give him an opportunity to raise objections. The judge must, without delay, either issue a warrant of arrest setting forth the reasons therefore or order the release from detention.

(4) A relative of the person detained or a person enjoying his confidence must be notified without delay of any judicial decision ordering or extending a deprivation of liberty.

X. FINANCE

Article 104a

(Apportionment of expenditure between the Federation and the Länder)

(1) The Federation and the Länder shall separately meet the expenditure resulting from the discharge of their respective tasks insofar as this Basic Law does not provide otherwise.

(2) Where the Länder act as agents of the Federation, the Federation shall meet the resulting expenditure.

(3) Federal statutes to be executed by the Länder and granting money payments may make provision for such payments to be met wholly or in part by the Federation. Where any such statute provides that the Federation shall meet one half of the expenditure or more, it shall be implemented by the Länder as agents of the Federation. Where any such statute provides that

the Länder shall meet one quarter of the expenditure or more, it shall require the consent of the Bundesrat.

(4) The Federation may grant the Länder financial assistance for particularly important investments by the Länder or communes or associations of communes, provided that such investments are necessary to avert a disturbance of the overall economic equilibrium or to equalize differences of economic capacities within the federal territory or to promote economic growth. Details, especially concerning the kinds of investments to be promoted, shall be regulated by a federal statute requiring the consent of the Bundesrat or by administrative arrangements under the federal budget law.

(5) The Federation and the Länder shall meet the administrative expenditure incurred by their respective authorities and shall be responsible to each other for ensuring proper administration. Details shall be regulated by a federal statute requiring the consent of the Bundesrat.

Article 105

(Legislative powers) amended 12 May 1969

(1) The Federation has the exclusive power to legislate on customs and fiscal monopolies.

(2) The Federation shall have concurrent power to legislate on all other taxes the revenue from which accrues to it wholly or in part or where the conditions provided for in paragraph (2) of Article 72 apply.

(2a) The Länder shall have power to legislate on local excise taxes as long and insofar as they are not identical with taxes imposed by federal legislation.

(3) Federal laws relating to taxes the yield of which accrues in whole or in pan to the Länder or the communities (community associations) require the consent of the Bundesrat.

Article 106

(Apportionment of tax revenue)

As amended 23 December 1955 and 24 December 1956

(1) The yield of fiscal monopolies and receipts from the following tares shall accrue to the Federation: 1. customs duties,

2. such excise taxes as do not accrue to the Länder in accordance with paragraph (2), 3. turnover tax, 4. transportation tax, 5. non-recurrent capital levies, and equalization taxes imposed for the purpose of implementing the equalization of burdens legislation, 6. Berlin emergency aid tax, 7. supplementary levies on income and corporation taxes.

(2) Receipts from the following taxes shall accrue to the Länder: 1. Property tax, 2. inheritance tax, 3. motor-vehicle tax, 4. such taxes on transactions that do not accrue to the Federation in accordance with paragraph (1), 5. beer tax, 6. levies on gambling establishments, 7. taxes on real estate and business, 8. taxes with localized application.

(3) Receipts from income tax and corporation tax shall accrue: until 31 March 1958, to the Federation and the Länder in a ratio of 33 1/3 per cent to 65 per cent, and from 1 April 1958, to the Federation and the Länder in a ratio of 35 per cent to 65 per cent.

(4) The ratio of appointment of the income and corporation taxes paragraph (3) should be modified by a Federal law requiring the consent of the Bundesrat whenever the development of the relation of revenues to expenditures in the Federation differs from that in the Länder and whenever the budgetary needs of the Federation or those of the Länder exceed the estimated revenues by a margin substantial enough to call for a corresponding adjustment of the ratio of apportionment in favor of either the Federation or the Länder. Any such adjustment shall be based on the following principles: 1. The Federation and the Länder shall each bear the expenditures resulting from the administration of their respective tasks; Article 120 paragraph (1) shall not be affected; 2. There shall be equality of rank between the claim of the Federation and the claim of the Länder to have their respective necessary expenditures covered from ordinary revenues; 3. The requirements of the Federation and of the Länder in respect of budget coverage shall be coordinated in such a way that a fair equalization is achieved, any overburdening of taxpayers precluded, and uniformity of living standards in the Federal territory ensured. The ratio of apportionment may be modified for the first time with effect from 1 April 1958 and

subsequently at intervals of not less than two years after the entry into force of any law determining such ratio; provided that this stipulation shall not affect any notification of such ratio effected in accordance with paragraph (5).

(5) If a Federal law imposes additional expenditures on, or withdraws revenues from the Länder, the ratio of apportionment of the income and corporation taxes shall be modified in favor of the Länder, provided that conditions as envisaged in paragraph (4) have developed. If the additional burden placed upon the Länder is limited to a period of short duration, such burden may be compensated by grants from the Federation under a Federal law requiring the consent of the Bundesrat and which shall lay down the principles for assessing the amounts of such grants and for distributing them among the Länder.

(6) Receipts from taxes on real estate and businesses shall accrue to the communes. In case there are no communes in a Land the receipts shall accrue to the Land. In accordance with Land legislation, taxes on real estate and businesses may be used to ascertain assessments and surtaxes. The receipts of the Länder from income tax and corporation tax shall accrue to the communes and associations of communes in a percentage to be determined by Land legislation. Furthermore, the Land legislation shall determine whether and how much of the receipts of the Land taxes shall accrue to the communes (associations of communes).

(7) If the Federation establishes special institutions in the Länder or communes (association of communes) which cause immediate higher expenditures or lower receipts to those Länder or communes (associations of communes), the Federation shall grant the necessary financial equalization, if and insofar as it is anticipated that the Länder or communes (associations of communes) are unable to bear these special burdens. Compensation by a third party and financial advantages which accrue to these Länder or communes (associations of communes as a consequence of these institutions shall be considered in such equalization.

(8) For the purposes of the present Article, revenues and expenditures of communes (associations of communes) shall be deemed to be Land revenues and expenditures.

Article 107

(Financial equalization) amended 12 May 1969

(1) Revenue from Land taxes and the Land share of revenue from income and corporation taxes shall accrue to the individual Länder to the extent that such taxes are collected by revenue authorities within their respective territories (local revenue). A federal statute requiring the consent of the Bundesrat may provide in detail for the delimitation as well as the manner and scope of allotment of local revenue from corporation and wage taxes. such statute may also provide for the delimitation and allotment of local revenue from other taxes. The Land share of revenue from the turnover tax shall accrue to the individual Länder on a per capita basis; a federal statute requiring the consent of the Bundesrat may provide for supplementary shares not exceeding one quarter of a Land share to be granted to Länder whose per capita revenue from Land taxes and from the income and corporation taxes is below the average of all the Länder combined.

(2) Such statute shall ensure a reasonable equalization between financially strong and financially weak Länder, due account being taken of the financial capacity and financial requirements of communes or associations of communes. Such statute shall specify the conditions governing equalization claims of Länder entitled to equalization payments and equalization liabilities of Länder owing equalization payments as well as the criteria for determining the amounts of equalization payments. Such statute may also provide for grants to be made by the Federation from federal funds to financially weak Länder in order to complement the coverage of their general financial requirements (supplementary grants).

Article 108

(Revenue administration) amended 12 May 1969

(1) Customs, fiscal monopolies, the excise taxes subject to federal legislation, including the import turnover tax, and

charges imposed within the framework of the European Communities shall be administered by federal revenue authorities. The organization of these authorities shall be regulated by Federal law. The heads of the authorities at intermediate level shall be appointed after consultation of the Land governments.

(2) All other taxes shall be administered by Land revenue authorities. The organization of these authorities and the uniform training of their civil servants may be regulated by a federal statute requiring the consent of the Bundesrat. The heads of authorities at the intermediate level shall be appointed in agreement with the Federal Government.

(3) To the extent that taxes accruing wholly or in part to the Federation are administered by Land revenue authorities, those authorities shall act as agents of the Federation. Paragraphs (3) and (4) of Article 85 shall apply, the Federal Minister of Finance, however, being substituted for the Federal Government.

(4) In respect of the administration of taxes, a federal statute requiring the consent of the Bundesrat may provide for collaboration between federal and Land revenue authorities, or in the case of taxes under paragraph (1) of this Article for their administration by Land revenue authorities, or in the case of other taxes for their administration by federal revenue authorities, where and to the extent that the execution of revenue statutes is substantially improved or facilitated thereby. As regards taxes the revenue from which accrues exclusively to communes or associations of communes, their administration may wholly or in part be transferred by the Länder from the appropriate Land revenue authorities to communes or associations of communes.

(5) The procedure to be applied by federal revenue authorities shall be laid down by federal legislation. The procedure to be applied by Land revenue authorities or, as envisaged in the second sentence of paragraph 4 of this Article, by communes or associations of communes may be laid down by federal statute requiring the consent of the Bundesrat.

(6) The jurisdiction of revenue courts shall be uniformly regulated by federal legislation.

(7) The Federal Government may issue appropriate general administrative rules which, to the extent that administration is entrusted to Land revenue authorities or communes or associations of communes, shall require the consent of the Bundesrat.

Article 109*

(Budget management in the Federation and the Länder)

(1) The Federation and the Länder shall be autonomous and independent of each other in their budget management.

(2) The Federation and the Länder shall have due regard in their budget management to the requirements of overall economic equilibrium.

(3)** Through federal legislation requiring the consent of the Bundesrat, principles applicable to both the Federation and the Länder may be established governing budgetary law, responsiveness of budget management to economic trends, and financial planning to cover several years ahead.

(4) With a view to averting disturbances of the overall economic equilibrium, federal legislation requiring the consent of the Bundesrat may be enacted providing for:

1. maximum amounts, terms and timing of loans to be raised by territorial entities (Gebietskoerperschaften) or special purpose associations (Zweckverbaende), and

2. an obligation on the part of the Federation and the Länder to maintain interest-free deposits at the Deutsche Bundesbank (reserves for counterbalancing economic trends).

Authorizations to issue the relevant ordinances may be conferred on Federal Government only. Such ordinances shall require the consent of the Bundesrat. They shall be repealed insofar as the Bundestag may demand; details shall be regulated by federal legislation.

---

* As amended by federal statute of 8 June 1967 (Federal Law Gazette I, p. 581).

** As amended by federal statute of 12 May 1969 (Federal Law Gazette I, p. 357).

Article 110*

(Budget and budget law of the Federation)

(1) All revenues and expenditures of the Federation shall be included in the budget; in respect of federal enterprises and special assets, allocations thereto or remittances therefrom need be included. The budget shall be balanced as regards revenue and expenditure.

(2) The budget shall be laid down in a statute covering one year or several fiscal years separately before the beginning of the first of those fiscal years. Provision may be made for parts of the budget to apply to periods of different duration, but divided into fiscal years.

(3) Bills within the meaning of the first sentence of paragraph (2) of this Article as well as bills to amend the budget statute and the budget be submitted simultaneously to the Bundesrat and to the Bundestag; the Bundesrat shall be entitled to state its position on such bills within weeks or, in the case of amending bills, within three weeks.

(4) The budget statute may contain only such provisions as apply to revenues and expenditures of the Federation and to the period for which the budget statute is being enacted. The budget statute may stipulate these provisions and shall cease to apply only upon the promulgation of the next budget statute or, in the event of an authorization pursuant to Article 115, at a later date.

Article 111

(Interim budget management)

(1) If, by the end of a fiscal year, the budget for the following year has not been established by a law, the Federal Government may, until such law comes into force, make all payments which are necessary: (a) to maintain institutions existing by law and to carry out measures authorized by law; (b) to meet legal obligations of the Federation; (c) to continue building projects, procurements and other services or to continue

*As amended by federal statute of 12 May 1969 (Federal Law Gazette I)

the grant of subsidies for these purposes, provided amounts have already been authorized in the budget of a previous year.

(2) Insofar as revenues provided by special legislation and derived from taxes, levies, or other sources, or the working capital reserves, do not cover the expenditures set forth in paragraph 1, the Federal Government may borrow the funds necessary for the conduct of current operations to a maximum of one-quarter of the total amount of the previous budget.

Article 112*

(Expenditures in excess of budgetary estimates) amended 12 May 1969

Expenditures in excess of budgetary appropriations and extrabudgetary expenditures shall require the consent of the Federal Minister of Finance. Such consent may be given only in the case of an unforeseen and compelling necessity. Details may be regulated by federal legislation.

Article 113*

(Consent of Federal Government to increases in expenditures or decreases in revenue)

(1) Statutes increasing the budget expenditures proposed by the Federal Government or involving or likely in future to cause new expenditures shall require the consent of the Federal Government. This shall also apply to statutes involving or likely in future to cause decreases in revenue. The Federal Government may demand that the Bundestag postpone vote on such bills. In this case the Federal Government shall state its position to the Bundestag within six weeks.

(2) Within four weeks after the Bundestag has adopted such a bill, Federal Government may demand that it votes on that bill again.

(3) Where the bill has become a statute pursuant to Article 78, the Federal Government may withhold its consent only within six weeks and only after having initiated the procedure

* As amended by federal statute of 12 May 1969 (Federal Law Gazette I, p. 357).

provided for in the third and fourth sentences of paragraph (1) or in paragraph (2) of the present Article. Upon the expiry of this period such consent shall be deemed to have been given.

Article 114*

(Rendering and auditing of accounts)

(1) The Federal Minister of Finance shall, on behalf of the Federal Government, submit annually to the Bundestag and to the Bundesrat their approval an account, covering the preceding fiscal year, of revenues and expenditures as well as of property and debt.

(2) The Federal Audit Office, the members of which shall enjoy judicial independence, shall audit the account and examine the management of the budget and the conduct of business as to economy and correctness. The Federal Audit Office shall submit an annual report directly to Federal Government as well as to the Bundestag and to the Bundesrat. In all other respects the powers of the Federal Audit Office shall be regulated by federal legislation.

Article 115*

(Procurement of credit)

(1) The borrowing of funds and the assumption of pledges, guarantee or other commitments, as a result of which expenditure may be incurred in future fiscal years, shall require federal legislative authorization indicating, or permitting computation of, the maximum amount involved. Revenue obtained by borrowing shall not exceed the total expenditures for investments provided for in the budget; exceptions shall be permissible only to avert a disturbance of the overall economic equilibrium. Details shall be regulated by federal legislation.

(2) In respect of special assets of the Federation, exceptions to the provisions of paragraph (1) of this Article may be authorized by federal legislation.

---

* As amended by federal statute of 12 May 1969 (Federal Law Gazette I, p. 357).

Xa.* STATE OF DEFENSE

Article 115a

(Concept and determination of a state of Defense)

(1) The determination that federal territory is being attacked by armed force or that such an attack is directly imminent (state of Defense) shall be made by the Bundestag with the consent of the Bundesrat. Such determination shall be made at the request of the Federal Government and shall require a two-thirds majority of the votes cast, which shall include at least the majority of the members of the Bundestag.

(2) Where the situation imperatively calls for immediate action and where insurmountable obstacles prevent the timely assembly of the Bundestag, or where there is no quorum in the Bundestag, the Joint Committee shall make this determination with a two-thirds majority of the votes cast, which shall include at least the majority of its members.

(3) The determination shall be promulgated in the Federal Law Gazette by the Federal President pursuant to Article 82. Where this cannot be done in time, the promulgation shall be effected in another manner; it shall subsequently be printed in the Federal Law Gazette as soon as circumstances permit.

(4) Where the federal territory is being attacked by armed force and where the competent bodies of the Federation are not in a position at once to make the determination provided for in the first sentence of paragraph (1) of this Article, such determination shall be deemed to have been made and promulgated at the time the attack began. The Federal President shall announce such time as soon as circumstances permit.

(5) Where the determination of the existence of a state of Defense has been promulgated and where the federal territory is being attacked by armed force, the Federal President may, with the consent of the Bundestag, issue declarations under international law regarding the existence of such state of Defense. Where the conditions mentioned in paragraph (2) of

* Entire section Xa inserted by federal statute of 4 June 1968 (Federal Gazette I, p. 711).

this Article apply, the Joint Committee shall act in substitution for the Bundestag.

Article 115b

(Transfer of command to the Federal Chancellor)

Upon the promulgation of a state of Defense, the power of command over the Armed Forces shall pass to the Federal Chancellor.

Article 115c

(Extension of legislative powers of the Federation)

(1) The Federation shall have the right to legislate concurrently in respect of a state of Defense even on matters within the legislative powers of the Länder. Such statutes shall require the consent of the Bundesrat.

(2) Federal legislation to be applicable upon the occurrence of a state of Defense to the extent required by conditions obtaining while such state of Defense exists may make: 1. preliminary provision for compensation to be made in the event of property being taken, in derogation of the second sentence of paragraph (3) of Article 14; 2. provision for a time-limit other than that referred to in the third sentence of paragraph (2) and the first sentence of paragraph (3) of Article 104 in respect of deprivations of liberty, but not exceeding four days at the most, in a case where no judge has been able to act within the time- limit applying in normal times.

(3)* Federal legislation to be applicable upon the occurrence of a state of Defense to the extent required for averting an existing or directly imminent attack may, subject to the consent of the Bundesrat, regulate the administration and the financial system of the Federation and the Länder in derogation of Sections VIII, VIIIa and X, provided that the viability of the Länder, communes and associations of communes is safeguarded, particularly in financial matters.

* As amended by federal statute of 12 May 1969 (Federal Law Gazette I, p. 359).

(4) Federal statutes enacted pursuant to paragraph (1) or subparagraph 1 of paragraph (2) of this Article may, for the purpose of preparing for their enforcement, be applied even prior to the occurrence of a state of Defense.

Article 115d

(Legislative process in case of urgent bills)

(1) While a state of Defense exists, the provisions of paragraphs (2) and (3) of this Article shall apply in respect of federal legislation, in derogation of the provisions of paragraph (2) of Article 76, the second sentence of paragraph (1) and paragraph (2) to (4) of Article 77, Article 78, and paragraph (1) of Article 82.

(2) Bills submitted as urgent by the Federal Government shall be forwarded to the Bundesrat at the same time as they are submitted to the Bundestag. The Bundestag and the Bundesrat shall debate such bills together without delay. Insofar as the consent of the Bundesrat is necessary, the majority of its votes shall be required for any such bill to become a statute. Details shall be regulated by rules of procedure adopted by the Bundestag and requiring the consent of the Bundesrat.

(3) The second sentence of paragraph (3) of Article 115a shall apply mutatis mutandis in respect of the promulgation of such statutes.

Article 115e

(Powers of the Joint Committee)

(1) Where, in a state of Defense, the Joint Committee determines with a two-thirds majority of the votes cast, which shall include at least the majority of its members, that insurmountable obstacles prevent the timely assembly of the Bundestag or that there is no quorum in the Bundestag, the Joint Committee shall have the status of both the Bundestag and the Bundesrat and shall exercise their rights as one body.

(2) The Joint Committee may not enact any statute to amend this Basic Law or to deprive it of effect or application either in whole or in part. The Joint Committee shall not be

authorized to enact statutes pursuant to paragraph (1) of Article 24 or to Article 29.

Article 115f

(Powers of the Federal Government)

(1) In a state of Defense, the Federal Government may, to the extent necessitated by circumstances: 1. use the Federal Border Guard throughout the federal territory; 2. issue instructions not only to federal administrative authorities but also to Land governments and, where it deems the matter urgent, to Land authorities, and may delegate this power to members of Land governments to be designated by it.

(2) The Bundestag, the Bundesrat and the Joint Committee shall be informed without delay of the measures taken in accordance with paragraph (1) of this Article.

Article 115g

(Status and functions of Federal Constitutional Court)

The constitutional status and the performance of the constitutional functions of the Federal Constitutional Court and its judges shall not be impaired. The Federal Constitutional Court Act may not be amended by a statute enacted by the Joint Committee except insofar as such amendment is required. Also in the opinion of the Federal Constitutional Court, to maintain the capability of the Court to function. Pending the enactment of such a statute, the Federal Constitutional Court may take such measures as are necessary to maintain the capability of the Court to carry out its work. Any decisions by the Federal Constitutional Court in pursuance of the second and third sentences of this Article shall require a two-thirds majority of the judges present.

Article 115h

(Functioning capability of constitutional organs)

(1) Any legislative terms of the Bundestag or of Land parliaments due to expire while a state of Defense exists shall end six months after the termination of such state of Defense. A term of office of the Federal President due to expire while a state of Defense exists, and the exercise of his functions by the

President of the Bundesrat in case of the premature vacancy of the Federal President's office. shall end nine months after the termination of such state of Defense. The term of office of a member of the Federal Constitutional Court due to expire while a state of Defense exists shall end six months after the termination of such state of Defense.

(2) Should the necessity arise for the Joint Committee to elect a Federal Chancellor, the Committee shall do so with the majority of members; the Federal President shall propose a candidate to the Joint Committee. The Joint Committee can express its lack of confidence to the Federal Chancellor only by electing a successor with a two-thirds majority of its members.

(3) The Bundestag shall not be dissolved while a state of Defense exists.

Article 115i

(Powers of Land governments)

(1) Where the competent federal bodies are incapable of taking measures necessary to avert the danger, and where the situation imperatively calls for immediate independent action in individual pats of the federal territory, the Land governments or the authorities or commissioners designated by them shall be authorized to take, within their respective spheres of competence, the measures provided for in paragraph (1) of Article 115f.

(2) Any measures taken in accordance with paragraph (1) of the present Article may be revoked at any time by the Federal Government, or, in relation to Land authorities and subordinate federal authorities, by Land minister-presidents.

Article 115k

(Duration of validity of extraordinary legal provisions

(1) Statutes enacted in accordance with Articles 115c, 115e and 115g as well as ordinances issued by virtue of such statutes, shall, for the duration of their applicability, suspend law which is inconsistent with such statutes or ordinances. This shall not apply to earlier legislation enacted by virtue of Articles 115c, 115e or 115g.

(2) Statutes adopted by the Joint Committee, as well as ordinances is~ by virtue of such statutes, shall cease to have effect not later than, months after the termination of a state of Defense.

(3)* Statutes containing provisions that diverge from Articles 91a, 104a, 106 and 107 shall apply no longer than the end of the second fiscal —

Article 115l

(Repeal of extraordinary statutes and measures, termination of a state of Defense, conclusion of peace)

(1) The Bundestag, with the consent of the Bundesrat, may at any time repeal statutes enacted by the Joint Committee. The Bundesrat may demand that the Bundestag make a decision on such matter. Any measures taken by the Joint Committee or the Federal Government to avert a danger shall be revoked where the Bundestag and the Bundesrat so decide.

(2) The Bundestag, with the consent of the Bundesrat, may at any time declare a state of Defense terminated by a decision to be promulgated by the Federal President. The Bundesrat may demand that the Bundestag make a decision on such matter. A state of Defense shall, without delay, be declared terminated where the prerequisites for the determination thereof no longer exist.

(3) The conclusion of peace shall be the subject of a federal statute.

XI. TRANSITIONAL AND CONCLUDING PROVISIONS

Article 116

(1) Unless otherwise provided by law, a German within the meaning of this Basic Law is a person who possesses German citizenship who has been admitted to the territory of the German Reich, as it existed on 31 December 1937, as a refugee

---

* As amended by federal statute of 12 May 1969 (Federal Law Gazette I) following upon the termination of a state of Defense. After such termination they may, with the consent of the Bundesrat, be amended by federal legislation so as to return to the provisions made in Sections VIIIa and X.

or expellee of German stock or as the spouse or descendant of such person.

(2) Former German citizens who between 30 January 1933 and 8 May 1945, were deprived of their citizenship for political, racial or religious reasons, and their descendants, shall be re-granted German citizenship on application. They are considered as not having been deprived of their German citizenship if they have established their domicile in Germany after 8 May 1945 and have not expressed a contrary intention.

Article 117

(1) Law which conflicts with Article 3, paragraph 2, remains in force until adapted to this provision of the Basic Law, but not beyond 31 March 1953.

(2) Laws which restrict the right of freedom of movement in view of the present housing shortage remain in force until repealed by Federal legislation.

Article 118

The reorganization of the territory comprising the Länder of Baden, Wuerttemberg-Baden and Wuerttemberg-Hohenzollern may be effected notwithstanding the provisions of Article 29, by agreement between the Länder concerned. If no agreement is reached, the reorganization, will be regulated by a Federal law which must provide for a referendum.

Article 119

In matters relating to refugees and expellees, in particular as regards their distribution among the Länder, the Federal Government with the consent of the Bundesrat issue ordinances having the force of law, pending settlement of the matter by Federal legislation. The Federal Government may in this matter be authorized to issue individual instructions for particular cases. Except where there is danger in delay, the instructions shall be addressed to the highest Land authorities.

Article 120*

(Occupation costs and burdens resulting from war)

(1)** The Federation shall meet the expenditure for occupation costs and the other internal and external burdens caused by the war, as regulated in detail by federal legislation. To the extent that these costs and other burdens have been regulated by federal legislation on or before I October 1969. the Federation and the Länder shall meet such expenditure between them in accordance with such federal legislation. Insofar as expenditures for such of these costs and burdens as neither have been nor will be regulated by federal legislation have been met on or before 1 October 1965 by Länder, communes, associations of communes or other entities performing functions of the Länder or the communes, the Federation shall not be obliged to meet expenditure of that nature even where it arises after that date. The Federation shall pay the subsidies towards the burdens of social insurance institutions. including unemployment insurance and public assistance to the unemployed. The distribution between the Federation and the Länder of costs and other burdens caused by the war, as regulated in this paragraph, shall not affect any statutory regulation of claims for indemnification in respect of the consequences of the war.

(2) Revenue shall pass to the Federation at the same time as the latter assumes responsibility for the expenditure referred to in this Article.

Article 120a

Added 14 August 1952

(1) Laws concerning the implementation of the equalization of burdens may, with the consent of the Bundesrat, stipulate that in the field of equalization benefits, they shall be executed partly by the Federation and partly by the Länder acting as agents of the Federation, and that the relevant powers vested in

---

* As amended by federal statutes of 30 July 1965 (Federal Law Gazette I, p. 649) and of 28 July 1969 (Federal Law Gazette I, p. 985).

** As amended by federal statute of 28 July 1969 (Federal Law Gazette I, p. 985).

the Federal Government and the competent highest Federal authorities by virtue of Article 5 shall be wholly or partly delegated to the Federal Equalization Office. In the exercise of these powers the Federal Equalization Office shall not require the consent of the Bundesrat; with the exception of urgent cases, its instructions shall be given to the highest Land authorities (Land Equalization Offices).

(2) The provisions of Article 87, paragraph 3, second sentence, shall not be affected hereby.

Article 121

Within the meaning of this Basic Law, a majority of the members of the Bundestag and of the Federal Convention is the majority of the number of their members established by law.

Article 122

(1) From the time of the first meeting of the Bundestag, laws shall be passed exclusively by the legislative organs recognized in this Basic Law.

(2) Legislative bodies and bodies participating in legislation in an advisory capacity whose competence ends by virtue of paragraph 1, are dissolved from that date.

Article 123

(1) Law in force before the first meeting of the Bundestag remains in force, insofar as it does not conflict with the Basic Law.

(2) Subject to all rights and objections of the interested parties, the State treaties concluded by the German Reich concerning matters for which, under this Basic Law, Land legislation is competent remain in force, if they are and continue to be valid in accordance with general principles of law, until new State treaties are concluded by the agencies competent under this Basic Law, or until they are in any other way terminated pursuant to their provisions.

Article 124

Law affecting matters within the exclusive power to legislate of the Federation becomes Federal law wherever it is applicable.

Article 125

Law affecting matters within the concurrent power to legislate of the Federation becomes Federal law wherever it is applicable: 1. insofar as it applies uniformly within one or more zones of occupation; 2. insofar as it is law by which former Reich law has been amended after 8 May 1945.

Article 126

The Federal Constitutional Court decides disputes regarding the continuance of law as Federal law.

Article 127

Within one year of the promulgation of this Basic Law the Federal Government may, with the consent of the governments of the Länder concerned, extend to the Länder of Baden, Greater Berlin, Rhineland-Palatinate and Wuerttemberg-Hohenzollern any legislation of the Bizonal Economic Administration, insofar as it continues to be in force as Federal law under Article 124 or 125.

Article 128

Insofar as law continuing in force provides for powers to give instructions within the meaning of Article 84, paragraph 5, these powers remain in existence until otherwise provided by law.

Article 129

(1) Insofar as legal provisions which continue in force as Federal law contain an authorization to issue ordinances having the force of law or general administrative rules or to perform administrative acts, the authorization passes to the agencies henceforth competent in the matter. In cases of doubt, the Federal Government will decide in agreement with the Bundesrat; the decision must be published.

(2) Insofar as legal provisions which continue in force as Land law contain such an authorization, it will be exercised by the agencies competent under Land law.

(3) Insofar as legal provision within the meaning of paragraphs 1 and 2 authorize their amendment or

supplementation or the issue of legal provisions in place of laws, these authorizations have expired.

(4) The provisions of paragraphs I and 2 apply mutatis mutandis whenever legal provisions refer to regulations no longer valid or to institutions no longer in existence.

Article 130

(1) Administrative agencies and other institutions which serve the public administration or the administration of justice and are not based on Land law or treaties between Länder, as well as the Association of Management of Southwest German Railroads and the Administrative Council for the Postal Services and Telecommunications of the French Zone of Occupation, are placed under the Federal Government. The Federal Government provides with the consent of the Bundesrat for their transfer, dissolution or liquidation.

(2) The highest disciplinary superior of the personnel of these administrations and institutions is the appropriate Federal Minister.

(3) Bodies corporate and institutions of public law not directly under a Land and not based on treaties between Länder, are under the supervision of the appropriate highest Federal authorities.

Article 131

Federal legislation shall regulate the legal status of persons, including refugees and expellees, who on 8 May 1945, were employed in the public service, have left the service for reasons other than those arising from civil service regulations or collective agreement rules, and have not until now been employed or are employed in a position not corresponding to their former one. The same applies mutatis mutandis to persons, including refugees and expellees, who, on 8 May 1945 were entitled to a pension or other assistance and who no longer receive any assistance or any commensurate assistance for reasons other than those arising from civil service regulations or collective agreement rules. Until the Federal law comes into force, no legal claims can be made, unless otherwise provided by Land legislation.

Article 132

(1) Civil servants and Judges who, when the Basic Law comes into force, are appointed for life, may within six months after the first meeting of the Bundestag, be placed on the retired list or waiting list or be transferred to another one with lower remuneration, if they lack the personal or professional aptitude for their office. This provision applies mutatis mutandis also to salaried employees whose service cannot be terminated by notice. In the case of salaried employer whose services can be terminated by notice, periods of notice in excess of the periods fixed by collective agreement rules may be cancelled within the same period.

(2) This provision does not apply to members of the public service who are not affected by the provisions regarding the liberation from National Socialism and militarism or who are recognized victims of National Socialism unless there is an important reason with respect to their personality.

(3) Those affected may have recourse to the courts in accordance with Article 19, paragraph 4.

(4) Details will be regulated by an ordinance of the Federal Government which requires the consent of the Bundesrat.

Article 133

The Federation succeeds to the rights and obligations of the Bizonal Economic Administration.

Article 134

(1) Reich property becomes in principle Federal properly.

(2) Insofar as the property was originally intended to be used predominantly for administrative tasks which, under this Basic Law, are no administrative tasks of the Federation, it shall be transferred without compensation to the authorities not charged with such tasks, and to the Länder insofar as it is being used at present, and not merely temporarily, for administrative tasks which under the Basic Law are now within the administrative functions of the Länder. The Federation may also transfer other property to the Länder.

(3) Property which was placed at the disposal of the Reich by the Länder and communities (associations of communities) without compensation shall again become the property of the Länder and communities (community associations), insofar as it is not required by the Federation for its own administrative tasks.

(4) Details will be regulated by a Federal law which requires the consent of the Bundesrat.

Article 135

(1) If after 8 May 1945, and before the coming into force of this Basic Law an area has passed from one Land to another, the Land to which the area now belongs is entitled to the property located therein of the Land to which it formerly belonged.

(2) Property of Länder and other bodies-corporate and institutions under public law, which no longer exist, passes insofar as it was originally intended to be used predominantly for administrative tasks or is being used at present, and not merely temporarily, predominantly for administrative tasks, to the Land or the body-corporate or institution under public law which now discharges these tasks.

(3) Real estate of Länder which no longer exists, including appurtenances, passes to the Land within which it is located insofar as it is not included among property within the meaning of paragraph 1.

(4) If an overriding interest of the Federation or the particular interest of an area so requires, a settlement deviating from paragraph 1 to 3 may be effected by Federal Law.

(5) For the rest, the succession in law and the settlement of the property, insofar as it has not been affected before 1 January 1952, by agreement between the Länder or bodies-corporate or institutions under public law concerned will be regulated by a Federal law which requires the counsel of the Bundesrat.

(6) Interests of the former Land of Prussia in enterprises under private law pass to the Federation. A Federal law which may also deviate from this provision, will regulate details.

(7) Insofar as, on the coming into force of the Basic Law, property which would fall to a Land or body-corporate or institution under public law pursuant to paragraph 1 to 3 had been disposed of through or under authority of a Land law or in any other manner by the party thus entitled, the passing of the property is deemed to have taken place before such disposition.

Article 135a

(amended 31 August 1990 & 23 September 1990)

(1) The legislation reserved to the Federation in Article 134, paragraph (4), and Article 135, paragraph (5), may also stipulate that the following liabilities shall not be discharged, or not to their full extent: 1. liabilities of the Reich or liabilities of the former Land Prussia or liabilities of such other bodies-corporate and institutions under public law as no longer exist; 2. such liabilities of the Federation or other bodies-corporate and institutions under public law as are connected with the transfer of properties pursuant to Articles 89, 90, 134 or 135, and such liabilities of the same as arise from measures taken by the holders of rights defined under item 1; 3. such liabilities of Länder or communes (associations of communes) as have arisen from measures taken by these holders of rights before 1 August 1945, within the sphere of administrative functions incumbent upon, or delegated by, the Reich to comply with regulations of occupying powers or to remove a state of emergency due to the war.

(2) Paragraph 1 above shall be applied mutatis mutandis to liabilities of the German Democratic Republic or its legal entities as well as to liabilities of the Federation or other corporate bodies and institutions under public law which are connected with the transfer of properties of the German Democratic Republic to the Federation, Länder and communes (Gemeinden), and to liabilities arising from measures taken by the German Democratic Republic or its legal entities.

Article 136

(1) The Bundesrat assembles for the first time on the day of the first meeting of the Bundestag.

(2) Until the election of the first Federal President his powers will be exercised by the President of the Bundesrat. He has not the right to dissolve the Bundestag.

Article 137

(1) The right of civil servants, of salaried employees of the public services, of professional soldiers, of temporary volunteer soldiers and of judges to stand for election in the Federation, in the Länder or in the communes may be restricted by legislation.

(2) The Electoral Law to be adopted by the Parliamentary Council applies to the election of the first Bundestag of the first Federal Convention and of the first Federal President of the Federal Republic.

(3) The function of the Federal Constitutional Court pursuant to Article 41, paragraph 2, shall, pending its establishment, be exercised by the German High Court for the Combined Economic Area, which shall decide in accordance with its rules of procedure.

Article 138

Changes in the rules relating to notaries as they now exist in the Länder of Baden, Bavaria, Wuerttemberg-Baden and Wuerttemberg-Hohenzollern, require the consent of the governments of these Länder.

Article 139

The provisions of law enacted for the liberation of the German people from National Socialism and Militarism are not affected by the provisions of this Basic Law.

Article 140

The provisions of Articles 136, 137, 138, 139 and 141 of the German Constitution of 11 August 1919, are an integral part of this Basic Law.

Article 141

Article 7, paragraph 3 first sentence, has no application in a Land in which different provisions of Land law were in force on 1 January 1949.

Article 142

Notwithstanding the provision of Article 31, such provisions of Land Constitutions as guarantee basic rights in conformity with Articles 1 to 18 of this Basic Law also remain in force.

Article 142a (Repealed)

Article 143

(1) Law in the territory specified in Article 3 of the Unification Treaty may deviate from provisions of this Basic Law for a period not extending beyond 31 December 1992 insofar as and as long as no complete adjustment to the order of the Basic Law can be achieved as a consequence of the different conditions. Deviations must not violate Article 19 (2) and must be compatible with the principles set out in Article 79 (3).

(2) Deviations from sections II, VIII, VIIIa, IX, X and XI are permissible for a period not extending beyond 31 December 1995.

(3) Notwithstanding paragraphs 1 and 2 above, Article 41 of the Unification Treaty and the rules for its implementation shall remain valid insofar as they provide for the irreversibility of intrusion on property in the territory specified in Article 3 of the said Treaty.

Article 144

(1) This Basic Law requires ratification by the representative assemblies in two-thirds of the German Länder in which it is for the time being to apply.

(2) Insofar as the application of this Basic Law is subject to restrictions in any Land listed in Article 23 or in any part of such Land, the Land or the part thereof has the right to send representatives to the Bundestag in accordance with Article 38 and to the Bundesrat in accordance with Article 50.

Article 145

(1) The Parliamentary Council shall note in public session, with the participation of the representatives of Greater Berlin, the ratification of this Basic Law and shall sign and promulgate it.

(2) This Basic Law shall come into force at the end of the day of promulgation.

(3) It shall be published in the Federal Gazette.

Article 146

(Duration of validity of the Basic Law) amended by Unification Treaty of 31 August 1990 and federal statute 23 September 1990

This Basic Law, which is valid for the entire German people following the achievement of the unity and freedom of Germany, shall cease to be in force on the day on which a constitution adopted by a free decision of the German people comes into force.

Note: following is extract from the German Constitution of 11 August 1919 (Weimar Constitution)

APPENDIX TO BASIC LAW

Articles 136-137-138-139 and 141 of the Section "Religion and Religious Associations" of the Weimar Constitution incorporated into the Basic Law for the Federal Republic of Germany pursuant to Article 140 thereof.

Article 136

(Weimar Constitution)

Civil and political rights and duties are neither dependent upon nor restricted by the practice of religious freedom.

The enjoyment of civil and political rights, as well as admission to official posts, is independent of religious creed. No one is bound to disclose his religious convictions. The authorities have the right to make enquiries as to membership of a religious body only when rights and duties depend upon it, or when the collection of statistics ordered by law requires it. No one may be compelled to take part in any ecclesiastical act or ceremony, or the use of any religious form of oath.

Article 137

(Weimar Constitution)

There is no state church.

Freedom of association is guaranteed to religious bodies. There are no restrictions as to the union of religious bodies within the territory of the Federation. Each religious body regulates and administers its affairs independently within the limits of general laws. It appoints its officials without the cooperation of the Land, or of the civil community. Religious bodies acquire legal rights in accordance with the general regulations of the civil code. Religious bodies remain corporations with public rights in so far as they have been so up to the present. Equal rights shall be granted to other religious bodies upon application, if their Constitution and the number of their members offer a guarantee of permanency. When several such religious bodies holding public rights combine to form one union this union becomes a corporation of a similar class. Religious bodies forming corporations with public rights are entitled to levy taxes on the basis of the civil tax rolls, in accordance with the provisions of Land law. Associations adopting as their work the common encouragement of a world-philosophy shall be placed upon an equal footing with religious bodies. So far as the execution of these provisions may require further regulation, this is the duty of the Land legislature.

Article 138

(Weimar Constitution)

Land connections with religious bodies, depending upon law, agreement or special legal titles, are dissolved by Land legislation. The principle for such action shall be laid down by the Federal Government. Ownership and other rights of religious bodies and unions to their institutions, foundations, and other properties devoted to purposes of public worship, education or charity, are guaranteed.

Article 139

(Weimar Constitution)

Sundays and holidays recognized by the Land shall remain under legal protection as days of rest from work and for the promotion of spiritual purposes.

Article 141

(Weimar Constitution)

Religious bodies shall have the right of entry for religious purposes into the army, hospitals, prisons, or other public institutions, so far as is necessary for the arrangement of public worship or the exercise of pastoral offices, but every form of compulsion must be avoided.

Constitution of Canada

5

CONSTITUTION ACT, 1982

SCHEDULE B

CONSTITUTION ACT, 1982

PART I

CANADIAN CHARTER OF RIGHTS AND FREEDOMS

Whereas Canada is founded upon principles that recognize the supremacy of God and the rule of law:

GUARANTEE OF RIGHTS AND FREEDOMS

RIGHTS AND FREEDOMS IN CANADA

1. The Canadian Charter of Rights and Freedoms guarantees the rights and freedoms set out in it subject only to such reasonable limits prescribed by law as can be demonstrably justified in a free and democratic society.

FUNDAMENTAL FREEDOMS

2. Everyone has the following fundamental freedoms:

(a) freedom of conscience and religion;

(b) freedom of thought, belief, opinion and expression, including freedom of the press and other media of communication;

(c) freedom of peaceful assembly; and

(d) freedom of association.

DEMOCRATIC RIGHTS

DEMOCRATIC RIGHTS OF CITIZENS

3. Every citizen of Canada has the right to vote in an election of members of the House of Commons or of a legislative assembly and to be qualified for membership therein.

MAXIMUM DURATION OF LEGISLATIVE BODIES

4. (1) No House of Commons and no legislative assembly shall continue for longer than five years from the date fixed for the return of the writs of a general election of its members.

Continuation in special circumstances

(2) In time of real or apprehended war, invasion or insurrection, a House of Commons may be continued by Parliament and a Legislative assembly may be continued by the legislature beyond five years if such continuation is not opposed by the votes of more than one-third of the members of the House of Commons or the legislative assembly, as the case may be.

ANNUAL SITTING OF LEGISLATIVE BODIES

5. There shall be a sitting of Parliament and of each legislature at least once every twelve months.

MOBILITY RIGHTS

MOBILITY OF CITIZENS

6. (1) Every citizen of Canada has the right to enter, remain in and leave Canada.

Rights to move and gain livelihood

(2) Every citizen of Canada and every person who has the status of a permanent resident of Canada has the right

(a) to move to and take up residence in any province; and

(b) to pursue the gaining of a livelihood in any province.

Limitation

(3) The rights specified in subsection (2) are subject to

(a) any laws or practices of general application in force in a province other than those that discriminate among persons primarily on the basis of province of present or previous residence; and

(b) any laws providing for reasonable residency requirements as a qualification for the receipt of publicly provided social service.

Affirmative action programs

(4) Subsections (2) and (3) do not preclude any law, program or activity that has as its object the amelioration in a province of conditions of individuals in that province who are socially or economically disadvantaged if the rate of employment in that province is below the rate of employment in Canada.

LEGAL RIGHTS

LIFE, LIBERTY AND SECURITY OF PERSON

7. Everyone has the right to life, liberty and security of the person and the right not to be deprived thereof except in accordance with the principles of fundamental justice.

SEARCH OR SEIZURE

8. Everyone has the right to be secure against unreasonable search or seizure.

DETENTION OR IMPRISONMENT

9. Everyone has the right not to be arbitrarily detained or imprisoned.

ARREST OR DETENTION

10. Everyone has the right on arrest or detention

(a) to be informed promptly of the reasons therefor;

(b) to retain and instruct counsel without delay and to be informed of that right; and

(c) to have the validity of the detention determined by way of habeas corpus and to be released if the detention is not lawful.

PROCEEDINGS IN CRIMINAL AND PENAL MATTERS

11. Any person charged with an offense has the right

(a) to be informed without unreasonable delay of the specific offense;

(b) to be tried within a reasonable time;

(c) not to be compelled to be a witness in proceedings against that person in respect of the offense;

(d) to be presumed innocent until proven guilty according to law in a fair and public hearing by an independent and impartial tribunal;

(e) not to be denied reasonable bail without just cause;

(f) except in the case of an offense under military law tried before a military tribunal, to the benefit of trial by jury where the maximum punishment for the offense is imprisonment for five years or a more severe punishment;

(g) not to be found guilty on account of any act or omission unless, at the time of the act or omission, it constituted an offense under Canadian or international law or was criminal according to the general principles of law recognized by the community of nations;

(h) if finally acquitted of the offense, not to be tried for it again and, if finally found guilty and punished for the offense, not to be tried or punished for it again; and

(i) if found guilty of the offense and if the punishment for the offense has been varied between the time of commission and the time of sentencing, to the benefit of the lesser punishement.

TREATMENT OR PUNISHMENT

12. Everyone has the right not to be subjected to any cruel and unusual treatment or punishment.

SELF-CRIMINATION

13. A witness who testifies in any proceedings has the right not to have any incriminating evidence so given used to incriminate that witness in any other proceedings, except in a prosecution for perjury or for the giving of contradictory evidence.

INTERPRETER

14. A party or witness in any proceedings who does not understand or speak the language in which the proceedings are

conducted or who is deaf has the right to the assistance of an interpreter.

EQUALITY RIGHTS

EQUALITY BEFORE AND UNDER LAW AND EQUAL PROTECTION AND BENEFIT OF LAW

15. Every individual is equal before and under the law and has the right to the equal protection and equal benefit of the law without discrimination and, in particular, without discrimination based on race, national or ethnic origin, color, religion, sex, age or mental or physical disability.

OFFICIAL LANGUAGES OF CANADA

16. (1) English and French are the official languages of Canada and have equality of status and equal rights and privileges as to their use in all institutions of the Parliament and government of Canada.

Official languages of New Brunswick

(2) English and French are the official languages of New Brunswick and have equality of status and equal rights and privileges as to their use in all institutions of the legislature and government of New Brunswick.

Advancement of status and use

(3) Nothing in this Charter limits the authority of Parliament or a legislature to advance the equality of status or use of English and French.

PROCEEDINGS OF PARLIAMENT

17. (1) Everyone has the right to use English or French in any debates and other proceedings of Parliament.

Proceedings of New Brunswick legislature

(2) Everyone has the right to use English or French in any debates and other proceedings of the legislature of New Brunswick.

PARLIAMENTARY STATUTES AND RECORDS

18. (1) The statutes, records and journals of Parliament shall be printed and published in English and French and both language versions are equally authoritative.

New Brunswick statutes and records

(2) The statutes, records and journals of the legislature of New Brunswick shall be printed and published in English and French and both language versions are equally authoritative.

PROCEEDINGS IN COURTS ESTABLISHED BY PARLIAMENT

19. (1) Either English or French may be used by any person in, or in any pleading in or process issuing from, any court established by Parliament.

Proceedings in New Brunswick courts

(2) Either English or French may be used by any person in or in any pleading in or process issuing from, any court of New Brunswick.

COMMUNICATIONS BY PUBLIC WITH FEDERAL INSTITUTIONS

20. Any member of the public in Canada has the right to communicate with, and to receive available services from, any head or central office of an institution of the Parliament or government of Canada in English or French, and has the same right with respect to any other office of any such institution where

(a) there is a significant demand for communications with and services from that office in such language; or

(b) due to the nature of the office, it is reasonable that communications with and services from that office be available in both English and French.

Communications by public with New Brunswick institutions

21. Nothing in sections 16 to 20 abrogates or derogates from any right, privilege or obligation with respect to the English and French languages, or either of them, that exists or is continued by virtue of any other provision of the Constitution of Canada.

RIGHTS AND PRIVILEGES PRESERVED

22. Nothing in sections 16 to 20 abrogates or derogates from any legal or customary right or privilege acquired or enjoyed either before or after the coming into force of this Charter with respect to any language that is not English or French.

MINORITY LANGUAGE EDUCATIONAL RIGHTS

LANGUAGE OF INSTRUCTION

23. (1) Citizens of Canada

(a) whose first language learned and still understood is that of the English or French linguistic minority population of the province in which they reside, or

(b) who have received their primary school instruction in Canada in English or French and reside in a province where the language in which they received that instruction is the language of the English or French linguistic minority population of the province,

have the right to have their children receive primary and secondary school instruction in that language in that province.

Continuity of language instruction

(2) Citizens of Canada of whom any child has received or is receiving primary or secondary school instruction in English or French in Canada, have the right to have all their children receive primary and secondary school instruction in the same language.

Application where numbers warrant

(3) The right of citizens of Canada under subsections (1) and (2) to have their children receive primary and secondary school instruction in the language of the English or French linguistic minority population of a province.

(a) applies wherever in the province the number of children of citizens who have such a right is sufficient to warrant the provision to them out of public funds of minority language instruction; and

(b) includes, where the number of those children so warrants, the right to have them receive that instruction in minority language educational facilities provided out of public funds.

ENFORCEMENT

ENFORCEMENT OF GUARANTEED RIGHTS AND FREEDOMS

24. (1) Anyone whose rights or freedoms, as guaranteed by this Charter, have been infringed or denied may apply to a court of competent jurisdiction to obtain such remedy as the court considers appropriate and just in the circumstances.

Exclusion of evidence bringing administration of justice into disrepute

(2) Where, in proceedings under subsection (1), a court concludes that evidence was obtained in a manner that infringed or denied any rights or freedoms guaranteed by this Charter, the evidence shall be excluded if it is established that, having regard to all the circumstances, the admission of it in the proceedings would bring the administration of justice into disrepute.

GENERAL

ABORIGINAL RIGHTS AND FREEDOMS NOT AFFECTED BY CHARTER

25. The guarantee in this Charter of certain rights and freedoms shall not be construed so as to abrogate or derogate from any aboriginal, treaty or other rights or freedoms that pertain to the aboriginal peoples of Canada including

(a) any rights or freedoms that have been recognized by the Royal Proclamation of 7 October 1763; and

(b) any rights or freedoms that now exist by way of land claims agreements or may be so acquired.

OTHER RIGHTS AND FREEDOMS NOT AFFECTED BY CHARTER

26. The guarantee in this Charter of certain rights and freedoms shall not be construed as denying the existence of any other rights or freedoms that exist in Canada.

MULTICULTURAL HERITAGE

27. This Charter shall be interpreted in a manner consistent with the preservation and enhancement of the multicultural heritage of Canadians.

RIGHTS GUARANTEED EQUALLY TO BOTH SEXES

28. Notwithstanding anything in this Charter, the rights and freedoms referred to in it are guaranteed equally to male and female persons.

RIGHTS RESPECTING CERTAIN SCHOOLS PRESERVED

29. Nothing in this Charter abrogates or derogates from any rights or privileges guaranteed by or under the Constitution of Canada in respect of denominational, separate or dissentient schools.

APPLICATION TO TERRITORIES AND TERRITORIAL AUTHORITIES

30. A reference in this Charter to a Province or to the legislative assembly or legislature of a province shall be deemed to include a reference to the Yukon Territory and the Northwest Territories, or to the appropriate legislative authority thereof, as the case may be.

LEGISLATIVE POWERS NOT EXTENDED

31. Nothing in this Charter extends the legislative powers of any body or authority.

APPLICATION OF CHARTER

32. (1) This Charter applies

(a) to the Parliament and government of Canada in respect of all matters within the authority of Parliament including all matters relating to the Yukon Territory and Northwest Territories; and

(b) to the legislature and government of each province in respect of all matters within the authority of the legislature of each province.

Exception

(2) Notwithstanding subsection (1), section 15 shall not have effect until three years after this section comes into force.

EXCEPTION WHERE EXPRESS DECLARATION

33. (1) Parliament or the legislature of a province may expressly declare in an Act of Parliament or of the legislature, as the case may be, that the Act or a provision thereof shall operate notwithstanding a provision included in section 2 or sections 7 to 15 of this Charter.

Operation of exception

(2) An Act or a provision of an Act in respect of which a declaration made under this section is in effect shall have such operation as it would have but for the provision of this Charter referred to in the declaration.

Five year limitation

(3) A declaration made under subsection (1) shall cease to have effect five years after it comes into force or on such earlier date as may be specified in the declaration.

Re-enactment

(4) Parliament or the legislature of a province may reenact a declaration made under subsection (1).

Five-year limitation

(5) Subsection (3) applies in respect of a re-enactment made under subsection (4).

CITATION

34. This Part may be cited as the Canadian Charter of Rights and Freedoms.

PART II

RIGHTS OF THE ABORIGINAL PEOPLES OF CANADA

RECOGNITION OF EXISTING ABORIGINAL AND TREATY RIGHTS

35. (1)[A] The existing aboriginal and treaty rights of the aboriginal peoples of Canada are hereby recognized and affirmed.

Definition of "aboriginal peoples of Canada"

(2) In this Act, "aboriginal peoples of Canada" includes the Indian, Inuit and Métis peoples of Canada.

Land claims agreements

(3) For greater certainty, in subsection (1) "treaty rights" includes rights that now exist by way of land claims agreements or may be so acquired.

Aboriginal and treaty rights are guaranteed equally to both sexes

(4) Notwithstanding any other provision of this Act, the aboriginal and treaty rights referred to in subsection (1) are guaranteed equally to male and female persons.

COMMITMENT TO PARTICIPATION IN CONSTITUTIONAL CONFERENCE

35(1)[B] The government of Canada and the provincial governments are committed to the principal that, before any amendment is made to Class 24 of section 91 of the "Constitution Act, 1867", to section 25 of this Act or to this Part,

(a) a constitutional conference that includes in its agenda an item relating to the proposed amendment, composed of the Prime Minister of Canada and the first ministers of the provinces, will be convened by the Prime Minister of Canada; and

(b) the Prime Minister of Canada will invite representatives of the aboriginal peoples of Canada to participate in the discussions on that item.

PART III

EQUALIZATION AND REGIONAL DISPARITIES

COMMITMENT TO PROMOTE EQUAL OPPORTUNITIES

36. (1) Without altering the legislative authority of Parliament or of the provincial legislatures, or the rights of any of them with respect to the exercise of their legislative authority, Parliament and the legislatures, together with the government of Canada and the provincial governments, are committed to

(a) promoting equal opportunities for the well-being of Canadians;

(b) furthering economic development to reduce disparity in opportunities; and

(c) providing essential public services of reasonable quality to all Canadians.

Commitment respecting public services

(2) Parliament and the government of Canada are committed to the principle of making equalization payments to ensure that provincial governments have sufficient revenues to provide reasonable comparable levels of public services at reasonably comparable levels of taxation.

PART IV

CONSTITUTIONAL CONFERENCE

37. Section 54 provide for the repeal of Part IV one year after part VII came into force. Part VII came into force on 17 April 1982 thereby repealing Part IV on 17 April 1983.

PART IV.I

CONSTITUTIONAL CONFERENCES

(1) Which was added by the Constitution Amendment Proclamation, 1983 (see SI/84-102), was repealed on 18 April 1987 by section 54.1.

PART V

PROCEDURE FOR AMENDING CONSTITUTION OF CANADA

GENERAL PROCEDURE FOR AMENDING CONSTITUTION OF CANADA

38. (1) An amendment to the Constitution of Canada may be made by proclamation issued by the Governor General under the Grant Seal of Canada where so authorized by

(a) resolutions of the Senate and House of Commons; and

(b) resolutions of the legislative assemblies of at least two-thirds of the provinces that have, in the aggregate, according to the then latest general census, at lcast fifty per cent of the population of all the provinces.

Majority of members

(2) An amendment made under subsection (1) that derogates from the legislative powers, the proprietary rights or any other rights or privileges of the legislature or government of a province shall require a resolution supported by a majority of the members of each of the Senate, the House of Commons and the legislative assemblies required under subsection (1).

Expression of dissent

(3) An amendment referred to in subsection (2) shall not have effect in a province the legislative assembly of which has expressed its dissent thereto by resolution supported by a majority of its members prior to the issue of the proclamation to which the amendment relates unless that legislative assembly, subsequently, by resolution supported by a majority of its members, revokes its dissent and authorizes the amendment.

Revocation of dissent

(4) A resolution of dissent made for the purposes of subsection (3) may be revoked at any time before or after the issue of the proclamation to which it relates.

RESTRICTION ON PROCLAMATION

39. (1) A proclamation shall not be issued under subsection 38(1) before the expiration of one year from the adoption of the resolution initiating the amendment procedure thereunder, unless the legislative assembly of each province has previously adopted a resolution of assent or dissent.

Idem

(2) A proclamation shall not be issued under subsection 38(1) after the expiration of three years from the adoption of the resolution initiating the amendment procedure thereunder.

COMPENSATION

40. Where an amendment is made under subsection 38(1) that transfers provincial legislative powers relating to education or other cultural matters from provincial legislatures to Parliament, Canada shall provide reasonable compensation to any province to which the amendment does not apply.

AMENDMENT BY UNANIMOUS CONSENT

41. An amendment to the Constitution of Canada in relation to the following matters may be made by proclamation issued by the Governor General under the Great Seal of Canada only where authorized by resolutions of the Senate and House of Commons and of the Legislative assembly of each province:

(a) the office of the Queen, the Governor General and the Lieutenant Governor of a province;

(b) the right of a province to a number of members in the House of Commons not less than the number of Senators by which the province is entitled to be represented at the time this Part comes into force;

(c) subject to section 43, the use of the English or the French language;

(d) the composition of the Supreme Court of Canada; and

(e) an amendment to this Part.

AMENDMENT BY GENERAL PROCEDURE

42. (1) An amendment to the Constitution of Canada in relation to the following matters may be made only in accordance with subsection 38(1):

(a) the principle of proportionate representation of the provinces in the House of Commons prescribed by the Constitution of Canada;

(b) the powers of the Senate and the method of selecting Senators;

(c) the number of members by which a province is entitled to be represented in the Senate and the residence qualifications of Senators;

(d) subject to paragraph 41(d), the Supreme Court of Canada;

(e) the extension of existing provinces into the territories; and

(f) notwithstanding any other law or practice, the establishment of new provinces.

Exception

(2) Subsections 38(2) to (4) do not apply in respect of amendments in relation to matters referred to in subsection (1).

AMENDMENT OF PROVISIONS RELATING TO SOME BUT NOT ALL PROVINCES

43. An amendment to the Constitution of Canada in relation to any provision that applies to one or more, but not all, provinces, including

(a) any alteration to boundaries between provinces, and

(b) any amendment to any provision that relates to the use of the English or the French language within a province may be made by proclamation issued by the Governor General under the Great Seal of Canada only where so authorized by resolutions of the Senate and House of Commons and of the legislative assembly of each province to which the amendment applies.

AMENDMENTS BY PARLIAMENT

44. Subject to sections 41 and 42, Parliament may exclusively make laws amending the Constitution of Canada in relation to the executive government of Canada or the Senate and House of Commons.

AMENDMENTS BY PROVINCIAL LEGISLATURES

45. Subject to section 41, the legislature of each province may exclusively make laws amending the Constitution of the province.

INITIATION OF AMENDMENT PROCEDURES

46. (1) The procedures for amendment under sections 38, 41, 42 and 43 may be initiated either by the Senate or the House of Commons or by the legislative assembly of a province.

(2) A resolution of assent made for the purposes of this Part may be revoked at any time before the issue of a proclamation authorized by it.

AMENDMENTS WITHOUT SENATE RESOLUTION

47. (1) An amendment to the Constitution of Canada made by proclamation under sections 38, 41, 42 or 43 may be made without a resolution of the Senate authorizing the issue of the proclamation if, within one hundred and eighty days after the adoption by the House of Commons of a resolution authorizing its issue, the Senate has not adopted such a resolution and if, at any time after the expiration of that period, the House of Commons again adopts the resolution.

Computation of period

(2) Any period when Parliament is prorogued or dissolved shall not be counted in computing the one hundred and eighty day period referred to in subsection (1).

ADVICE TO ISSUE PROCLAMATION

48. The Queen's Privy Council for Canada shall advise the Governor General to issue a proclamation under this Part forthwith on the adoption of the resolutions required for an amendment made by proclamation under this Part.

CONSTITUTIONAL CONFERENCE

49. A constitutional conference composed of the Prime Minister of Canada and the first ministers of the provinces shall be convened by the Primer Minister of Canada within fifteen years after this Part comes into force to review the provisions of this Part.

PART VI

AMENDMENT TO THE CONSTITUTION ACT, 1867

50. The amendment is set out in the Consolidation of the Constitution Act, 1867, as section 92A thereof.

51. The amendment is set out in the Consolidation of the Constitution Act, 1867, as the Sixth Schedule thereof.

PART VII

GENERAL

Primacy of Constitution of Canada

52. (1) The Constitution of Canada is the supreme law of Canada, and any law that is inconsistent with the provisions of

the Constitution is, to the extent of the inconsistency, of no force or effect.

Constitution of Canada

(2) The Constitution of Canada includes

(a) the Canada Act 1982, including this Act;

(b) the Acts add orders referred to in the schedule; and

(c) any amendment to any Act or order referred to in paragraph (a) or (b).

Amendments to Constitution of Canada

(3) Amendments to the Constitution of Canada shall be made only in accordance with the authority contained in the Constitution of Canada.

REPEALS AND NEW NAMES

53. (1) The enactments referred to in Column I of the schedule are hereby repealed or amended to the extent indicated in Column II thereof and, unless repealed, shall continue as law in Canada under the names set out in Column III thereof.

Consequential amendments

(2) Every enactment, except the Canada Act 1982, that refers to an enactment referred to in the schedule by the name in Column I thereof is hereby amended by substituting for that name the corresponding name in Column III thereof, and any British North America Act not referred to in the schedule may be cited as the Constitution Act followed by the year and number, if any, of its enactment.

REPEAL AND CONSEQUENTIAL AMENDMENTS

54. Part IV is repealed on the day that is one year after this Part comes into force and this section may be repealed and this Act renumbered, consequentially upon the repeal of Part IV and this section, by proclamation issued by the Governor General under the Great Seal of Canada.

(1) Which was added by the Constitution Amendment Proclamation, 1983 (see SI/84-102), provided for the repeal of Part IV, I and section 54.1 on 18 April 1987.

FRENCH VERSION OF CONSTITUTION OF CANADA

55. A French version of the portions of the Constitution of Canada referred to in the schedule shall be prepared by the Minister of Justice of Canada as expeditiously as possible and, when any portion thereof sufficient to warrant action being taken has been so prepared, it shall be put forward for enactment by proclamation issued by the Governor General under the Great Seal of Canada pursuant to the procedure then applicable to an amendment of the same provisions of the Constitution of Canada.

ENGLISH AND FRENCH VERSIONS OF CERTAIN CONSTITUTIONAL TEXTS

56. Where any portion of the Constitution of Canada has been or is enacted in English and French or where a French version of any portion of the Constitution is enacted pursuant to section 55, the English and French versions of that portion of the Constitution are equally authoritative.

ENGLISH AND FRENCH VERSIONS OF THIS ACT

57. The English and French versions of this Act are equally authoritative.

COMMENCEMENT

58. Subject to section 59, this Act shall come into force one day to be fixed by proclamation issued by the Queen or the Governor General under the Great Seal of Canada.

COMMENCEMENT OF PARAGRAPH

59. (1) Paragraph 23(1)(a) shall come into force in respect of Quebec one day to be fixed by proclamation issued by the Queen or the Governor General under the Great Seal of Canada.

(2) A proclamation under subsection (1) shall be issued only where authorized by the legislative assembly or government of Quebec.

(3) This section may be repealed on the day paragraph 23(1)(a) comes into force in respect of Quebec and this Act amended and renumbered, consequentially upon the repeal of

this section, by proclamation issued by the Queen or the Governor General under the Great Seal of Canada.

SHORT TITLE AND CITATIONS

60. This Act may be cited as the Constitution Act. 1982, and the Constitution Acts 1867 to 1975 (No. 2) and this Act may be cited together as the Constitution Acts, 1867 to 1982.

REFERENCES

61. A reference to the "Constitution Acts, 1867 to 1982" shall be deemed to include a reference to the "Constitution Amendment Proclamation, 1983".

Constitution of the Republic of South Africa

6

Date of Commencement: 4 February 1997

[Short title, previously 'Constitution of the Republic of South Africa, Act 108 of 1996', substituted by s. 1 (1) of Act 5 of 2005.] [Assented to 16 December 1996] [Date of Commencement: 4 February 1997] [Unless otherwise indicated - see also s. 243 (5)] (English text signed by the President) as amended by

Constitution of the Republic of South Africa, 1996

Constitution First Amendment Act of 1997

Constitution Second Amendment Act of 1998

Constitution Third Amendment Act of 1998

Constitution Fourth Amendment Act of 1999

Constitution Fifth Amendment Act of 1999

Constitution Sixth Amendment Act of 2001

Constitution Seventh Amendment Act of 2001

Constitution Eighth Amendment Act of 2002

Constitution Ninth Amendment Act of 2002

Constitution Tenth Amendment Act of 2003

Constitution Eleventh Amendment Act of 2003

Constitution Twelfth Amendment Act of 2005

The Act to introduce a new Constitution for the Republic of South Africa and to provide for matters incidental thereto.

Preamble

We, the people of South Africa, Recognise the injustices of our past; Honour those who suffered for justice and freedom in our land; Respect those who have worked to build and develop our country; and Believe that South Africa belongs to all who live in it, united in our diversity. We therefore, through our freely elected representatives, adopt this Constitution as the supreme law of the Republic so as to - Heal the divisions of the past and establish a society based on democratic values, social justice and fundamental human rights; Lay the foundations for a democratic and open society in which government is based on the will of the people and every citizen is equally protected by law; Improve the quality of life of all citizens and free the potential of each person; and Build a united and democratic South Africa able to take its rightful place as a sovereign state in the family of nations. May God protect our people. 'Nkosi Sikelel' iAfrika. Morena boloka setjhaba sa heso. God seën Suid-Afrika. God bless South Africa. Mudzimu fhatutshedza Afurika. Hosi katekisa Afrika.

Chapter 1

Founding Provisions (ss 1-6)

1. Republic of South Africa

The Republic of South Africa is one, sovereign, democratic state founded on the following values:

(a) Human dignity, the achievement of equality and the advancement of human rights and freedoms.

(b) Non-racialism and non-sexism.

(c) Supremacy of the Constitution and the rule of law.

(d) Universal adult suffrage, a national common voters roll, regular elections and a multiparty system of democratic government, to ensure accountability, responsiveness and openness.

2. Supremacy of Constitution

This Constitution is the supreme law of the Republic; law or conduct inconsistent with it is invalid, and the obligations imposed by it must be fulfilled.

3. Citizenship

(1) There is a common South African citizenship.

(2) All citizens are:

(a) equally entitled to the rights, privileges and benefits of citizenship; and

(b) equally subject to the duties and responsibilities of citizenship.

(3) National legislation must provide for the acquisition, loss and restoration of citizenship.

4. National anthem

The national anthem of the Republic is determined by the President by proclamation.

5. National flag

The national flag of the Republic is black, gold, green, white, red and blue, as described and sketched in Schedule 1.

6. Languages

(1) The official languages of the Republic are Sepedi, Sesotho, Setswana, siSwati, Tshivenda, Xitsonga, Afrikaans, English, isiNdebele, isiXhosa and isiZulu.

(2) Recognising the historically diminished use and status of the indigenous languages of our people, the state must take practical and positive measures to elevate the status and advance the use of these languages.

(3)

(a) The national government and provincial governments may use any particular official languages for the purposes of government, taking into account usage, practicality, expense, regional circumstances and the balance of the needs and preferences of the population as a whole or in the province concerned; but the national government and each provincial government must use at least two official languages.

(b) Municipalities must take into account the language usage and preferences of their residents.

(4) The national government and provincial governments, by legislative and other measures, must regulate and monitor their use of official languages. Without detracting from the

provisions of subsection (2), all official languages must enjoy parity of esteem and must be treated equitably.

(5) A Pan South African Language Board established by national legislation must

(a) promote, and create conditions for, the development and use of-
   (i) all official languages;
   (ii) the Khoi, Nama and San languages; and
   (iii) sign language; and

(b) promote and ensure respect for-
   (i) all languages commonly used by communities in South Africa, including German, Greek, Gujarati, Hindi, Portuguese, Tamil, Telugu and Urdu; and
   (ii) Arabic, Hebrew, Sanskrit and other languages used for religious purposes in South Africa.

Chapter 2

Bill of Rights (ss 7-39)

7. Rights

(1) This Bill of Rights is a cornerstone of democracy in South Africa. It enshrines the rights of all people in our country and affirms the democratic values of human dignity, equality and freedom.

(2) The state must respect, protect, promote and fulfil the rights in the Bill of Rights.

(3) The rights in the Bill of Rights are subject to the limitations contained or referred to in section 36, or elsewhere in the Bill.

8. Application

(1) The Bill of Rights applies to all law, and binds the legislature, the executive, the judiciary and all organs of state.

(2) A provision of the Bill of Rights binds a natural or a juristic person if, and to the extent that, it is applicable, taking into account the nature of the right and the nature of any duty imposed by the right.

(3) When applying a provision of the Bill of Rights to a natural or juristic person in terms of subsection (2), a court-

(a) in order to give effect to a right in the Bill, must apply, or if necessary develop, the common law to the extent that legislation does not give effect to that right; and

(b) may develop rules of the common law to limit the right, provided that the limitation is in accordance with section 36 (1).

(4) A juristic person is entitled to the rights in the Bill of Rights to the extent required by the nature of the rights and the nature of that juristic person.

9. Equality

(1) Everyone is equal before the law and has the right to equal protection and benefit of the law.

(2) Equality includes the full and equal enjoyment of all rights and freedoms. To promote the achievement of equality, legislative and other measures designed to protect or advance persons, or categories of persons, disadvantaged by unfair discrimination may be taken.

(3) The state may not unfairly discriminate directly or indirectly against anyone on one or more grounds, including race, gender, sex, pregnancy, marital status, ethnic or social origin, colour, sexual orientation, age, disability, religion, conscience, belief, culture, language and birth.

(4) No person may unfairly discriminate directly or indirectly against anyone on one or more grounds in terms of subsection (3). National legislation must be enacted to prevent or prohibit unfair discrimination.

(5) Discrimination on one or more of the grounds listed in subsection (3) is unfair unless it is established that the discrimination is fair.

10. Human dignity

Everyone has inherent dignity and the right to have their dignity respected and protected.

11. Life

Everyone has the right to life.

12. Freedom and security of the person

(1) Everyone has the right to freedom and security of the person, which includes the right-

(a) not to be deprived of freedom arbitrarily or without just cause;

(b) not to be detained without trial;

(c) to be free from all forms of violence from either public or private sources;

(d) not to be tortured in any way; and

(e) not to be treated or punished in a cruel, inhuman or degrading way.

(2) Everyone has the right to bodily and psychological integrity, which includes the right-

(a) to make decisions concerning reproduction;

(b) to security in and control over their body; and

(c) not to be subjected to medical or scientific experiments without their informed consent.

13. Slavery, servitude and forced labour

No one may be subjected to slavery, servitude or forced labour.

14. Privacy

Everyone has the right to privacy, which includes the right not to have-

(a) their person or home searched;

(b) their property searched;

(c) their possessions seized; or

(d) the privacy of their communications infringed.

15. Freedom of religion, belief and opinion

(1) Everyone has the right to freedom of conscience, religion, thought, belief and opinion.

(2) Religious observances may be conducted at state or state-aided institutions, provided that-

(a) those observances follow rules made by the appropriate public authorities;

(b) they are conducted on an equitable basis; and

(c) attendance at them is free and voluntary.

(3)

(a) This section does not prevent legislation recognising-

(i) marriages concluded under any tradition, or a system of religious, personal or family law; or

(ii) systems of personal and family law under any tradition, or adhered to by persons professing a particular religion.

(b) Recognition in terms of paragraph (a) must be consistent with this section and the other provisions of the Constitution.

16. Freedom of expression

(1) Everyone has the right to freedom of expression, which includes-

(a) freedom of the press and other media;

(b) freedom to receive or impart information or ideas;

(c) freedom of artistic creativity; and

(d) academic freedom and freedom of scientific research.

(2) The right in subsection (1) does not extend to

(a) propaganda for war;

(b) incitement of imminent violence; or

(c) advocacy of hatred that is based on race, ethnicity, gender or religion, and that constitutes incitement to cause harm.

17. Assembly, demonstration picket and petition

Everyone has the right, peacefully and unarmed, to assemble, to demonstrate, to picket and to present petitions.

18. Freedom of association

Everyone has the right to freedom of association.

19. Political rights

(1) Every citizen is free to make political choices, which includes the right

(a) to form a political party;

(b) to participate in the activities of, or recruit members for, a political party; and

(c) to campaign for a political party or cause.

(2) Every citizen has the right to free, fair and regular elections for any legislative body established in terms of the Constitution.

(3) Every adult citizen has the right-

(a) to vote in elections for any legislative body established in terms of the Constitution, and to do so in secret; and

(b) to stand for public office and, if elected, to hold office.

20. Citizenship

No citizen may be deprived of citizenship.

21. Freedom of movement and residence

(1) Everyone has the right to freedom of movement.

(2) Everyone has the right to leave the Republic.

(3) Every citizen has the right to enter, to remain in and to reside anywhere in, the Republic.

(4) Every citizen has the right to a passport.

22. Freedom of trade, occupation and profession

Every citizen has the right to choose their trade, occupation or profession freely. The practice of a trade, occupation or profession may be regulated by law.

23. Labour relations

(1) Everyone has the right to fair labour practices.

(2) Every worker has the right

(a) to form and join a trade union;

(b) to participate in the activities and programmes of a trade union; and

(c) to strike.

(3) Every employer has the right

(a) to form and join an employers' organisation; and

(b) to participate in the activities and programmes of an employers' organisation.

(4) Every trade union and every employers' organisation has the right-

(a) to determine its own administration, programmes and activities;

(b) to organise; and

(c) to form and join a federation.

(5) Every trade union, employers' organisation and employer has the right to engage in collective bargaining. National legislation may be enacted to regulate collective bargaining. To the extent that the legislation may limit a right in this Chapter, the limitation must comply with section 36 (1).

(6) National legislation may recognise union security arrangements contained in collective agreements. To the extent that the legislation may limit a right in this Chapter the limitation must comply with section 36 (1).

24. Environment

Everyone has the right

(a) to an environment that is not harmful to their health or well-being; and

(b) to have the environment protected, for the benefit of present and future generations, through reasonable legislative and other measures that-

(i) prevent pollution and ecological degradation;

(ii) promote conservation; and

(iii) secure ecologically sustainable development and use of natural resources while promoting justifiable economic and social development.

25. Property

(1) No one may be deprived of property except in terms of law of general application, and no law may permit arbitrary deprivation of property.

(2) Property may be expropriated only in terms of law of general application-

(a) for a public purpose or in the public interest; and

(b) subject to compensation, the amount of which and the time and manner of payment of which have either been agreed to by those affected or decided or approved by a court.

(3) The amount of the compensation and the time and manner of payment must be just and equitable, reflecting an equitable balance between the public interest and the interests of those affected, having regard to all relevant circumstances, including-

(a) the current use of the property;

(b) the history of the acquisition and use of the property;

(c) the market value of the property;

(d) the extent of direct state investment and subsidy in the acquisition and beneficial capital improvement of the property; and

(e) the purpose of the expropriation.

(4) For the purposes of this section-

(a) the public interest includes the nation's commitment to land reform, and to reforms to bring about equitable access to all South Africa's natural resources; and

(b) property is not limited to land.

(5) The state must take reasonable legislative and other measures, within its available resources, to foster conditions

which enable citizens to gain access to land on an equitable basis.

(6) A person or community whose tenure of land is legally insecure as a result of past racially discriminatory laws or practices is entitled, to the extent provided by an Act of Parliament, either to tenure which is legally secure or to comparable redress.

(7) A person or community dispossessed of property after 19 June 1913 as a result of past racially discriminatory laws or practices is entitled, to the extent provided by an Act of Parliament, either to restitution of that property or to equitable redress.

(8) No provision of this section may impede the state from taking legislative and other measures to achieve land, water and related reform, in order to redress the results of past racial discrimination, provided that any departure from the provisions of this section is in accordance with the provisions of section 36 (1).

(9) Parliament must enact the legislation referred to in subsection (6).

26. Housing

(1) Everyone has the right to have access to adequate housing.

(2) The state must take reasonable legislative and other measures, within its available resources, to achieve the progressive realisation of this right.

(3) No one may be evicted from their home, or have their home demolished, without an order of court made after considering all the relevant circumstances. No legislation may permit arbitrary evictions.

27. Health care, food, water and social security

(1) Everyone has the right to have access to-

(a) health care services, including reproductive health care;

(b) sufficient food and water; and

(c) social security, including, if they are unable to support themselves and their dependents, appropriate social assistance.

(2) The state must take reasonable legislative and other measures, within its available resources, to achieve the progressive realisation of each of these rights.

(3) No one may be refused emergency medical treatment.

28. Children

(1) Every child has the right-

(a) to a name and a nationality from birth;

(b) to family care or parental care, or to appropriate alternative care when removed from the family environment;

(c) to basic nutrition, shelter, basic health care services and social services;

(d) to be protected from maltreatment, neglect, abuse or degradation;

(e) to be protected from exploitative labour practices;

(f) not to be required or permitted to perform work or provide services that-

(i) are inappropriate for a person of that child's age; or

(ii) place at risk the child's well-being, education, physical or mental health or spiritual, moral or social development;

(g) not to be detained except as a measure of last resort, in which case, in addition to the rights a child enjoys under sections 12 and 35, the child may be detained only for the shortest appropriate period of time, and has the right to be-

(i) kept separately from detained persons over the age of 18 years; and

(ii) treated in a manner, and kept in conditions, that take account of the child's age;

(h) to have a legal practitioner assigned to the child by the state, and at state expense, in civil proceedings affecting the child, if substantial injustice would otherwise result; and

(i) not to be used directly in armed conflict, and to be protected in times of armed conflict.

(2) A child's best interests are of paramount importance in every matter concerning the child.

(3) In this section 'child' means a person under the age of 18 years.

29. Education

(1) Everyone has the right-

(a) to a basic education, including adult basic education; and

(b) to further education, which the state, through reasonable measures, must make progressively available and accessible.

(2) Everyone has the right to receive education in the official language or languages of their choice in public educational institutions where that education is reasonably practicable. In order to ensure the effective access to, and implementation of, this right, the state must consider all reasonable educational alternatives, including single medium institutions, taking into account

(a) equity;

(b) practicability; and

(c) the need to redress the results of past racially discriminatory laws and practices.

(3) Everyone has the right to establish and maintain, at their own expense, independent educational institutions that-

(a) do not discriminate on the basis of race;

(b) are registered with the state; and

(c) maintain standards that are not inferior to standards at comparable public educational institutions.

(4) Subsection (3) does not preclude state subsidies for independent educational institutions.

30. Language and culture

Everyone has the right to use the language and to participate in the cultural life of their choice, but no one exercising these rights may do so in a manner inconsistent with any provision of the Bill of Rights.

31. Cultural, religious and linguistic communities

(1) Persons belonging to a cultural, religious or linguistic community may not be denied the right, with other members of that community-

(a) to enjoy their culture, practise their religion and use their language; and

(b) to form, join and maintain cultural, religious and linguistic associations and other organs of civil society.

(2) The rights in subsection (1) may not be exercised in a manner inconsistent with any provision of the Bill of Rights.

32. Access to information

(1) Everyone has the right of access to-

(a) any information held by the state; and

(b) any information that is held by another person and that is required for the exercise or protection of any rights.

(2) National legislation must be enacted to give effect to this right, and may provide for reasonable measures to alleviate the administrative and financial burden on the state.

33. Just administrative action

(1) Everyone has the right to administrative action that is lawful, reasonable and procedurally fair.

(2) Everyone whose rights have been adversely affected by administrative action has the right to be given written reasons.

(3) National legislation must be enacted to give effect to these rights, and must-

(a) provide for the review of administrative action by a court or, where appropriate, an independent and impartial tribunal;

(b) impose a duty on the state to give effect to the rights in subsections (1) and (2); and

(c) promote an efficient administration.

34. Access to courts

Everyone has the right to have any dispute that can be resolved by the application of law decided in a fair public hearing before a court or, where appropriate, another independent and impartial tribunal or forum.

35. Arrested, detained and accused persons

(1) Everyone who is arrested for allegedly committing an offence has the right-

(a) to remain silent;

(b) to be informed promptly-

(i) of the right to remain silent; and

(ii) of the consequences of not remaining silent;

(c) not to be compelled to make any confession or admission that could be used in evidence against that person;

(d) to be brought before a court as soon as reasonably possible, but not later than-

(i) 48 hours after the arrest; or

(ii) the end of the first court day after the expiry of the 48 hours, if the 48 hours expire outside ordinary court hours or on a day which is not an ordinary court day;

(e) at the first court appearance after being arrested, to be charged or to be informed of the reason for the detention to continue, or to be released and

(f) to be released from detention if the interests of justice permit, subject to reasonable conditions.

(2) Everyone who is detained, including every sentenced prisoner, has the right-

(a) to be informed promptly of the reason for being detained;

(b) to choose, and to consult with, a legal practitioner, and to be informed of this right promptly;

(c) to have a legal practitioner assigned to the detained person by the state and at state expense, if substantial injustice would otherwise result, and to be informed of this right promptly;

(d) to challenge the lawfulness of the detention in person before a court and, if the detention is unlawful, to be released;

(e) to conditions of detention that are consistent with human dignity, including at least exercise and the provision, at state expense, of adequate accommodation, nutrition, reading material and medical treatment; and

(f) to communicate with, and be visited by, that person's-

(i) spouse or partner;

(ii) next of kin;

(iii) chosen religious counsellor; and

(iv) chosen medical practitioner.

(3) Every accused person has a right to a fair trial, which includes the right.

(a) to be informed of the charge with sufficient detail to answer it;

(b) to have adequate time and facilities to prepare a defence;

(c) to a public trial before an ordinary court;

(d) to have their trial begin and conclude without unreasonable delay;

(e) to be present when being tried;

(f) to choose, and be represented by, a legal practitioner, and to be informed of this right promptly;

(g) to have a legal practitioner assigned to the accused person by the state and at state expense, if substantial injustice would otherwise result, and to be informed of this right promptly;

(h) to be presumed innocent, to remain silent, and not to testify during the proceedings;

(i) to adduce and challenge evidence;

(j) not to be compelled to give self-incriminating evidence;

(k) to be tried in a language that the accused person understands or, if that is not practicable, to have the proceedings interpreted in that language;

(l) not to be convicted for an act or omission that was not an offence under either national or international law at the time it was committed or omitted;

(m) not to be tried for an offence in respect of an act or omission for which that person has previously been either acquitted or convicted;

(n) to the benefit of the least severe of the prescribed punishments if the prescribed punishment for the offence has been changed between the time that the offence was committed and the time of sentencing; and

(o) of appeal to, or review by, a higher court.

(4) Whenever this section requires information to be given to a person, that information must be given in a language that the person understands.

(5) Evidence obtained in a manner that violates any right in the Bill of Rights must be excluded if the admission of that evidence would render the trial unfair or otherwise be detrimental to the administration of justice.

36. Limitation of rights

(1) The rights in the Bill of Rights may be limited only in terms of law of general application to the extent that the

limitation is reasonable and justifiable in an open and democratic society based on human dignity, equality and freedom, taking into account all relevant factors, including-

(a) the nature of the right;

(b) the importance of the purpose of the limitation;

(c) the nature and extent of the limitation;

(d) the relation between the limitation and its purpose; and

(e) less restrictive means to achieve the purpose.

(2) Except as provided in subsection (1) or in any other provision of the Constitution, no law may limit any right entrenched in the Bill of Rights.

37. States of emergency

(1) A state of emergency may be declared only in terms of an Act of Parliament, and only when-

(a) the life of the nation is threatened by war, invasion, general insurrection, disorder, natural disaster or other public emergency; and

(b) the declaration is necessary to restore peace and order.

(2) A declaration of a state of emergency, and any legislation enacted or other action taken in consequence of that declaration, may be effective only-

(a) prospectively; and

(b) for no more than 21 days from the date of the declaration, unless the National Assembly resolves to extend the declaration. The Assembly may extend a declaration of a state of emergency for no more than three months at a time. The first extension of the state of emergency must be by a resolution adopted with a supporting vote of a majority of the members of the Assembly. Any subsequent extension must be by a resolution adopted with a supporting vote of at least 60 per cent of the members of the Assembly. A resolution in terms of this paragraph may be adopted only following a public debate in the Assembly.

(3) Any competent court may decide on the validity of-

(a) a declaration of a state of emergency;

(b) any extension of a declaration of a state of emergency; or

(c) any legislation enacted, or other action taken, in consequence of a declaration of a state of emergency.

(4) Any legislation enacted in consequence of a declaration of a state of emergency may derogate from the Bill of Rights only to the extent that-

(a) the derogation is strictly required by the emergency; and

(b) the legislation-

(i) is consistent with the Republic's obligations under international law applicable to states of emergency;

(ii) conforms to subsection (5); and

(iii) is published in the national Government Gazette as soon as reasonably possible after being enacted.

(5) No Act of Parliament that authorises a declaration of a state of emergency, and no legislation enacted or other action taken in consequence of declaration, may permit or authorise

(a) indemnifying the state, or any person, in respect of any unlawful act;

(b) any derogation from this section; or

(c) any derogation from a section mentioned in column 1 of the Table of Non-Derogable Rights, to the extent indicated opposite that section in column 3 of the Table.

Table of Non-Derogable Rights

Section Number	Section Title	Extent to which the right is protected
9	Equality	With respect to unfair discrimination solely on the grounds of race, colour, ethnic or social origin, sex religion or language
10	Human Dignity	Entirely
11	Life	Entirely
12	Freedom and Security of the person	With respect to subsections (1)(d) and (e) and (2)(c).
13	Slavery, servitude and forced labour	With respect to slavery and servitude
28	Children	With respect to: - subsection (1)(d) and (e); - the rights in subparagraphs (i) and (ii) of subsection (1)(g); and - subsection 1(i) in respect of children of 15 years and younger
35	Arrested, detained and accused persons	With respect to: - subsections (1)(a), (b) and (c) and (2)(d); - the rights in paragraphs (a) to (o) of subsection (3), excluding paragraph (d) - subsection (4); and - subsection (5) with respect to the exclusion of evidence if the admission of that evidence would render the trial unfair.

(6) Whenever anyone is detained without trial in consequence of a derogation of rights resulting from a declaration of a state of emergency, the following conditions must be observed:

(a) An adult family member or friend of the detainee must be contacted as soon as reasonably possible, and informed that the person has been detained.

(b) A notice must be published in the national Government Gazette within five days of the person being detained, stating the detainee's name and place of detention and referring to the emergency measure in terms of which that person has been detained.

(c) The detainee must be allowed to choose, and be visited at any reasonable time by, a medical practitioner.

(d) The detainee must be allowed to choose, and be visited at any reasonable time by, a legal representative.

(e) A court must review the detention as soon as reasonably possible, but no later than 10 days after the date the person was detained, and the court must release the detainee unless it is necessary to continue the detention to restore peace and order.

(f) A detainee who is not released in terms of a review under paragraph (e), or who is not released in terms of a review under this paragraph, may apply to a court for a further review of the detention at any time after 10 days have passed since the previous review, and the court must release the detainee unless it is still necessary to continue the detention to restore peace and order.

(g) The detainee must be allowed to appear in person before any court considering the detention, to be represented by a legal practitioner at those hearings, and to make representations against continued detention.

(h) The state must present written reasons to the court to justify the continued detention of the detainee, and must give a copy of those reasons to the detainee at least two days before the court reviews the detention.

(7) If a court releases a detainee, that person may not be detained again on the same grounds unless the state first shows a court good cause for re-detaining that person. (8) Subsections (6) and (7) do not apply to persons who are not South African citizens and who are detained in consequence of an international armed conflict. Instead, the state must comply with the standards binding on the Republic under international humanitarian law in respect of the detention of such persons.

38. Enforcement of rights

Anyone listed in this section has the right to approach a competent court, alleging that a right in the Bill of Rights has been infringed or threatened, and the court may grant appropriate relief, including a declaration of rights. The persons who may approach a court are

(a) anyone acting in their own interest;

(b) anyone acting on behalf of another person who cannot act in their own name;

(c) anyone acting as a member of, or in the interest of, a group or class of persons;

(d) anyone acting in the public interest; and

(e) an association acting in the interest of its members.

39. Interpretation of Bill of Rights

(1) When interpreting the Bill of Rights, a court, tribunal or forum

(a) must promote the values that underlie an open and democratic society based on human dignity, equality and freedom;

(b) must consider international law; and

(c) may consider foreign law.

(2) When interpreting any legislation, and when developing the common law or customary law, every court, tribunal or forum must promote the spirit, purport and objects of the Bill of Rights.

(3) The Bill of Rights does not deny the existence of any other rights or freedoms that are recognised or conferred by common law, customary law or legislation, to the extent that they are consistent with the Bill.

Chapter 3

Cooperative Government (ss 40-41)

40. Government of the Republic

(1) In the Republic, government is constituted as national, provincial and local spheres of government which are distinctive, interdependent and interrelated.

(2) All spheres of government must observe and adhere to the principles in this Chapter and must conduct their activities within the parameters that the Chapter provides.

41. Principles of cooperative government and intergovernmental relations

(1) All spheres of government and all organs of state within each sphere must-

(a) preserve the peace, national unity and the indivisibility of the Republic;

(b) secure the well-being of the people of the Republic;

(c) provide effective, transparent, accountable and coherent government for the Republic as a whole;

(d) be loyal to the Constitution, the Republic and its people;

(e) respect the constitutional status, institutions, powers and functions of government in the other spheres;

(f) not assume any power or function except those conferred on them in terms of the Constitution;

(g) exercise their powers and perform their functions in a manner that does not encroach on the geographical, functional or institutional integrity of government in another sphere; and

(h) cooperate with one another in mutual trust and good faith by-

(i) fostering friendly relations;

(ii) assisting and supporting one another;

(iii) informing one another of, and consulting one another on, matters of common interest;

(iv) coordinating their actions and legislation with one another;

(v) adhering to agreed procedures; and

(vi) avoiding legal proceedings against one another.

(2) An Act of Parliament must-

(a) establish or provide for structures and institutions to promote and facilitate intergovernmental relations; and

(b) provide for appropriate mechanisms and procedures to facilitate settlement of intergovernmental disputes.

(3) An organ of state involved in an intergovernmental dispute must make every reasonable effort to settle the dispute by means of mechanisms and procedures provided for that purpose, and must exhaust all other remedies before it approaches a court to resolve the dispute.

(4) If a court is not satisfied that the requirements of subsection (3) have been met, it may refer a dispute back to the organs of state involved.

Chapter 4

Parliament (ss 42-82)

42. Composition of Parliament

(1) Parliament consists of-

(a) the National Assembly; and

(b) the National Council of Provinces.

(2) The National Assembly and the National Council of Provinces participate in the legislative process in the manner set out in the Constitution.

(3) The National Assembly is elected to represent the people and to ensure government by the people under the Constitution. It does this by choosing the President, by providing a national forum for public consideration of issues, by passing legislation and by scrutinizing and overseeing executive action.

(4) The National Council of Provinces represents the provinces to ensure that provincial interests are taken into account in the national sphere of government. It does this mainly by participating in the national legislative process and by providing a national forum for public consideration of issues affecting the provinces.

(5) The President may summon Parliament to an extraordinary sitting at any time to conduct special business.

(6) The seat of Parliament is Cape Town, but an Act of Parliament enacted in accordance with section 76 (1) and (5) may determine that the seat of Parliament is elsewhere.

43. Legislative authority of the Republic

In the Republic, the legislative authority

(a) of the national sphere of government is vested in Parliament, as set out in section 44;

(b) of the provincial sphere of government is vested in the provincial legislatures, as set out in section 104; and

(c) of the local sphere of government is vested in the Municipal Councils, as set out in section 156.

44. National legislative authority

(1) The national legislative authority as vested in Parliament

(a) confers on the National Assembly the power-

(i) to amend the Constitution;

(ii) to pass legislation with regard to any matter, including a matter within a functional area listed in Schedule 4, but excluding, subject to subsection (2), a matter within a functional area listed in Schedule 5; and

(iii) to assign any of its legislative powers, except the power to amend the Constitution, to any legislative body in another sphere of government; and

(b) confers on the National Council of Provinces the power-

(i) to participate in amending the Constitution in accordance with section 74;

(ii) to pass, in accordance with section 76, legislation with regard to any matter within a functional area listed in Schedule 4 and any other matter required by the Constitution to be passed in accordance with section 76; and

(iii) to consider, in accordance with section 75, any other legislation passed by the National Assembly.

(2) Parliament may intervene, by passing legislation in accordance with section 76 (1), with regard to a matter falling within a functional area listed in Schedule 5, when it is necessary

(a) to maintain national security;

(b) to maintain economic unity;

(c) to maintain essential national standards;

(d) to establish minimum standards required for the rendering of services; or

(e) to prevent unreasonable action taken by a province which is prejudicial to the interests of another province or to the country as a whole.

(3) Legislation with regard to a matter that is reasonably necessary for, or incidental to, the effective exercise of a power concerning any matter listed in Schedule 4 is, for all purposes, legislation with regard to a matter listed in Schedule 4.

(4) When exercising its legislative authority; Parliament is bound only by the Constitution, and must act in accordance with, and within the limits of, the Constitution.

45. Joint rules and orders and joint committees

(1) The National Assembly and the National Council of Provinces must establish a joint rules committee to make rules and orders concerning the joint business of the Assembly and Council, including rules and orders-

(a) to determine procedures to facilitate the legislative process, including setting a time limit for completing any step in the process;

(b) to establish joint committees composed of representatives from both the Assembly and the Council to consider and report on Bills envisaged in sections 74 and 75 that are referred to such a committee;

(c) to establish a joint committee to review the Constitution at least annually; and

(d) to regulate the business of-

(i) the joint rules committee;

(ii) the Mediation Committee;

(iii) the constitutional review committee; and

(iv) any joint committees established in terms of paragraph (b).

(2) Cabinet members, members of the National Assembly and delegates to the National Council of Provinces have the same privileges and immunities before a joint committee of the

Assembly and the Council as they have before the Assembly or the Council.

The National Assembly (ss 46-59).

46. Composition and election

(1) Subject to schedule 6A, the National Assembly consists of no fewer than 350 and no more than 400 women and men elected as members in terms of an electoral system that-

(a) is prescribed by national legislation;

(b) is based on the national common voters roll;

(c) provides for a minimum voting age of 18 years; and

(d) results, in general, in proportional representation. [Sub-s. (1) amended by s. 1 of the Constitution Tenth Amendment Act of 2003]

(2) An Act of Parliament must provide a formula for determining the number of members of the National Assembly.

47. Membership

(1) Every citizen who is qualified to vote for the National Assembly is eligible to be a member of the Assembly, except-

(a) anyone who is appointed by, or is in the service of, the state and receives remuneration for that appointment or service, other than-

(i) the President, Deputy President, Ministers and Deputy Ministers; and

(ii) other office-bearers whose functions are compatible with the functions of a member of the Assembly, and have been declared compatible with those functions by national legislation;

(b) permanent delegates to the National Council of Provinces or members of a provincial legislature or a Municipal Council;

(c) unrehabilitated insolvents;

(d) anyone declared to be of unsound mind by a court of the Republic; or

(e) anyone who, after this section took effect, is convicted of an offence and sentenced to more than 12 months' imprisonment without the option of a fine, either in the Republic, or outside the Republic if the conduct constituting the offence would have been an offence in the Republic, but no one may be regarded as having been sentenced until an appeal against the conviction or sentence has been determined, or until the time for an appeal has expired. A disqualification under this paragraph ends five years after the sentence has been completed.

(2) A person who is not eligible to be a member of the National Assembly in terms of subsection (1)

(a) or (b) may be a candidate for the Assembly, subject to any limits or conditions established by national legislation.

(3) A person loses membership of the National Assembly if that person-

(a) ceases to be eligible;

(b) is absent from the Assembly without permission in circumstances for which the rules and orders of the Assembly prescribe loss of membership; or

(c) ceases to be a member of the party that nominated that person as a member of the Assembly, unless that member has become a member of another party in accordance with Schedule 6A. [Sub-s. (3) substituted by s. 2 of the Constitution Tenth Amendment Act of 2003]

(4) Vacancies in the National Assembly must be filled in terms of national legislation.

48. Oath or affirmation

Before members of the National Assembly begin to perform their functions in the Assembly, they must swear or affirm faithfulness to the Republic and obedience to the Constitution, in accordance with Schedule 2.

49. Duration of National Assembly

(1) The National Assembly is elected for a term of five years.

(2) If the National Assembly is dissolved in terms of section 50, or when its term expires, the President, by proclamation, must call and set dates for an election, which must be held within 90 days of the date the Assembly was dissolved or its term expired. A proclamation calling and setting dates for an election may be issued before or after the expiry of the term of the National Assembly. [Sub-s. (2) substituted by s. 1 of the Constitution Fifth Amendment Act of 1999]

(3) If the result of an election of the National Assembly is not declared within the period established in terms of section 190, or if an election is set aside by a court, the President, by proclamation, must call and set dates for another election, which must be held within 90 days of the expiry of that period or of the date on which the election was set aside.

(4) The National Assembly remains competent to function from the time it is dissolved or its term expires, until the day before the first day of polling for the next Assembly.

50. Dissolution of National Assembly before expiry of its term

(1) The President must dissolve the National Assembly if-

- (a) the Assembly has adopted a resolution to dissolve with a supporting vote of a majority of its members; and
- (b) three years have passed since the Assembly was elected.

(2) The Acting President must dissolve the National Assembly if-

- (a) there is a vacancy in the office of President; and
- (b) the Assembly fails to elect a new President within 30 days after the vacancy occurred.

51. Sittings and recess periods

(1) After an election, the first sitting of the National Assembly must take place at a time and on a date determined by

the Chief Justice, but not more than 14 days after the election result has been declared. The Assembly may determine the time and duration of its other sittings and its recess periods. [Sub-s. (1) substituted by s. 1 of the Constitution Sixth Amendment Act of 2001]

(2) The President may summon the National Assembly to an extraordinary sitting at any time to conduct special business.

(3) Sittings of the National Assembly are permitted at places other than the seat of Parliament only on the grounds of public interest, security or convenience, and if provided for in the rules and orders of the Assembly.

52. Speaker and Deputy Speaker

(1) At the first sitting after its election, or when necessary to fill a vacancy, the National Assembly must elect a Speaker and a Deputy Speaker from among its members.

(2) The Chief Justice must preside over the election of a Speaker, or designate another judge to do so. The Speaker presides over the election of a Deputy Speaker. [Sub-s. (2) substituted by s. 2 of the Constitution Sixth Amendment Act of 2001]

(3) The procedure set out in Part A of Schedule 3 applies to the election of the Speaker and the Deputy Speaker.

(4) The National Assembly may remove the Speaker or Deputy Speaker from office by resolution. A majority of the members of the Assembly must be present when the resolution is adopted.

(5) In terms of its rules and orders, the National Assembly may elect from among its members other presiding officers to assist the Speaker and the Deputy Speaker.

53. Decisions

(1) Except where the Constitution provides otherwise-

(a) a majority of the members of the National Assembly must be present before a vote may be taken on a Bill or an amendment to a Bill;

(b) at least one third of the members must be present before a vote may be taken on any other question before the Assembly; and

(c) all questions before the Assembly are decided by a majority of the votes cast.

(2) The member of the National Assembly presiding at a meeting of the Assembly has no deliberative vote, but-

(a) must cast a deciding vote when there is an equal number of votes on each side of a question; and

(b) may cast a deliberative vote when a question must be decided with a supporting vote of at least two-thirds of the members of the Assembly.

54. Rights of certain Cabinet members and Deputy Ministers in the National Assembly

The President and any member of the Cabinet or any Deputy Minister who is not a member of the National Assembly may, subject to the rules and orders of the Assembly, attend and speak in the Assembly, but may not vote.

[S. 54 substituted by s. 3 of the Constitution Sixth Amendment Act of 2001]

55. Powers of National Assembly

(1) In exercising its legislative power, the National Assembly may

(a) consider, pass, amend or reject any legislation before the Assembly; and

(b) initiate or prepare legislation, except money Bills.

(2) The National Assembly must provide for mechanisms-

(a) to ensure that all executive organs of state in the national sphere of government are accountable to it; and

(b) to maintain oversight of-

(i) the exercise of national executive authority, including the implementation of legislation; and

(ii) any organ of state.

56. Evidence or information before National Assembly

The National Assembly or any of its committees may

(a) summon any person to appear before it to give evidence on oath or affirmation, or to produce documents;

(b) require any person or institution to report to it;

(c) compel, in terms of national legislation or the rules and orders, any person or institution to comply with a summons or requirement in terms of paragraph (a) or (b); and

(d) receive petitions, representations or submissions from any interested persons or institutions.

57. Internal arrangements, proceedings and procedures of National Assembly

(1) The National Assembly may-

(a) determine and control its internal arrangements, proceedings and procedures; and

(b) make rules and orders concerning its business, with due regard to representative and participatory democracy, accountability, transparency and public involvement.

(2) The rules and orders of the National Assembly must provide for-

(a) the establishment, composition, powers, functions, procedures and duration of its committees;

(b) the participation in the proceedings of the Assembly and its committees of minority parties represented in the Assembly, in a manner consistent with democracy;

(c) financial and administrative assistance to each party represented in the Assembly in proportion to its representation, to enable the party and its leader to perform their functions in the Assembly effectively; and

(d) the recognition of the leader of the largest opposition party in the Assembly as the Leader of the Opposition.

58. Privilege

(1) Cabinet members, Deputy Ministers and members of the National Assembly-

(a) have freedom of speech in the Assembly and in its committees, subject to its rules and orders; and

(b) are not liable to civil or criminal proceedings, arrest, imprisonment or damages for-

(i) anything that they have said in, produced before or submitted to the Assembly or any of its committees; or

(ii) anything revealed as a result of anything that they have said in, produced before or submitted to the Assembly or any of its committees. [Sub-s. (1) amended by s. 4 of the Constitution Sixth Amendment Act of 2001]

(2) Other privileges and immunities of the National Assembly, Cabinet members and members of the Assembly may be prescribed by national legislation.

(3) Salaries, allowances and benefits payable to members of the National Assembly are a direct charge against the National Revenue Fund.

59. Public access to and involvement in National Assembly

(1) The National Assembly must-

(a) facilitate public involvement in the legislative and other processes of the Assembly and its committees; and

(b) conduct its business in an open manner, and hold its sittings, and those of its committees, in public, but reasonable measures may be taken-

(i) to regulate public access, including access of the media, to the Assembly and its committees; and

(ii) to provide for the searching of any person and, where appropriate, the refusal of entry to, or the removal of, any person.

(2) The National Assembly may not exclude the public, including the media, from a sitting of a committee unless it is reasonable and justifiable to do so in an open and democratic society.

National Council of Provinces (ss 60-72)

60. Composition of National Council

(1) The National Council of Provinces is composed of a single delegation from each province consisting of ten delegates.

(2) The ten delegates are-

(a) four special delegates consisting of-

(i) the Premier of the province or, if the Premier is not available, any member of the provincial legislature designated by the Premier either generally or for any specific business before the National Council of Provinces; and

(ii) three other special delegates; and

(b) six permanent delegates appointed in terms of section 61 (2).

(3) The Premier of a province, or if the Premier is not available, a member of the province's delegation designated by the Premier, heads the delegation.

61. Allocation of delegates

(1) Parties represented in a provincial legislature are entitled to delegates in the province's delegation in accordance with the formula set out in Part B of Schedule 3.

(2) (a) A provincial legislature must, within 30 days after the result of an election of that legislature is declared-

(i) determine, in accordance with national legislation, how many of each party's delegates are to be permanent delegates and how many are to be special delegates; and

(ii) appoint the permanent delegates in accordance with the nominations of the parties.

(b) If the composition of a provincial legislature is changed on account of changes of party membership, mergers between parties, subdivision of parties or subdivision and merger of parties within that legislature, it must within 30 days after such change-

(i) determine, in accordance with the national legislation referred to in paragraph (a), how many of each party's delegates are to be permanent delegates and how many are to be special delegates; and

(ii) appoint the permanent delegates in accordance with the nominations of the parties. [Sub-s. (2) substituted by s. 1 of the Constitution Ninth Amendment Act of 2002]

(3) The national legislation envisaged in subsection (2) (a) must ensure the participation of minority parties in both the permanent and special delegates' components of the delegation in a manner consistent with democracy.

(4) The legislature, with the concurrence of the Premier and the leaders of the parties entitled to special delegates in the province's delegation, must designate special delegates, as required from time to time, from among the members of the legislature.

62. Permanent delegates

(1) A person nominated as a permanent delegate must be eligible to be a member of the provincial legislature.

(2) If a person who is a member of a provincial legislature is appointed as a permanent delegate, that person ceases to be a member of the legislature.

(3) Permanent delegates are appointed for a term that expires-

(a) immediately before the first sitting of a provincial legislature after its next election; or

(b) on the day before the appointment of permanent delegates in accordance with section 61 (2) (b)

(ii) takes effect. [Sub-s. (3) substituted by s. 2 of the Constitution Ninth Amendment Act of 2002]

(4) A person ceases to be a permanent delegate if that person-

(a) ceases to be eligible to be a member of the provincial legislature for any reason other than being appointed as a permanent delegate;

(b) becomes a member of the Cabinet;

(c) has lost the confidence of the provincial legislature and is recalled by the party that nominated that person;

(d) ceases to be a member of the party that nominated that person and is recalled by that party; or

(e) is absent from the National Council of Provinces without permission in circumstances for which the rules and orders of the Council prescribe loss of office as a permanent delegate.

(5) Vacancies among the permanent delegates must be filled in terms of national legislation.

(6) Before permanent delegates begin to perform their functions in the National Council of Provinces, they must swear or affirm faithfulness to the Republic and obedience to the Constitution, in accordance with Schedule 2.

63. Sittings of National Council

(1) The National Council of Provinces may determine the time and duration of its sittings and its recess periods.

(2) The President may summon the National Council of Provinces to an extraordinary sitting at any time to conduct special business.

(3) Sittings of the National Council of Provinces are permitted at places other than the seat of Parliament only on the grounds of public interest, security or convenience, and if provided for in the rules and orders of the Council.

64. Chairperson and Deputy Chairpersons

(1) The National Council of Provinces must elect a Chairperson and two Deputy Chairpersons from among the delegates.

(2) The Chairperson and one of the Deputy Chairpersons are elected from among the permanent delegates for five years unless their terms as delegates expire earlier.

(3) The other Deputy Chairperson is elected for a term of one year, and must be succeeded by a delegate from another province, so that every province is represented in turn.

(4) The Chief Justice must preside over the election of the Chairperson, or designate another judge to do so. The Chairperson presides over the election of the Deputy Chairpersons. [Sub-s. (4) substituted by s. 5 of the Constitution Sixth Amendment Act of 2001]

(5) The procedure set out in Part A of Schedule 3 applies to the election of the Chairperson and the Deputy Chairpersons.

(6) The National Council of Provinces may remove the Chairperson or a Deputy Chairperson from office.

(7) In terms of its rules and orders, the National Council of Provinces may elect from among the delegates other presiding officers to assist the Chairperson and Deputy Chairpersons.

65. Decisions

(1) Except where the Constitution provides otherwise-

- (a) each province has one vote, which is cast on behalf of the province by the head of its delegation; and
- (b) all questions before the National Council of Provinces are agreed when at least five provinces vote in favour of the question.

(2) An Act of Parliament, enacted in accordance with the procedure established by either subsection (1) or subsection (2) of section 76, must provide for a uniform procedure in terms of which provincial legislatures confer authority on their delegations to cast votes on their behalf.

66. Participation by members of National Executive

(1) Cabinet members and Deputy Ministers may attend, and may speak in, the National Council of Provinces, but may not vote.

(2) The National Council of Provinces may require a Cabinet member, a Deputy Minister or an official in the national executive or a provincial executive to attend a meeting of the Council or a committee of the Council.

67. Participation by local government representatives

Not more than ten part-time representatives designated by organised local government in terms of section 163, to represent the different categories of municipalities, may participate when necessary in the proceedings of the National Council of Provinces, but may not vote.

68. Powers of National Council

In exercising its legislative power, the National Council of Provinces may

(a) consider, pass, amend, propose amendments to or reject any legislation before the Council, in accordance with this Chapter; and

(b) initiate or prepare legislation falling within a functional area listed in Schedule 4 or other legislation referred to in section 76 (3), but may not initiate or prepare money Bills.

69. Evidence or information before National Council

The National Council of Provinces or any of its committees may

(a) summon any person to appear before it to give evidence on oath or affirmation or to produce documents;

(b) require any institution or person to report to it;

(c) compel, in terms of national legislation or the rules and orders, any person or institution to comply with a summons or requirement in terms of paragraph (a) or (b); and

(d) receive petitions, representations or submissions from any interested persons or institutions.

70. Internal arrangements, proceedings and procedures of National Council

(1) The National Council of Provinces may

(a) determine and control its internal arrangements, proceedings and procedures; and

(b) make rules and orders concerning its business, with due regard to representative and participatory democracy, accountability, transparency and public involvement.

(2) The rules and orders of the National Council of Provinces must provide for-

(a) the establishment, composition, powers, functions, procedures and duration of its committees;

(b) the participation of all the provinces in its proceedings in a manner consistent with democracy; and

(c) the participation in the proceedings of the Council and its committees of minority parties represented in the Council, in a manner consistent with democracy, whenever a matter is to be decided in accordance with section 75.

71. Privileges

(1) Delegates to the National Council of Provinces and the persons referred to in sections 66 and 67-

(a) have freedom of speech in the Council and in its committees, subject to its rules and orders; and

(b) are not liable to civil or criminal proceedings, arrest, imprisonment or damages for-

(i) anything that they have said in, produced before or submitted to the Council or any of its committees; or

(ii) anything revealed as a result of anything that they have said in, produced before or submitted to the Council or any of its committees.

(2) Other privileges and immunities of the National Council of Provinces, delegates to the Council and persons referred to in sections 66 and 67 may be prescribed by national legislation.

(3) Salaries, allowances and benefits payable to permanent members of the National Council of Provinces are a direct charge against the National Revenue Fund.

72. Public access to and involvement in National Council

(1) The National Council of Provinces must-

- (a) facilitate public involvement in the legislative and other processes of the Council and its committees; and
- (b) conduct its business in an open manner, and hold its sittings, and those of its committees, in public, but reasonable measures may be taken-
  - (i) to regulate public access, including access of the media, to the Council and its committees; and
  - (ii) to provide for the searching of any person and, where appropriate, the refusal of entry to, or the removal of, any person.

(2) The National Council of Provinces may not exclude the public, including the media, from a sitting of a committee unless it is reasonable and justifiable to do so in an open and democratic society.

National Legislative Process (ss 73-82)

73. All Bills

(1) Any Bill may be introduced in the National Assembly.

(2) Only a Cabinet member or a Deputy Minister, or a member or committee of the National Assembly, may introduce a Bill in the Assembly, but only the Cabinet member responsible for national financial matters may introduce the following Bills in the Assembly:

- (a) a money Bill; or
- (b) a Bill which provides for legislation envisaged in section 214. [Sub-s. (2) substituted by s. 1 (a) of the Constitution Seventh Amendment Act of 2001]

(3) A Bill referred to in section 76 (3), except a Bill referred to in subsection (2) (a) or (b) of this section, may be introduced in the National Council of Provinces. [Sub-s. (3) substituted by s. 1 (b) of the Constitution Seventh Amendment Act of 2001]

(4) Only a member or committee of the National Council of Provinces may introduce a Bill in the Council.

(5) A Bill passed by the National Assembly must be referred to the National Council of Provinces if it must be considered by the Council. A Bill passed by the Council must be referred to the Assembly.

74. Bills amending the Constitution

(1) Section 1 and this subsection may be amended by a Bill passed by-

(a) the National Assembly, with a supporting vote of at least 75 per cent of its members; and

(b) the National Council of Provinces, with a supporting vote of at least six provinces.

(2) Chapter 2 may be amended by a Bill passed by-

(a) the National Assembly, with a supporting vote of at least two thirds of its members; and

(b) the National Council of Provinces, with a supporting vote of at least six provinces.

(3) Any other provision of the Constitution may be amended by a Bill passed-

(a) by the National Assembly, with a supporting vote of at least two thirds of its members; and

(b) also by the National Council of Provinces, with a supporting vote of at least six provinces, if the amendment

(i) relates to a matter that affects the Council;

(ii) alters provincial boundaries, powers, functions or institutions; or

(iii) amends a provision that deals specifically with a provincial matter.

(4) A Bill amending the Constitution may not include provisions other than constitutional amendments and matters connected with the amendments.

(5) At least 30 days before a Bill amending the Constitution is introduced in terms of section 73 (2), the person or committee intending to introduce the Bill must-

(a) publish in the national Government Gazette, and in accordance with the rules and orders of the National Assembly, particulars of the proposed amendment for public comment;

(b) submit, in accordance with the rules and orders of the Assembly, those particulars to the provincial legislatures for their views; and

(c) submit, in accordance with the rules and orders of the National Council of Provinces, those particulars to the Council for a public debate, if the proposed amendment is not an amendment that is required to be passed by the Council.

(6) When a Bill amending the Constitution is introduced, the person or committee introducing the Bill must submit any written comments received from the public and the provincial legislatures-

(a) to the Speaker for tabling in the National Assembly; and

(b) in respect of amendments referred to in subsection (1), (2) or (3)(b), to the Chairperson of the National Council of Provinces for tabling in the Council.

(7) A Bill amending the Constitution may not be put to the vote in the National Assembly within 30 days of-

(a) its introduction, if the Assembly is sitting when the Bill is introduced; or

(b) its tabling in the Assembly, if the Assembly is in recess when the Bill is introduced.

(8) If a Bill referred to in subsection (3) (b), or any part of the Bill, concerns only a specific province or provinces, the

National Council of Provinces may not pass the Bill or the relevant part unless it has been approved by the legislature or legislatures of the province or provinces concerned.

(9) A Bill amending the Constitution that has been passed by the National Assembly and, where applicable, by the National Council of Provinces, must be referred to the President for assent.

75. Ordinary Bills not affecting provinces

(1) When the National Assembly passes a Bill other than a Bill to which the procedure set out in section 74 or 76 applies, the Bill must be referred to the National Council of Provinces and dealt with in accordance with the following procedure:

- (a) The Council must-
  - (i) pass the Bill;
  - (ii) pass the Bill subject to amendments proposed by it; or
  - (iii) reject the Bill.
- (b) If the Council passes the Bill without proposing amendments, the Bill must be submitted to the President for assent.
- (c) If the Council rejects the Bill or passes it subject to amendments, the Assembly must reconsider the Bill, taking into account any amendment proposed by the Council, and may
  - (i) pass the Bill again, either with or without amendments; or
  - (ii) decide not to proceed with the Bill.
- (d) A Bill passed by the Assembly in terms of paragraph (c) must be submitted to the President for assent.

(2) When the National Council of Provinces votes on a question in terms of this section, section 65 does not apply; instead-

- (a) each delegate in a provincial delegation has one vote;

(b) at least one third of the delegates must be present before a vote may be taken on the question; and

(c) the question is decided by a majority of the votes cast, but if there is an equal number of votes on each side of the question, the delegate presiding must cast a deciding vote.

76. Ordinary Bills affecting provinces

(1) When the National Assembly passes a Bill referred to in subsection (3), (4) or (5), the Bill must be referred to the National Council of Provinces and dealt with in accordance with the following procedure:

(a) The Council must-

(i) pass the Bill;

(ii) pass an amended Bill; or

(iii) reject the Bill.

(b) If the Council passes the Bill without amendment, the Bill must be submitted to the President for assent.

(c) If the Council passes an amended Bill, the amended Bill must be referred to the Assembly, and if the Assembly passes the amended Bill, it must be submitted to the President for assent.

(d) If the Council rejects the Bill, or if the Assembly refuses to pass an amended Bill referred to it in terms of paragraph (c), the Bill and, where applicable, also the amended Bill, must be referred to the Mediation Committee, which may agree on-

(i) the Bill as passed by the Assembly;

(ii) the amended Bill as passed by the Council; or

(iii) another version of the Bill.

(e) If the Mediation Committee is unable to agree within 30 days of the Bill's referral to it, the Bill lapses unless the Assembly again passes the Bill, but with a supporting vote of at least two-thirds of its members.

(f) If the Mediation Committee agrees on the Bill as passed by the Assembly, the Bill must be referred to the Council, and if the Council passes the Bill, the Bill must be submitted to the President for assent.

(g) If the Mediation Committee agrees on the amended Bill as passed by the Council, the Bill must be referred to the Assembly, and if it is passed by the Assembly, it must be submitted to the President for assent.

(h) If the Mediation Committee agrees on another version of the Bill, that version of the Bill must be referred to both the Assembly and the Council, and if it is passed by the Assembly and the Council, it must be submitted to the President for assent.

(i) If a Bill referred to the Council in terms of paragraph (f) or (h) is not passed by the Council, the Bill lapses unless the Assembly passes the Bill with a supporting vote of at least two-thirds of its members.

(j) If a Bill referred to the Assembly in terms of paragraph (g) or (h) is not passed by the Assembly, that Bill lapses, but the Bill as originally passed by the Assembly may again be passed by the Assembly, but with a supporting vote of at least two-thirds of its members.

(k) A Bill passed by the Assembly in terms of paragraph (e), (i) or (j) must be submitted to the President for assent.

(2) When the National Council of Provinces passes a Bill referred to in subsection (3), the Bill must be referred to the National Assembly and dealt with in accordance with the following procedure:

(a) The Assembly must-

(i) pass the Bill;

(ii) pass an amended Bill; or

(iii) reject the Bill.

(b) A Bill passed by the Assembly in terms of paragraph (a) (i) must be submitted to the President for assent.

(c) If the Assembly passes an amended Bill, the amended Bill must be referred to the Council, and if the Council passes the amended Bill, it must be submitted to the President for assent.

(d) If the Assembly rejects the Bill, or if the Council refuses to pass an amended Bill referred to it in terms of paragraph (c), the Bill and, where applicable, also the amended Bill must be referred to the Mediation Committee, which may agree on-

(i) the Bill as passed by the Council;

(ii) the amended Bill as passed by the Assembly; or

(iii) another version of the Bill.

(e) If the Mediation Committee is unable to agree within 30 days of the Bill's referral to it, the Bill lapses.

(f) If the Mediation Committee agrees on the Bill as passed by the Council, the Bill must be referred to the Assembly, and if the Assembly passes the Bill, the Bill must be submitted to the President for assent.

(g) If the Mediation Committee agrees on the amended Bill as passed by the Assembly, the Bill must be referred to the Council, and if it is passed by the Council, it must be submitted to the President for assent.

(h) If the Mediation Committee agrees on another version of the Bill, that version of the Bill must be referred to both the Council and the Assembly, and if it is passed by the Council and the Assembly, it must be submitted to the President for assent.

(i) If a Bill referred to the Assembly in terms of paragraph (f) or (h) is not passed by the Assembly, the Bill lapses.

(3) A Bill must be dealt with in accordance with the procedure established by either subsection (1) or subsection (2) if it falls within a functional area listed in Schedule 4 or provides for legislation envisaged in any of the following sections:

(a) section 65 (2);

(b) section 163;

(c) section 182;

(d) section 195 (3) and (4);

(e) section 196; and

(f) section 197.

(4) A Bill must be dealt with in accordance with the procedure established by subsection (1) if it provides for legislation-

(a) envisaged in section 44 (2) or 220 (3); or

(b) envisaged in Chapter 13, and which includes any provision affecting the financial interests of the provincial sphere of government. [para (b) substituted by s. 1 of the Constitution Eleventh Amendment Act of 2003]

(5) A Bill envisaged in section 42 (6) must be dealt with in accordance with the procedure established by subsection (1), except that-

(a) when the National Assembly votes on the Bill, the provisions of section 53 (1) do not apply; instead, the Bill may be passed only if a majority of the members of the Assembly vote in favour of it; and

(b) if the Bill is referred to the Mediation Committee, the following rules apply:

(i) If the National Assembly considers a Bill envisaged in subsection (1) (g) or (h), that Bill may be passed only if a majority of the members of the Assembly vote in favour of it.

(ii) If the National Assembly considers or reconsiders a Bill envisaged in subsection (1) (e), (i) or (j),

that Bill may be passed only if at least two-thirds of the members of the Assembly vote in favour of it.

(6) This section does not apply to money Bills.

77. Money Bills

(1) A Bill is a money Bill if it

(a) appropriates money;

(b) imposes national taxes, levies, duties or surcharges;

(c) abolishes or reduces, or grants exemptions from, any national taxes, levies, duties or surcharges; or

(d) authorises direct charges against the National Revenue Fund, except a Bill envisaged in section 214 authorising direct charges.

(2) A money Bill may not deal with any other matter except-

(a) a subordinate matter incidental to the appropriation of money;

(b) the imposition, abolition or reduction of national taxes, levies, duties or surcharges;

(c) the granting of exemption from national taxes, levies, duties or surcharges; or

(d) the authorisation of direct charges against the National Revenue Fund.

(3) All money Bills must be considered in accordance with the procedure established by section 75. An Act of Parliament must provide for a procedure to amend money Bills before Parliament.

[S. 77 substituted by s. 2 of the Constitution Seventh Amendment Act of 2001]

78. Mediation Committee

(1) The Mediation Committee consists of-

(a) nine members of the National Assembly elected by the Assembly in accordance with a procedure that is prescribed by the rules and orders of the Assembly and results in the representation of parties in substantially the same proportion that the parties are represented in the Assembly; and

(b) one delegate from each provincial delegation in the National Council of Provinces, designated by the delegation.

(2) The Mediation Committee has agreed on a version of a Bill, or decided a question, when that version, or one side of the question, is supported by-

(a) at least five of the representatives of the National Assembly; and

(b) at least five of the representatives of the National Council of Provinces.

79. Assent to Bills

(1) The President must either assent to and sign a Bill passed in terms of this Chapter or, if the President has reservations about the constitutionality of the Bill, refer it back to the National Assembly for reconsideration.

(2) The joint rules and orders must provide for the procedure for the reconsideration of a Bill by the National Assembly and the participation of the National Council of Provinces in the process.

(3) The National Council of Provinces must participate in the reconsideration of a Bill that the President has referred back to the National Assembly if-

(a) the President's reservations about the constitutionality of the Bill relate to a procedural matter that involves the Council; or

(b) section 74 (1), (2) or (3) (b) or 76 was applicable in the passing of the Bill.

(4) If, after reconsideration, a Bill fully accommodates the President's reservations, the President must assent to and sign the Bill; if not, the President must either-

(a) assent to and sign the Bill; or

(b) refer it to the Constitutional Court for a decision on its constitutionality.

(5) If the Constitutional Court decides that the Bill is constitutional, the President must assent to and sign it.

80. Application by members of National Assembly to Constitutional Court

(1) Members of the National Assembly may apply to the Constitutional Court for an order declaring that all or part of an Act of Parliament is unconstitutional.

(2) An application-

(a) must be supported by at least one-third of the members of the National Assembly; and

(b) must be made within 30 days of the date on which the President assented to and signed the Act.

(3) The Constitutional Court may order that all or part of an Act that is the subject of an application in terms of subsection (1) has no force until the Court has decided the application if-

(a) the interests of justice require this; and

(b) the application has a reasonable prospect of success.

(4) If an application is unsuccessful, and did not have a reasonable prospect of success, the Constitutional Court may order the applicants to pay costs.

81. Publication of Acts

A Bill assented to and signed by the President becomes an Act of Parliament, must be published promptly, and takes effect when published or on a date determined in terms of the Act.

82. Safekeeping of Acts of Parliament

The signed copy of an Act of Parliament is conclusive evidence of the provisions of that Act and, after publication, must be entrusted to the Constitutional Court for safekeeping.

Chapter 5

The President and National Executive (ss 83-102)

83. The President

The President-

(a) is the Head of State and head of the national executive;

(b) must uphold, defend and respect the Constitution as the supreme law of the Republic; and

(c) promotes the unity of the nation and that which will advance the Republic.

84. Powers and functions of President

(1) The President has the powers entrusted by the Constitution and legislation, including those necessary to perform the functions of Head of State and head of the national executive.

(2) The President is responsible for

(a) assenting to and signing Bills;

(b) referring a Bill back to the National Assembly for reconsideration of the Bill's constitutionality;

(c) referring a Bill to the Constitutional Court for a decision on the Bill's constitutionality;

(d) summoning the National Assembly, the National Council of Provinces or Parliament to an extraordinary sitting to conduct special business;

(e) making any appointments that the Constitution or legislation requires the President to make, other than as head of the national executive;

(f) appointing commissions of inquiry;

(g) calling a national referendum in terms of an Act of Parliament;

(h) receiving and recognising foreign diplomatic and consular representatives;

(i) appointing ambassadors, plenipotentiaries, and diplomatic and consular representatives;

(j) pardoning or reprieving offenders and remitting any fines, penalties or forfeitures; and

(k) conferring honours.

85. Executive authority of the Republic

(1) The executive authority of the Republic is vested in the President.

(2) The President exercises the executive authority, together with the other members of the Cabinet, by

(a) implementing national legislation except where the Constitution or an Act of Parliament provides otherwise;

(b) developing and implementing national policy;

(c) coordinating the functions of state departments and administrations;

(d) preparing and initiating legislation; and

(e) performing any other executive function provided for in the Constitution or in national legislation.

86. Election of President

(1) At its first sitting after its election, and whenever necessary to fill a vacancy, the National Assembly must elect a woman or a man from among its members to be the President.

(2) The Chief Justice must preside over the election of the President, or designate another judge to do so. The procedure set out in Part A of Schedule 3 applies to the election of the President. [Sub-s. (2) substituted by s. 6 of the Constitution Sixth Amendment Act of 2001]

(3) An election to fill a vacancy in the office of President must be held at a time and on a date determined by the Chief Justice, but not more than 30 days after the vacancy occurs. [Sub-s. (3) substituted by s. 6 of the Constitution Sixth Amendment Act of 2001]

87. Assumption of office by President

When elected President, a person ceases to be a member of the National Assembly and, within five days, must assume office by swearing or affirming faithfulness to the Republic and obedience to the Constitution, in accordance with Schedule 2.

88. Term of office of President

(1) The President's term of office begins on assuming office and ends upon a vacancy occurring or when the person next elected President assumes office.

(2) No person may hold office as President for more than two terms, but when a person is elected to fill a vacancy in the office of President, the period between that election and the next election of a President is not regarded as a term.

89. Removal of President

(1) The National Assembly, by a resolution adopted with a supporting vote of at least two-thirds of its members, may remove the President from office only on the grounds of-

(a) a serious violation of the Constitution or the law;

(b) serious misconduct; or

(c) inability to perform the functions of office.

(2) Anyone who has been removed from the office of President in terms of subsection (1) (a) or (b) may not receive any benefits of that office, and may not serve in any public office.

90. Acting President

(1) When the President is absent from the Republic or otherwise unable to fulfil the duties of President, or during a vacancy in the office of President, an office-bearer in the order below acts as President:

(a) The Deputy President.

(b) A Minister designated by the President.

(c) A Minister designated by the other members of the Cabinet.

(d) The Speaker, until the National Assembly designates one of its other members.

(2) An Acting President has the responsibilities, powers and functions of the President.

(3) Before assuming the responsibilities, powers and functions of the President, the Acting President must swear or affirm faithfulness to the Republic and obedience to the Constitution, in accordance with Schedule 2.

(4) A person who as Acting President has sworn or affirmed faithfulness to the Republic need not repeat the swearing of

affirming procedure for any subsequent term as acting President during the period ending when the person next elected President assumes office. [Sub-s. (4) added by s. 1 of the Constitution First Amendment Act of 1997]

91. Cabinet

(1) The Cabinet consists of the President, as head of the Cabinet, a Deputy President and Ministers.

(2) The President appoints the Deputy President and Ministers, assigns their powers and functions, and may dismiss them.

(3) The President-

(a) must select the Deputy President from among the members of the National Assembly;

(b) may select any number of Ministers from among the members of the National Assembly; and

(c) may select no more than two Ministers from outside the Assembly.

(4) The President must appoint a member of the Cabinet to be the leader of government business in the National Assembly.

(5) The Deputy President must assist the President in the execution of the functions of government.

92. Accountability and responsibilities

(1) The Deputy President and Ministers are responsible for the powers and functions of the executive assigned to them by the President.

(2) Members of the Cabinet are accountable collectively and individually to Parliament for the exercise of their powers and the performance of their functions.

(3) Members of the Cabinet must-

(a) act in accordance with the Constitution; and

(b) provide Parliament with full and regular reports concerning matters under their control.

93. Deputy Ministers

(1) The President may appoint-

(a) any number of Deputy Ministers from among the members of the National Assembly; and

(b) no more than two Deputy Ministers from outside the Assembly, to assist the members of the Cabinet, and may dismiss them.

(2) Deputy Ministers appointed in terms of subsection (1) (b) are accountable to Parliament for the exercise of their powers and the performance of their functions.

[S. 93 substituted by s. 7 of the Constitution Sixth Amendment Act of 2001]

94. Continuation of Cabinet after elections

When an election of the National Assembly is held, the Cabinet, the Deputy President, Ministers and any Deputy Ministers remain competent to function until the person elected President by the next Assembly assumes office.

95. Oath or affirmation

Before the Deputy President, Ministers and any Deputy Ministers begin to perform their functions, they must swear or affirm faithfulness to the Republic and obedience to the Constitution, in accordance with Schedule 2.

96. Conduct of Cabinet members and Deputy Ministers

(1) Members of the Cabinet and Deputy Ministers must act in accordance with a code of ethics prescribed by national legislation.

(2) Members of the Cabinet and Deputy Ministers may not-

(a) undertake any other paid work;

(b) act in any way that is inconsistent with their office, or expose themselves to any situation involving the risk of a conflict between their official responsibilities and private interests; or

(c) use their position or any information entrusted to them, to enrich themselves or improperly benefit any other person.

97. Transfer of functions

The President by proclamation may transfer to a member of the Cabinet-

(a) the administration of any legislation entrusted to another member; or

(b) any power or function entrusted by legislation to another member.

98. Temporary assignment of functions

The President may assign to a Cabinet member any power or function of another member who is absent from office or is unable to exercise that power or perform that function.

99. Assignment of functions

A Cabinet member may assign any power or function that is to be exercised or performed in terms of an Act of Parliament to a member of a provincial Executive Council or to a Municipal Council. An assignment-

(a) must be in terms of an agreement between the relevant Cabinet member and the Executive Council member or Municipal Council;

(b) must be consistent with the Act of Parliament in terms of which the relevant power or function is exercised or performed; and

(c) takes effect upon proclamation by the President.

100. National intervention in provincial administration

(1) When a province cannot or does not fulfil an executive obligation in terms of the Constitution or legislation, the national executive may intervene by taking any appropriate steps to ensure fulfilment of that obligation, including-

(a) issuing a directive to the provincial executive, describing the extent of the failure to fulfil its obligations and stating any steps required to meet its obligations; and

(b) assuming responsibility for the relevant obligation in that province to the extent necessary to-

(i) maintain essential national standards or meet established minimum standards for the rendering of a service;

(ii) maintain economic unity;

(iii) maintain national security; or

(iv) prevent that province from taking unreasonable action that is prejudicial to the interests of another province or to the country as a whole. [Sub-s. (1) amended by s. 2 (b) of the Constitution Eleventh Amendment Act of 2003]

(2) If the national executive intervenes in a province in terms of subsection (1) (b)-

(a) it must submit a written notice of the intervention to the National Council of Provinces within 14 days after the intervention began;

(b) the intervention must end if the Council disapproves the intervention within 180 days after the intervention began or by the end of that period has not approved the intervention; and

(c) the Council must, while the intervention continues, review the intervention regularly and may make any appropriate recommendations to the national executive. [Sub-s. (2) substituted by s. 2 (c) of the Constitution Eleventh Amendment Act of 2003]

(3) National legislation may regulate the process established by this section.

[S. 100 amended by s. 2 (a) of the Constitution Eleventh Amendment Act of 2003]

101. Executive decisions

(1) A decision by the President must be in writing if it-

(a) is taken in terms of legislation; or

(b) has legal consequences.

(2) A written decision by the President must be countersigned by another Cabinet member if that decision concerns a function assigned to that other Cabinet member.

(3) Proclamations, regulations and other instruments of subordinate legislation must be accessible to the public.

(4) National legislation may specify the manner in which, and the extent to which, instruments mentioned in subsection (3) must be-

(a) tabled in Parliament; and

(b) approved by Parliament.

102. Motions of no confidence

(1) If the National Assembly, by a vote supported by a majority of its members, passes a motion of no confidence in the Cabinet excluding the President, the President must reconstitute the Cabinet.

(2) If the National Assembly, by a vote supported by a majority of its members, passes a motion of no confidence in the President, the President and the other members of the Cabinet and any Deputy Ministers must resign.

Chapter 6

Provinces (ss 103-150)

103. Provinces

(1) The Republic has the following provinces:

(a) Eastern Cape

(b) Free State

(c) Gauteng

(d) KwaZulu-Natal

(e) Limpopo

(f) Mpumalanga

(g) Northern Cape

(h) North West

(i) Western Cape [Sub-s. (1) amended by s. 3 of the Constitution Eleventh Amendment Act of 2003

and substituted by s. 1 of the Constitution Twelfth Amendment Act of 2005]

(2) The geographical areas of the respective provinces comprise the sum of the indicated geographical areas reflected in the various maps referred to in the Notice listed in Schedule 1A. [Sub-s. (2) substituted by s. 1 of the Constitution Twelfth Amendment Act of 2005]

(3)

(a) Whenever the geographical area of a province is re-determined by an amendment to the Constitution, an Act of Parliament may provide for measures to regulate, within a reasonable time, the legal, practical and any other consequences of the re-determination.

(b) An Act of Parliament envisaged in paragraph (a) may be enacted and implemented before such amendment to the Constitution takes effect, but any provincial functions, assets, rights, obligations, duties or liabilities may only be transferred in terms of that Act after that amendment to the Constitution takes effect. [Sub-s. (3) added by s. 1 of the Constitution Twelfth Amendment Act of 2005] [Date of commencement of s. 103 (3): 23 December 2005]

Provincial Legislatures (ss 104-124)

104. Legislative authority of provinces

(1) The legislative authority of a province is vested in its provincial legislature, and confers on the provincial legislature the power-

(a) to pass a constitution for its province or to amend any constitution passed by it in terms of sections 142 and 143;

(b) to pass legislation for its province with regard to-

(i) any matter within a functional area listed in Schedule 4;

(ii) any matter within a functional area listed in Schedule 5;

(iii) any matter outside those functional areas, and that is expressly assigned to the province by national legislation; and

(iv) any matter for which a provision of the Constitution envisages the enactment of provincial legislation; and

(c) to assign any of its legislative powers to a Municipal Council in that province.

(2) The legislature of a province, by a resolution adopted with a supporting vote of at least two thirds of its members, may request Parliament to change the name of that province.

(3) A provincial legislature is bound only by the Constitution and, if it has passed a constitution for its province, also by that constitution, and must act in accordance with, and within the limits of, the Constitution and that provincial constitution.

(4) Provincial legislation with regard to a matter that is reasonably necessary for, or incidental to, the effective exercise of a power concerning any matter listed m Schedule 4, is for all purposes legislation with regard to a matter listed in Schedule 4.

(5) A provincial legislature may recommend to the National Assembly legislation concerning any matter outside the authority of that legislature, or in respect of which an Act of Parliament prevails over a provincial law.

105. Composition and election of provincial legislatures

(1) Subject to Schedule 6A, a provincial legislature consists of women and men elected as members in terms of an electoral system that-

(a) is prescribed by national legislation;

(b) is based on that province's segment of the national common voters roll;

(c) provides for a minimum voting age of 18 years; and

(d) results, in general, in proportional representation. [Sub-s. (1) amended by s. 3 of the Constitution Tenth Amendment Act of 2003]

(2) A provincial legislature consists of between 30 and 80 members. The number of members, which may differ among the provinces, must be determined in terms of a formula prescribed by national legislation.

106. Membership

(1) Every citizen who is qualified to vote for the National Assembly is eligible to be a member of a provincial legislature, except-

(a) anyone who is appointed by, or is in the service of, the state and receives remuneration for that appointment or service, other than-

(i) the Premier and other members of the Executive Council of a province; and

(ii) other office-bearers whose functions are compatible with the functions of a member of a provincial legislature, and have been declared compatible with those functions by national legislation;

(b) members of the National Assembly, permanent delegates to the National Council of Provinces or members of a Municipal Council;

(c) unrehabilitated insolvents;

(d) anyone declared to be of unsound mind by a court of the Republic; or

(e) anyone who, after this section took effect, is convicted of an offence and sentenced to more than 12 months' imprisonment without the option of a fine, either in the Republic, or outside the Republic if the conduct constituting the offence would have been an offence in the Republic, but no one may be regarded as having been sentenced until an appeal against the conviction or sentence has been determined, or until the time for an appeal has expired. A disqualification under this paragraph ends five years after the sentence has been completed.

(2) A person who is not eligible to be a member of a provincial legislature in terms of subsection (1) (a) or (b) may be a candidate for the legislature, subject to any limits or conditions established by national legislation.

(3) A person loses membership of a provincial legislature if that person-

(a) ceases to be eligible;

(b) is absent from the legislature without permission in circumstances for which the rules and orders of the legislature prescribe loss of membership; or

(c) ceases to be a member of the party that nominated that person as a member of the legislature, unless that member has become a member of another party in accordance with Schedule 6A. [Sub-s. (3) substituted by s. 4 of the Constitution Tenth Amendment Act of 2003]

(4) Vacancies in a provincial legislature must be filled in terms of national legislation.

107. Oath or affirmation

Before members of a provincial legislature begin to perform their functions in the legislature, they must swear or affirm faithfulness to the Republic and obedience to the Constitution, in accordance with Schedule 2.

108. Duration of provincial legislatures

(1) A provincial legislature is elected for a term of five years.

(2) If a provincial legislature is dissolved in terms of section 109, or when its term expires, the Premier of the province, by proclamation, must call and set dates for an election, which must be held within 90 days of the date the legislature was dissolved or its term expired. A proclamation calling and setting dates for an election may be issued before or after the expiry of the term of a provincial legislature. [Sub-s. (2) substituted by s. 1 of the Constitution Fourth Amendment Act of 1999]

(3) If the result of an election of a provincial legislature is not declared within the period referred to in section 190, or if an election is set aside by a court, the President, by proclamation, must call and set dates for another election, which must be held within 90 days of the expiry of that period or of the date on which the election was set aside.

(4) A provincial legislature remains competent to function from the time it is dissolved or its term expires, until the day before the first day of polling for the next legislature.

109. Dissolution of provincial legislatures before expiry of term

(1) The Premier of a province must dissolve the provincial legislature if-

(a) the legislature has adopted a resolution to dissolve with a supporting vote of a majority of its members; and

(b) three years have passed since the legislature was elected.

(2) An Acting Premier must dissolve the provincial legislature if-

(a) there is a vacancy in the office of Premier; and

(b) the legislature fails to elect a new Premier within 30 days after the vacancy occurred.

110. Sittings and recess periods

(1) After an election, the first sitting of a provincial legislature must take place at a time and on a date determined by a judge designated by the Chief Justice, but not more than 14 days after the election result has been declared. A provincial legislature may determine the time and duration of its other sittings and its recess periods. [Sub-s. (1) substituted by s. 8 of the Constitution Sixth Amendment Act of 2001]

(2) The Premier of a province may summon the provincial legislature to an extraordinary sitting at any time to conduct special business.

(3) A provincial legislature may determine where it ordinarily will sit.

111. Speakers and Deputy Speakers

(1) At the first sitting after its election, or when necessary to fill a vacancy, a provincial legislature must elect a Speaker and a Deputy Speaker from among its members.

(2) A judge designated by the Chief Justice must preside over the election of a Speaker. The Speaker presides over the election of a Deputy Speaker. [Sub-s. (2) substituted by s. 9 of the Constitution Sixth Amendment Act of 2001]

(3) The procedure set out in Part A of Schedule 3 applies to the election of Speakers and Deputy Speakers.

(4) A provincial legislature may remove its Speaker or Deputy Speaker from office by resolution. A majority of the members of the legislature must be present when the resolution is adopted.

(5) In terms of its rules and orders, a provincial legislature may elect from among its members other presiding officers to assist the Speaker and the Deputy Speaker.

112. Decisions

(1) Except where the Constitution provides otherwise-

(a) a majority of the members of a provincial legislature must be present before a vote may be taken on a Bill or an amendment to a Bill;

(b) at least one-third of the members must be present before a vote may be taken on any other question before the legislature; and

(c) all questions before a provincial legislature are decided by a majority of the votes cast.

(2) The member presiding at a meeting of a provincial legislature has no deliberative vote, but-

(a) must cast a deciding vote when there is an equal number of votes on each side of a question; and

(b) may cast a deliberative vote when a question must be decided with a supporting vote of at least two-thirds of the members of the legislature.

113. Permanent delegates' rights in provincial legislatures

A province's permanent delegates to the National Council of Provinces may attend, and may speak in, their provincial legislature and its committees, but may not vote. The legislature may require a permanent delegate to attend the legislature or its committees.

114. Powers of provincial legislatures

(1) In exercising its legislative power, a provincial legislature may

- (a) consider, pass, amend or reject any Bill before the legislature; and
- (b) initiate or prepare legislation, except money Bills.

(2) A provincial legislature must provide for mechanisms-

- (a) to ensure that all provincial executive organs of state in the province are accountable to it; and
- (b) to maintain oversight of-
  - (i) the exercise of provincial executive authority in the province, including the implementation of legislation; and
  - (ii) any provincial organ of state.

115. Evidence or information before provincial legislatures

A provincial legislature or any of its committees may

- (a) summon any person to appear before it to give evidence on oath or affirmation, or to produce documents;
- (b) require any person or provincial institution to report to it;
- (c) compel, in terms of provincial legislation or the rules and orders, any person or institution to comply with a summons or requirement in terms of paragraph (a) or (b); and
- (d) receive petitions, representations or submissions from any interested persons or institutions.

116. Internal arrangements, proceedings and procedures of provincial legislatures

(1) A provincial legislature may

(a) determine and control its internal arrangements, proceedings and procedures; and

(b) make rules and orders concerning its business, with due regard to representative and participatory democracy, accountability, transparency and public involvement.

(2) The rules and orders of a provincial legislature must provide for-

(a) the establishment, composition, powers, functions, procedures and duration of its committees;

(b) the participation in the proceedings of the legislature and its committees of minority parties represented in the legislature, in a manner consistent with democracy;

(c) financial and administrative assistance to each party represented in the legislature, in proportion to its representation, to enable the party and its leader to perform their functions in the legislature effectively; and

(d) the recognition of the leader of the largest opposition party in the legislature, as the Leader of the Opposition.

117. Privileges

(1) Members of a provincial legislature and the province's permanent delegates to the National Council of Provinces-

(a) have freedom of speech in the legislature and in its committees, subject to its rules and orders; and

(b) are not liable to civil or criminal proceedings, arrest, imprisonment or damages for-

(i) anything that they have said in, produced before or submitted to the legislature or any of its committees; or

(ii) anything revealed as a result of anything that they have said in, produced before or submitted to the legislature or any of its committees.

(2) Other privileges and immunities of a provincial legislature and its members may be prescribed by national legislation.

(3) Salaries, allowances and benefits payable to members of a provincial legislature are a direct charge against the Provincial Revenue Fund.

118. Public access to and involvement in provincial legislatures

(1) A provincial legislature must-

(a) facilitate public involvement in the legislative and other processes of the legislature and its committees; and

(b) conduct its business in an open manner, and hold its sittings, and those of its committees, in public, but reasonable measures may be taken-

(i) to regulate public access, including access of the media, to the legislature and its committees; and

(ii) to provide for the searching of any person and, where appropriate, the refusal of entry to, or the removal of, any person.

(2) A provincial legislature may not exclude the public, including the media, from a sitting of a committee unless it is reasonable and justifiable to do so in an open and democratic society.

119. Introduction of Bills

Only members of the Executive Council of a province or a committee or member of a provincial legislature may introduce a Bill in the legislature; but only the member of the Executive Council who is responsible for financial matters in the province may introduce a money Bill in the legislature.

120. Money Bills

(1) A Bill is a Money Bill if it

(a) appropriates money;

(b) imposes provincial taxes, levies, duties or surcharges;

(c) abolishes or reduces, or grants exemptions from, any provincial taxes, levies, duties or surcharges; or

(d) authorises direct charges against a Provincial Revenue Fund.

(2) A Money Bill may not deal with any other matter except-

(a) a subordinate matter incidental to the appropriation of money;

(b) the imposition, abolition or reduction of provincial taxes, levies, duties or surcharges;

(c) the granting of exemption from provincial taxes, levies, duties or surcharges; or

(d) the authorisation of direct charges against a Provincial Revenue Fund.

(3) A provincial Act must provide for a procedure by which the province's legislature may amend a Money Bill.

[S. 120 substituted by s. 3 of the Constitution Seventh Amendment Act of 2001]

121. Assent to Bills

(1) The Premier of a province must either assent to and sign a Bill passed by the provincial legislature in terms of this Chapter or, if the Premier has reservations about the constitutionality of the Bill, refer it back to the legislature for reconsideration.

(2) If, after reconsideration, a Bill fully accommodates the Premier's reservations, the Premier must assent to and sign the Bill; if not, the Premier must either-

(a) assent to and sign the Bill; or

(b) refer it to the Constitutional Court for a decision on its constitutionality.

(3) If the Constitutional Court decides that the Bill is constitutional, the Premier must assent to and; sign it.

122. Application by members to Constitutional Court

(1) Members of a provincial legislature may apply to the Constitutional Court for an order declaring that all or part of a provincial Act is unconstitutional.

(2) An application-

(a) must be supported by at least 20 per cent of the members of the legislature; and

(b) must be made within 30 days of the date on which the Premier assented to and signed the Act.

(3) The Constitutional Court may order that all or part of an Act that is the subject of an application in terms of subsection (1) has no force until the Court has decided the application if-

(a) the interests of justice require this; and

(b) the application has a reasonable prospect of success.

(4) If an application is unsuccessful, and did not have a reasonable prospect of success, the Constitutional Court may order the applicants to pay costs.

123. Publication of provincial Acts

A Bill assented to and signed by the Premier of a province becomes a provincial Act, must be published promptly and takes effect when published or on a date determined in terms of the Act.

124. Safekeeping of provincial Acts

The signed copy of a provincial Act is conclusive evidence of the provisions of that Act and, after publication, must be entrusted to the Constitutional Court for safekeeping.

Provincial Executives (ss 125-141)

125. Executive authority of provinces

(1) The executive authority of a province is vested in the Premier of that province.

(2) The Premier exercises the executive authority, together with the other members of the Executive Council, by-

(a) implementing provincial legislation in the province;
(b) implementing all national legislation within the functional areas listed in Schedule 4 or 5 except where the Constitution or an Act of Parliament provides otherwise;
(c) administering in the province, national legislation outside the functional areas listed in Schedules 4 and 5, the administration of which has been assigned to the provincial executive in terms of an Act of Parliament;
(d) developing and implementing provincial policy;
(e) coordinating the functions of the provincial administration and its departments;
(f) preparing and initiating provincial legislation; and
(g) performing any other function assigned to the provincial executive in terms of the Constitution or an Act of Parliament.

(3) A province has executive authority in terms of subsection (2) (b) only to the extent that the province has the administrative capacity to assume effective responsibility. The national government, by legislative and other measures, must assist provinces to develop the administrative capacity required for the effective exercise of their powers and performance of their functions referred to in subsection (2).

(4) Any dispute concerning the administrative capacity of a province in regard to any function must be referred to the National Council of Provinces for resolution within 30 days of the date of the referral to the Council.

(5) Subject to Section 100, the implementation of provincial legislation in a province is an exclusive provincial executive power.

(6) The provincial executive must act in accordance with-
(a) the Constitution; and
(b) the provincial constitution, if a constitution has been passed for the province.

126. Assignment of functions

A member of the Executive Council of a province may assign any power or function that is to be exercised or performed in terms of an Act of Parliament or a provincial Act, to a Municipal Council. An assignment-

(a) must be in terms of an agreement between the relevant Executive Council member and the Municipal Council;

(b) must be consistent with the Act in terms of which the relevant power or function is exercised or performed; and

(c) takes effect upon proclamation by the Premier.

127. Powers and functions of Premiers

(1) The Premier of a province has the powers and functions entrusted to that office by the Constitution and any legislation.

(2) The Premier of a province is responsible for-

(a) assenting to and signing Bills;

(b) referring a Bill back to the provincial legislature for reconsideration of the Bill's constitutionality;

(c) referring a Bill to the Constitutional Court for a decision on the Bill's constitutionality;

(d) summoning the legislature to an extraordinary sitting to conduct special business;

(e) appointing commissions of inquiry; and

(f) calling a referendum in the province in accordance with national legislation.

128. Election of Premiers

(1) At its first sitting after its election, and whenever necessary to fill a vacancy, a provincial legislature must elect a woman or a man from among its members to be the Premier of the province.

(2) A judge designated by the Chief Justice must preside over the election of the Premier. The procedure set out in Part A of Schedule 3 applies to the election of the Premier. [Sub-s. (2)

substituted by s. 10 of the Constitution Sixth Amendment Act of 2001]

(3) An election to fill a vacancy in the office of Premier must be held at a time and on a date determined by the Chief Justice, but not later than 30 days after the vacancy occurs.[Sub-s. (3) substituted by s. 10 of the Constitution Sixth Amendment Act of 2001]

129. Assumption of office by Premiers

A Premier-elect must assume office within five days of being elected, by swearing or affirming faithfulness to the Republic and obedience to the Constitution, in accordance with Schedule 2.

130. Term of office and removal of Premiers

(1) A Premier's term of office begins when the Premier assumes office and ends upon a vacancy occurring or when the person next elected Premier assumes office.

(2) No person may hold office as Premier for more than two terms, but when a person is elected to fill a vacancy in the office of Premier, the period between that election and the next election of a Premier is not regarded as a term.

(3) The legislature of a province, by a resolution adopted with a supporting vote of at least two-thirds of its members, may remove the Premier from office only on the grounds of-

(a) a serious violation of the Constitution or the law;

(b) serious misconduct; or

(c) inability to perform the functions of office.

(4) Anyone who has been removed from the office of Premier in terms of subsection (3) (a) or (b) may not receive any benefits of that office, and may not serve in any public office.

131. Acting Premiers

(1) When the Premier is absent or otherwise unable to fulfil the duties of the office of Premier, or during a vacancy in the office of Premier, an office-bearer in the order below acts as the Premier:

(a) A member of the Executive Council designated by the Premier.

(b) A member of the Executive Council designated by the other members of the Council.

(c) The Speaker, until the legislature designates one of its other members.

(2) An Acting Premier has the responsibilities, powers and functions of the Premier.

(3) Before assuming the responsibilities, powers and functions of the Premier, the Acting Premier must swear or affirm faithfulness to the Republic and obedience to the Constitution, in accordance with Schedule 2.

132. Executive Councils

(1) The Executive Council of a province consists of the Premier, as head of the Council, and no fewer than five and no more than ten members appointed by the Premier from among the members of the provincial legislature.

(2) The Premier of a province appoints the members of the Executive Council, assigns their powers and functions, and may dismiss them.

133. Accountability and responsibilities

(1) The members of the Executive Council of a province are responsible for the functions of the executive assigned to them by the Premier.

(2) Members of the Executive Council of a province are accountable collectively and individually to the legislature for the exercise of their powers and the performance of their functions.

(3) Members of the Executive Council of a province must-

(a) act in accordance with the Constitution and, if a provincial constitution has been passed for the province, also that constitution; and

(b) provide the legislature with full and regular reports concerning matters under their control.

134. Continuation of Executive Councils after elections

When an election of a provincial legislature is held, the Executive Council and its members remain competent to function until the person elected Premier by the next legislature assumes office.

135. Oath or affirmation

Before members of the Executive Council of a province begin to perform their functions, they must swear or affirm faithfulness to the Republic and obedience to the Constitution, in accordance with Schedule 2.

136. Conduct of members of Executive Councils

(1) Members of the Executive Council of a province must act in accordance with a code of ethics prescribed by national legislation.

(2) Members of the Executive Council of a province may not-

(a) undertake any other paid work;

(b) act in any way that is inconsistent with their office, or expose themselves to any situation involving the risk of a conflict between their official responsibilities and private interests; or

(c) use their position or any information entrusted to them, to enrich themselves or improperly benefit any other person.

137. Transfer of functions

The Premier by proclamation may transfer to a member of the Executive Council-

(a) the administration of any legislation entrusted to another member; or

(b) any power or function entrusted by legislation to another member.

138. Temporary assignment of functions

The Premier of a province may assign to a member of the Executive Council any power or function of another member who is absent from office or is unable to exercise that power or perform that function.

139. Provincial intervention in local government

(1) When a municipality cannot or does not fulfil an executive obligation in terms of the Constitution or legislation, the relevant provincial executive may intervene by taking any appropriate steps to ensure fulfilment of that obligation, including-

(a) issuing a directive to the Municipal Council, describing the extent of the failure to fulfil its obligations and stating any steps required to meet its obligations;

(b) assuming responsibility for the relevant obligation in that municipality to the extent necessary to-

(i) maintain essential national standards or meet established minimum standards for the rendering of a service;

(ii) prevent that Municipal Council from taking unreasonable action that is prejudicial to the interests of another municipality or to the province as a whole; or

(iii) maintain economic unity; or

(c) dissolving the Municipal Council and appointing an administrator until a newly elected Municipal Council has been declared elected, if exceptional circumstances warrant such a step.

(2) If a provincial executive intervenes in a municipality in terms of subsection (1) (b)-

(a) it must submit a written notice of the intervention to-

(i) the Cabinet member responsible for local government affairs; and

(ii) the relevant provincial legislature and the National Council of Provinces, within 14 days after the intervention began;

(b) the intervention must end if-

(i) the Cabinet member responsible for local government affairs disapproves the intervention within 28 days after the intervention began or by the end of that period has not approved the intervention; or

(ii) the Council disapproves the intervention within 180 days after the intervention began or by the end of that period has not approved the intervention; and

(c) the Council must, while the intervention continues, review the intervention regularly and may make any appropriate recommendations to the provincial executive.

(3) If a Municipal Council is dissolved in terms of subsection (1) (c)-

(a) the provincial executive must immediately submit a written notice of the dissolution to-

(i) the Cabinet member responsible for local government affairs; and

(ii) the relevant provincial legislature and the National Council of Provinces; and

(b) the dissolution takes effect 14 days from the date of receipt of the notice by the Council unless set aside by that Cabinet member or the Council before the expiry of those 14 days.

(4) If a municipality cannot or does not fulfil an obligation in terms of the Constitution or legislation to approve a budget or any revenue-raising measures necessary to give effect to the budget, the relevant provincial executive must intervene by taking any appropriate steps to ensure that the budget or those revenue-raising measures are approved, including dissolving the Municipal Council and-

(a) appointing an administrator until a newly elected Municipal Council has been declared elected; and

(b) approving a temporary budget or revenue-raising measures to provide for the continued functioning of the municipality.

(5) If a municipality, as a result of a crisis in its financial affairs, is in serious or persistent material breach of its obligations to provide basic services or to meet its financial commitments, or admits that it is unable to meet its obligations or financial commitments, the relevant provincial executive must

(a) impose a recovery plan aimed at securing the municipality's ability to meet its obligations to provide basic services or its financial commitments, which-

(i) is to be prepared in accordance with national legislation; and

(ii) binds the municipality in the exercise of its legislative and executive authority, but only to the extent necessary to solve the crisis in its financial affairs; and

(b) dissolve the Municipal Council, if the municipality cannot or does not approve legislative measures, including a budget or any revenue-raising measures, necessary to give effect to the recovery plan, and-

(i) appoint an administrator until a newly elected Municipal Council has been declared elected; and

(ii) approve a temporary budget or revenue-raising measures or any other measures giving effect to the recovery plan to provide for the continued functioning of the municipality; or

(c) if the Municipal Council is not dissolved in terms of paragraph (b), assume responsibility for the implementation of the recovery plan to the extent that the municipality cannot or does not otherwise implement the recovery plan.

(6) If a provincial executive intervenes in a municipality in terms of subsection (4) or (5), it must submit a written notice of the intervention to-

(a) the Cabinet member responsible for local government affairs; and

(b) the relevant provincial legislature and the National Council of Provinces, within seven days after the intervention began.

(7) If a provincial executive cannot or does not or does not adequately exercise the powers or perform the functions referred to in subsection (4) or (5), the national executive must intervene in terms of subsection (4) or (5) in the stead of the relevant provincial executive.

(8) National legislation may regulate the implementation of this section, including the processes established by this section.

[S. 139 substituted by s. 4 of the Constitution Eleventh Amendment Act of 2003]

140. Executive decisions

(1) A decision by the Premier of a province must be in writing if it-

(a) is taken in terms of legislation; or

(b) has legal consequences.

(2) A written decision by the Premier must be countersigned by another Executive Council member if that decision concerns a function assigned to that other member.

(3) Proclamations, regulations and other instruments of subordinate legislation of a province must be accessible to the public.

(4) Provincial legislation may specify the manner in which, and the extent to which, instruments mentioned in subsection (3) must be-

(a) tabled in the provincial legislature; and

(b) approved by the provincial legislature.

141. Motions of no confidence

(1) If a provincial legislature, by a vote supported by a majority of its members, passes a motion of no confidence in the province's Executive Council excluding the Premier, the Premier must reconstitute the Council.

(2) If a provincial legislature, by a vote supported by a majority of its members, passes a motion of no confidence in the

Premier, the Premier and the other members of the Executive Council must resign.

Provincial Constitutions (ss 142-145)

142. Adoption of provincial constitutions

A provincial legislature may pass a constitution for the province or, where applicable, amend its constitution, if at least two-thirds of its members vote in favour of the Bill.

143. Contents of provincial constitutions

(1) A provincial constitution, or constitutional amendment, must not be inconsistent with this Constitution, but may provide for-

(a) provincial legislative or executive structures and procedures that differ from those provided for in this Chapter; or

(b) the institution, role, authority and status of a traditional monarch, where applicable.

(2) Provisions included in a provincial constitution or constitutional amendment in terms of paragraph (a) or (b) of subsection (1)-

(a) must comply with the values in section 1 and with Chapter 3; and

(b) may not confer on the province any power or function that falls-

(i) outside the area of provincial competence in terms of Schedules 4 and 5; or

(ii) outside the powers and functions conferred on the province by other sections of the Constitution.

144. Certification of provincial constitutions

(1) If a provincial legislature has passed or amended a constitution, the Speaker of the legislature must submit the text of the constitution or constitutional amendment to the Constitutional Court for certification.

(2) No text of a provincial constitution or constitutional amendment becomes law until the Constitutional Court has certified-

(a) that the text has been passed in accordance with section 142; and

(b) that the whole text complies with section 143.

145. Signing, publication and safekeeping of provincial constitutions

(1) The Premier of a province must assent to and sign the text of a provincial constitution or constitutional amendment that has been certified by the Constitutional Court.

(2) The text assented to and signed by the Premier must be published in the national Government Gazette and takes effect on publication or on a later date determined in terms of that constitution or amendment.

(3) The signed text of a provincial constitution or constitutional amendment is conclusive evidence of its provisions and, after publication, must be entrusted to the Constitutional Court for safekeeping.

Conflicting Laws (ss 146-150)

146. Conflicts between national and provincial legislation

(1) This section applies to a conflict between national legislation and provincial legislation falling within a functional area listed in Schedule 4.

(2) National legislation that applies uniformly with regard to the country as a whole prevails over provincial legislation if any of the following conditions is met:

(a) The national legislation deals with a matter that cannot be regulated effectively by legislation enacted by the respective provinces individually;

(b) The national legislation deals with a matter that, to be dealt with effectively, requires uniformity across the nation, and the national legislation provides that uniformity by establishing

(i) norms and standards;

(ii) frameworks; or

(iii) national policies.

(c) The national legislation is necessary for-

(i) the maintenance of national security;

(ii) the maintenance of economic unity;

(iii) the protection of the common market in respect of the mobility of goods, services, capital and labour;

(iv) the promotion of economic activities across provincial boundaries;

(v) the promotion of equal opportunity or equal access to government services; or

(vi) the protection of the environment.

(3) National legislation prevails over provincial legislation if the national legislation is aimed at preventing unreasonable action by a province that-

(a) is prejudicial to the economic, health or security interests of another province or the country as a whole; or

(b) impedes the implementation of national economic policy.

(4) When there is a dispute concerning whether national legislation is necessary for a purpose set out in subsection (2) (c) and that dispute comes before a court for resolution, the court must have due regard to the approval or the rejection of the legislation by the National Council of Provinces.

(5) Provincial legislation prevails over national legislation if subsection (2) or (3) does not apply.

(6) A law made in terms of an Act of Parliament or a provincial Act can prevail only if that law has been approved by the National Council of Provinces.

(7) If the National Council of Provinces does not reach a decision within 30 days of its first sitting after a law was referred to it, that law must be considered for all purposes to have been approved by the Council.

(8) If the National Council of Provinces does not approve a law referred to in subsection (6), it must, within 30 days of its decision, forward reasons for not approving the law to the authority that referred the law to it.

147. Other conflicts

(1) If there is a conflict between national legislation and a provision of a provincial constitution with regard to-

(a) a matter concerning which this Constitution specifically requires or envisages the enactment of national legislation, the national legislation prevails over the affected provision of the provincial constitution;

(b) national legislative intervention in terms of section 44 (2), the national legislation prevails over the provision of the provincial constitution; or

(c) a matter within a functional area listed in Schedule 4, section 146 applies as if the affected provision of the provincial constitution were provincial legislation referred to in that section.

(2) National legislation referred to in section 44 (2) prevails over provincial legislation in respect of matters within the functional areas listed in Schedule 5.

148. Conflicts that cannot be resolved

If a dispute concerning a conflict cannot be resolved by a court, the national legislation prevails over the provincial legislation or provincial constitution.

149. Status of legislation that does not prevail

A decision by a court that legislation prevails over other legislation does not invalidate that other legislation, but that other legislation becomes inoperative for as long as the conflict remains.

150. Interpretation of conflicts

When considering an apparent conflict between national and provincial legislation, or between national legislation and a provincial constitution, every court must prefer any reasonable interpretation of the legislation or constitution that avoids a conflict, over any alternative interpretation that results in a conflict.

Chapter 7

Local Government (ss 151-164)

151. Status of municipalities

(1) The local sphere of government consists of municipalities, which must be established for the whole of the territory of the Republic.

(2) The executive and legislative authority of a municipality is vested in its Municipal Council.

(3) A municipality has the right to govern, on its own initiative, the local government affairs of its community, subject to national and provincial legislation, as provided for in the Constitution.

(4) The national or a provincial government may not compromise or impede a municipality's ability or right to exercise its powers or perform its functions.

152. Objects of local government

(1) The objects of local government are-

(a) to provide democratic and accountable government for local communities;

(b) to ensure the provision of services to communities in a sustainable manner;

(c) to promote social and economic development;

(d) to promote a safe and healthy environment; and

(e) to encourage the involvement of communities and community organisations in the matters of local government.

(2) A municipality must strive, within its financial and administrative capacity, to achieve the objects set out in subsection (1).

153. Developmental duties of municipalities

A municipality must-

(a) structure and manage its administration and budgeting and planning processes to give priority to

the basic needs of the community, and to promote the social and economic development of the community; and

(b) participate in national and provincial development programmes.

154. Municipalities in cooperative government

(1) The national government and provincial governments, by legislative and other measures, must support and strengthen the capacity of municipalities to manage their own affairs, to exercise their powers and to perform their functions.

(2) Draft national or provincial legislation that affects the status, institutions, powers or functions of local government must be published for public comment before it is introduced in Parliament or a provincial legislature, in a manner that allows organised local government, municipalities and other interested persons an opportunity to make representations with regard to the draft legislation.

155. Establishment of municipalities

(1) There are the following categories of municipality:

(a) Category A: A municipality that has exclusive municipal executive and legislative authority in its area;

(b) Category B: A municipality that shares municipal executive and legislative authority in its area with a category C municipality within whose area it falls;

(c) Category C: A municipality that has municipal executive and legislative authority in an area that includes more than one municipality.

(2) National legislation must define the different types of municipality that may be established within each category.

(3) National legislation must-

(a) establish the criteria for determining when an area should have a single category A municipality or when it should have municipalities of both category B and category C;

(b) establish criteria and procedures for the determination of municipal boundaries by an independent authority; and

(c) subject to section 229, make provision for an appropriate division of powers and functions between municipalities when an area has municipalities of both category B and category C. A division of powers and functions between a category B municipality and a category C municipality may differ from the division of powers and functions between another category B municipality and that category C municipality.

(4) The legislation referred to in subsection (3) must take into account the need to provide municipal services in an equitable and sustainable manner.

(5) Provincial legislation must determine the different types of municipality to be established in the province.

(6) Each provincial government must establish municipalities in its province in a manner consistent with the legislation enacted in terms of subsections (2) and (3) and, by legislative or other measures, must

(a) provide for the monitoring and support of local government in the province; and

(b) promote the development of local government capacity to enable municipalities to perform their functions and manage their own affairs. (6A) ... [Sub-s. (6A) inserted by s. 1 of the Constitution Third Amendment Act of 1998 and deleted by s. 2 of the Constitution Twelfth Amendment Act of 2005]

(7) The national government, subject to section 44, and the provincial governments have the legislative and executive authority to see to the effective performance by municipalities of their functions in respect of matters listed in Schedules 4 and 5, by regulating the exercise by municipalities of their executive authority referred to in section 156 (1).

156. Powers and functions of municipalities

(1) A municipality has executive authority in respect of, and has the right to administer-

(a) the local government matters listed in Part B of Schedule 4 and Part B of Schedule 5; and

(b) any other matter assigned to it by national or provincial legislation.

(2) A municipality may make and administer by-laws for the effective administration of the matters which it has the right to administer.

(3) Subject to section 151 (4), a by-law that conflicts with national or provincial legislation is invalid. If there is a conflict between a by-law and national or provincial legislation that is inoperative because of a conflict referred to in section 149, the by-law must be regarded as valid for as long as that legislation is inoperative.

(4) The national government and provincial governments must assign to a municipality, by agreement and subject to any conditions, the administration of a matter listed in Part A of Schedule 4 or Part A of Schedule 5 which necessarily relates to local government, if

(a) that matter would most effectively be administered locally; and

(b) the municipality has the capacity to administer it.

(5) A municipality has the right to exercise any power concerning a matter reasonably necessary for, or incidental to, the effective performance of its functions.

157. Composition and election of Municipal Councils

(1) Subject to Schedule 6A, a Municipal Council consists of-

(a) members elected in accordance with subsections (2) and (3); or

(b) if provided for by national legislation-

(i) members appointed by other Municipal Councils to represent those other Councils; or

(ii) both members elected in accordance with paragraph (a) and members appointed in accordance with subparagraph (i) of this paragraph. [Sub-s. (1) substituted by s. 1 (a) of called the Constitution Eighth Amendment Act of 2002]

(2) The election of members to a Municipal Council as anticipated in subsection (1) (a) must be in accordance with national legislation, which must prescribe a system

(a) of proportional representation based on that municipality's segment of the national common voters roll, and which provides for the election of members from lists of party candidates drawn up in a party's order of preference; or

(b) of proportional representation as described in paragraph (a) combined with a system of ward representation based on that municipality's segment of the national common voters roll.

(3) An electoral system in terms of subsection (2) must result, in general, in proportional representation. [Sub-s. (3) substituted by s. 1 (b) of called the Constitution Eighth Amendment Act of 2002]

(4)

(a) If the electoral system includes ward representation, the delimitation of wards must be done by an independent authority appointed in terms of, and operating according to, procedures and criteria prescribed by national legislation.

(b) ... [Para (b) deleted by s. 2 of the Constitution Twelfth Amendment Act of 2005] [Sub-s. (4) substituted by s. 2 of the Constitution Third Amendment Act of 1998]

(5) A person may vote in a municipality only if that person is registered on that municipality's segment of the national common voters roll.

(6) The national legislation referred to in subsection (1) (b) must establish a system that allows for parties and interests reflected within the Municipal Council making the appointment, to be fairly represented in the Municipal Council to which the appointment is made.

158. Membership of Municipal Councils

(1) Every citizen who is qualified to vote for a Municipal Council is eligible to be a member of that Council, except-

(a) anyone who is appointed by, or is in the service of, the municipality and receives remuneration for that appointment or service, and who has not been exempted from this disqualification in terms of national legislation;

(b) anyone who is appointed by, or is in the service of, the state in another sphere, and receives remuneration for that appointment or service, and who has been disqualified from membership of a Municipal Council in terms of national legislation;

(c) anyone who is disqualified from voting for the National Assembly or is disqualified in terms of section 47(1) (c), (d) or (e) from being a member of the Assembly;

(d) a member of the National Assembly, a delegate to the National Council of Provinces or a member of a provincial legislature; but this disqualification does not apply to a member of a Municipal Council representing local government in the National Council; or

(e) a member of another Municipal Council; but this disqualification does not apply to a member of a Municipal Council representing that Council in another Municipal Council of a different category.

(2) A person who is not eligible to be a member of a Municipal Council in terms of subsection (1) (a), (b), (d) or (e) may be a candidate for the Council, subject to any limits or conditions established by national legislation.

159. Terms of Municipal Councils

(1) The term of a Municipal Council may be no more than five years, as determined by national legislation.

(2) If a Municipal Council is dissolved in terms of national legislation, or when its term expires, an election must be held within 90 days of the date that Council was dissolved or its term expired.

(3) A Municipal Council, other than a Council that has been dissolved following an intervention in terms of section 139, remains competent to function from the time it is dissolved or its term expires, until the newly elected Council has been declared elected.

[S. 159 substituted by s. 1 of the Constitution Second Amendment Act of 1998]

160. Internal procedures

(1) A Municipal Council-

(a) makes decisions concerning the exercise of all the powers and the performance of all the functions of the municipality;

(b) must elect its chairperson; [date of commencement of para (b): 30 June 1997]

(c) may elect an executive committee and other committees, subject to national legislation; and

(d) may employ personnel that are necessary for the effective performance of its functions.

(2) The following functions may not be delegated by a Municipal Council:

(a) The passing of by-laws;

(b) the approval of budgets;

(c) the imposition of rates and other taxes, levies and duties; and

(d) the raising of loans.

(3)

(a) A majority of the members of a Municipal Council must be present before a vote may be taken on any matter;

(b) All questions concerning matters mentioned in subsection (2) are determined by a decision taken by a Municipal Council with a supporting vote of a majority of its members;

(c) All other questions before a Municipal Council are decided by a majority of the votes cast.

(4) No by-law may be passed by a Municipal Council unless-

(a) all the members of the Council have been given reasonable notice; and

(b) the proposed by-law has been published for public comment.

(5) National legislation may provide criteria for determining

(a) the size of a Municipal Council;

(b) whether Municipal Councils may elect an executive committee or any other committee; or

(c) the size of the executive committee or any other committee of a Municipal Council.

(6) A Municipal Council may make by-laws which prescribe rules and orders for-

(a) its internal arrangements;

(b) its business and proceedings; and

(c) the establishment, composition, procedures, powers and functions of its committees.

(7) A Municipal Council must conduct its business in an open manner, and may close its sittings, or those of its committees, only when it is reasonable to do so having regard to the nature of the business being transacted.

(8) Members of a Municipal Council are entitled to participate in its proceedings and those of its committees in a manner that-

(a) allows parties and interests reflected within the Council to be fairly represented;

(b) is consistent with democracy; and

(c) may be regulated by national legislation.

161. Privilege

Provincial legislation within the framework of national legislation may provide for privileges and immunities of Municipal Councils and their members.

162. Publication of municipal by-laws

(1) A municipal by-law may be enforced only after it has been published in the official gazette of the relevant province.

(2) A provincial official gazette must publish a municipal by-law upon request by the municipality.

(3) Municipal by-laws must be accessible to the public.

163. Organised local government

An Act of Parliament enacted in accordance with the procedure established by section 76 must-

(a) provide for the recognition of national and provincial organisations representing municipalities; and

(b) determine procedures by which local government may

(i) consult with the national or a provincial government;

(ii) designate representatives to participate in the National Council of Provinces; and

(iii) participate in the process prescribed in the national legislation envisaged in section 221 (1) (c). [Para (b) substituted by s. 4 of the Constitution Seventh Amendment Act of 2001]

164. Other matters

Any matter concerning local government not dealt with in the Constitution may be prescribed by national legislation or by provincial legislation within the framework of national legislation.

Chapter 8

Courts and Administration of Justice (ss 165-180)

165. Judicial authority

(1) The judicial authority of the Republic is vested in the courts.

(2) The courts are independent and subject only to the Constitution and the law, which they must apply impartially and without fear, favour or prejudice.

(3) No person or organ of state may interfere with the functioning of the courts.

(4) Organs of state, through legislative and other measures, must assist and protect the courts to ensure the independence, impartiality, dignity, accessibility and effectiveness of the courts.

(5) An order or decision issued by a court binds all persons to whom and organs of state to which it applies.

166. Judicial system

The courts are

(a) the Constitutional Court;

(b) the Supreme Court of Appeal;

(c) the High Courts, including any high court of appeal that may be established by an Act of Parliament to hear appeals from High Courts;

(d) the Magistrates' Courts; and

(e) any other court established or recognised in terms of an Act of Parliament, including any court of a status similar to either the High Courts or the Magistrates' Courts.

167. Constitutional Court

(1) The Constitutional Court consists of the Chief Justice of South Africa, the Deputy Chief Justice and nine other judges. [Sub-s. (1) substituted by s. 11 of the Constitution Sixth Amendment Act of 2001]

(2) A matter before the Constitutional Court must be heard by at least eight judges.

(3) The Constitutional Court-

(a) is the highest court in all constitutional matters;

(b) may decide only constitutional matters, and issues connected with decisions on constitutional matters; and

(c) makes the final decision whether a matter is a constitutional matter or whether an issue is connected with a decision on a constitutional matter.

(4) Only the Constitutional Court may-

(a) decide disputes between organs of state in the national or provincial sphere concerning the constitutional status, powers or functions of any of those organs of state;

(b) decide on the constitutionality of any parliamentary or provincial Bill, but may do so only in the circumstances anticipated in section 79 or 121;

(c) decide applications envisaged in section 80 or 122;

(d) decide on the constitutionality of any amendment to the Constitution;

(e) decide that Parliament or the President has failed to fulfil a constitutional obligation; or

(f) certify a provincial constitution in terms of section 144.

(5) The Constitutional Court makes the final decision whether an Act of Parliament, a provincial Act or conduct of the President is constitutional, and must confirm any order of invalidity made by the Supreme Court of Appeal, a High Court, or a court of similar status, before that order has any force.

(6) National legislation or the rules of the Constitutional Court must allow a person, when it is in the interests of justice and with leave of the Constitutional Court-

(a) to bring a matter directly to the Constitutional Court; or

(b) to appeal directly to the Constitutional Court from any other court.

(7) A constitutional matter includes any issue involving the interpretation, protection or enforcement of the Constitution.

168. Supreme Court of Appeal

(1) The Supreme Court of Appeal consists of a President, a Deputy President and the number of judges of appeal determined

in terms of an Act of Parliament. [Sub-s. (1) substituted by s. 12 of the Constitution Sixth Amendment Act of 2001]

(2) A matter before the Supreme Court of Appeal must be decided by the number of judges determined in terms of an Act of Parliament. [Sub-s. (2) substituted by s. 12 of the Constitution Sixth Amendment Act of 2001]

(3) The Supreme Court of Appeal may decide appeals in any matter. It is the highest court of appeal except in constitutional matters, and may decide only

(a) appeals;

(b) issues connected with appeals; and

(c) any other matter that may be referred to it in circumstances defined by an Act of Parliament.

169. High Courts

A High Court may decide-

(a) any constitutional matter except a matter that-

(i) only the Constitutional Court may decide; or

(ii) is assigned by an Act of Parliament to another court of a status similar to a High Court; and

(b) any other matter not assigned to another court by an Act of Parliament.

170. Magistrates' courts and other courts

Magistrates' courts and all other courts may decide any matter determined by an Act of Parliament, but a court of a status lower than a High Court may not enquire into or rule on the constitutionality of any legislation or any conduct of the President.

171. Court procedures

All courts function in terms of national legislation, and their rules and procedure must be provided for in terms of national legislation.

172. Powers of courts in constitutional matters

(1) When deciding a constitutional matter within its power, a court-

(a) must declare that any law or conduct that is inconsistent with the Constitution is invalid to the extent of its inconsistency; and

(b) may make any order that is just and equitable, including-

(i) an order limiting the retrospective effect of the declaration of invalidity; and

(ii) an order suspending the declaration of invalidity for any period and on any conditions, to allow the competent authority to correct the defect.

(2) (a) The Supreme Court of Appeal, a High Court or a court of similar status may make an order concerning the constitutional validity of an Act of Parliament, a provincial Act or any conduct of the President, but an order of constitutional invalidity has no force unless it is confirmed by the Constitutional Court.

(b) A court which makes an order of constitutional invalidity may grant a temporary interdict or other temporary relief to a party, or may adjourn the proceedings, pending a decision of the Constitutional Court on the validity of that Act or conduct.

(c) National legislation must provide for the referral of an order of constitutional invalidity to the Constitutional Court.

(d) Any person or organ of state with a sufficient interest may appeal, or apply, directly to the Constitutional Court to confirm or vary an order of constitutional invalidity by a court in terms of this subsection.

173. Inherent power

The Constitutional Court, Supreme Court of Appeal and High Courts have the inherent power to protect and regulate their own process, and to develop the common law, taking into account the interests of justice.

174. Appointment of judicial officers

(1) Any appropriately qualified woman or man who is a fit and proper person may be appointed as a judicial officer. Any person to be appointed to the Constitutional Court must also be a South African citizen.

(2) The need for the judiciary to reflect broadly the racial and gender composition of South Africa must be considered when judicial officers are appointed.

(3) The President as head of the national executive, after consulting the Judicial Service Commission and the leader of parties represented in the National Assembly, appoints the Chief Justice and the Deputy Chief Justice and, after consulting the Judicial Service Commission, appoints the President and Deputy President of the Supreme Court of Appeal. [Sub-s. (3) substituted by s. 13 of the Constitution Sixth Amendment Act of 2001]

(4) The other judges of the Constitutional Court are appointed by the President, as head of the national executive, after consulting the Chief Justice and the leaders of parties represented in the National Assembly, in accordance with the following procedure:

(a) The Judicial Service Commission must prepare a list of nominees with three names more than the number of appointments to be made, and submit the list to the President.

(b) The President may make appointments from the list, and must advise the Judicial Service Commission, with reasons, if any of the nominees are unacceptable and any appointment remains to be made.

(c) The Judicial Service Commission must supplement the list with further nominees and the President must make the remaining appointments from the supplemented list. [Sub-s. (4) substituted by s. 13 of the Constitution Sixth Amendment Act of 2001]

(5) At all times, at least four members of the Constitutional Court must be persons who were judges at the time they were appointed to the Constitutional Court.

(6) The President must appoint the judges of all other courts on the advice of the Judicial Service Commission.

(7) Other judicial officers must be appointed in terms of an Act of Parliament which must ensure that the appointment, promotion, transfer or dismissal of, or disciplinary steps against, these judicial officers take place without favour or prejudice.

(8) Before judicial officers begin to perform their functions, they must take an oath or affirm, in accordance with Schedule 2, that they will uphold and protect the Constitution.

175. Acting judges

(1) The President may appoint a woman or a man to be an acting judge of the Constitutional Court if there is a vacancy or if a judge is absent. The appointment must be made on the recommendation of the Cabinet member responsible for the administration of justice acting with the concurrence of the Chief Justice. [Sub-s. (1) substituted by s. 14 of the Constitution Sixth Amendment Act of 2001]

(2) The Cabinet member responsible for the administration of justice must appoint acting judges to other courts after consulting the senior judge of the court on which the acting judge will serve.

176. Terms of office and remuneration

(1) A Constitutional Court judge holds office for a non-renewable term of 12 years, or until he or she attains the age of 70, whichever occurs first, except where an Act of Parliament extends the term of office of a Constitutional Court judge. [Sub-s. (1) substituted by s. 15 of the Constitution Sixth Amendment Act of 2001]

(2) Other judges hold office until they are discharged from active service in terms of an Act of Parliament.

(3) The salaries, allowances and benefits of judges may not be reduced.

177. Removal

(1) A judge may be removed from office only if

(a) the Judicial Service Commission funds that the judge suffers from an incapacity, is grossly incompetent or is guilty of gross misconduct; and

(b) the National Assembly calls for that judge to be removed, by a resolution adopted with a supporting vote of at least two-thirds of its members.

(2) The President must remove a judge from office upon adoption of a resolution calling for that judge to be removed.

(3) The President, on the advice of the Judicial Service Commission, may suspend a judge who is the subject of a procedure in terms of subsection (1).

178. Judicial Service Commission

(1) There is a Judicial Service Commission consisting of-

(a) the Chief Justice, who presides at meetings of the Commission;

(b) the President of the Supreme Court of Appeal; [para (b) substituted by s. 16 (a) of the Constitution Sixth Amendment Act of 2001]

(c) one Judge President designated by the Judges President;

(d) the Cabinet member responsible for the administration of justice, or an alternate designated by that Cabinet member;

(e) two practising advocates nominated from within the advocates' profession to represent the profession as a whole, and appointed by the President;

(f) two practising attorneys nominated from within the attorneys' profession to represent the profession as a whole, and appointed by the President;

(g) one teacher of law designated by teachers of law at South African universities;

(h) six persons designated by the National Assembly from among its members, at least three of whom must be members of opposition parties represented in the Assembly;

(i) four permanent delegates to the National Council of Provinces designated together by the Council with a supporting vote of at least six provinces;

(j) four persons designated by the President as head of the national executive, after consulting the leaders of all the parties in the National Assembly; and

(k) when considering matters relating to a specific High Court, the Judge President of that Court and the Premier of the province concerned, or an alternate designated by each of them. [Para (k) substituted by s. 2 of the Constitution Second Amendment Act of 1998 and by s. 16 (b) of the Constitution Sixth Amendment Act of 2001]

(2) If the number of persons nominated from within the advocates' or attorneys' profession in terms of subsection (1) (e) or (f) equals the number of vacancies to be filled, the President must appoint them. If the number of persons nominated exceeds the number of vacancies to be filled, the President, after consulting the relevant profession, must appoint sufficient of the nominees to fill the vacancies, taking into account the need to ensure that those appointed represent the profession as a whole.

(3) Members of the Commission designated by the National Council of Provinces serve until they are replaced together, or until any vacancy occurs in their number. Other members who were designated or nominated to the Commission serve until they are replaced by those who designated or nominated them.

(4) The Judicial Service Commission has the powers and functions assigned to it in the Constitution and national legislation.

(5) The Judicial Service Commission may advise the national government on any matter relating to the judiciary or the administration of justice, but when it considers any matter except the appointment of a judge, it must sit without the members designated in terms of subsection (1) (h) and (i).

(6) The Judicial Service Commission may determine its own procedure, but decisions of the Commission must be supported by a majority of its members.

(7) If the Chief Justice or the President of the Supreme Court of Appeal is temporarily unable to serve on the Commission, the Deputy Chief Justice or the Deputy President of the Supreme Court of Appeal, as the case may be, acts as his or her alternate on the Commission. [Sub-s. (7) added by s. 2 (b) of the Constitution Second Amendment Act of 1998 and substituted by s. 16 (c) of the Constitution Sixth Amendment Act of 2001]

(8) The President and the persons who appoint, nominate or designate the members of the Commission in terms of subsection (1) (c), (e), (f) and (g), may, in the same manner appoint, nominate or designate an alternate for each of those members, to serve on the Commission whenever the member concerned is temporarily unable to do so by reason of his or her incapacity or absence from the Republic or for any other sufficient reason. [Sub-s. (8) added by s. 2 (b) of the Constitution Second Amendment Act of 1998]

179. Prosecuting authority

(1) There is a single national prosecuting authority in the Republic, structured in terms of an Act of Parliament, and consisting of-

(a) a National Director of Public Prosecutions, who is the head of the prosecuting authority, and is appointed by the President, as head of the national executive; and

(b) Directors of Public Prosecutions and prosecutors as determined by an Act of Parliament.

(2) The prosecuting authority has the power to institute criminal proceedings on behalf of the state, and to carry out any necessary functions incidental to instituting criminal proceedings.

(3) National legislation must ensure that the Directors of Public Prosecutions-

(a) are appropriately qualified; and

(b) are responsible for prosecutions in specific jurisdictions, subject to subsection (5).

(4) National legislation must ensure that the prosecuting authority exercises its functions without fear, favour or prejudice.

(5) The National Director of Public Prosecutions

(a) must determine, with the concurrence of the Cabinet member responsible for the administration of justice, and after consulting the Directors of Public Prosecutions, prosecution policy, which must be observed in the prosecution process;

(b) must issue policy directives which must be observed in the prosecution process;

(c) may intervene in the prosecution process when policy directives are not complied with; and

(d) may review a decision to prosecute or not to prosecute, after consulting the relevant Director of Public Prosecutions and after taking representations within a period specified by the National Director of Public Prosecutions, from the following:

(i) The accused person;

(ii) The complainant;

(iii) Any other person or party whom the National Director considers to be relevant.

(6) The Cabinet member responsible for the administration of justice must exercise final responsibility over the prosecuting authority.

(7) All other matters concerning the prosecuting authority must be determined by national legislation.

180. Other matters concerning administration of justice

National legislation may provide for any matter concerning the administration of justice that is not dealt with in the Constitution, including-

(a) training programmes for judicial officers;

(b) procedures for dealing with complaints about judicial officers; and

(c) the participation of people other than judicial officers in court decisions.

Chapter 9

State Institutions Supporting Constitutional Democracy (ss 181-194)

181. Establishment and governing principles

(1) The following state institutions strengthen constitutional democracy in the Republic:

(a) The Public Protector.

(b) The South African Human Rights Commission. [Para (b) amended by s. 4 of the Constitution Second Amendment Act of 1998]

(c) The Commission for the Promotion and Protection of the Rights of Cultural, Religious and Linguistic Communities.

(d) The Commission for Gender Equality.

(e) The Auditor General.

(f) The Electoral Commission.

(2) These institutions are independent, and subject only to the Constitution and the law, and they must be impartial and must exercise their powers and perform their functions without fear, favour or prejudice.

(3) Other organs of state, through legislative and other measures, must assist and protect these institutions to ensure the independence, impartiality, dignity and effectiveness of these institutions.

(4) No person or organ of state may interfere with the functioning of these institutions.

(5) These institutions are accountable to the National Assembly, and must report on their activities and the performance of their functions to the Assembly at least once a year.

Public Protector (ss 182-183)

182. Functions of Public Protector

(1) The Public Protector has the power, as regulated by national legislation-

(a) to investigate any conduct in state affairs, or in the public administration in any sphere of government, that is alleged or suspected to be improper or to result in any impropriety or prejudice;

(b) to report on that conduct; and

(c) to take appropriate remedial action.

(2) The Public Protector has the additional powers and functions prescribed by national legislation.

(3) The Public Protector may not investigate court decisions.

(4) The Public Protector must be accessible to all persons and communities.

(5) An report issued by the Public Protector must be open to the public unless exceptional circumstances, to be determined in terms of national legislation, require that a report be kept confidential.

183. Tenure

The Public Protector is appointed for a non-renewable period of seven years. South African Human Rights Commission (s 184)

184. Functions of South African Human Rights Commission

(1) The South African Human Rights Commission must-

(a) promote respect for human rights and a culture of human rights;

(b) promote the protection, development and attainment of human rights; and

(c) monitor and assess the observance of human rights in the Republic.

(2) The South African Human Rights Commission has the powers, as regulated by national legislation, necessary to perform its functions, including the power-

(a) to investigate and to report on the observance of human rights;

(b) to take steps to secure appropriate redress where human rights have been violated;

(c) to carry out research; and

(d) to educate.

(3) Each year, the South African Human Rights Commission must require relevant organs of state to provide the Commission with information on the measures that they have taken towards the realisation of the rights in the Bill of Rights concerning housing, health care, food, water, social security, education and the environment.

(4) The South African Human Rights Commission has the additional powers and functions prescribed by national legislation.

[S. 184 amended by s. 4 of the Constitution Second Amendment Act of 1998] Commission for the Promotion and Protection of the Rights of Cultural, Religious and Linguistic Communities (ss 185-186).

185. Functions of Commission

(1) The primary objects of the Commission for the Promotion and Protection of the Rights of Cultural, Religious and Linguistic Communities are-

(a) to promote respect for the rights of cultural, religious and linguistic communities;

(b) to promote and develop peace, friendship, humanity, tolerance and national unity among cultural, religious and linguistic communities, on the basis of equality, non-discrimination and free association; and

(c) to recommend the establishment or recognition, in accordance with national legislation, of a cultural or other council or councils for a community or communities in South Africa.

(2) The Commission has the power, as regulated by national legislation, necessary to achieve its primary objects, including the power to monitor, investigate, research, educate, lobby, advise and report on issues concerning the rights of cultural, religious and linguistic communities.

(3) The Commission may report any matter which falls within its powers and functions to the South African Human

Rights Commission for investigation. [Sub-s. (3) amended by s. 4 of the Constitution Second Amendment Act of 1998]

(4) The Commission has the additional powers and functions prescribed by national legislation.

186. Composition of Commission

(1) The number of members of the Commission for the Promotion and Protection of the Rights of Cultural, Religious and Linguistic Communities and their appointment and terms of office must be prescribed by national legislation.

(2) The composition of the Commission must-

(a) be broadly representative of the main cultural, religious and linguistic communities in South Africa; and

(b) broadly reflect the gender composition of South Africa.

Commission for Gender Equality (s 187)

187. Functions of Commission for Gender Equality

(1) The Commission for Gender Equality must promote respect for gender equality and the protection, development and attainment of gender equality.

(2) The Commission for Gender Equality has the power, as regulated by national legislation, necessary to perform its functions, including the power to monitor, investigate, research, educate, lobby, advise and report on issues concerning gender equality.

(3) The Commission for Gender Equality has additional powers and functions prescribed by national legislation.

Auditor General (ss 188-189)

188. Functions of Auditor General

(1) The Auditor General must audit and report on the accounts, financial statements and financial management of-

(a) all national and provincial state departments and administrations;

(b) all municipalities; and

(c) any other institution or accounting entity required by national or provincial legislation to be audited by the Auditor General.

(2) In addition to the duties prescribed in subsection (1), and subject to any legislation, the Auditor General may audit and report on the accounts, financial statements and financial management of-

(a) any institution funded from the National Revenue Fund or a Provincial Revenue Fund or by a municipality; or

(b) any institution that is authorised in terms of any law to receive money for a public purpose.

(3) The Auditor General must submit audit reports to any legislature that has a direct interest in the audit, and to any other authority prescribed by national legislation. All reports must be made public.

(4) The Auditor General has additional powers and functions prescribed by national legislation.

189. Tenure

The Auditor General must be appointed for a fixed, non-renewable term of between five and ten years.

Electoral Commission (ss 190-191)

190. Functions of Electoral Commission

(1) The Electoral Commission must-

(a) manage elections of national, provincial and municipal legislative bodies in accordance with national legislation;

(b) ensure that those elections are free and fair; and

(c) declare the results of those elections within a period that must be prescribed by national legislation and that is as short as reasonably possible.

(2) The Electoral Commission has additional powers and functions prescribed by national legislation.

191. Composition of Electoral Commission

The Electoral Commission must be composed of at least three persons. The number of members and their terms of office must be prescribed by national legislation.

Independent Authority to Regulate Broadcasting (s 192)

192. Broadcasting Authority

National legislation must establish an independent authority to regulate broadcasting in the public interest, and to ensure fairness and a diversity of views broadly representing South African society.

General Provisions (ss 193-194)

193. Appointments

(1) The Public Protector and the members of any Commission established by this Chapter must be women or men who-

- (a) are South African citizens;
- (b) are fit and proper persons to hold the particular office; and
- (c) comply with any other requirements prescribed by national legislation.

(2) The need for a Commission established by this Chapter to reflect broadly the race and gender composition of South Africa must be considered when members are appointed.

(3) The Auditor General must be a woman or a man who is a South African citizen and a fit and proper person to hold that office. Specialised knowledge of, or experience in, auditing, state finances and public administration must be given due regard in appointing the Auditor General.

(4) The President, on the recommendation of the National Assembly, must appoint the Public Protector, the Auditor-General and the members of-

- (a) the South African Human Rights Commission; [Para (a) amended by s. 4 of the Constitution Second Amendment Act of 1998]
- (b) the Commission for Gender Equality; and
- (c) the Electoral Commission.

(5) The National Assembly must recommend persons-

(a) nominated by a committee of the Assembly proportionally composed of members of all parties represented in the Assembly; and

(b) approved by the Assembly by a resolution adopted with a supporting vote-

(i) of at least 60 per cent of the members of the Assembly, if the recommendation concerns the appointment of the Public Protector or the Auditor General; or

(ii) of a majority of the members of the Assembly, if the recommendation concerns the appointment of a member of a Commission.

(6) The involvement of civil society in the recommendation process may be provided for as envisaged in section 59 (1) (a).

194. Removal from office

(1) The Public Protector, the Auditor General or a member of a Commission established by this Chapter may be removed from office only on-

(a) the ground of misconduct, incapacity or incompetence;

(b) a finding to that effect by a committee of the National Assembly; and

(c) the adoption by the Assembly of a resolution calling for that person's removal from office.

(2) A resolution of the National Assembly concerning the removal from office of-

(a) the Public Protector or the Auditor General must be adopted with a supporting vote of at least two-thirds of the members of the Assembly; or

(b) a member of a Commission must be adopted with a supporting vote of a majority of the members of the Assembly.

(3) The President-

(a) may suspend a person from office at any time after the start of the proceedings of a committee of the National Assembly for the removal of that person; and

(b) must remove a person from office upon adoption by the Assembly of the resolution calling for that person's removal.

Chapter 10

Public Administration (ss 195-197)

195. Basic values and principles governing public administration

(1) Public administration must be governed by the democratic values and principles enshrined in the Constitution, including the following principles:

(a) A high standard of professional ethics must be promoted and maintained.

(b) Efficient, economic and effective use of resources must be promoted.

(c) Public administration must be development-oriented.

(d) Services must be provided impartially, fairly, equitably and without bias.

(e) People's needs must be responded to, and the public must be encouraged to participate in policy-making.

(f) Public administration must be accountable.

(g) Transparency must be fostered by providing the public with timely, accessible and accurate information.

(h) Good human-resource management and career-development practices, to maximise human potential, must be cultivated.

(i) Public administration must be broadly representative of the South African people, with employment and personnel management practices based on ability, objectivity, fairness, and the need to redress the imbalances of the past to achieve broad representation.

(2) The above principles apply to-

(a) administration in every sphere of government;

(b) organs of state; and

(c) public enterprises.

(3) National legislation must ensure the promotion of the values and principles listed in subsection (1).

(4) The appointment in public administration of a number of persons on policy considerations is not precluded, but national legislation must regulate these appointments in the public service.

(5) Legislation regulating public administration may differentiate between different sectors, administrations or institutions.

(6) The nature and functions of different sectors, administrations or institutions of public administration are relevant factors to be taken into account in legislation regulating public administration.

196. Public Service Commission

(1) There is a single Public Service Commission for the Republic.

(2) The Commission is independent and must be impartial, and must exercise its powers and perform its functions without fear, favour or prejudice in the interest of the maintenance of effective and efficient public administration and a high standard of professional ethics in the public service. The Commission must be regulated by national legislation.

(3) Other organs of state, through legislative and other measures, must assist and protect the Commission to ensure the independence, impartiality, dignity and effectiveness of the Commission. No person or organ of state may interfere with the functioning of the Commission.

(4) The powers and functions of the Commission are

(a) to promote the values and principles set out in section 195, throughout the public service;

(b) to investigate, monitor and evaluate the organisation and administration, and the personnel practices, of the public service;

(c) to propose measures to ensure effective and efficient performance within the public service;

(d) to give directions aimed at ensuring that personnel procedures relating to recruitment, transfers, promotions and dismissals comply with the values and principles set out in section 195;

(e) to report in respect of its activities and the performance of its functions, including any finding it may make and directions and advice it may give, and to provide an evaluation of the extent to which the values and principles set out in section 195 are complied with; and

(f) either of its own accord or on receipt of any complaint-

(i) to investigate and evaluate the application of personnel and public administration practices, and to report to the relevant executive authority and legislature;

(ii) to investigate grievances of employees in the public service concerning official acts or omissions, and recommend appropriate remedies;

(iii) to monitor and investigate adherence to applicable procedures in the public service; and

(iv) to advise national and provincial organs of state regarding personnel practices in the public service, including those relating to the recruitment, appointment, transfer, discharge and other aspects of the careers of employees in the public service.

(g) to exercise or perform the additional powers or functions prescribed by an Act of Parliament. [Para (g) added by s. 3 of the Constitution Second Amendment Act of 1998]

(5) The Commission is accountable to the National Assembly.

(6) The Commission must report at least once a year in terms of subsection (4) (e)-

(a) to the National Assembly; and

(b) in respect of its activities in a province, to the legislature of that province.

(7) The Commission has the following 14 commissioners appointed by the President:

(a) Five commissioners approved by the National Assembly in accordance with subsection (8) (a); and

(b) one commissioner for each province nominated by the Premier of the province in accordance with subsection (8) (b).

(8)

(a) A commissioner appointed in terms of subsection (7) (a) must be

(i) recommended by a committee of the National Assembly that is proportionally composed of members of all parties represented in the Assembly; and

(ii) approved by the Assembly by a resolution adopted with a supporting vote of a majority of its members.

(b) A commissioner nominated by the Premier of a province must be

(i) recommended by a committee of the provincial legislature that is proportionally composed of members of all parties represented in the legislature; and

(ii) approved by the legislature by a resolution adopted with a supporting vote of a majority of its members.

(9) An Act of Parliament must regulate the procedure for the appointment of commissioners.

(10) A commissioner is appointed for a term of five years, which is renewable for one additional term only, and must be a woman or a man who is-

(a) a South African citizen; and

(b) a fit and proper person with knowledge of, or experience in, administration, management or the provision of public services.

(11) A commissioner may be removed from office only on-

(a) the ground of misconduct, incapacity or incompetence;

(b) a finding to that effect by a committee of the National Assembly or, in the case of a commissioner nominated by the Premier of a province, by a committee of the legislature of that province; and

(c) the adoption by the Assembly or the provincial legislature concerned, of a resolution with a supporting vote of majority of its members calling for the commissioner's removal from office.

(12) The President must remove the relevant commissioner from office upon-

(a) the adoption by the Assembly of a resolution calling for that commissioner's removal; or

(b) written notification by the Premier that the provincial legislature has adopted a resolution calling for that commissioner's removal.

(13) Commissioners referred to in subsection (7) (b) may exercise the powers and perform the functions of the Commission in their provinces as prescribed by national legislation.

197. Public Service

(1) Within public administration there is a public service for the Republic, which must function, and be structured, in terms of national legislation, and which must loyally execute the lawful policies of the government of the day.

(2) The terms and conditions of employment in the public service must be regulated by national legislation. Employees are entitled to a fair pension as regulated by national legislation.

(3) No employee of the public service may be favoured or prejudiced only because that person supports a particular political party or cause.

(4) Provincial governments are responsible for the recruitment, appointment, promotion, transfer and dismissal of members of the public service in their administrations within a framework of uniform norms and standards applying to the public service.

Chapter 11

Security Services (ss 198-210)

198. Governing principles

The following principles govern national security in the Republic:

(a) National security must reflect the resolve of South Africans, as individuals and as a nation, to live as equals, to live in peace and harmony, to be free from fear and want and to seek a better life.

(b) The resolve to live in peace and harmony precludes any South African citizen from participating in armed conflict, nationally or internationally, except as provided for in terms of the Constitution or national legislation.

(c) National security must be pursued in compliance with the law, including international law.

(d) National security is subject to the authority of Parliament and the national executive.

199. Establishment, structuring and conduct of security services

(1) The security services of the Republic consist of a single defence force, a single police service and any intelligence services established in terms of the Constitution.

(2) The defence force is the only lawful military force in the Republic.

(3) Other than the security services established in terms of the Constitution, armed organisations or services may be established only in terms of national legislation.

(4) The security services must be structured and regulated by national legislation.

(5) The security services must act, and must teach and require their members to act, in accordance with the Constitution and the law, including customary international law and international agreements binding on the Republic.

(6) No member of any security service may obey a manifestly illegal order.

(7) Neither the security services, nor any of their members, may, in the performance of their functions-

(a) prejudice a political party interest that is legitimate in terms of the Constitution; or

(b) further, in a partisan manner, any interest of a political party.

(8) To give effect to the principles of transparency and accountability, multiparty parliamentary committees, have oversight of all security services in a manner determined by national legislation or the rules and orders of Parliament.

Defence (ss 200-204)

200. Defence force

(1) The defence force must be structured and managed as a disciplined military force.

(2) The primary object of the defence force is to defend and protect the Republic, its territorial integrity and its people in accordance with the Constitution and the principles of international law regulating the use of force.

201. Political responsibility

(1) A member of the Cabinet must be responsible for defence.

(2) Only the President, as head of the national executive, may authorise the employment of the defence force

(a) in cooperation with the police service;

(b) in defence of the Republic; or

(c) in fulfilment of an international obligation.

(3) When the defence force is employed for any purpose mentioned in subsection (2), the President must inform Parliament, promptly and in appropriate detail, of-

(a) the reasons for the employment of the defence force;

(b) any place where the force is being employed;

(c) the number of people involved; and

(d) the period for which the force is expected to be employed.

(4) If Parliament does not sit during the first seven days after the defence force is employed as envisaged in subsection (2), the President must provide the information required in subsection (3) to the appropriate oversight committee.

202. Command of defence force

(1) The President as head of the national executive is Commander-in-Chief of the defence force, and must appoint the Military Command of the defence force.

(2) Command of the defence force must be exercised in accordance with the directions of the Cabinet member responsible for defence, under the authority of the President.

203. State of national defence

(1) The President as head of the national executive may declare a state of national defence, and must inform Parliament promptly and in appropriate detail of-

(a) the reasons for the declaration;

(b) any place where the defence force is being employed; and

(c) the number of people involved.

(2) If Parliament is not sitting when a state of national defence is declared, the President must summon Parliament to an extraordinary sitting within seven days of the declaration.

(3) A declaration of a state of national defence lapses unless it is approved by Parliament within seven days of the declaration.

204. Defence civilian secretariat

A civilian secretariat for defence must be established by national legislation to function under the direction of the Cabinet member responsible for defence.

Police (ss 205-208)

205. Police service

(1) The national police service must be structured to function in the national, provincial and, where appropriate, local spheres of government.

(2) National legislation must establish the powers and functions of the police service and must enable the police service to discharge its responsibilities effectively, taking into account the requirements of the provinces.

(3) The objects of the police service are to prevent, combat and investigate crime, to maintain public order, to protect and secure the inhabitants of the Republic and their property, and to uphold and enforce the law.

206. Political responsibility

(1) A member of the Cabinet must be responsible for policing and must determine national policing policy after consulting the provincial governments and taking into account the policing needs and priorities of the provinces as determined by the provincial executives.

(2) The national policing policy may make provision for different policies in respect of different provinces after taking into account the policing needs and priorities of these provinces.

(3) Each province is entitled-

(a) to monitor police conduct;

(b) to oversee the effectiveness and efficiency of the police service, including receiving reports on the police service;

(c) to promote good relations between the police and the community;

(d) to assess the effectiveness of visible policing; and

(e) to liaise with the Cabinet member responsible for policing with respect to crime and policing in the province.

(4) A provincial executive is responsible for policing functions-

(a) vested in it by this Chapter;

(b) assigned to it in terms of national legislation; and

(c) allocated to it in the national policing policy.

(5) In order to perform the functions set out in subsection (3), a province

(a) may investigate, or appoint a commission of inquiry into, any complaints of police inefficiency or a breakdown in relations between the police and any community; and

(b) must make recommendations to the Cabinet member responsible for policing.

(6) On receipt of a complaint lodged by a provincial executive, an independent police complaints body established by national legislation must investigate any alleged misconduct of, or offence committed by, a member of the police service in the province.

(7) National legislation must provide a framework for the establishment, powers, functions and control of municipal police services.

(8) A committee composed of the Cabinet member and the members of the Executive Councils responsible for policing must be established to ensure effective coordination of the police service and effective cooperation among the spheres of government.

(9) A provincial legislature may require the provincial commissioner of the province to appear before it or any of its committees to answer questions.

207. Control of police service

(1) The President as head of the national executive must appoint a woman or a man as the National Commissioner of the police service, to control and manage the police service.

(2) The National Commissioner must exercise control over and manage the police service in accordance with the national policing policy and the directions of the Cabinet member responsible for policing.

(3) The National Commissioner, with the concurrence of the provincial executive, must appoint a woman or a man as the provincial commissioner for that province, but if the National Commissioner and the provincial executive are unable to agree on the appointment, the Cabinet member responsible for policing must mediate between the parties.

(4) The provincial commissioners are responsible for policing in their respective provinces-

(a) as prescribed by national legislation; and

(b) subject to the power of the National Commissioner to exercise control over and manage the police service in terms of subsection (2).

(5) The provincial commissioner must report to the provincial legislature annually on policing in the province, and must send a copy of the report to the National Commissioner.

(6) If the provincial commissioner has lost the confidence of the provincial executive, that executive may institute appropriate proceedings for the removal or transfer of, or disciplinary action against, that commissioner, in accordance with national legislation.

208. Police civilian secretariat

A civilian secretariat for the police service must be established by national legislation to function under the direction of the Cabinet member responsible for policing.

Intelligence (ss 209-210)

209. Establishment and control of intelligence services

(1) Any intelligence service, other than any intelligence division of the defence force or police service, may be established only by the President, as head of the national executive, and only in terms of national legislation.

(2) The President as head of the national executive must appoint a woman or a man as head of each intelligence service

established in terms of subsection (1), and must either assume political responsibility for the control and direction of any of those services, or designate a member of the Cabinet to assume that responsibility.

210. Powers, functions and monitoring

National legislation must regulate the objects, powers and functions of the intelligence services, including any intelligence division of the defence force or police service, and must provide for-

(a) the coordination of all intelligence services; and

(b) civilian monitoring of the activities of those services by an inspector appointed by the President, as head of the national executive, and approved by a resolution adopted by the National Assembly with a supporting vote of at least two-thirds of its members.

Chapter 12

Traditional Leaders (ss 211-212)

211. Recognition

(1) The institution, status and role of traditional leadership, according to customary law, are recognised, subject to the Constitution.

(2) A traditional authority that observes a system of customary law may function subject to any applicable legislation and customs, which includes amendments to, or repeal of, that legislation or those customs.

(3) The courts must apply customary law when that law is applicable, subject to the Constitution and any legislation that specifically deals with customary law.

212. Role of traditional leaders

(1) National legislation may provide for a role for traditional leadership as an institution at local level on matters affecting local communities.

(2) To deal with matters relating to traditional leadership, the role of traditional leaders, customary law and the customs of communities observing a system of customary law-

(a) national or provincial legislation may provide for the establishment of houses of traditional leaders; and

(b) national legislation may establish a council of traditional leaders.

Chapter 13

Finance (ss 213-230A)

General Financial Matters (ss 213-219)

213. National Revenue Fund

(1) There is a National Revenue Fund into which all money received by the national government must be paid, except money reasonably excluded by an Act of Parliament.

(2) Money may be withdrawn from the National Revenue Fund only-

(a) in terms of an appropriation by an Act of Parliament; or

(b) as a direct charge against the National Revenue Fund, when it is provided for in the Constitution or an Act of Parliament.

(3) A province's equitable share of revenue raised nationally is a direct charge against the National Revenue Fund. [date of commencement of s. 213: 1 January 1998]

214. Equitable shares and allocations of revenue

(1) An Act of Parliament must provide for-

(a) the equitable division of revenue raised nationally among the national, provincial and local spheres of government;

(b) the determination of each province's equitable share of the provincial share of that revenue; and

(c) any other allocations to provinces, local government or municipalities from the national government's share of that revenue, and any conditions on which those allocations may be made.

(2) The Act referred to in subsection (1) may be enacted only after the provincial governments, organised local government and the Financial and Fiscal Commission have been consulted, and any recommendations of the Commission have been considered, and must take into account-

(a) the national interest;

(b) any provision that must be made in respect of the national debt and other national obligations;

(c) the needs and interests of the national government, determined by objective criteria;

(d) the need to ensure that the provinces and municipalities are able to provide basic services and perform the functions allocated to them;

(e) the fiscal capacity and efficiency of the provinces and municipalities;

(f) developmental and other needs of provinces, local government and municipalities;

(g) economic disparities within and among the provinces;

(h) obligations of the provinces and municipalities in terms of national legislation;

(i) the desirability of stable and predictable allocations of revenue shares; and

(j) the need for flexibility in responding to emergencies or other temporary needs, and other factors based on similar objective criteria. [date of commencement of s. 214: 1 January 1998]

215. National, provincial and municipal budgets

(1) National, provincial and municipal budgets and budgetary processes must promote transparency, accountability and the effective financial management of the economy, debt and the public sector.

(2) National legislation must prescribe-

(a) the form of national, provincial and municipal budgets;

(b) when national and provincial budgets must be tabled; and

(c) that budgets in each sphere of government must show the sources of revenue and the way in which proposed expenditure will comply with national legislation.

(3) Budgets in each sphere of government must contain-

(a) estimates of revenue and expenditure, differentiating between capital and current expenditure;

(b) proposals for financing any anticipated deficit for the period to which they apply; and

(c) an indication of intentions regarding borrowing and other forms of public liability that will increase public debt during the ensuing year. [date of commencement of s. 215: 1 January 1998]

216. Treasury control

(1) National legislation must establish a national treasury and prescribe measures to ensure both transparency and expenditure control in each sphere of government, by introducing-

(a) generally recognised accounting practice;

(b) uniform expenditure classifications; and

(c) uniform treasury norms and standards.

(2) The national treasury must enforce compliance with the measures established in terms of subsection (1), and may stop the transfer of funds to an organ of state if that organ of state commits a serious or persistent material breach of those measures. [Sub-s. (2) substituted by s. 5 (a) of the Constitution Seventh Amendment Act of 2001]

(3) A decision to stop the transfer of funds due to a province in terms of section 214 (1) (b) may be taken only in the circumstances mentioned in subsection (2) and-

(a) may not stop the transfer of funds for more than 120 days; and

(b) may be enforced immediately, but will lapse retrospectively unless Parliament approves it following a process substantially the same as that established in terms of section 76 (1) and prescribed by the joint rules and orders of Parliament. This process must be completed within 30 days of the decision by the national treasury. [Sub-s. (3) amended by s. 5 (b) of the Constitution Seventh Amendment Act of 2001]

(4) Parliament may renew a decision to stop the transfer of funds for no more than 120 days at a time, following the process established in terms of subsection (3).

(5) Before Parliament may approve or renew a decision to stop the transfer of funds to a province-

(a) the Auditor General must report to Parliament; and

(b) the province must be given an opportunity to answer the allegations against it, and to state its case, before a committee. [date of commencement of s. 216: 1 January 1998]

217. Procurement

(1) When an organ of state in the national, provincial or local sphere of government, or any other institution identified in national legislation, contracts for goods or services, it must do so in accordance with a system which is fair, equitable, transparent, competitive and cost-effective.

(2) Subsection (1) does not prevent the organs of state or institutions referred to in that subsection from implementing a procurement policy providing for-

(a) categories of preference in the allocation of contracts; and

(b) the protection or advancement of persons, or categories of persons, disadvantaged by unfair discrimination.

(3) National legislation must prescribe a framework within which the policy referred to in subsection (2) must be implemented. [Sub-s. (3) substituted by s. 6 of the Constitution Seventh Amendment Act of 2001]

218. Government guarantees

(1) The national government, a provincial government or a municipality may guarantee a loan only if the guarantee complies with any conditions set out in national legislation.

(2) National legislation referred to in subsection (1) may be enacted only after any recommendations of the Financial and Fiscal Commission have been considered.

(3) Each year, every government must publish a report on the guarantees it has granted. [date of commencement of s. 218: 1 January 1998]

219. Remuneration of persons holding public office

(1) An Act of Parliament must establish a framework for determining-

(a) the salaries, allowances and benefits of members of the National Assembly, permanent delegates to the National Council of Provinces, members of the Cabinet, Deputy Ministers, traditional leaders and members of any councils of traditional leaders; and

(b) the upper limit of salaries, allowances or benefits of members of provincial legislatures, members of Executive Councils and members of Municipal Councils of the different categories.

(2) National legislation must establish an independent commission to make recommendations concerning the salaries, allowances and benefits referred to in subsection (1).

(3) Parliament may pass the legislation referred to in subsection (1) only after considering any recommendations of the commission established in terms of subsection (2).

(4) The national executive, a provincial executive, a municipality or any other relevant authority may implement the national legislation referred to in subsection (1) only after considering any recommendations of the commission established in terms of subsection (2).

(5) National legislation must establish frameworks for determining the salaries, allowances and benefits of judges, the Public Protector, the Auditor General, and members of any

commission provided for in the Constitution, including the broadcasting authority referred to in section 192.

Financial and Fiscal Commission (ss 220-222)

220. Establishment and functions

(1) There is a Financial and Fiscal Commission for the Republic which makes recommendations envisaged in this Chapter, or in national legislation, to Parliament, provincial legislatures and any other authorities determined by national legislation.

(2) The Commission is independent and subject only to the Constitution and the law, and must be impartial.

(3) The Commission must function in terms of an Act of Parliament and, in performing its functions, must consider all relevant factors, including those listed in section 214 (2).

221. Appointment and tenure of members

(1) The Commission consists of the following women and men appointed by the President, as head of the national executive:

(a) A chairperson and deputy chairperson;

(b) three persons selected, after consulting the Premiers, from a list compiled in accordance with a process prescribed by national legislation;

(c) two persons selected, after consulting organised local government, from a list compiled in accordance with a process prescribed by national legislation; and

(d) two other persons. [Sub-s. (1) substituted by s. 7 (a) of the Constitution Seventh Amendment Act of 2001] (1A) National legislation referred to in subsection (1) must provide for the participation of-

(i) the Premiers in the compilation of a list envisaged in subsection (1) (b); and

(ii) organised local government in the compilation of a list envisaged in subsection (1) (c). [Sub-s. (1A) inserted by 7 (b) of the Constitution Seventh Amendment Act of 2001]

(2) Members of the Commission must have appropriate expertise.

(3) Members serve for a term established in terms of national legislation. The President may remove a member from office on the ground of misconduct, incapacity or incompetence.

222. Reports

The Commission must report regularly both to Parliament and to the provincial legislatures.

Central Bank (ss 223-225)

223. Establishment

The South African Reserve Bank is the central bank of the Republic and is regulated in terms of an Act of Parliament.

224. Primary object

(1) The primary object of the South African Reserve Bank is to protect the value of the currency in the interest of balanced and sustainable economic growth in the Republic.

(2) The South African Reserve Bank, in pursuit of its primary object, must perform its functions independently and without fear, favour or prejudice, but there must be regular consultation between the Bank and the Cabinet member responsible for national financial matters.

225. Powers and functions

The powers and functions of the South African Reserve Bank are those customarily exercised and performed by central banks, which powers and functions must be determined by an Act of Parliament and must be exercised or performed subject to the conditions prescribed in terms of that Act.

Provincial and Local Financial Matters (ss 226-230A)

226. Provincial Revenue Funds

(1) There is a Provincial Revenue Fund for each province into which all money received by the provincial government must be paid, except money reasonably excluded by an Act of Parliament.

(2) Money may be withdrawn from a Provincial Revenue Fund only-

(a) in terms of an appropriation by a provincial Act; or

(b) as a direct charge against the Provincial Revenue Fund, when it is provided for in the Constitution or a provincial Act.

(3) Revenue allocated through a province to local government in that province in terms of section 214 (1), is a direct charge against that province's Revenue Fund.

(4) National legislation may determine a framework within which-

(a) a provincial Act may in terms of subsection (2) (b) authorise the withdrawal of money as a direct charge against a Provincial Revenue Fund; and

(b) revenue allocated through a province to local government in that province in terms of subsection

(3) must be paid to municipalities in the province.[Sub-s. (4) added by s. 8 of the Constitution Seventh Amendment Act of 2001] [date of commencement of s. 226: 1 January 1998]

227. National sources of provincial and local government funding

(1) Local government and each province-

(a) is entitled to an equitable share of revenue raised nationally to enable it to provide basic services and perform the functions allocated to it; and

(b) may receive other allocations from national government revenue, either conditionally or unconditionally.

(2) Additional revenue raised by provinces or municipalities may not be deducted from their share of revenue raised nationally, or from other allocations made to them out of national government revenue. Equally, there is no obligation on the national government to compensate provinces or municipalities that do not raise revenue commensurate with their fiscal capacity and tax base.

(3) A province's equitable share of revenue raised nationally must be transferred to the province promptly and without deduction, except when the transfer has been stopped in terms of section 216.

(4) A province must provide for itself any resources that it requires, in terms of a provision of its provincial constitution, that are additional to its requirements envisaged in the Constitution. [date of commencement of s. 227: 1 January 1998]

228. Provincial taxes

(1) A provincial legislature may impose-

(a) taxes, levies and duties other than income tax, value-added tax, general sales tax, rates on property or customs duties; and

(b) flat-rate surcharges on any tax, levy or duty that is imposed by national legislation, other than on corporate income tax, value-added tax, rates on property or customs duties. [Para (b) substituted by s. 9 of the Constitution Seventh Amendment Act of 2001]

(2) The power of a provincial legislature to impose taxes, levies, duties and surcharges-

(a) may not be exercised in way that materially and unreasonably prejudices national economic policies, economic activities across provincial boundaries, or the national mobility of goods, services, capital or labour; and

(b) must be regulated in terms of an Act of Parliament, which may be enacted only after any recommendations of the Financial and Fiscal Commission have been considered. [date of commencement of s. 228: 1 January 1998]

229. Municipal fiscal powers and functions

(1) Subject to subsections (2), (3) and (4), a municipality may impose-

(a) rates on property and surcharges on fees for services provided by or on behalf of the municipality; and

(b) if authorised by national legislation, other taxes, levies and duties appropriate to local government or to the category of local government into which that municipality falls, but no municipality may impose income tax, value-added tax, general sales tax or customs duty.

(2) The power of a municipality to impose rates on property, surcharges on fees for services provided by or on behalf of the municipality, or other taxes, levies or duties-

(a) may not be exercised in a way that materially and unreasonably prejudices national economic policies, economic activities across municipal boundaries, or the national mobility of goods, services, capital or labour; and

(b) may be regulated by national legislation.

(3) When two municipalities have the same fiscal powers and functions with regard to the same area, an appropriate division of those powers and functions must be made in terms of national legislation. The division may be made only after taking into account at least the following criteria:

(a) The need to comply with sound principles of taxation.

(b) The powers and functions performed by each municipality.

(c) The fiscal capacity of each municipality.

(d) The effectiveness and efficiency of raising taxes, levies and duties.

(e) Equity.

(4) Nothing in this section precludes the sharing of revenue raised in terms of this section between municipalities that have fiscal power and functions in the same area.

(5) National legislation envisaged in this section may be enacted only after organised local government and the Financial and Fiscal Commission have been consulted, and any recommendations of the Commission have been considered. [date of commencement of s. 229: 1 January 1998]

230. Provincial loans

(1) A province may raise loans for capital or current expenditure in accordance with national legislation, but loans for current expenditure may be raised only when necessary for bridging purposes during a fiscal year.

(2) National legislation referred to in subsection (1) may be enacted only after any recommendations of the Financial and Fiscal Commission have been considered.

[S. 230 substituted by s. 10 of the Constitution Seventh Amendment Act of 2001] [date of commencement of s. 230: 1 January 1998]

230A. Municipal loans

(1) A Municipal Council may, in accordance with national legislation-

(a) raise loans for capital or current expenditure for the municipality, but loans for current expenditure may be raised only when necessary for bridging purposes during a fiscal year; and

(b) bind itself and a future Council in the exercise of its legislative and executive authority to secure loans or investments for the municipality.

(2) National legislation referred to in subsection (1) may be enacted only after any recommendations of the Financial and Fiscal Commission have been considered.

[S. 230A inserted by s. 17 of the Constitution Sixth Amendment Act of 2001]

Chapter 14

General Provisions (ss 231-243)

International Law (ss 231-233)

231. International agreements

(1) The negotiating and signing of all international agreements is the responsibility of the national executive.

(2) An international agreement binds the Republic only after it has been approved by resolution in both the National

Assembly and the National Council of Provinces, unless it is an agreement referred to in subsection (3).

(3) An international agreement of a technical, administrative or executive nature, or an agreement which does not require either ratification or accession, entered into by the national executive, binds the Republic without approval by the National Assembly and the National Council of Provinces, but must be tabled in the Assembly and the Council within a reasonable time.

(4) Any international agreement becomes law in the Republic when it is enacted into law by national legislation; but a self-executing provision of an agreement that has been approved by Parliament is law in the Republic unless it is inconsistent with the Constitution or an Act of Parliament.

(5) The Republic is bound by international agreements which were binding on the Republic when this Constitution took effect.

232. Customary international law

Customary international law is law in the Republic unless it is inconsistent with the Constitution or an Act of Parliament.

233. Application of international law

When interpreting any legislation, every court must prefer any reasonable interpretation of the legislation that is consistent with international law over any alternative interpretation that is inconsistent with international law.

Other Matters (ss 234-243)

234. Charters of Rights

In order to deepen the culture of democracy established by the Constitution, Parliament may adopt Charters of Rights consistent with the provisions of the Constitution.

235. Self-determination

The right of the South African people as a whole to self-determination, as manifested in this Constitution, does not preclude, within the framework of this right, recognition of the right of self-determination of any community sharing a common cultural and language heritage, within a territorial entity in the Republic or in any other way, determined by national legislation.

236. Funding of political parties

To enhance multiparty democracy, national legislation must provide for the funding of political parties participating in national and provincial legislatures on an equitable and proportional basis.

237. Diligent performance of obligations

All constitutional obligations must be performed diligently and without delay.

238. Agency and delegation

An executive organ of state in any sphere of government may

(a) delegate any power or function that is to be exercised or performed in terms of legislation to any other executive organ of state, provided the delegation is consistent with the legislation in terms of which the power is exercised or the function is performed; or

(b) exercise any power or perform any function for any other executive organ of state on an agency or delegation basis.

239. Definitions

In the Constitution, unless the context indicates otherwise- 'national legislation' includes

(a) subordinate legislation made in terms of an Act of Parliament; and

(b) legislation that was in force when the Constitution took effect and that is administered by the national government; 'organ of state' means-

(a) any department of state or administration in the national, provincial or local sphere of government; or

(b) any other functionary or institution-

  (i) exercising a power or performing a function in terms of the Constitution or a provincial constitution; or

(ii) exercising a public power or performing a public function in terms of any legislation, but does not include a court or a judicial officer;

'provincial legislation' includes-

(a) subordinate legislation made in terms of a provincial Act; and

(b) legislation that was in force when the Constitution took effect and that is administered by a provincial government.

240. Inconsistencies between different texts

In the event of an inconsistency between different texts of the Constitution, the English text prevails.

241. Transitional arrangements

Schedule 6 applies to the transition to the new constitutional order established by this Constitution, and any matter incidental to that transition.

242. Repeal of laws

The laws mentioned in Schedule 7 are repealed, subject to section 243 and Schedule 6.

243. Short title and commencement

(1) This Act is called the Constitution of the Republic of South Africa, 1996, and comes into effect as soon as possible on a date set by the President by proclamation, which may not be a date later than 1 July 1997.

(2) The President may set different dates before the date mentioned in subsection (1) in respect of different provisions of the Constitution.

(3) Unless the context otherwise indicates, a reference in a provision of the Constitution to a time when the Constitution took effect must be construed as a reference to the time when that provision took effect.

(4) If a different date is set for any particular provision of the Constitution in terms of subsection (2), any corresponding provision of the Constitution of the Republic of South Africa,

1993 (Act 200 of 1993), mentioned in the proclamation, is repealed with effect from the same date.

(5) Sections 213, 214, 215, 216, 218, 226, 227, 228, 229 and 230 come into effect on 1 January 1998, but this does not preclude the enactment in terms of this Constitution of legislation envisaged in any of these provisions before that date. Until that date any corresponding and incidental provisions of the Constitution of the Republic of South Africa, 1993, remain in force.

Schedules to the Constitution of South Africa (1996)

Schedule 1 – National Flag

(1) The national flag is rectangular; it is one and a half times longer than it is wide.

(2) It is black, gold, green, white, chilli red and blue.

(3) It has a green Y-shaped band that is one-fifth as wide as the flag. The centre lines of the band start in the top and bottom corners next to the flag post, converge in the centre of the flag, and continue horizontally to the middle of the free edge.

(4) The green band is edged, above and below in white, and towards the flag post end, in gold. Each edging is one-fifteenth as wide as the flag.

(5) The triangle next to the flag post is black.

(6) The upper horizontal band is chilli red and the lower horizontal band is blue. These bands are each one-third as wide as the flag. [Schedule 1 amended by s. 2 of Act No. 35 of 1997 (English text only) and substituted by s. 18 of Act No. 34 of 2001]

Schedule 2 – Oaths and solemn affirmations

Oath or solemn affirmation of President and Acting President

1. The President or Acting President, before the Chief Justice, or another judge designated by the Chief Justice, must swear/affirm as follows: In the presence of everyone assembled here, and in full realisation of the high calling I assume as President/Acting President of the Republic of South Africa, I, A.B., swear/solemnly affirm that I will be faithful to the

Republic of South Africa, and will obey, observe, uphold and maintain the Constitution and all other law of the Republic; and I solemnly and sincerely promise that I will always.

- promote all that will advance the Republic, and oppose all that may harm it;
- protect and promote the rights of all South Africans;
- discharge my duties with all my strength and talents to the best of my knowledge and ability and true to the dictates of my conscience;
- do justice to all; and
- devote myself to the well-being of the Republic and all of its people.

(In the case of an oath: So help me God.) Oath or solemn affirmation of Deputy President

2. The Deputy President, before the Chief Justice or another judge designated by the Chief Justice, must swear/affirm as follows: In the presence of everyone assembled here, and in full realisation of the high calling I assume as Deputy President of the Republic of South Africa, I, A.B., swear/solemnly affirm that I will be faithful to the Republic of South Africa and will obey, observe, uphold and maintain the Constitution and all other law of the Republic; and I solemnly and sincerely promise that I will always.

- promote all that will advance the Republic, and oppose all that may harm it;
- be a true and faithful counsellor;
- discharge my duties with all my strength and talents to the best of my knowledge and ability and true to the dictates of my conscience;
- do justice to all; and
- devote myself to the well-being of the Republic and all of its people.

(In the case of an oath: So help me God.) Oath or solemn affirmation of Ministers and Deputy Ministers

1. Each Minister and Deputy Minister, before the Chief Justice or another judge designated by the Chief Justice, must swear/affirm as follows: I, A.B., swear/solemnly affirm that I will be faithful to the Republic of South Africa and will obey, respect and uphold the Constitution and all other law of the Republic; and I undertake to hold my office as Minister/Deputy Minister with honour and dignity; to be a true and faithful counsellor; not to divulge directly or indirectly any secret matter entrusted to me; and to perform the functions of my office conscientiously and to the best of my ability. (In the case of an oath: So help me God.) Oath or solemn affirmation of members of the National Assembly, permanent delegates to the National Council of Provinces and members of the provincial legislatures

2. (1) Members of the National Assembly, permanent delegates to the National Council of Provinces and members of provincial legislatures, before the Chief Justice or a judge designated by the Chief Justice, must swear or affirm as follows: I, A.B., swear/solemnly affirm that I will be faithful to the Republic of South Africa and will obey, respect and uphold the Constitution and all other law of the Republic, and I solemnly promise to perform my functions as a member of the National Assembly/permanent delegate to the National Council of Provinces/member of the legislature of the province of C.D. to the best of my ability. (In the case of an oath: So help me God.)

(2) Persons filling a vacancy in the National Assembly, a permanent delegation to the National Council of Provinces or a provincial legislature may swear or affirm in terms of sub item (1) before the presiding officer of the Assembly, Council or legislature, as the case may be. Oath or solemn affirmation of Premiers, Acting Premiers and members of provincial Executive Councils

1. The Premier or Acting Premier of a province, and each member of the Executive Council of a province, before the Chief Justice or a judge designated by the Chief Justice, must swear/affirm as follows: I, A.B., swear/solemnly affirm that I will be faithful to the Republic of South Africa and will obey,

respect and uphold the Constitution and all other law of the Republic; and I undertake to hold my office as Premier/Acting Premier/member of the Executive Council of the province of C.D. with honour and dignity; to be a true and faithful counsellor; not to divulge directly or indirectly any secret matter entrusted to me; and to perform the functions of my office conscientiously and to the best of my ability. (In the case of an oath: So help me God.) Oath or solemn affirmation of Judicial Officers

2. (1) Each judge or acting judge, before the Chief Justice or another judge designated by the Chief Justice, must swear or affirm as follows: I, A.B., swear/solemnly affirm that, as a Judge of the Constitutional Court/Supreme Court of Appeal/High Court/ E.F. Court, I will be faithful to the Republic of South Africa, will uphold and protect the Constitution and the human rights entrenched in it, and will administer justice to all persons alike without fear, favour or prejudice, in accordance with the Constitution and the law. (In the case of an oath: So help me God.)

(2) A person appointed to the office of Chief Justice who is not already a judge at the time of that appointment must swear or affirm before the Deputy Chief Justice, or failing that judge, the next most senior available judge of the Constitutional Court.

(3) Judicial officers, and acting judicial officers, other than judges, must swear/affirm in terms of national legislation. [Schedule 2 amended by s. 2 of Act No. 35 of 1997 (English text only) and substituted by s. 18 of Act No. 34 of 2001]

Schedule 3 – Election Procedures

Part A - Election procedures for constitutional office-bearers application

The procedure set out in this Schedule applies whenever

(a) the National Assembly meets to elect the President, or the Speaker or Deputy Speaker of the Assembly;

(b) the National Council of Provinces meets to elect its Chairperson or a Deputy Chairperson; or

(c) a provincial legislature meets to elect the Premier of the province or the Speaker or Deputy Speaker of the legislature. Nominations

The person presiding at a meeting to which this Schedule applies must call for the nomination of candidates at the meeting. Formal requirements are:

(1) A nomination must be made on the form prescribed by the rules mentioned in item 9.

(2) The form on which a nomination is made must be signed,

(a) by two members of the National Assembly, if the President or the Speaker or Deputy Speaker of the Assembly is to be elected;

(b) on behalf of two provincial delegations, if the Chairperson or a Deputy Chairperson of the National Council of Provinces is to be elected; or

(c) by two members of the relevant provincial legislature, if the Premier of the province or the Speaker or Deputy Speaker of the legislature is to be elected.

(3) A person who is nominated must indicate acceptance of the nomination by signing either the nomination form or any other form of written confirmation. Announcement of names of candidates

1. At a meeting to which this Schedule applies, the person presiding must announce the names of the persons who have been nominated as candidates, but may not permit any debate. Single candidate

2. If only one candidate is nominated, the person presiding must declare that candidate elected. Election procedure

3. If more than one candidate is nominated.

(a) a vote must be taken at the meeting by secret ballot;

(b) each member present, or if it is a meeting of the National Council of Provinces, each province represented, at the meeting may cast one vote; and

(c) the person presiding must declare elected the candidate who receives a majority of the votes. Elimination procedure

7. (1) If no candidate receives a majority of the votes, the candidate who receives the lowest number of votes must be eliminated and a further vote taken on the remaining candidates in accordance with item 6. This procedure must be repeated until a candidate receives a majority of the votes.

(2) When applying subitem (1), if two or more candidates each have the lowest number of votes, a separate vote must be taken on those candidates, and repeated as often as may be necessary to determine which candidate is to be eliminated. Further meetings

8. (1) If only two candidates are nominated, or if only two candidates remain after an elimination procedure has been applied, and those two candidates receive the same number of votes, a further meeting must be held within seven days, at a time determined by the person presiding.

(2) If a further meeting is held in terms of subitem (1), the procedure prescribed in this Schedule must be applied at that meeting as if it were the first meeting for the election in question. Rules

9. (1) The Chief Justice must make rules prescribing

(a) the procedure for meetings to which this Schedule applies;

(b) the duties of any person presiding at a meeting, and of any person assisting the person presiding;

(c) the form on which nominations must be submitted; and

(d) the manner in which voting is to be conducted.

(2) These rules must be made known in the way that the Chief Justice determines.

Part B. Formula to Determine Party Participation in Provincial Delegations to the National Council of Provinces

1. The number of delegates in a provincial delegation to the National Council of Provinces to which a party is entitled, must

be determined by multiplying the number of seats the party holds in the provincial legislature by ten and dividing the result by the number of seats in the legislature plus one.

2. If a calculation in terms of item 1 yields a surplus not absorbed by the delegates allocated to a party in terms of that item, the surplus must compete with similar surpluses accruing to any other party or parties, and any undistributed delegates in the delegation must be allocated to the party or parties in the sequence of the highest surplus.

3. If the competing surpluses envisaged in item 2 are equal, the undistributed delegates in the delegation must be allocated to the party or parties, including any merged party as contemplated in section 61 (2) (b), with the same surplus in sequence of votes recorded, starting with the party or merged party which recorded the highest number of votes, including combined votes in the case of a merged party, during the last election for the provincial legislature concerned, but if any of the parties with the same surplus-

(a) came into existence on account of changes of party membership or subdivision of parties within that legislature as contemplated in section 61 (2) (b); and

(b) did not participate in the last election for the provincial legislature concerned, the legislature must allocate the undistributed delegates in the delegation to the party or parties with the same surplus in a manner which is consistent with democracy.

[Schedule 3 amended by s. 2 of Act No. 3 of 1999, by s. 19 of Act No. 34 of 2001 and by s. 3 of Act No. 21 of 2002]

Schedule 4 - Functional areas of concurrent national and provincial legislative competence

Part A

- Administration of indigenous forests
- Agriculture
- Airports other than international and national airports

- Animal control and diseases
- Casinos, racing, gambling and wagering, excluding lotteries and sports pools
- Consumer protection
- Cultural matters
- Disaster management
- Education at all levels, excluding tertiary education
- Environment
- Health services
- Housing
- Indigenous law and customary law, subject to Chapter 12 of the Constitution
- Industrial promotion
- Language policy and the regulation of official languages to the extent that the provisions of section 6 of the Constitution expressly confer upon the provincial legislatures legislative competence
- Media services directly controlled or provided by the provincial government, subject to section 192
- Nature conservation, excluding national parks, national botanical gardens and marine resources
- Police to the extent that the provisions of Chapter 11 of the Constitution confer upon the provincial legislatures legislative competence
- Pollution control
- Population development
- Property transfer fees
- Provincial public enterprises in respect of the functional areas in this Schedule
- Public transport
- Public works only in respect of the needs of provincial government departments in the discharge of their responsibilities to administer functions specifically

assigned to them in terms of the Constitution or any other law

- Regional planning and development
- Road traffic regulation
- Soil conservation
- Tourism
- Trade
- Traditional leadership, subject to Chapter 12 of the Constitution
- Urban and rural development
- Vehicle licensing
- Welfare services

Part B

The following local government matters to the extent set out in section 155(6)(a) and (7):

- Air pollution
- Building regulations
- Child care facilities
- Electricity and gas reticulation
- Firefighting services
- Local tourism
- Municipal airports
- Municipal planning
- Municipal health services
- Municipal public transport
- Municipal public works only in respect of the needs of municipalities in the discharge of their responsibilities to administer functions specifically assigned to them under this Constitution or any other law
- Pontoons, ferries, jetties, piers and harbours, excluding the regulation of international and national shipping and matters related thereto

- Storm water management systems in built-up areas
- Trading regulations
- Water and sanitation services limited to potable water supply systems and domestic wastewater and sewage disposal systems

Schedule 5 - Functional areas of exclusive provincial legislative competence

Part A

- Abattoirs
- Ambulance services
- Archives other than national archives
- Libraries other than national libraries
- Liquor licences
- Museums other than national museums
- Provincial planning
- Provincial cultural matters
- Provincial recreation and amenities
- Provincial sport
- Provincial roads and traffic
- Veterinary services, excluding regulation of the profession

Part B

The following local government matters to the extent set out for provinces in section 155(6)(a) and (7):

- Beaches and amusement facilities
- Billboards and the display of advertisements in public places
- Cemeteries, funeral parlours and crematoria
- Cleansing
- Control of public nuisances
- Control of undertakings that sell liquor to the public

- Facilities for the accommodation, care and burial of animals
- Fencing and fences
- Licensing of dogs
- Licensing and control of undertakings that sell food to the public
- Local amenities
- Local sport facilities
- Markets
- Municipal abattoirs
- Municipal parks and recreation
- Municipal roads
- Noise pollution
- Pounds
- Public places
- Refuse removal, refuse dumps and solid waste disposal
- Street trading
- Street lighting
- Traffic and parking

[Schedule 6 amended by s. 3 of Act No. 35 of 1997, by s. 5 of Act No. 65 of 1998 and by s. 20 of Act No. 34 of 2001]

Schedule 6 - Transitional arrangements

Definitions

1. In this Schedule, unless inconsistent with the context. "homeland" means a part of the Republic which, before the previous Constitution took effect, was dealt with in South African legislation as an independent or a self-governing territory; "new Constitution" means the Constitution of the Republic of South Africa, 1996; "old order legislation" means legislation enacted before the previous Constitution took effect; "previous Constitution" means the Constitution of the Republic of South Africa, 1993 (Act 200 of 1993).

Continuation of existing law

2. (1) All law that was in force when the new Constitution took effect, continues in force, subject to.

(a) any amendment or repeal; and

(b) consistency with the new Constitution.

(2) Old order legislation that continues in force in terms of subitem

(a) does not have a wider application, territorially or otherwise, than it had before the previous Constitution took effect unless subsequently amended to have a wider application; and

(b) continues to be administered by the authorities that administered it when the new Constitution took effect, subject to the new Constitution.

Interpretation of existing legislation

3. (1) Unless inconsistent with the context or clearly inappropriate, a reference in any legislation that existed when the new Constitution took effect.

(a) to the Republic of South Africa or a homeland (except when it refers to a territorial area), must be construed as a reference to the Republic of South Africa under the new Constitution;

(b) to Parliament, the National Assembly or the Senate, must be construed as a reference to Parliament, the National Assembly or the National Council of Provinces under the new Constitution;

(c) to the President, an Executive Deputy President, a Minister, a Deputy Minister or the Cabinet, must be construed as a reference to the President, the Deputy President, a Minister, a Deputy Minister or the Cabinet under the new Constitution, subject to item 9 of this Schedule;

(d) to the President of the Senate, must be construed as a reference to the Chairperson of the National Council of Provinces;

(e) to a provincial legislature, Premier, Executive Council or member of an Executive Council of a province, must be construed as a reference to a provincial legislature, Premier, Executive Council or member of an Executive Council under the new Constitution, subject to item 12 of this Schedule; or

(f) to an official language or languages, must be construed as a reference to any of the official languages under the new Constitution.

(2) Unless inconsistent with the context or clearly inappropriate, a reference in any remaining old order legislation.

(a) to a Parliament, a House of a Parliament or a legislative assembly or body of the Republic or of a homeland, must be construed as a reference to.

(i) Parliament under the new Constitution, if the administration of that legislation has been allocated or assigned in terms of the previous Constitution or this Schedule to the national executive; or

(ii) the provincial legislature of a province, if the administration of that legislation has been allocated or assigned in terms of the previous Constitution or this Schedule to a provincial executive; or

(b) to a State President, Chief Minister, Administrator or other chief executive, Cabinet, Ministers' Council or executive council of the Republic or of a homeland, must be construed as a reference to.

(i) the President under the new Constitution, if the administration of that legislation has been allocated or assigned in terms of the previous Constitution or this Schedule to the national executive; or

(ii) the Premier of a province under the new Constitution, if the administration of that legislation has been allocated or assigned in terms of the previous Constitution or this Schedule to a provincial executive.

National Assembly

4. (1) Anyone who was a member or office-bearer of the National Assembly when the new Constitution took effect, becomes a member or office-bearer of the National Assembly under the new Constitution, and holds office as a member or office-bearer in terms of the new Constitution.

(2) The National Assembly as constituted in terms of subitem (1) must be regarded as having been elected under the new Constitution for a term that expires on 30 April 1999.

(3) The National Assembly consists of 400 members for the duration of its term that expires on 30 April 1999, subject to section 49(4) of the new Constitution.

(4) The rules and orders of the National Assembly in force when the new Constitution took effect, continue in force, subject to any amendment or repeal.

Unfinished business before Parliament

5. (1) Any unfinished business before the National Assembly when the new Constitution takes effect must be proceeded with in terms of the new Constitution.

(2) Any unfinished business before the Senate when the new Constitution takes effect must be referred to the National Council of Provinces, and the Council must proceed with that business in terms of the new Constitution.

Elections of National Assembly

6. (1) No election of the National Assembly may be held before 30 April 1999 unless the Assembly is dissolved in terms of section 50(2) after a motion of no confidence in the President in terms of section 102(2) of the new Constitution.

(2) Section 50(1) of the new Constitution is suspended until 30 April 1999.

(3) Despite the repeal of the previous Constitution, Schedule 2 to that Constitution, as amended by Annexure A to this Schedule, applies.

(a) to the first election of the National Assembly under the new Constitution;

(b) to the loss of membership of the Assembly in circumstances other than those provided for in section 47(3) of the new Constitution; and

(c) to the filling of vacancies in the Assembly, and the supplementation, review and use of party lists for the filling of vacancies, until the second election of the Assembly under the new Constitution.

(4) Section 47(4) of the new Constitution is suspended until the second election of the National Assembly under the new Constitution.

National Council of Provinces

7. (1) For the period which ends immediately before the first sitting of a provincial legislature held after its first election under the new Constitution.

(a) the proportion of party representation in the province's delegation to the National Council of Provinces must be the same as the proportion in which the province's 10 senators were nominated in terms of section 48 of the previous Constitution; and

(b) the allocation of permanent delegates and special delegates to the parties represented in the provincial legislature, is as follows:

Province	Permanent Delegates	Special Delegates
1. Eastern Cape	ANC 5 NP 1	ANC 4
2. Free State	ANC 4 FF 1 NP 1	ANC 4
3. Gauteng	ANC 3 DP 1 NP 1 FF 1 NP 1	ANC 3
4. KwaZulu-Natal	ANC 1 DP 1 IFP 2 IFP 3 NP 1	ANC 2

5. Mpumalanga	ANC 4 FF 1 NP 1	ANC 4
6. Northern Cape	ANC 3 FF 1 NP 2 NP 2	ANC 2
7. Northern Province	ANC 6	ANC 4
8. North West	ANC 4 FF 1 NP 1	ANC 4
9. Western Cape	ANC 2 DP 1 NP 3 NP 3	ANC 1

(2) A party represented in a provincial legislature.

(a) must nominate its permanent delegates from among the persons who were senators when the new Constitution took effect and are available to serve as permanent delegates; and

(b) may nominate other persons as permanent delegates only if none or an insufficient number of its former senators are available.

(3) A provincial legislature must appoint its permanent delegates in accordance with the nominations of the parties.

(4) Subitems (2) and (3) apply only to the first appointment of permanent delegates to the National Council of Provinces.

(5) Section 62(1) of the new Constitution does not apply to the nomination and appointment of former senators as permanent delegates in terms of this item.

(6) The rules and orders of the Senate in force when the new Constitution took effect, must be applied in respect of the business of the National Council to the extent that they can be applied, subject to any amendment or repeal.

Former senators

8. (1) A former senator who is not appointed as a permanent delegate to the National Council of Provinces is entitled to become a full voting member of the legislature of the province

from which that person was nominated as a senator in terms of section 48 of the previous Constitution.

(2) If a former senator elects not to become a member of a provincial legislature that person is regarded as having resigned as a senator the day before the new Constitution took effect.

(3) The salary, allowances and benefits of a former senator appointed as a permanent delegate or as a member of a provincial legislature may not be reduced by reason only of that appointment.

National executive

9. (1) Anyone who was the President, an Executive Deputy President, a Minister or a Deputy Minister under the previous Constitution when the new Constitution took effect, continues in and holds that office in terms of the new Constitution, but subject to subitem (2).

(2) Until 30 April 1999, sections 84, 89, 90, 91, 93 and 96 of the new Constitution must be regarded to read as set out in Annexure B to this Schedule.

(3) Subitem (2) does not prevent a Minister who was a senator when the new Constitution took effect, from continuing as a Minister referred to in section 91(1)(a) of the new Constitution, as that section reads in Annexure B.

Provincial legislatures

10. (1) Anyone who was a member or office-bearer of a province's legislature when the new Constitution took effect, becomes a member or office-bearer of the legislature for that province under the new Constitution, and holds office as a member or office-bearer in terms of the new Constitution and any provincial constitution that may be enacted.

(2) A provincial legislature as constituted in terms of subitem (1) must be regarded as having been elected under the new Constitution for a term that expires on 30 April 1999.

(3) For the duration of its term that expires on 30 April 1999, and subject to section 108(4), a provincial legislature consists of the number of members determined for that legislature under the previous Constitution plus the number of former

senators who became members of the legislature in terms of item 8 of this Schedule.

(4) The rules and orders of a provincial legislature in force when the new Constitution took effect, continue in force, subject to any amendment or repeal.

Elections of provincial legislatures

11. (1) Despite the repeal of the previous Constitution, Schedule 2 to that Constitution, as amended by Annexure A to this Schedule, applies.

(a) to the first election of a provincial legislature under the new Constitution;

(b) to the loss of membership of a legislature in circumstances other than those provided for in section 106(3) of the new Constitution; and

(c) to the filling of vacancies in a legislature, and the supplementation, review and use of party lists for the filling of vacancies, until the second election of the legislature under the new Constitution.

(2) Section 106(4) of the new Constitution is suspended in respect of a provincial legislature until the second election of the legislature under the new Constitution.

Provincial executives

12. (1) Anyone who was the Premier or a member of the Executive Council of a province when the new Constitution took effect, continues in and holds that office in terms of the new Constitution and any provincial constitution that may be enacted, but subject to subitem (2).

(2) Until the Premier elected after the first election of a province's legislature under the new Constitution assumes office, or the province enacts its constitution, whichever occurs first, sections 132 and 136 of the new Constitution must be regarded to read as set out in Annexure C to this Schedule.

Provincial constitutions

13. A provincial constitution passed before the new Constitution took effect must comply with section 143 of the new Constitution.

Assignment of legislation to provinces

14. (1) Legislation with regard to a matter within a functional area listed in Schedule 4 or 5 to the new Constitution and which, when the new Constitution took effect, was administered by an authority within the national executive, may be assigned by the President, by proclamation, to an authority within a provincial executive designated by the Executive Council of the province.

(2) To the extent that it is necessary for an assignment of legislation under subitem (1) to be effectively carried out, the President, by proclamation, may.

(a) amend or adapt the legislation to regulate its interpretation or application;

(b) where the assignment does not apply to the whole of any piece of legislation, repeal and re-enact, with or without any amendments or adaptations referred to in paragraph (a), those provisions to which the assignment applies or to the extent that the assignment applies to them; or

(c) regulate any other matter necessary as a result of the assignment, including the transfer or secondment of staff, or the transfer of assets, liabilities, rights and obligations, to or from the national or a provincial executive or any department of state, administration, security service or other institution.

(3)

(a) A copy of each proclamation issued in terms of subitem (1) or (2) must be submitted to the National Assembly and the National Council of Provinces within 10 days of the publication of the proclamation.

(b) If both the National Assembly and the National Council by resolution disapprove the proclamation or any provision of it, the proclamation or provision lapses, but without affecting.

(i) the validity of anything done in terms of the proclamation or provision before it lapsed; or

(ii) a right or privilege acquired or an obligation or liability incurred before it lapsed.

(4) When legislation is assigned under subitem (1), any reference in the legislation to an authority administering it, must be construed as a reference to the authority to which it has been assigned.

(5) Any assignment of legislation under section 235(8) of the previous Constitution, including any amendment, adaptation or repeal and re-enactment of any legislation and any other action taken under that section, is regarded as having been done under this item.

Existing legislation outside Parliament's legislative power

15. (1) An authority within the national executive that administers any legislation falling outside Parliament's legislative power when the new Constitution takes effect, remains competent to administer that legislation until it is assigned to an authority within a provincial executive in terms of item 14 of this Schedule.

(2) Subitem (1) lapses two years after the new Constitution took effect.

Courts

16. (1) Every court, including courts of traditional leaders, existing when the new Constitution took effect, continues to function and to exercise jurisdiction in terms of the legislation applicable to it, and anyone holding office as a judicial officer continues to hold office in terms of the legislation applicable to that office, subject to.

(a) any amendment or repeal of that legislation; and

(b) consistency with the new Constitution.

(2)

(a) The Constitutional Court established by the previous Constitution becomes the Constitutional Court under the new Constitution.

(b) ...

(3)

(a) The Appellate Division of the Supreme Court of South Africa becomes the Supreme Court of Appeal under the new Constitution.

(b) ...

(4)

(a) A provincial or local division of the Supreme Court of South Africa or a supreme court of a homeland or a general division of such a court, becomes a High Court under the new Constitution without any alteration in its area of jurisdiction, subject to any rationalisation contemplated in subitem (6).

(b) Anyone holding office or deemed to hold office as the Judge President, the Deputy Judge President or a judge of a court referred to in paragraph (a) when the new Constitution takes effect, becomes the Judge President, the Deputy Judge President or a judge of such a court under the new Constitution, subject to any rationalisation contemplated in subitem (6).

(5) Unless inconsistent with the context or clearly inappropriate, a reference in any legislation or process to.

(a) the Constitutional Court under the previous Constitution, must be construed as a reference to the Constitutional Court under the new Constitution;

(b) the Appellate Division of the Supreme Court of South Africa, must be construed as a reference to the Supreme Court of Appeal; and

(c) a provincial or local division of the Supreme Court of South Africa or a supreme court of a homeland or general division of that court, must be construed as a reference to a High Court.

(6)

(a) As soon as is practical after the new Constitution took effect all courts, including their structure, composition, functioning and jurisdiction, and all relevant legislation, must be rationalised with a view to establishing a judicial system suited to the requirements of the new Constitution.

(b) The Cabinet member responsible for the administration of justice, acting after consultation with the Judicial Service Commission, must manage the rationalisation envisaged in paragraph (a).

(7)

(a) Anyone holding office, when the Constitution of the Republic of South Africa Amendment Act, 2001, takes effect, as-

(i) the President of the Constitutional Court, becomes the Chief Justice as contemplated in section 167 (1) of the new Constitution;

(ii) the Deputy President of the Constitutional Court, becomes the Deputy Chief Justice as contemplated in section 167 (1) of the new Constitution;

(iii) the Chief Justice, becomes the President of the Supreme Court of Appeal as contemplated in section 168 (1) of the new Constitution; and

(iv) the Deputy Chief Justice, becomes the Deputy President of the Supreme Court of Appeal as contemplated in section 168 (1) of the new Constitution.

(a) All rules, regulations or directions made by the President of the Constitutional Court or the Chief Justice in force immediately before the Constitution of the Republic of South Africa Amendment Act, 2001, takes effect, continue in force until repealed or amended.

(b) Unless inconsistent with the context or clearly inappropriate, a reference in any law or process to the Chief Justice or to the President of the Constitutional Court, must be construed as a reference to the Chief Justice as contemplated in section 167 (1) of the new Constitution.

Cases pending before courts

17. All proceedings which were pending before a court when the new Constitution took effect, must be disposed of as if the new Constitution had not been enacted, unless the interests of justice require otherwise.

Prosecuting authority

18. (1) Section 108 of the previous Constitution continues in force until the Act of Parliament envisaged in section 179 of the new Constitution takes effect. This subitem does not affect the appointment of the National Director of Public Prosecutions in terms of section 179.

(2) An Attorney General holding office when the new Constitution takes effect, continues to function in terms of the legislation applicable to that office, subject to subitem (1).

Oaths and affirmations

19. A person who continues in office in terms of this Schedule and who has taken the oath of office or has made a solemn affirmation under the previous Constitution, is not obliged to repeat the oath of office or solemn affirmation under the new Constitution.

Other constitutional institutions

20. (1) In this section "constitutional institution" means.

(a) the Public Protector;

(b) the Human Rights Commission;

(c) the Commission on Gender Equality;

(d) the Auditor General;

(e) the South African Reserve Bank;

(f) the Financial and Fiscal Commission;

(g) the Judicial Service Commission; or

(h) the Pan South African Language Board.

(2) A constitutional institution established in terms of the previous Constitution continues to function in terms of the legislation applicable to it, and anyone holding office as a commission member, a member of the board of the Reserve

Bank or the Pan South African Language Board, the Public Protector or the Auditor General when the new Constitution takes effect, continues to hold office in terms of the legislation applicable to that office, subject to -

(a) any amendment or repeal of that legislation; and

(b) consistency with the new Constitution.

(3) Sections 199(1), 200(1), (3) and (5) to (11) and 201 to 206 of the previous Constitution continue in force until repealed by an Act of Parliament passed in terms of section 75 of the new Constitution.

(4) The members of the Judicial Service Commission referred to in section 105(1)(h) of the previous Constitution cease to be members of the Commission when the members referred to in section 178(1)(i) of the new Constitution are appointed.

(5)

(a) The Volkstaat Council established in terms of the previous Constitution continues to function in terms of the legislation applicable to it, and anyone holding office as a member of the Council when the new Constitution takes effect, continues to hold office in terms of the legislation applicable to that office, subject to.

(i) any amendment or repeal of that legislation; and

(ii) consistency with the new Constitution.

(b) Sections 184A and 184B(1)(a), (b) and (d) of the previous Constitution continue in force until repealed by an Act of Parliament passed in terms of section 75 of the new Constitution.

Enactment of legislation required by new Constitution

21. (1) Where the new Constitution requires the enactment of national or provincial legislation, that legislation must be enacted by the relevant authority within a reasonable period of the date the new Constitution took effect.

(2) Section 198(b) of the new Constitution may not be enforced until the legislation envisaged in that section has been enacted.

(3) Section 199(3)(a) of the new Constitution may not be enforced before the expiry of three months after the legislation envisaged in that section has been enacted.

(4) National legislation envisaged in section 217(3) of the new Constitution must be enacted within three years of the date on which the new Constitution took effect, but the absence of this legislation during this period does not prevent the implementation of the policy referred to in section 217(2).

(5) Until the Act of Parliament referred to in section 65(2) of the new Constitution is enacted each provincial legislature may determine its own procedure in terms of which authority is conferred on its delegation to cast votes on its behalf in the National Council of Provinces.

(6) Until the legislation envisaged in section 229(1)(b) of the new Constitution is enacted, a municipality remains competent to impose any tax, levy or duty which it was authorised to impose when the Constitution took effect.

National unity and reconciliation

22. (1) Notwithstanding the other provisions of the new Constitution and despite the repeal of the previous Constitution, all the provisions relating to amnesty contained in the previous Constitution under the heading "National Unity and Reconciliation" are deemed to be part of the new Constitution for the purposes of the Promotion of National Unity and Reconciliation Act, 1995 (Act 34 of 1995), as amended, including for the purposes of its validity.

(2) For the purposes of subitem (1), the date "6 September 1993", where it appears in the provisions of the previous Constitution under the heading "National Unity and Reconciliation", must be read as "11 May 1994".

Bill of Rights

23. (1) National legislation envisaged in sections 9(4), 32(2) and 33(3) of the new Constitution must be enacted within three years of the date on which the new Constitution took effect.

(2) Until the legislation envisaged in sections 32(2) and 33(3) of the new Constitution is enacted.

(a) section 32(1) must be regarded to read as follows:

(i) "(1) Every person has the right of access to all information held by the state or any of its organs in any sphere of government in so far as that information is required for the exercise or protection of any of their rights."; and

(b) section 33(1) and (2) must be regarded to read as follows: "Every person has the right to.

(i) lawful administrative action where any of their rights or interests is affected or threatened;

(ii) procedurally fair administrative action where any of their rights or legitimate expectations is affected or threatened;

(iii) be furnished with reasons in writing for administrative action which affects any of their rights or interests unless the reasons for that action have been made public; and

(iv) administrative action which is justifiable in relation to the reasons given for it where any of their rights is affected or threatened."

(3) Sections 32(2) and 33(3) of the new Constitution lapse if the legislation envisaged in those sections, respectively, is not enacted within three years of the date the new Constitution took effect.

Public administration and security services

24. (1) Sections 82(4)(b), 215, 218(1), 219(1), 224 to 228, 236(1), (2), (3), (6), (7)(b) and (8), 237(1) and (2)(a) and 239 (4) and (5) of the previous Constitution continue in force as if the previous Constitution had not been repealed, subject to.

(a) the amendments to those sections as set out in Annexure D;

(b) any further amendment or any repeal of those sections by an Act of Parliament passed in terms of section 75 of the new Constitution; and

(c) consistency with the new Constitution.

(2) The Public Service Commission and the provincial service commissions referred to in Chapter 13 of the previous Constitution continue to function in terms of that Chapter and the legislation applicable to it as if that Chapter had not been repealed, until the Commission and the provincial service commissions are abolished by an Act of Parliament passed in terms of section 75 of the new Constitution.

(3) The repeal of the previous Constitution does not affect any proclamation issued under section 237(3) of the previous Constitution, and any such proclamation continues in force, subject to.

(a) any amendment or repeal; and

(b) consistency with the new Constitution.

Additional disqualification for legislatures

25. (1) Anyone who, when the new Constitution took effect, was serving a sentence in the Republic of more than 12 months' imprisonment without the option of a fine, is not eligible to be a member of the National Assembly or a provincial legislature.

(2) The disqualification of a person in terms of subitem (1).

(a) lapses if the conviction is set aside on appeal, or the sentence is reduced on appeal to a sentence that does not disqualify that person; and

(b) ends five years after the sentence has been completed.

Local government

26. (1) Notwithstanding the provisions of sections 151, 155, 156 and 157 of the new Constitution -

(a) the provisions of the Local Government Transition Act, 1993 (Act 209 of 1993), as may be amended from time to time by national legislation consistent with the new Constitution, remain in force in respect of a Municipal Council until a Municipal Council replacing that Council has been declared elected as a result of the first general election of Municipal Councils after the commencement of the new Constitution; and;

(b) a traditional leader of a community observing a system of indigenous law and residing on land within the area of a transitional local council, transitional rural council or transitional representative council, referred to in the Local Government Transition Act, 1993, and who has been identified as set out in section 182 of the previous Constitution, is ex officio entitled to be a member of that council until a Municipal Council replacing that council has been declared elected as a result of the first general election of Municipal Councils after the commencement of the new Constitution.

(2) Section 245 (4) of the previous Constitution continues in force until the application of that section lapses. Section 16 (5) and (6) of the Local Government Transition Act, 1993, may not be repealed before 30 April 2000.

Safekeeping of Acts of Parliament and Provincial Acts

27. Sections 82 and 124 of the new Constitution do not affect the safekeeping of Acts of Parliament or provincial Acts passed before the new Constitution took effect.

Registration of immovable property owned by the state

28. (1) On the production of a certificate by a competent authority that immovable property owned by the state is vested in a particular government in terms of section 239 of the previous Constitution, a registrar of deeds must make such entries or endorsements in or on any relevant register, title deed or other document to register that immovable property in the name of that government.

(2) No duty, fee or other charge is payable in respect of a registration in terms of subitem (1).

ANNEXURE A

Amendments to Schedule 2 to the previous Constitution

The replacement of item 1 with the following item:

"1. Parties registered in terms of national legislation and contesting an election of the National Assembly, shall nominate candidates for such election on lists of candidates prepared in accordance with this Schedule and national legislation."

2. The replacement of item 2 with the following item: "2. The seats in the National Assembly as determined in terms of section 46 of the new Constitution, shall be filled as follows:

(a) One half of the seats from regional lists submitted by the respective parties, with a fixed number of seats reserved for each region as determined by the Commission for the next election of the Assembly, taking into account available scientifically based data in respect of voters, and representations by interested parties.

(b) The other half of the seats from national lists submitted by the respective parties, or from regional lists where national lists were not submitted."

1. The replacement of item 3 with the following item: "3. The lists of candidates submitted by a party, shall in total contain the names of not more than a number of candidates equal to the number of seats in the National Assembly, and each such list shall denote such names in such fixed order of preference as the party may determine."

(4) The amendment of item 5 by replacing the words preceding paragraph (a) with the following words:

"(5) The seats referred to in item 2(a) shall be allocated per region to the parties contesting an election, as follows:"

2. The amendment of item 6 -

(a) by replacing the words preceding paragraph (a) with the following words: "6. The seats referred to in item 2(b) shall be allocated to the parties contesting an election, as follows:"; and

(b) by replacing paragraph (a) with the following paragraph: "(a) A quota of votes per seat shall be determined by dividing the total number of votes cast nationally by the number of seats in the National Assembly, plus one, and the result plus one, disregarding fractions, shall be the quota of votes per seat."

1. The amendment of item 7(3) by replacing paragraph (b) with the following paragraph: "(b) An amended quota of votes per seat shall be determined by dividing the total number of votes cast nationally, minus the number of votes cast nationally in favour of the party referred to in paragraph (a), by the number of seats in the Assembly, plus one, minus the number of seats finally allocated to the said party in terms of paragraph (a)."

2. The replacement of item 10 with the following item: "10. The number of seats in each provincial legislature shall be as determined in terms of section 105 of the new Constitution."

3. The replacement of item 11 with the following item: "11. Parties registered in terms of national legislation and contesting an election of a provincial legislature, shall nominate candidates for election to such provincial legislature on provincial lists prepared in accordance with this Schedule and national legislation."

4. The replacement of item 16 with the following item: Designation of representatives

16. (1) After the counting of votes has been concluded, the number of representatives of each party has been determined and the election result has been declared in terms of section 190 of the new Constitution, the Commission shall, within two days after such declaration, designate from each list of candidates, published in terms of national legislation, the representatives of each party in the legislature.

(2) Following the designation in terms of subitem (1), if a candidate's name appears on more than one list for the National Assembly or on lists for both the National Assembly and a provincial legislature (if an election of the Assembly and a

provincial legislature is held at the same time), and such candidate is due for designation as a representative in more than one case, the party which submitted such lists shall, within two days after the said declaration, indicate to the Commission from which list such candidate will be designated or in which legislature the candidate will serve, as the case may be, in which event the candidate's name shall be deleted from the other lists.

(3) The Commission shall forthwith publish the list of names of representatives in the legislature or legislatures."

1. The amendment of item 18 by replacing paragraph (b) with the following paragraph: "(b) a representative is appointed as a permanent delegate to the National Council of Provinces;"

2. The replacement of item 19 with the following item: "19. Lists of candidates of a party referred to in item 16(1) may be supplemented on one occasion only at any time during the first 12 months following the date on which the designation of representatives in terms of item 16 has been concluded, in order to fill casual vacancies: Provided that any such supplementation shall be made at the end of the list."

3. The replacement of item 23 with the following item: "Vacancies

23.(1) In the event of a vacancy in a legislature to which this Schedule applies, the party which nominated the vacating member shall fill the vacancy by nominating a person.

(a) whose name appears on the list of candidates from which the vacating member was originally nominated; and

(b) who is the next qualified and available person on the list.

(2) A nomination to fill a vacancy shall be submitted to the Speaker in writing.

(3) If a party represented in a legislature dissolves or ceases to exist and the members in question vacate their seats in consequence of item 23A(1), the seats in question shall be allocated to the remaining parties mutatis mutandis as if such seats were forfeited seats in terms of item 7 or 14, as the case may be."

13. The insertion of the following item after item 23: "Additional ground for loss of membership of legislatures 23A. (1) A person loses membership of a legislature to which this Schedule applies if that person ceases to be a member of the party which nominated that person as a member of the legislature.

(2) Despite subitem (1) any existing political party may at any time change its name.

(3) An Act of Parliament may, within a reasonable period after the new Constitution took effect, be passed in accordance with section 76(1) of the new Constitution to amend this item and item 23 to provide for the manner in which it will be possible for a member of a legislature who ceases to be a member of the party which nominated that member, to retain membership of such legislature.

(4) An Act of Parliament referred to in subitem (3) may also provide for

(a) any existing party to merge with another party; or

(b) any party to subdivide into more than one party.

1. The deletion of item 24.

2. The amendment of item 25

(a) by replacing the definition of "Commission" with the following definition: "'Commission' means the Electoral Commission referred to in section 190 of the new Constitution"; and

(b) by inserting the following definition after the definition of "national list": "'new Constitution' means the Constitution of the Republic of South Africa, 1996".

16. The deletion of item 26.

ANNEXURE B

Government of National Unity: National Sphere

1. Section 84 of the new Constitution is deemed to contain the following additional subsection: "(3) The President must consult the Executive Deputy Presidents.

(a) in the development and execution of the policies of the national government;

(b) in all matters relating to the management of the Cabinet and the performance of Cabinet business;

(c) in the assignment of functions to the Executive Deputy Presidents;

(d) before making any appointment under the Constitution or any legislation, including the appointment of ambassadors or other diplomatic representatives;

(e) before appointing commissions of inquiry;

(f) before calling a referendum; and

(g) before pardoning or reprieving offenders.

2. Section 89 of the new Constitution is deemed to contain the following additional subsection:

"(3) Subsections (1) and (2) apply also to an Executive Deputy President."

2. Paragraph (a) of section 90(1) of the new Constitution is deemed to read as follows: "(a) an Executive Deputy President designated by the President;"

3. Section 91 of the new Constitution is deemed to read as follows:

91. (1) The Cabinet consists of the President, the Executive Deputy Presidents and

(a) not more than 27 Ministers who are members of the National Assembly and appointed in terms of subsections (8) to (12); and

(b) not more than one Minister who is not a member of the National Assembly and appointed in terms of subsection (13), provided the President, acting in consultation with the Executive Deputy Presidents and the leaders of the participating parties, deems the appointment of such a Minister expedient.

(2) Each party holding at least 80 seats in the National Assembly is entitled to designate an Executive Deputy President from among the members of the Assembly.

(3) If no party or only one party holds 80 or more seats in the Assembly, the party holding the largest number of seats and the party holding the second largest number of seats are each entitled to designate one Executive Deputy President from among the members of the Assembly.

(4) On being designated, an Executive Deputy President may elect to remain or cease to be a member of the Assembly.

(5) An Executive Deputy President may exercise the powers and must perform the functions vested in the office of Executive Deputy President by the Constitution or assigned to that office by the President.

(6) An Executive Deputy President holds office

(a) until 30 April 1999 unless replaced or recalled by the party entitled to make the designation in terms of subsections (2) and (3); or

(b) until the person elected President after any election of the National Assembly held before 30 April 1999, assumes office.

(7) A vacancy in the office of an Executive Deputy President may be filled by the party which designated that Deputy President.

(8) A party holding at least 20 seats in the National Assembly and which has decided to participate in the government of national unity, is entitled to be allocated one or more of the Cabinet portfolios in respect of which Ministers referred to in subsection (1)(a) are to be appointed, in proportion to the number of seats held by it in the National Assembly relative to the number of seats held by the other participating parties.

(9) Cabinet portfolios must be allocated to the respective participating parties in accordance with the following formula:

(a) A quota of seats per portfolio must be determined by dividing the total number of seats in the National Assembly held jointly by the participating parties by the number of portfolios in respect of which Ministers referred to in subsection (1) (a) are to be appointed, plus one.

(b) The result, disregarding third and subsequent decimals, if any, is the quota of seats per portfolio.

(c) The number of portfolios to be allocated to a participating party is determined by dividing the total number of seats held by that party in the National Assembly by the quota referred to in paragraph (b).

(d) The result, subject to paragraph (e), indicates the number of portfolios to be allocated to that party.

(e) Where the application of the above formula yields a surplus not absorbed by the number of portfolios allocated to a party, the surplus competes with other similar surpluses accruing to another party or parties, and any portfolio or portfolios which remain unallocated must be allocated to the party or parties concerned in sequence of the highest surplus.

(10) The President after consultation with the Executive Deputy Presidents and the leaders of the participating parties must.

(a) determine the specific portfolios to be allocated to the respective participating parties in accordance with the number of portfolios allocated to them in terms of subsection (9);

(b) appoint in respect of each such portfolio a member of the National Assembly who is a member of the party to which that portfolio was allocated under paragraph (a), as the Minister responsible for that portfolio;

(c) if it becomes necessary for the purposes of the Constitution or in the interest of good government, vary any determination under paragraph (a), subject to subsection (9);

(d) terminate any appointment under paragraph (b).

(i) if the President is requested to do so by the leader of the party of which the Minister in question is a member; or

(ii) if it becomes necessary for the purposes of the Constitution or in the interest of good government.

(e) fill, when necessary, subject to paragraph (b), a vacancy in the office of Minister.

(11) Subsection (10) must be implemented in the spirit embodied in the concept of a government of national unity, and the President and the other functionaries concerned must in the implementation of that subsection seek to achieve consensus at all times: Provided that if consensus cannot be achieved on.

(a) the exercise of a power referred to in paragraph (a), (c) or (d)(ii) of that subsection, the President's decision prevails;

(b) the exercise of a power referred to in paragraph (b), (d)(i) or (e) of that subsection affecting a person who is not a member of the President's party, the decision of the leader of the party of which that person is a member prevails; and

(c) the exercise of a power referred to in paragraph (b) or (e) of that subsection affecting a person who is a member of the President's party, the President's decision prevails.

(12) If any determination of portfolio allocations is varied under subsection (10)(c), the affected Ministers must vacate their portfolios but are eligible, where applicable, for reappointment to other portfolios allocated to their respective parties in terms of the varied determination.

(13) The President.

(a) in consultation with the Executive Deputy Presidents and the leaders of the participating parties, must.

(i) determine a specific portfolio for a Minister referred to in subsection (1) (b) should it become necessary pursuant to a decision of the President under that subsection;

(ii) appoint in respect of that portfolio a person who is not a member of the National Assembly, as the Minister responsible for that portfolio; and

(iii) fill, if necessary, a vacancy in respect of that portfolio; or

(b) after consultation with the Executive Deputy Presidents and the leaders of the participating parties, must terminate any appointment under paragraph (a) if it becomes necessary for the purposes of the Constitution or in the interest of good government.

(14) Meetings of the Cabinet must be presided over by the President, or, if the President so instructs, by an Executive Deputy President: Provided that the Executive Deputy Presidents preside over meetings of the Cabinet in turn unless the exigencies of government and the spirit embodied in the concept of a government of national unity otherwise demand.

(15) The Cabinet must function in a manner which gives consideration to the consensus-seeking spirit embodied in the concept of a government of national unity as well as the need for effective government.

5. Section 93 of the new Constitution is deemed to read as follows: Appointment of Deputy Ministers

93. (1) The President may, after consultation with the Executive Deputy Presidents and the leaders of the parties participating in the Cabinet, establish deputy ministerial posts.

(2) A party is entitled to be allocated one or more of the deputy ministerial posts in the same proportion and according to the same formula that portfolios in the Cabinet are allocated.

(3) The provisions of section 91 (10) to (12) apply, with the necessary changes, in respect of Deputy Ministers, and in such application a reference in that section to a Minister or a portfolio must be read as a reference to a Deputy Minister or a deputy ministerial post, respectively.

(4) If a person is appointed as the Deputy Minister of any portfolio entrusted to a Minister.

(a) that Deputy Minister must exercise and perform on behalf of the relevant Minister any of the powers and functions assigned to that Minister in terms of any legislation or otherwise which may, subject to the directions of the President, be assigned to that Deputy Minister by that Minister; and

(b) any reference in any legislation to that Minister must be construed as including a reference to the Deputy Minister acting in terms of an assignment under paragraph (a) by the Minister for whom that Deputy Minister acts.

(5) Whenever a Deputy Minister is absent or for any reason unable to exercise or perform any of the powers or functions of office, the President may appoint any other Deputy Minister or any other person to act in the said Deputy Minister's stead, either generally or in the exercise or performance of any specific power or function.

6. Section 96 of the new Constitution is deemed to contain the following additional subsections: (3) Ministers are accountable individually to the President and to the National Assembly for the administration of their portfolios, and all members of the Cabinet are correspondingly accountable collectively for the performance of the functions of the national government and for its policies.

(4) Ministers must administer their portfolios in accordance with the policy determined by the Cabinet.

(5) If a Minister fails to administer the portfolio in accordance with the policy of the Cabinet, the President may require the Minister concerned to bring the administration of the portfolio into conformity with that policy.

(6) If the Minister concerned fails to comply with a requirement of the President under subsection (5), the President may remove the Minister from office.

(a) if it is a Minister referred to in section 91(1)(a), after consultation with the Minister and, if the Minister is not a member of the President's party or is not the leader of a participating party, also after consultation with the leader of that Minister's party; or

(b) if it is a Minister referred to in section 91(1)(b), after consultation with the Executive Deputy Presidents and the leaders of the participating parties.

ANNEXURE C

Government of National Unity: Provincial Sphere

1. Section 132 of the new Constitution is deemed to read as follows: Executive Councils

132. (1) The Executive Council of a province consists of the Premier and not more than 10 members appointed by the Premier in accordance with this section.

(2) A party holding at least 10 per cent of the seats in a provincial legislature and which has decided to participate in the government of national unity, is entitled to be allocated one or more of the Executive Council portfolios in proportion to the number of seats held by it in the legislature relative to the number of seats held by the other participating parties.

(3) Executive Council portfolios must be allocated to the respective participating parties according to the same formula set out in section 91 (9), and in applying that formula a reference in that section

(4) The Premier of a province after consultation with the leaders of the participating parties must.

(a) determine the specific portfolios to be allocated to the respective participating parties in accordance with the number of portfolios allocated to them in terms of subsection (3);

(b) appoint in respect of each such portfolio a member of the provincial legislature who is a member of the party to which that portfolio was allocated under paragraph (a), as the member of the Executive Council responsible for that portfolio;

(c) if it becomes necessary for the purposes of the Constitution or in the interest of good government, vary any determination under paragraph (a), subject to subsection (3);

(d) terminate any appointment under paragraph (b).

(i) if the Premier is requested to do so by the leader of the party of which the Executive Council member in question is a member; or

(ii) if it becomes necessary for the purposes of the Constitution or in the interest of good government; or

(e) fill, when necessary, subject to paragraph (b), a vacancy in the office of a member of the Executive Council.

(5) Subsection (4) must be implemented in the spirit embodied in the concept of a government of national unity, and the Premier and the other functionaries concerned must in the implementation of that subsection seek to achieve consensus at all times: Provided that if consensus cannot be achieved on.

(a) the exercise of a power referred to in paragraph (a), (c) or (d)(ii) of that subsection, the Premier's decision prevails;

(b) the exercise of a power referred to in paragraph (b), (d)(i) or (e) of that subsection affecting a person who is not a member of the Premier's party, the decision of the leader of the party of which such person is a member prevails; and

(c) the exercise of a power referred to in paragraph (b) or (e) of that subsection affecting a person who is a member of the Premier's party, the Premier's decision prevails.

(6) If any determination of portfolio allocations is varied under subsection (4)(c), the affected members must vacate their portfolios but are eligible, where applicable, for reappointment to other portfolios allocated to their respective parties in terms of the varied determination.

(7) Meetings of an Executive Council must be presided over by the Premier of the province.

(8) An Executive Council must function in a manner which gives consideration to the consensus-seeking spirit embodied in the concept of a government of national unity, as well as the need for effective government.

2. Section 136 of the new Constitution is deemed to contain the following additional subsections: (3) Members of Executive

Councils are accountable individually to the Premier and to the provincial legislature for the administration of their portfolios, and all members of the Executive Council are correspondingly accountable collectively for the performance of the functions of the provincial government and for its policies.

(4) Members of Executive Councils must administer their portfolios in accordance with the policy determined by the Council.

(5) If a member of an Executive Council fails to administer the portfolio in accordance with the policy of the Council, the Premier may require the member concerned to bring the administration of the portfolio into conformity with that policy.

(6) If the member concerned fails to comply with a requirement of the Premier under subsection (5), the Premier may remove the member from office after consultation with the member, and if the member is not a member of the Premier's party or is not the leader of a participating party, also after consultation with the leader of that member's party.

ANNEXURE D

Public administration and security services: Amendments to sections of the previous Constitution

1. The amendment of section 218 of the previous Constitution.

(a) by replacing in subsection (1) the words preceding paragraph (a) with the following words: "(1) Subject to the directions of the Minister of Safety and Security, the National Commissioner shall be responsible for";

(b) by replacing paragraph (b) of subsection (1) with the following paragraph: "(b) the appointment of provincial commissioners";

(c) by replacing paragraph (d) of subsection (1) with the following paragraph: "(d) the investigation and prevention of organised crime or crime which requires national investigation and prevention or specialised skills"; and

(d) by replacing paragraph (k) of subsection (1) with the following paragraph: "(k) the establishment and maintenance of a national public order policing unit to be deployed in support of and at the request of the Provincial Commissioner".

1. The amendment of section 219 of the previous Constitution by replacing in subsection (1) the words preceding paragraph (a) with the following words: "(1) Subject to section 218(1), a Provincial Commissioner shall be responsible for".

2. The amendment of section 224 of the previous Constitution by replacing the proviso to subsection (2) with the following proviso: "Provided that this subsection shall also apply to members of any armed force which submitted its personnel list after the commencement of the Constitution of the Republic of South Africa, 1993 (Act 200 of 1993), but before the adoption of the new constitutional text as envisaged in section 73 of that Constitution, if the political organisation under whose authority and control it stands or with which it is

associated and whose objectives it promotes did participate in the Transitional Executive Council or did take part in the first election of the National Assembly and the provincial legislatures under the said Constitution."

3. The amendment of section 227 of the previous Constitution by replacing subsection (2) with the following subsection: "(2) The National Defence Force shall exercise its powers and perform its functions solely in the national interest in terms of Chapter 11 of the Constitution of the Republic of South Africa, 1996."

4. The amendment of section 236 of the previous Constitution

(a) by replacing subsection (1) with the following subsection: "(1) A public service, department of state, administration or security service which immediately before the commencement of the Constitution of the Republic of South Africa, 1996 (hereinafter referred to as 'the new Constitution'), performed governmental functions, continues to function in terms of the legislation applicable to it until it is abolished or incorporated or integrated into any appropriate institution or is rationalised or consolidated with any other institution."

(b) by replacing subsection (6) with the following subsection: "(6) (a) The President may appoint a commission to review the conclusion or amendment of a contract, the appointment or promotion, or the award of a term or condition of service or other benefit, which occurred between 27 April 1993 and 30 September 1994 in respect of any person referred to in subsection (2) or any class of such persons.

(c) The commission may reverse or alter a contract, appointment, promotion or award if not proper or justifiable in the circumstances of the case"; and

(d) by replacing "this Constitution", wherever this occurs in section 236, with "the new Constitution".

6. The amendment of section 237 of the previous Constitution

(a) by replacing paragraph (a) of subsection (1) with the following paragraph: (a) The rationalisation of all institutions referred to in section 236(1), excluding military forces referred to in section 224(2), shall after the commencement of the Constitution of the Republic of South Africa, 1996, continue, with a view to establishing

(i) an effective administration in the national sphere of government to deal with matters within the jurisdiction of the national sphere; and

(ii) an effective administration for each province to deal with matters within the jurisdiction of each provincial government; and

(b) by replacing subparagraph (i) of subsection (2) (a) with the following subparagraph: "(i) institutions referred to in section 236(1), excluding military forces, shall rest with the national government, which shall exercise such responsibility in co-operation with the provincial governments".

7. The amendment of section 239 of the previous Constitution by replacing subsection (4) with the following subsection: "(4) Subject to and in accordance with any applicable law, the assets, rights, duties and liabilities of all forces referred to in section 224(2) shall devolve upon the National Defence Force in accordance with the directions of the Minister of Defence."

Schedule 6A

Retention of membership of National Assembly or provincial legislature, after a change of party membership, mergers between parties, subdivision of parties and subdivision and merger of parties

[Schedule 6A inserted by s. 6 of Act No. 2 of 2003]

Definition

1. In this Schedule "legislature" means the National Assembly or any provincial legislature.

Retention of membership of legislature in event of change of party membership

2. (1) Subject to item 4, a member of a legislature who becomes a member of a party (the new party) other than the party which nominated that person as a member (the nominating party), whether the new party participated in an election or not, remains a member of that legislature if that member, whether by himself or herself or together with one or more other members who, during a period referred to in item 4 (1) (a) or (b), ceased to be members of the nominating party, represents not less that 10 per cent of the total number of seats held by the nominating party in that legislature.

(2) The seat held by a member referred to in subitem (1) is regarded as having been allocated to the new party which the member represents.

Retention of membership of legislature in event of mergers, subdivision and subdivision and merger of parties

3. (1) Subject to item 4, any party (the original party) which is represented in a legislature may-

(a) merge with another party, whether that party participated in an election or not; or

(b) subdivide into more than one party or subdivide and any subdivision may merge with another party, whether that party participated in an election or not, if the members of subdivision leaving the original party represent not less than 10 per cent of the total number of seats held by the original party in that legislature.

(2) If a party merges with another party or subdivides into more than one party or subdivides and any subdivision merges with another party in terms of subitem (1), the members concerned remain members of that legislature and the seats held by them are regarded as having been allocated to the party which they represent pursuant to any merger, subdivision or subdivision and merger contemplated in subitem (1).

Period of application of items 2 and 3 and further requirements

4. (1) The provisions of items 2 and 3 only apply-

(a) for a period of 15 days from the first to the fifteenth day of September in the second year following the date of an election of the legislature; and

(b) for a period of 15 days from the first to the fifteenth day of September in the fourth year following the date of an election of the legislature.

(2) For the purpose of subitem (1) "year" means a period of 365 days.

(3) During each period referred to in subitem (1) (a) and (b)

(a) a member of legislature may only once change membership of a party, by informing the Speaker of the legislature thereof in writing and by submitting to the Speaker written confirmation from such other party that he or she has been accepted as a member of that party; and

(b) a party may only once -

(i) merge with another party;

(ii) subdivide into more than one party; and

(iii) subdivide and any subdivision may merge with another party, by informing the Speaker of the legislature thereof in writing and by submitting to the Speaker written confirmation from the other party of the names of all members involved in the merger or subdivision, and that the party has accepted the merger; and

(c) no party represented in a legislature may -

(i) suspend or terminate the party membership of a member representing that party in that legislature; or

(ii) perform any act whatsoever which may cause such a member to be disqualified from holding office as such a member, without the written consent of the member concerned.

(4) A party which has not been registered in terms of any law applicable to the registration of political parties is regarded as a party for the purposes of this Schedule, but such a party must apply for registration as a party in accordance with applicable law within the period referred to in subitem (1)

(a) or (b). If the party is not registered within four months after the expiry of that period, it is regarded as having ceased to exist, and the seats in question must be allocated to the remaining parties in accordance with applicable law.

Composition of legislature maintained until election or reconstitution in terms of Schedule

5. (1) After the expiry of a period referred to in item 4 (1) (a) or (b), the composition of a legislature which has been reconstituted as a result of any conduct in terms of item 2 or 3 is maintained until the next election of that legislature or until the composition of the legislature is reconstituted in accordance with item 2 or 3.

(2) Within seven days after the expiry of a period referred to in item 4 (1) (a) or (b), each party represented in a legislature contemplated in subitem (1) must submit a list of its candidates to the Secretary of the legislature.

(3) The Speaker of a legislature contemplated in subitem (1) must, within seven days after the expiry of a period referred to in item 4 (1) (a) or (b), publish a notice in the Gazette which must reflect -

(a) the number of seats allocated to each party represented in that legislature; and

(b) the name of, and party represented by, each member.

Transitional arrangement in respect of retention of membership of legislature in event of change of party membership, mergers between parties, subdivision of parties and subdivision and merger of parties.

6. (1) During the first 15 days immediately following the date of the commencement of this Schedule -

(a) a member of a legislature may become a member of another party (the new party), whether the new party participated in an election or not, whilst remaining a member of the legislature concerned and the seat held by that member must be regarded as having been allocated to the new party of which that member has become a member; and

(b) any party which is represented in a legislature may -

(i) merge with another party, whether that party participated in an election or not; or

(ii) subdivide into more than one party or subdivide and any subdivision may merge with another party, whether that party participated in an election or not, whilst the members concerned remain members of that legislature and the seats held by them must be regarded as having been allocated to the party which they represent pursuant to any merger, subdivision or subdivision and merger contemplated in this paragraph.

(2) The provisions of item 4 (3) and (4) and item 5 are also applicable in respect of subitem (1), and any reference therein to a period referred to in item 4 (1) (a) or (b) must be construed as a reference to the period referred to in subitem (1).

Schedule 6B - Loss or retention of membership of Municipal Councils, after a change of party membership, mergers between parties, subdivision of parties and subdivion and merger of parties, and filling of vacancies

[Schedule 6B, formerly Schedule 6A, inserted by s. 2 of Act No. 18 of 2002 and amended by s. 5 of Act No. 2 of 2003]

Loss or retention of Council membership

1. (1) A councillor not representing a ward ceases to be a member of a Municipal Council if that councillor, other than in accordance with item 2, 3 or 7, ceases to be a member of the party which nominated that councillor as a member of that Council.

(2) A councillor representing a ward in a Municipal Council ceases to be member of that Council if that councillor, other than in accordance with item 2, 3 or 7 -

(a) ceases to be a member of a party which nominated that councillor as a candidate in the ward election; or

(b) was not nominated by any party as a candidate in the ward election and becomes a member of a party.

Retention of Council membership in event of change of party membership

2. (1) Subject to item 4, a councillor -

(a) not representing a ward, who is a member of a party represented in that Municipal Council (the original party) and who becomes a member of another party (the new party), whether the new party participated in an election or not, remains a councillor of that Council; or

(b) who represents a ward in that Council, remains a councillor for that ward, if that councillor -

(i) was nominated by a party (the original party) as a candidate in the ward election and - (aa) cease to be a member of the original party and becomes a member of another party (the new party), whether the new party participated in an election or not; or (bb) ceases to be a member of the original party and does not become a member of anther party; or

(ii) was not nominated by a party as a candidate in the ward election and becomes a member of a party, whether that party participated in an election or not, if the councillor referred to in paragraphs (a) and (b) (i), whether by himself or herself or together with one or more other councillors who, during a period referred to in item 4 (1) (a) (i) or (ii) ceased to be members of the original party, represent not less than 10 per cent of the total number of seats held by the original party in that Council.

(2) The seat held by a councillor referred to in subitem (1) (9a) must be regarded as having been allocated to the new party of which that councillor has become a member.

(3) The ward represented by a councillor referred to in subitem (1) (b) must be regarded as having been -

(a) allocated to the party of which that councillor has become a member; or

(b) acquired by that councillor, if such councillor has not become a member of another party.

Retention of Council in event of mergers, subdivision and subdivision and merger of parties

3. (1) Subject to item 4, any political party (the original party) which is represented in a Municipal Council may -

(a) merge with another party, whether that party participated in a an election or not; or

(b) subdivide into more than one party or subdivide and any one subdivision may merge with another party, whether that party participated in an election or not, if the members of a subdivision leaving the original party represented not less than 10 per cent of the total number of seats held by the original party in respect of that Council.

(2) If a party merges with another party or subdivides into more than one party or subdivides and merges with another party in terms of subitem (1), the councillors concerned remain members of that Municipal Council and the seats held by them must be regarded as having been allocated to the new party which they represent pursuant to any merger, subdivision or subdivision and merger as contemplated in subitem (1).

Period of application of items 2 and 3 and further requirements

4. (1)

(a) The provisions of items 2 and 3 only apply -

(i) for a period of 15 days from the first to the fifteenth day of September in the second year following the date of an election of all Municipal Councils; and

(ii) for a period of 15 days from the first to the fifteenth day of September in the fourth year following the date of an election of all Municipal Councils, but do not apply during the year ending on 31 December 2002.

(b) For the purpose of paragraph (a) "year" means a period of 365 days.

(2) During a period referred to in subitem (1) (a) (i) or (ii) -

(a) a councillor may only once -

(i) change membership of a party;

(ii) become a member of a party; or

(iii) cease to be a member of a party, by informing an officer designated by the Electoral Commission thereof in writing, and if that councillor has changed membership of a party or has become a member of a party, by submitting to that officer written confirmation from the party in question that he or she has been accepted as a member of that party; and

(b) a party may only once -

(i) merge with another party;

(ii) subdivide into more than one party; or

(iii) subdivide and any one subdivision merge with another party, by informing an officer designated by the Electoral Commission thereof in writing, and by submitting to that officer written confirmation from the party - (aa) of the names of all councillors involved in such merger of subdivision; and (bb) that it has accepted such merger; and

(c) no party represented in a Municipal Council may -

(i) suspend or terminate the party membership of a councillor representing that party in that Council; or

(ii) perform any act whatsoever which may cause such a councillor to be disqualified from holding office as such a councillor in that Council, without the written consent of the councillor concerned.

Composition of Council maintained until election or by-election, or reconstitution in terms of Schedule

5. After the expiry of a period referred to in item 4 (1) (a), the composition of a Municipal Council, which has been reconstituted as a result of any conduct in terms of item 2 or 3, is maintained until the next election of all Municipal Councils or until the composition of that Municipal Council is reconstituted in accordance with item 2 or 3 or until a by-election is held in that Municipal Council.

Reconstitution by Municipal Councils

6.

(a) A Municipal Council referred to in item 5 which appoints members of another Municipal Council, as contemplated in section 157 (1) (b) must within 15 days of the expiry of a period referred to in item 4 (1) (a) (i) or (ii) apply again the procedure provided for in national legislation for appointing such members to represent the appointing Council.

(b) Within 30 days of the expiry of a period referred to in 4 (1) (a) (i) of (ii), all the structures and committees of -

(i) a Category A and a Category B municipality referred to in item 5 must be reconstituted in accordance with applicable law; and

(ii) a Category C municipality referred to in item 5 must be reconstituted in accordance with applicable law after all the appointments contemplated in paragraph (a) have been made in respect of that Category C municipality.

Transitional arrangement in respect of retention of membership of Municipal Councils in event of change of party membership, merger between parties, subdivision of parties and subdivision and merger of parties

7. (1) During the first 15 days immediately following the date of the commencement of this Schedule -

(a) a councillor who was elected from the party list of a party represented in a Municipal Council (the original party) may become a member of another party (the new party), whether the new party participated in an election or not, whilst remaining a councillor of the Municipal Council concerned and the seat held by that councillor must be regarded as having been allocated to the new party of which that councillor has become a member;

(b) a councillor who was elected to represent a ward in a Municipal Council and who -

(i) was nominated by a party as a candidate in the ward election, may cease to be a member of the original party and become a member of the new party, whether the new party participated in an election or not, or cease to be a member of the original party and not become a member of another party; or

(ii) was not nominated by a party as a candidate in the ward election, may become a member of a party, whether that party participated in an election or not, and the ward represented by such a councillor must be regarded as having been - (aa) allocated to the new party of which that councillor has become a member, or (bb) acquired by that councillor, if such councillor has not become a member of a party; and

(c) any political party which is represented in a Municipal Council may -

(i) merge with another party, whether that party participated in an election or not; or

(ii) subdivide into more than one party or subdivide and any one subdivision merge with another party, whether that party participated in an election or not, whilst the councillors concerned remain members of that Council and the seats held by them must be regarded and having been allocated to the party which they represent pursuant to any merger, subdivision or subdivision and merger contemplated in this paragraph.

(2) The provisions of items 4 (2), 5 and 6 are also applicable in respect or subitem (1), and any reference therein to a period referred to in item 4 (1) (a) (i) or (ii) must be construed as a reference to the period referred to in subitem (1).

Filling of vacancies

8. Vacancies in a Municipal Council must be filled in terms of national legislation.

Amendment of Schedule

9. ... [Item 9 deleted by s. 5 of Act No. 2 of 2003]

Schedule 7 - Laws repealed

Number and Year of Law	Title
Act 200 of 1993	Constitution of the Republic of South Africa, 1993
Act 2 of 1994	Constitution of the Republic of South Africa Amendment Act, 1994
Act 3 of 1994	Constitution of the Republic of South Africa Second Amendment Act, 1994
Act 13 of 1994	Constitution of the Republic of South Africa Third Amendment Act, 1994
Act 14 of 1994	Constitution of the Republic of South Africa Fourth Amendment Act, 1994

Act 24 of 1994	Constitution of the Republic of South Africa Sixth Amendment Act, 1994
Act 29 of 1994	Constitution of the Republic of South Africa Fifth Amendment Act, 1994
Act 20 of 1995	Constitution of the Republic of South Africa Amendment Act, 1995
Act 44 of 1995	Constitution of the Republic of South Africa Second Amendment Act, 1995
Act 7 of 1996	Constitution of the Republic of South Africa Amendment Act, 1996
Act 26 of 1996	Constitution of the Republic of South Africa Third Amendment Act, 1996

Constitution of Japan

7

The Constitution of Japan, 3 November 1946

Preface

We, the Japanese people, acting through our duly elected representatives in the National Diet, determined that we shall secure for ourselves and our posterity the fruits of peaceful cooperation with all nations and the blessings of liberty throughout this land, and resolved that never again shall we be visited with the horrors of war through the action of government, do proclaim that sovereign power resides with the people and do firmly establish this Constitution. Government is a sacred trust of the people, the authority for which is derived from the people, the powers of which are exercised by the representatives of the people, and the benefits of which are enjoyed by the people. This is a universal principle of mankind upon which this Constitution is founded. We reject and revoke all constitutions, laws ordinances, and rescripts in conflict herewith. We, the Japanese people, desire peace for all time and are deeply conscious of the high ideals controlling human relationship and we have determined to preserve our security and existence, trusting in the justice and faith of the peace-loving peoples of the world. We desire to occupy an honored place in an international society striving for the preservation of peace, and the banishment of tyranny and slavery, oppression and intolerance for all time from the earth. We recognize that all peoples of the world have the right to live in peace, free from fear and want. We believe that no nation is responsible to itself alone, but that laws of political morality are universal; and that obedience to such laws is incumbent upon all nations who would sustain their own sovereignty and justify their sovereign relationship with other nations. We, the Japanese people, pledge our national honor to accomplish these high ideals and purposes with all our resources.

CHAPTER I

THE EMPEROR

Article 1

The Emperor shall be the symbol of the State and the unity of the people, deriving his position from the will of the people with whom resides sovereign power.

Article 2

The Imperial Throne shall be dynastic and succeeded to in accordance with the Imperial House Law passed by the Diet.

Article 3

The advice and approval of the Emperor in matters of state, and the Cabinet shall be responsible therefor.

Article 4

(1) The Emperor shall perform only such acts in matters of state as are provided for in this Constitution and he shall not have powers related to government. (2) The Emperor may delegate the performance of his acts in matters of state as may be provided for by law.

Article 5

When, in accordance with the Imperial House Law, a Regency is established, the Regent shall perform his acts in matters of state in the Emperor's name. In this case, paragraph one of the preceding Article will be applicable.

Article 6

The Emperor shall appoint the Prime Minister as designated by the Emperor; shall appoint the Chief Judge of the Supreme Court as designated by the Cabinet.

Article 7

The Emperor shall, with the advice and approval of the Cabinet, perform the following acts in matters of state on behalf of the people: (1) Promulgation of amendments of the

Constitution, laws, cabinet orders and treaties. (2) Convocation of the Diet. (3) Dissolution of the House of Representatives. (4) Proclamation of general election of members of the Diet. (5) Attestation of the appointment and dismissal of Ministers of State and other officials as provided for by law, and of full powers and credentials of Ambassadors and Ministers. (6) Attestation of general and special amnesty, commutation of punishment, reprieve, and restoration of rights. (7) Awarding of honors. (8) Attestation of instruments of ratification and other diplomatic documents as provided for by law. (9) Receiving foreign ambassadors and ministers. (10) Performance of ceremonial functions.

Article 8

No property can be given to, or received by, the Imperial House, nor can any gifts be made therefrom, without the authorization of the Diet.

CHAPTER II

RENUNCIATION OF WAR

Article 9

(1) Aspiring sincerely to an international peace based on justice and order, the Japanese people forever renounce war as a sovereign right of the nation and the threat or use of force as means of settling international disputes. (2) In order to accomplish the aim of the preceding paragraph, land, sea, and air forces, as well as other war potential, will never be maintained. The right of belligerency of the state will not be recognized.

CHAPTER III

RIGHTS AND DUTIES OF THE PEOPLE

Article 10

The conditions necessary for being a Japanese national shall be determined by law.

Article 11

The people shall not be prevented from enjoying any of the fundamental human rights. These fundamental human rights guaranteed to the people by this Constitution shall be conferred upon the people of this and future generations as eternal and inviolate rights.

Article 12

The freedoms and rights guaranteed to the people by this Constitution shall be maintained by the constant endeavor of the people, who shall refrain from any abuse of these freedoms and rights and shall always be responsible for utilizing them for the public welfare.

Article 13

All of the people shall be respected as individuals. Their right to life, liberty, and the pursuit of happiness shall, to the extent that it does not interfere with the public welfare, be the supreme consideration in legislation and in other governmental affairs.

Article 14

(1) All of the people are equal under the law and there shall be no discrimination in political, economic or social relations because of race, creed, sex, social status or family origin. (2) Peers and peerage shall not be recognized. (3) No privilege shall accompany any award of honor, decoration or any distinction, nor shall any such award be valid beyond the lifetime of the individual who now holds or hereafter may receive it.

Article 15

(1) The people have the inalienable right to choose their public officials and to dismiss them. (2) All public officials are servants of the whole community and not of any group thereof. (3) Universal adult suffrage is guaranteed with regard to the election of public officials. (4) In all elections, secrecy of the ballot shall not be violated. A voter shall not be answerable, publicly or privately, for the choice he has made.

Article 16

Every person shall have the right of peaceful petition for the redress of damage, for the removal of public officials, for the enactment, repeal or amendment of laws, ordinances or regulations and for other matters; nor shall any person be in any way discriminated against for sponsoring such a petition.

Article 17

Every person may sue for redress as provided by law from the State or a public entity, in case he has suffered damage through illegal act of any public official.

Article 18

No person shall be held in bondage of any kind. Involuntary servitude, except as punishment for crime, is prohibited.

Article 19

Freedom of thought and conscience shall not be violated.

Article 20

(1) Freedom of religion is guaranteed to all. No religious organization shall receive any privileges from the State, nor exercise any political authority. (2) No person shall be compelled to take part in any religious acts, celebration, rite or practice. (3) The State and its organs shall refrain from religious education or any other religious activity.

Article 21

(1) Freedom of assembly and association as well as speech, press and all other forms of expression are guaranteed. (2) No censorship shall be maintained, nor shall the secrecy of any means of communication be violated.

Article 22

(1) Every person shall have freedom to choose and change his residence and to choose his occupation to the extent that it does not interfere with the public welfare. (2) Freedom of all persons to move to a foreign country and to divest themselves of their nationality shall be inviolate.

Article 23

Academic freedom is guaranteed.

Article 24

(1) Marriage shall be based only on the mutual consent of both sexes and it shall be maintained through mutual cooperation with the equal rights of husband and wife as a basis. (2) With regard to choice of spouse, property rights, inheritance, choice

of domicile, divorce and other matters pertaining to marriage and the family, laws shall be enacted from the standpoint of individual dignity and the essential equality of the sexes.

Article 25

(1) All people shall have the right to maintain the minimum standards of wholesome and cultured living. (2) In all spheres of life, the State shall use its endeavors for the promotion and extension of social welfare and security, and of public health.

Article 26

(1) All people shall have the right to receive an equal education correspondent to their ability, as provided for by law. (2) All people shall be obligated to have all boys and girls under their protection to receive ordinary education as provided for by law. Such compulsory education shall be free.

Article 27

(1) All people shall have the right and the obligation to work. (2) Standards for wages, hours, rest and other working conditions shall be fixed by law. (3) Children shall not be exploited.

Article 28

The right of workers to organize and to bargain and act collectively is guaranteed.

Article 29

(1) The right to own or to hold property is inviolable. (2) Property rights shall be defined by law, in conformity with the public welfare. (3) Private property may be taken for public use upon just compensation therefor.

Article 30

The people shall be liable to taxation as provided for by law.

Article 31

No person shall be deprived of life or liberty, nor shall any other criminal penalty be imposed, except according to procedure established by law.

Article 32

No person shall be denied the right of access to the courts.

Article 33

No person shall be apprehended except upon warrant issued by a competent judicial officer which specifies the offense with which the person is charged, unless he is apprehended, the offense being committed.

Article 34

No person shall be arrested or detained without being at once informed of the charges against him or without the immediate privilege of counsel; nor shall he be detained without adequate cause; and upon demand of any person such cause must be immediately shown in open court in his presence and the presence of his counsel.

Article 35

(1) The right of all persons to be secure in their homes, papers and effects against entries, searches and seizures shall not be impaired except upon warrant issued for adequate cause and particularly describing the place to be searched and things to be seized, or except as provided by Article 33. (2) Each search or seizure shall be made upon separate warrant issued by a competent judicial officer.

Article 36

The infliction of torture by any public officer and cruel punishments are absolutely forbidden.

Article 37

(1) In all criminal cases the accused shall enjoy the right to a speedy and public trial by an impartial tribunal. (2) He shall be permitted full opportunity to examine all witnesses, and he shall have the right of compulsory process for obtaining witnesses on his behalf at public expense. (3) At all times the accused shall have the assistance of competent counsel who shall, if the accused is unable to secure the same by his own efforts, be assigned to his use by the State.

Article 38

(1) No person shall be compelled to testify against himself. (2) Confession made under compulsion, torture or threat, or after prolonged arrest or detention shall not be admitted in evidence. (3) No person shall be convicted or punished in cases where the only proof against him is his own confession.

Article 39

No person shall be held criminally liable for an act which was lawful at the time it was committed, or of which he had been acquitted, nor shall he be placed in double jeopardy.

Article 40

Any person may, in case he is acquitted after he has been arrested or detained, sue the State for redress as provided for by law.

CHAPTER IV

THE DIET

Article 41

The Diet shall be the highest organ of the state power, and shall be the sole law-making organ of the State.

Article 42

The Diet shall consist of two Houses, namely the House of Representatives and the House of Councillors.

Article 43

(1) Both Houses shall consist of elected members, representative of all the people. (2) The number of the members of each House shall be fixed by law.

Article 44

The qualifications of members of both Houses and their electors shall be fixed by law. However, there shall be no discrimination because of race, creed, sex, social status, family origin, education, property or income.

Article 45

The term of office of members of the House of Representatives shall be four years. However, the term shall be terminated before the full term is up in case the House of Representatives is dissolved.

Article 46

The term of office of members of the House of Councillors shall be six years, and election for half the members shall take place every three years.

Article 47

Electoral districts, method of voting and other matters pertaining to the method of election of members of both Houses shall be fixed by law.

Article 48

No person shall be permitted to be a member of both Houses simultaneously.

Article 49

Members of both Houses shall receive appropriate annual payment from the national treasury in accordance with law.

Article 50

Except in cases as provided for by law, members of both Houses shall be exempt from apprehension while the Diet is in session, and any members apprehended before the opening of the session shall be freed during the term of the session upon demand of the House.

Article 51

Members of both Houses shall not be held liable outside the House for speeches, debates or votes cast inside the House.

Article 52

An ordinary session of the Diet shall be convoked once per year.

Article 53

The Cabinet may determine to convoke extraordinary sessions of the Diet. When a quarter or more of the total members of either House makes the demand, the Cabinet must determine on such convocation.

Article 54

(1) When the House of Representatives is dissolved, there must be a general election of members of the House of Representatives within forty (40) days from the date of dissolution, and the Diet must be convoked within thirty (30) days from the date of the election. (2) When the House of Representatives is dissolved, the House of Councillors is closed at the same time. However, the Cabinet may, in time of national emergency, convoke the House of Councillors in emergency session. (3) Measures taken at such session as mentioned in the proviso of the preceding paragraph shall be provisional and shall become null and void unless agreed to by the House of Representatives within a period of ten (10) days after the opening of the next session of the Diet.

Article 55

Each House shall judge disputes related to qualifications of its members. However, in order to deny a seat to any member, it is necessary to pass a resolution by a majority of two-thirds or more of the members present.

Article 56

(1) Business cannot be transacted in either House unless one-third or more of total membership is present. (2) All matters shall be decided, in each House, by a majority of those present, except as elsewhere provided for in the Constitution, and in case of a tie, the presiding officer shall decide the issue.

Article 57

(1) Deliberation in each House shall be public. However, a secret meeting may be held where a majority of two-thirds or more of those members present passes a resolution therefor. (2) Each House shall keep a record of proceedings. This record shall be published and given general circulation, excepting such parts of proceedings of secret session as may be deemed to require secrecy. (3) Upon demand of one-fifth or more of the members present, votes of the members on any matter shall be recorded in the minutes.

Article 58

(1) Each House shall select its own president and other officials. (2) Each House shall establish its rules pertaining to meetings, proceedings and internal discipline, and may punish members for disorderly conduct. However, in order to expel a member, a majority of two-thirds or more of those members present must pass a resolution thereon.

Article 59

(1) A bill becomes a law on passage by both Houses, except as otherwise provided for by the Constitution. (2) A bill, which is passed by the House of Representatives, and upon which the House of Councillors makes a decision different from that of the House of Representatives, becomes a law when passed a second time by the House of Representatives by a majority of two-thirds or more of the members present. (3) The provision of the preceding paragraph does not preclude the House of Representatives from calling for the meeting of a joint committee of both Houses, provided for by law. (4) Failure by the House of Councillors to take final action within sixty (60) days after receipt of a bill passed by the House of Representatives, time in recess excepted, may be determined by the House of Representatives to constitute a rejection of the said bill by the House of Councillors.

Article 60

(1) The budget must first be submitted to the House of Representatives. (2) Upon consideration of the budget, when the House of Councillors makes a decision different from that of the House of Representatives, and when no agreement can be reached even through a joint committee of both Houses, provided for by law, or in the case of failure by the House of Councillors to take final action within thirty (30) days, the period of recess excluded, after the receipt of the budget passed by the House of Representatives, the decision of the House of Representatives shall be the decision of the Diet.

Article 61

The second paragraph of the preceding Article applies also the Diet approval required for the conclusion of treaties.

Article 62

Each House may conduct investigations in relation to government, and may demand the presence and testimony of witnesses, and the production of records.

Article 63

The Prime Minister and other Ministers of State may, at any time, appear in either House for the purpose of speaking on bills, regardless of whether they are members of the House or not. They must appear when their presence is required in order to give answers or explanations.

Article 64

(1) The Diet shall set up an impeachment court from among the members of both Houses for the purposes of trying those judges against whom removal proceedings have been instituted. (2) Matters relating to impeachment shall be provided for by law.

CHAPTER V

THE CABINET

Article 65

Executive power shall be vested in the Cabinet.

Article 66

(1) The Cabinet shall consist of the Prime Minister, who shall be its head, and other Ministers of State, as provided for by law. (2) The Prime Minister and other Ministers of State must be civilians. (3) The Cabinet shall, in the exercise of executive power, be collectively responsible to the Diet.

Article 67

(1) The Prime Minister shall be designated from among the members of the Diet by a resolution of the Diet. This designation shall precede all other business. (2) If the House of Representatives and the House of Councillors disagree and if no agreement can be reached even through a joint committee of both Houses, provided for by law, or the House of Councillors fails to make designation within ten (10) days, exclusive of the period of recess, after the House of Representatives has made

designation, the decision of the House of Representatives shall be the decision of the Diet.

Article 68

(1) The Prime Minister shall appoint the Ministers of State. However, a majority of their number must be chosen from among the members of the Diet. (2) The Prime Minister may remove the Ministers of State as he chooses.

Article 69

If the House of Representatives passes a non-confidence resolution, or rejects a confidence resolution, the Cabinet shall resign en masse, unless the House of Representatives is dissolved within ten (10) days.

Article 70

When there is a vacancy in the post of Prime Minister, or upon the first convocation of the Diet after a general election of members of the House of Representatives, the Cabinet shall resign en masse.

Article 71

In the cases mentioned in the two preceding Articles, the Cabinet shall continue its functions until the time when a new Prime Minister is appointed.

Article 72

The Prime Minister, representing the Cabinet, submits bills, reports on general national affairs and foreign relations to the Diet and exercises control and supervision over various administrative branches.

Article 73

The Cabinet shall, in addition to other general administrative functions, perform the following functions: (1) Administer the law faithfully; conduct affairs of state. (2) Manage foreign affairs. (3) Conclude treaties. However, it shall obtain prior or, depending on circumstances subsequent approval of the Diet. (4) Administer the civil service, in accordance with standards established by law. (5) Prepare the budget, and present it to the cabinet in order to execute the provisions of this Constitution and of the law. However, it cannot include penal provisions in such cabinet orders unless authorized by such law. (6) Decide on general amnesty, special amnesty, commutation of punishment, reprieve, and restoration of rights.

Article 74

All laws and cabinet orders shall be signed by the competent Minister of State and countersigned by the Prime Minister.

Article 75

The Ministers of State shall not, during their tenure of office, be subject to legal action without the consent of the Prime Minister. However, the right to take that action is not impaired hereby.

CHAPTER VI

JUDICIARY

Article 76

(1) The whole judicial power is vested in a Supreme Court and in such inferior courts as are established by law. (2) No extraordinary tribunal shall be established, nor shall any organ or agency of the Executive be given final judicial power. (3) All judges shall be independent in the exercise of their conscience and shall be bound only by this Constitution and the laws.

Article 77

(1) The Supreme Court is vested with the rule-making power under which it determines the rules of procedure and of practice, and of matters relating to attorneys, the internal discipline of the courts and the administration of judicial affairs. (2) Public procurators shall be subject to the rule-making power of the Supreme Court. (3) The Supreme Court may delegate the power to make rules for inferior courts to such courts.

Article 78

Judges shall not be removed except by public impeachment unless judicially declared mentally or physically incompetent to perform official duties. No disciplinary action against judges shall be administered by any executive organ or agency.

Article 79

(1) The Supreme Court shall consist of a Chief Judge and such number of judges as may be determined by law; all such judges excepting the Chief Judge shall be appointed by the Cabinet. (2) The appointment of the judges of the Supreme Court shall be reviewed by the people at the first general election of members of the House of Representatives following their appointment, and shall be reviewed again at the first general election of members of the House of Representatives after a lapse of ten (10) years, and in the same manner thereafter.

Article 80

(1) The judges of the inferior courts shall be appointed by the Cabinet from a list of persons nominated by the Supreme Court. All such judges shall hold office for a term of ten (10) years with privilege of reappointment, provided that they shall be retired upon the attainment of the age as fixed by law. (2) The judges of the inferior courts shall receive, at regular stated intervals, adequate compensation which shall not be decreased during their terms of office.

Article 81

The Supreme Court is the court of last resort with power to determine the constitutionality of any law, order, regulation or official act.

Article 82

(1) Trials shall be conducted and judgement declared publicly. (2) Where a court unanimously determines publicity to be dangerous to public order or morals, a trial may be conducted privately, but trials of political offenses, offenses involving the press or cases wherein the rights of people as guaranteed in Chapter III of this Constitution are in question shall always be conducted publicly.

CHAPTER VII

FINANCE

Article 83

The power to administer national finances shall be exercised as the Diet shall determine.

Article 84

No new taxes shall be imposed or existing ones modified except by law or under such conditions as law may prescribe.

Article 85

No money shall be expended, nor shall the State obligate itself, except as authorized by the Diet.

Article 86

The Cabinet shall prepare and submit to the Diet for its consideration and decision a budget for each fiscal year.

Article 87

In order to provide for unforeseen deficiencies in the budget, a reserve fund may be authorized by the Diet to be expended upon the responsibility of the Cabinet that must get subsequent approval of the Diet for all payments from the reserve fund.

Article 88

All property of the Imperial Household shall belong to the State. All expenses of the Imperial Household shall be appropriated by the Diet in the budget.

Article 89

No public money or other property shall be expended or appropriated for the use, benefit or maintenance of any religious institution or association, or for any charitable, educational or benevolent enterprises not under the control of public authority.

Article 90

(1) Final accounts of the expenditures and revenues of the State shall be audited annually by a Board of Audit and submitted by the Diet, together with the statement of audit, during the fiscal year immediately following the period covered.
(2) The organization and competency of the Board of Audit shall be determined by law.

Article 91

At regular intervals and at least annually the Diet and the people deliberate on the state of national finances.

CHAPTER VIII

LOCAL SELF-GOVERNMENT

Article 92

Regulations concerning organization and operations of local public entities shall be fixed by law in accordance with the principle of local autonomy.

Article 93

(1) The local public entities shall establish assemblies as their deliberative organs, in accordance with law. (2) The chief executive officers of all local public entities, the members of their assemblies, and such other local officials as may be determined by law shall be elected by direct popular vote within their several communities.

Article 94

Local public entities shall have the right to manage their property, affairs and administration and to enact their own regulations within law.

Article 95

A special law, applicable only to one local public entity, cannot be enacted by the Diet without the consent of the majority of the voters of the local public entity concerned, obtained in accordance with law.

CHAPTER IX

AMENDMENTS

Article 96

(1) Amendments to this Constitution shall be initiated by the Diet, through a concurring vote of two-thirds or more of all the members of each House and shall thereupon be submitted to the people for ratification, which shall require the affirmative vote of a majority of all votes cast thereon, at a special referendum or at such election as the Diet shall specify. (2) Amendments when so ratified shall immediately be promulgated by the Emperor in the name of the people, as an integral part of this Constitution.

CHAPTER X

SUPREME LAW

Article 97

The fundamental human rights by this Constitution guaranteed to the people of Japan are fruits of the age-old struggle of man to be free; they have survived the many exacting tests for durability and are conferred upon this and future generations in trust, to be held for all time inviolate.

Article 98

(1) This Constitution shall be the supreme law of the nation and no law, ordinance, imperial rescript or other act of government, or part thereof, contrary to the provisions hereof, shall have legal force or validity. (2) The treaties concluded by Japan and established laws of nations shall be faithfully observed.

Article 99

The Emperor or the Regent as well as Ministers of State, members of the Diet, judges, and all other public officials have the obligation to respect and uphold this Constitution.

CHAPTER XI

SUPPLEMENTARY PROVISIONS

Article 100

(1) This Constitution shall be enforced as from the day when the period of six months will have elapsed counting from the day of its promulgation. (2) The enactment of laws necessary for the enforcement of this Constitution, the election of members of the House of Councillors and the procedure for the convocation of the Diet and other preparatory procedures necessary for the enforcement of this Constitution may be executed before the day prescribed in the preceding paragraph.

Article 101

If the House of Councillors is not constituted before the effective date of this Constitution, the House of Representatives shall function as the Diet until such time as the House of Councillors shall be constituted.

Article 102

The term of office for half the members of the House of Councillors serving in the first term under this Constitution shall be three years. Members falling under this category shall be determined in accordance with law.

Article 103

The Ministers of State, members of the House of Representatives, and judges in office on the effective date of this Constitution, and all other public officials who occupy positions corresponding to such positions as are recognized by this Constitution shall not forfeit their positions automatically on account of the enforcement of this Constitution unless otherwise specified by law. When, however, successors are elected or appointed under the provisions of this Constitution, they shall forfeit their positions as a matter of course.

THE CONSTITUTION OF JAPAN (3 November 1946)

I rejoice that the foundation for the construction of a new Japan has been laid according to the will of the Japanese people, and hereby sanction and promulgate the amendments of the Imperial Japanese Constitution effected following the consultation with the Privy Council and the decision of the Imperial Diet made in accordance with Article 73 of the said Constitution.

Signed:

HIROHITO,

Seal of the Emperor,

This third day of the eleventh month of the twenty-first year of Showa (3 November 1946)

Countersigned

*Prime Minister and concurrently Minister for Foreign Affairs *YOSHIDA Shigeru,

*Minister of State *Baron SHIDEHARA Kijuro,

*Minister of Justice *KIMURA Tokutaro,

*Minister for Home Affairs *OMURA Seiichi,

*Minister of Education *TANAKA Kotaro,

*Minister of Agriculture and Forestry *WADA Hiroo,

*Minister of State *SAITO Takao,

*Minister of Communication*HITOTSUMATSU Sadayoshi,

*Minister of Commerce and Industry *HOSHIJIMA Jiro,

*Minister of Welfare *KAWAI Yoshinari,

*Minister of State *UEHARA Etsujiro,

*Minister of Transportation *HIRATSUKA Tsunejiro,

*Minister of Finance *ISHIBASHI Tanzan,

*Minister of State *KANAMORI Tokujiro,

*Minister of State *ZEN Keinosuke.

This text is part of the Internet Modern History Sourcebook. The Sourcebook is a collection of public domain and copy-permitted texts for introductory level classes in modern European and World history.